Editors

on Editing

Editors

on Editing

**What Writers Need to Know
About What Editors Do**

Completely Revised Third Edition

SELECTED, EDITED, AND
WITH COMMENTARY AND PREFACE BY
Gerald Gross

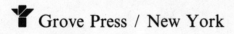 Grove Press / New York

Published by Grove Press
A division of Grove Press, Inc.
841 Broadway
New York, NY 10003-4793

Due to limitations of space, copyright acknowledgments appear on page 379, which serves as an extension of this copyright
page.

Library of Congress Cataloging-in-Publication Data
Editors on editing : What writers need to know about what
editors do /
    [edited by] Gerald Gross. — 3rd ed.
        p.   cm.
    Includes bibliographical references.
    ISBN 0-8021-1533-0
    ISBN 0-8021-3263-4 (pbk.)
    1. Editing. 2. Editors — Corrsepondence. I. Gross, Gerald.
PN162.E36 1993
808'.027 — dc20   92-29806
                                                  CIP

Manufactured in the United States of America
Printed on acid-free paper
Designed by Deidre Amthor

To unsung editors everywhere,
past, present and future:
May these pages sing your praises

To published and unpublished
writers everywhere:
May these pages guide you
to a better understanding of the art
and craft of the editor

Acknowledgments

My thanks and deep appreciation to all the editors who stole precious time from their crowded days and nights and gave so generously of their talents by contributing such splendid original essays to *Editors on Editing*. Editing editors is a high-wire-without-a-net exercise in delicacy and diplomacy; therefore, I also want to thank the contributors for responding with such grace under pressure to my editorial suggestions.

For their advice, counsel, and recommendations of editors to invite to contribute to the book, I want to thank (in alphabetical order) Carole Abel, Richard Curtis, Anita Diamant, Mitch Douglas, Joyce Engelson, Herman Gollob, Bert Holtje, Gerald Howard, Evan Marshall, Ruth Nathan, Ms. Bobbe Siegel, Ted Solotaroff, Bill Thompson, and Tom Wallace.

(My apologies to anyone I've forgotten to mention, but be assured that my *heart* remembers *everyone* who helped—even if my memory does not.)

For sharing my vision for *Editors on Editing* and making important contributions to the focusing and realization of that vision, I thank my dedicated and creative editor, Bryan Oettel.

For his intelligent, perceptive, sensitive, and, yes, even affectionate copy editing, I thank my copy editor, Ed Sedarbaum. His skill has orchestrated this anthology of thirty-nine different voices into a mellifluous chorus of clarity and coherence.

Finally, I thank my best friend and beloved wife, Arlene, for the support and encouragement she has given me in this and each of my other endeavors for over thirty-six years.

Contents

All essays have been written especially for this collection except those prefaced by an asterisk (*).

PRACTICE

Editing Reference Books

The Editor of Lives

Editing Popular Psychology and Self-Help Books

Editing the Romance Novel

Editing Male-Oriented Escapist Fiction

*An Annotated Bibliography of Books on Editing and
Publishing

Preface: Reflections on a Lifetime of Editing

Thirty years have passed since *Editors on Editing* was first published in 1962—and seven years have gone by since it was revised in 1985. The book you now hold in your hand is far more than a revision of those two editions of *Editors on Editing,* retaining as it does only one piece from the previous edition of the work. It contains thirty-two original essays especially commissioned for this volume, plus five essays on editing and publishing that did not appear in previous editions. This is a completely new edition of what has become the standard work on the art and craft of editing in our country, used in publishing courses, writing courses, and writers' conferences throughout the United States.

Because I give workshops and lecture widely at these writers' conferences, and know how eager writers are to have a happy, effective, creative relationship with an editor, I wanted to focus this new edition of *Editors on Editing* on what a writer needs to know about what editors do. Many writers suffer from a myriad of misconceptions about what editors will or won't do with and to their manuscript; they are unsure of the ways in which an editor can help them improve their manuscript; they are unclear as to the dynamics of the editor-author relationship: what each can and should expect from the other in the editing process; they are anxious and unsure about their rights to their own manuscript once it is accepted by an editor. Many writers are not aware of what developmental, line, and copy editors do and how they do it. Finally, they often don't know how and why some manuscripts are accepted and others rejected. The list of myths and erroneous assumptions goes on and on and on. To clarify the many creative, technical, and empowering ways in which an editor works with a writer, I wanted this edition of *Editors on Editing* to demystify for the writer—published and unpublished—that mysterious process known as editing. And I also wanted to reveal the editor as a passionately committed, caring professional who loves writers and who is dedicated to helping the writer say what the writer wants to say in the most effective way, one that will reach the widest possible audience.

To that end, as I did in compiling the first two editions of *Editors on Editing,* I went directly to the industry's top editors, the men and women who know their art and craft best and also know how to communicate their excitement and their expertise. Included among them are Ruth Cavin on "Editing Crime Fiction"; Charles Spicer on "Editing True Crime"; Maron Waxman on "Line Editing: Drawing Out the Best Book Possible"; Mel Parker on "The Pleasures and Perils of Editing Mass-Market Paperbacks"; and Scott Walker on "Editing for a Small Press: Publishing the Way It Used to Be."

These top professionals write with insight and candor about the special demands and skills necessary to their particular areas of editorial expertise. To make their comments as prescriptive, as practical as possible for both the beginning and experienced writer, I asked them to focus their essays on specific examples of the variety of ways an editor actually edits: everything from suggestions for a new beginning or a new ending to ideas for bringing a character to life, or smoothing out a difficult narrative passage, or clarifying a flashback or a flash-forward or dream scene, or a way to accelerate the pace and plotting of the story, and so forth.

Accordingly, the thirty-eight essays in this volume offer the writer solutions to the problems posed by the manuscript, guiding the writer through the various stages of publication from the inception of the idea through developmental editing, line editing, and copy editing to publication and afterwards. The result is, I hope, an informative short course in the editorial side of publishing that should make a writer feel confident, knowledgeable, and effective at any stage of his or her relationship with an editor.

In addition to offering insights into the nuts-and-bolts side of the editorial process, *Editors on Editing* also includes some provocative, even controversial articles on editorial theory and the relationship and responsibility of editing to the society at large. Alan D. Williams gives his own unique answer to "What Is an Editor?"; Marc Aronson offers a brief history of the American editor in "The Evolution of the American Editor"; and James O'Shea Wade treats an important but little-discussed aspect of editing in "Doing Good—And Doing It Right: The Ethical and Moral Dimensions of Editing." Gerald Howard updates his classic overview of the state of American editing and publishing entitled "Mistah Perkins—He Dead." Richard Marek examines "How Books Are Chosen: What Goes into Making an Editorial Decision." The emotional, controversial, and volatile issue of the impact of PC (political correctness) on editors and writers is discussed from a fiction point of view by Michael Denneny and from a nonfiction point of view by Wendy Wolf. And writer-editor-agent Richard Curtis poses the incendiary question "Are Editors Necessary?"

It was Oscar Wilde who said, "I can resist everything except temptation," and I understand the wisdom of that epigram more clearly now than ever before as I write this Preface. I have decided not to resist the temptation to reflect on a long career as an editor. For 1993 marks my fortieth year as an editor (it was my first, and has been my only, career choice since 1953, when I went to work as a first reader for Henry Simon of Simon & Schuster after graduating from the City College of New York). And so I thought that I would pause at this watershed in my professional life to offer some comments on the philosophy of editing by which I have lived for these many years.

1

When I started my editorial career, agents complained that editors edited too much. I remember being told: "Young man, if you didn't think the book was in good shape to begin with, you shouldn't have bought it." Nowadays, agents and authors try to work with editors who really understand developmental and line editing, who care enough and know enough about shaping the theme and content of a book to make it the best possible expression of the writer's intent and art.

When I was a young editor I was taught how to shape and line edit a book by Henry Simon and Donald A. Wollheim, who took me into their office after the working day to guide me in those arcane but essential skills. It was mentoring at its best. And it was done leisurely and lovingly. Today, the pace of publishing is such that there is little or no time or opportunity for young editors to serve such an apprenticeship. I wouldn't go so far as to say that developmental and line editing are lost arts, but they seem to be arts less practiced than before. And that perhaps is why critics and reviewers, more and more often, make a point of remarking on the absence of editing, or on the inferior editing, in a book they are reviewing. I would like to see a revival of the apprenticeship/mentoring situation that I enjoyed as a young editor. Everyone would profit from it—publishers, editors, agents, but writers most of all.

Ultimately, though, the best editing is not the least or the most; it is whatever measure of editing evokes the writer's greatest talent, that presents the writer's work in the best possible light so that it garners great reviews, enhances the writer's professional reputation and personal self-esteem, and reaches the audience the writer wrote for in numbers large enough so that the writer can live comfortably to write again and further develop his or her creative powers.

2

Much is made of who "owns" the book, whose judgment should prevail in the editor-author relationship. It is regrettable whenever a situation develops that forces the participants into such an either/or dilemma. It seems only right and just that in all cases, the editor must remember that the work in question is the author's book and that the author's decision must prevail. Seeing the publishing house as a "senate" in which debates over the manuscript take place, the editor can and should "advise" but the author must always "consent." For the manuscript is, in effect, leased to the editor until such time as the editor's work is done and the work is returned to the author. Or put another way, it is the author who gives birth to the book; the editor's role is that of midwife, whose job it is to bring forth a happy, healthy manuscript into the publishing world.

3

That said, and said with profound conviction, I would like to propose a revolutionary way of recognizing the midwifery of the editor. Since at least the legendary Maxwell Perkins's time, editors have been expected to be unsung, faceless, nameless technicians assisting the author in the creation of the completed manuscript. Quite often, of course, the author graciously and gratefully acknowledges the efforts of his or her editor in the prefatory pages of the published book. Quite often, though, the editor remains unsung. But why does it always have to be that way? More important, why *should* it be that way? Book jackets routinely mention the name of the jacket designer, graphic artist, illustrator, or photographer. Why should the editor remain anonymous? Why shouldn't the editor of the book be named on the jacket or on the copyright page? He or she has certainly made a contribution equal to that of the cover artist, photographer, designer, etc. And if more than one editor has been involved—because of firings, departures, and plain old-fashioned teamwork—then name all the editors who worked on the book. Is this an idea whose time has come because it is right and proper? Or should editors continue to edit "in the closet," as it were? I have opened this discussion with these words and in the dedication to the book, and would welcome hearing what agents, editors, writers, and publishers have to say on the subject. So please write to me care of the publisher of this book. I suspect it's time to put this sacred cow of anonymity out to pasture!

4

Much has been written about the various responsibilities the editor has: to the author, to the publisher, to the consumer, and to the book itself. Too little, however, has been said of the editor's responsibility to his or her own integrity: the duty to be true to one's political, moral, ethical, societal, and aesthetic convictions. Without that responsibility to one's own integrity, I don't believe the editor can be truly responsible to the author, the publisher, the consumer, or to the book itself. Several times during my long career I was offered projects that deeply offended my political and social convictions. I turned them down, often recommending the author or agent to another editor, one who would be more sympathetic to the theme and content of the work I refused to edit.

I do not for a single second advocate censorship of any kind. I am a devout and unconditional supporter of the First Amendment. Like cancer cells, a little censorship metastasizes into totalitarianism and the inevitable death of democracy. But I know I have to sleep at night and face myself in the shaving mirror in the morning and live with my wife and my children without shame or guilt. If I had to work on a manuscript that was violently in opposition to everything I stood for and believed in, I couldn't live with myself and couldn't do a good job for the author on the manuscript, or for the publisher. Remember, life is too short (understand, I say this as I face my sixtieth birthday) to live with self-inflicted intellectual, physical, or psychological pain. And remember, too, that there will always be someone to publish what you have walked away from.

5

At the many writers' conferences I attend each year, after one or more of my workshops on editing and publishing, inevitably there's a question from the floor along the lines of: "What would the ideal relationship between an editor and an author be like?" My answer to that is always some variation of these basic guidelines: that the two parties should work together collegially, not adversarially—symbiotically, not parasitically. Put even more simply: each needs the other; each has much to offer the other.

Writers must realize that editors are really necessary to inspire them, spur them, sometimes push them to write at the top of their form. And that editors have an authentic creativity of their own, one that few writers have: the gift of critical analysis, detachment, and expression that is there for the writer to make the most of. Editors can diagnose the positive and negative elements of a manuscript and prescribe a possible cure to what ails it in the same way that a diagnostically talented internist can read an X ray and discern the trouble in the patient's lung or chest and prescribe a course of treatment to eradicate that trouble. The writer should respect this kind of editorial talent, acknowledge its creative quality, and benefit from it.

The editor should always remember that it is the writer's work that validates the editor's work, and that all the diagnostic skills in the world are useless without the manuscript on which to practice those skills. The editor must not in any way at any time attempt to edit the book so that it will be written the way the editor would write it if the editor wanted to, or could, write. The editor must learn to edit in the writer's voice, think the writer's thoughts, achieve the writer's perspective. Otherwise the editor faces an unending frustration that could develop into a hostile, unproductive relationship with the writer, and that can result only in an inferior book.

Mutual recognition, respect, admiration, and reliance on each other's skills makes for the best kind of editor-author relationship, and the best kind of book comes out of such a relationship.

After reading these reflections, it should be clear that I have edited *Editors on Editing* as much to help the editor understand how to work with a writer as for the writer to understand how to work with an editor.

．　．　．

I knew that I wanted to become an editor at the age of sixteen. And ever since I have had the good fortune to work with and among some of the most brilliant editors of my time. I respect and have grown very fond of my colleagues, some of whom have become, over the years, my friends as well. A deep and abiding concern of my professional life is to discover and bring along the next generation of editors. The future of the written word, of books that are entertaining, important, and informative (especially books with all three virtues), of aspiring and developing authors everywhere depends on the intuition, talents, arts, and crafts of working editors today and in the years to come. Indeed, I do not think I understate when I say the future of the culture itself depends in great part on editors as much as writers.

As I prepared to write this Preface, I thought long and hard for the right words to sum up my feelings about forty years of editing, but I realized that my delight in and dedication to the world of books and authors is as strong today as I expressed it in the following quote from the Preface to the 1985 revised edition of *Editors on Editing,* a portion of which also appeared in the Preface to the 1962 original edition. I believe I will feel the same way until the last day of my life as a working editor, which will probably also be the last day of my life. Period.

. . .

It is my hope that this book will attract many more bright, creative men and women to the profession of editing. It is not a career for everyone. "Of that," to quote Mr. W. S. Gilbert, "there is no possible shadow of doubt whatever." For the frustrated writer, editing other writers could prove to be excruciating torture and put a damper on one's own creative efforts. For the dilettante "who just loves good books" but who has little knowledge of or concern for the reading trends and tastes of readers, editing can prove to be a most traumatically disillusioning experience. For the young man or woman who believes editing means endless rounds of glamorous cocktail parties with literary lions, and access to unlimited expense accounts, a few months in an entry-level job will disabuse him or her very, very quickly.

So much for what editing is not. It is, for one attuned to its demands and responsibilities and often tedious tasks, a most rewarding career—fully as creative, imaginative, and satisfying as being a writer. And some editors might even go so far as to say, "More so."

In my long career as an editor, I have been always fascinated, sometimes inspired and exhilarated, occasionally frustrated and disappointed, but never, never bored. I have looked upon my years as an editor as analogous to being a perpetually stimulated student who is attending a nonstop, incredibly diverse series of courses at the world's largest, and always expanding, university. I learn from editing each author more about the subject of his or her book than I had ever known before. Publishing has permitted me to meet unusual, even spellbinding and truly unforgettable people, some of whom are professional colleagues and some among my roster of authors. My need for creative self-expression has been more than amply satisfied by the editing I have done on many, many books and by the pleasure I have always experienced from getting a good and valuable book from a fine author. I still get a charge of exhilaration when I receive the advance copies of a book I have worked on for a year (and sometimes two). I look at that book and remember, perhaps, that it all began as an idea over lunch, or an outline and a chapter or two. I am proud of the contribution I have made to helping that idea come to fruition, to helping that outline and chapter grow into an important or entertaining book, one that the author and I believe will be in print for many, many years. I have never lost this involvement and commitment and pride in being an editor and I hope I never shall.

This book was compiled with a devotion and care that I hope express my deepest feelings about the profession of editing. I have loved it from the beginning and I love it even more now, after forty years of joy, fulfillment, grief, and frustration. I still am eager and excited as I begin to read yet another proposal, dip into yet another novel, hear about a fresh and innovative writer. May this new edition inspire would-be (and currently practicing) editors to similar heights of dedication and delight. May authors who read this book discover that the editor-author relationship need not be and should not be an adversarial one. At its best, it can be an unforgettably rewarding collaboration. Finally, I hope that the general reader will discover the subtle, complex, and often ineffable factors that inspire both editor and author to give unstintingly of their time and their talents to that singular act of creation—the book.

Croton-on-Hudson, New York
October 1992

Theory

What Is an Editor?

Alan D. Williams

Now an editorial consultant, ALAN D. WILLIAMS has held editorial and executive positions at a number of publishing houses, his major tenure having been two decades at Viking Press as managing editor and editorial director. His last post was as publisher of Grove Weidenfeld. During his career he has worked equally in both fiction and nonfiction with authors as varied as Isaiah Berlin, Stephen King, Tom Wicker, Iris Murdoch, Frederick Forsyth, Nadine Gordimer, and the Reverend Charlie W. Shedd.

The editor as hunter-gatherer? As therapist-nag? As magic worker–meddler? Which of these is the best editor for a writer to have? Which is the most effective approach to editing an editor can take? Check all of the above whether writer or editor. For in fact these are only a few of the editor's vital functions, suggests Alan D. Williams in his irreverent and witty quest for the answer to the question, What is an editor?

Is there no respite from all this role playing? No, but do not assume the editor is unhappy and put-upon. In truth, being so many things to so many people is all part of the fun and games and challenge of editing. For as Mr. Williams wisely says: "The day that an editor picks up a manuscript without some sense of anticipation is probably the last day he or she should be at work."

3

What Is an Editor?

An editor is so many things to so many people that this rhetorically questioning heading is virtually impossible to answer in any concise form. In addition, any one editor is likely to be cut from such radically different cloth from the next one that generalizing about character, somatotype, background, interests, or whatever would be as meaningless as grouping them by eye color. If form eludes us, then, function should be where we look for unifying aspects, and for those elements toward which writers peer in trepidation or hope, aversion or gratitude, contempt or respect and even affection.

Editors in publishing houses can be perceived as basically performing three different roles, all of them simultaneously. First they must find and select the books the house is to publish. Second, they edit (yes, Virginia, they still do edit, no matter what cries you hear about bottom lines, heartless conglomerates, and the defeat of taste by commerce). And third, they perform the Janus-like function of representing the house to the author and the author to the house.

The first function—the editor as hunter-gatherer—is the one most vital to the editor's own reputation and advancement, a point writers might particularly keep in mind. Editors *want* books; they are not there to demonstrate condescension to submitted writings, despite the flash of indignation experienced by almost everyone receiving a rejection letter. Indeed, the day that an editor picks up a manuscript without *some* sense of anticipation is probably the last day he or she should be at work. Whatever the endless winnowing (and it is estimated that only one in fifty manuscripts or proposals is accepted), the highest moments of exhilaration in an editor's professional life come with discovery and acquisition.

Authors know how *they* are individually discovered, but even they can have only an incomplete idea of how wide the plains of editorial search can be. Agents are of course the first conduit that springs to mind, and it is true that in the last fifty years more than 80 percent of all trade books were, by informal estimate, agented. (It is also a truism that it is as difficult to find a good agent as a good publisher, which supposedly presents the aspiring writer with a classic chicken-and-egg dilemma. But it should be remembered that the agent has many potential outlets and the acquiring editor but one, so that the former can play with many more possibilities and talents than the latter.)

The earth has circled the sun many times since a well-known publisher could display on his office wall a beautifully wrought needlepoint sampler reading "The relationship between publisher and agent is that of knife to throat." Cultivation of agents occupies a significant portion of an editor's waking hours, nor should this be thought of as seeking out dueling opponents. Instead, editor and agent are better perceived as two points of a triangle, the author obviously being the third. No one editor can conceivably "cover" all agents, so that as time goes by both sides gravitate more and more to the individuals they have successfully done business with before, and with whom they tend to have common interests. And yes, the burgeoning of these relationships not necessarily, but often, begins over that much-abused institution the business lunch, undisturbed by telephone or fax.

Of course, editors must cast their nets beyond the worlds of New York and California agenting, both for further gleanings and for their own fulfillment. Writers' conferences, creative writing courses, university campuses at large, magazines both literary and popular, writers who know your writers, scouting trips at home and abroad, foreign publishers—these are only some of the fields to be tilled. Luck certainly plays a part, but even there, some skein of logical happenstance has usually put one in the way of meeting and acquisition. Simply living in a university town for many years afforded me encounters with a number of admirable authors. And it should be noted that after one published book, the unagented author, sometimes even at the suggestion of the publisher, more often than not ties up with an agent. Agents too are hunter-gatherers.

Special mention should go to the books that are thought up by editors, usually works of nonfiction. The word will go out that a certain writer is looking for an idea, and an editor may have just the right biography or current controversy in mind. Or the editor may conceive it in the first place and try it on a likely author. (A famous example was Cecil Scott of Macmillan suggesting the subject of what became *The Guns of August* to Barbara Tuchman.) Series are another device joining authors to contracts they had not anticipated, and they are often the product of the fertile mind of an editor or publisher. To renowned editor Jason Epstein in his Doubleday days goes credit for inventing a whole new genre of publishing, the trade paperback.

Then there are editorial meetings, forums of electric inspiration, Athenian discourse, mutual support—also of backbiting, grandstanding, and the sort of compliments that are thinly veiled put-downs. They are, in short, strictly mortal conclaves. However, beyond the requisite items of agenda and record keeping, they vary as much from house to house as the individuals themselves, from a highly formal tribune of decision to a free-for-all devoted in considerable part to trade gossip. No matter what their nature, they tend to define editors in their singularity, especially in terms of what proposals, suggestions, opinions, and brain-picks they choose to bring to a meeting. Collectively, the editorial meeting says much about publishers in terms of the weight and credence given to the editorial sector as well as to individual editors, the process of decision, even the spirit and morale of the house. Though they are discreet in nature, ideally restricted to editorial folk except by invitation to colleagues in marketing, subsidiary rights, publicity, and other departments, prospective or aspiring authors can learn much about a publisher by some discreet querying of their own.

The second function is the editor as therapist-nag or magic worker—meddler. However he or she is regarded, an editor is, or should be, doing something that almost no friend, relative, or even spouse is qualified or willing to do, namely to read every line with care, to comment in detail with absolute candor, and to suggest changes where they seem desirable or even essential. In doing this the editor is acting as the first truly disinterested reader, giving the author not only constructive help but also, one hopes, the first inkling of how reviewers, readers, and the marketplace (especially for nonfiction) will react, so that the author can revise accordingly.

·   ·   ·

Two basic questions the editor should be addressing to the author are: Are you saying what you want to say? and, Are you saying it as clearly and consistently as possible? If these sound narrow at first glance, think further. They cover everything from awkward syntax and repetition, to the destruction of a novel's impact through a protagonist's behavior so unexplained and unmotivated as to be unintentionally baffling. All of this is of course subject to free and extended discussion and the author is the ultimate arbiter, as all responsible editors would agree. They would also concur that knowing when to leave things alone is as high an editorial skill as knowing when to suggest revision.

Does all this always work out in a glow of amity and constructive engagement? Certainly not, no more frequently than do love affairs. Overbearing, insensitive editors and mulish, unlistening authors, whether singly or in pairs, have caused many a shift of contract and failed book. Both species eventually tend to meet comeuppance and run out of partners. The more basic question, frequently alluded to in the press, and mentioned at the outset of this piece, is whether devoted editorial labor still takes place at all. This observer, at least, is convinced that it does, despite the undoubted increase in commercial pressure, the disappearance of the family (for which read: laid-back, kinder, gentler, in-it-for-literature) firm, and the swift currents of changing taste and accelerated technology. The fact is that the zest of the acquiring editor's initial involvement can no more be separated from concern about the finished product than flesh and blood from bone. In that sense, the editorial animal remains unchanged no matter what the economies, working conditions, or amenity slashes. Editors *do* care, or they wouldn't be there.

The eclectic nature of editorial taste, particularly in relation to nonfiction, deserves special mention. A wise man once remarked, only partly in derision: "A good trade editor can talk about anything for five minutes and nothing for six." It is absolutely true that catholic interests are a more important qualification than any one college major, including English. It is also an ill-kept secret that a few reasonably adroit questions directed at a prospective author of known enthusiasms can seduce the answerer into thinking his questioners know a lot more than they really do. On the other hand, as time goes by, most editors become singled out for certain known passions of their own, be it horses, opera, horse operas, great battles, sports, cuisine, or horticulture. Again, this is an element of compatibility a reasonably inquisitive writer should be able to figure out ahead of time.

The third function—editor as Janus, or two-face—occupies most of the working editor's office hours. (All serious reading and editing is done off premises, much of it nights and weekends; again, you have to love it to do it.) Unceasing reports, correspondence, phoning, meetings, business breakfasts, lunches, dinners, in- and out-of-office appointments leave active editors feeling like rapidly revolving doors as they attempt to explicate author and house to one another.

An editor is naturally the author's first and leading advocate in dealing with his or her publisher. It begins with the editor's initial enthusiasm for the project or novel and continues through acceptance by the house, negotiation of a contract, actual editing (where whatever real deepening of the relationship there will be tends to take place), and the publishing process itself, from copy editing, proofs, and production to sales and publicity. Throughout, the editor is usually attempting to bring as many relevant colleagues into the picture as possible, with the double purpose of interesting them in the book and author at hand, and of demonstrating to the author that a team of dedicated professionals, not just the editor, is devoted to the cause. Also, in this imperfect world, when late delivery, financial emergency, unexpected complexities of all kinds, intervene to prevent perfect fulfillment of a contract, it is the convinced editor who will argue the author's case.

Authors should, and usually do, appreciate the fact that one of the editor's most crucial challenges is to be able to articulate, clearly and appealingly, the signal virtues of a given book. From editorial reports on through catalog copy, jacket flaps, and publicity releases, it is the editor's initial core descriptions that implicitly explain why the book has been chosen in the first place and explicitly set the tone for how a book will be perceived both in and out of the house. Writing this copy is for most editors a true sweat—it is so much more pleasurable to skewer bad writing than to attempt, against all odds, to find fresh ways to lay credible encomia on the newest addition to fifty-five thousand annual U.S. titles. A related trial is the sales conference two or three times a year wherein the enthusiastic editor must stand and deliver to a skeptical audience of sales representatives a pear-shaped oration on the virtues of the titles he or she sponsors. It is the agony of the schoolroom book report magnified a hundredfold.

As for explicating the house to the author, this is often Janus's more minatory side. Economics does indeed seem a dismal science when the editor must repeatedly explain why a full-page ad in the *Times Book Review,* color illustrations, a coast-to-coast tour, or whatever is unwarranted and/ or unaffordable and why even some of the more modest requests cannot be met. The sotto voce diplomatic drumbeat beneath all this is that there's one partner (the publisher) on one side, and many (all the authors) on the other, and that time, energy, and resources must be allocated accordingly. Like polygamy, it's not equitable, but a fact of a certain kind of life. At the same time, when some extra effort is made on a book or author's behalf— midnight oil burned by a copy editor, an imaginative publicity break or unexpected special market ferreted out—it is up to the editor to be sure the author knows about it.

Trying to define the role of the book editor in America without mentioning Maxwell Perkins (1884–1947) of Scribner's can be likened to writing a short history of aviation without the Wright brothers, so pervasive is the image of the man who edited Hemingway, Fitzgerald, Thomas Wolfe, and so many others. Where is his like today? is the invariable echoing lament whenever his name comes up. There is justice in this, for few would compare themselves to Perkins, but it could be speculated, at the risk of sounding defensive, that if he were alive today, he would be spending far more time than he wanted cozening agents, working up competitive bids, scouting afar, and generally being distracted from the manuscripts at hand. He would thus have a much harder time *being* Maxwell Perkins, so to speak.

Be that as it may, Perkins still remains the beau ideal of his trade. Nobody remotely interested in the role of editors or their relationship to writers should fail to read *Editor to Author: The Letters of Maxwell Perkins,* edited by John Hall Wheelock. With their warmth, eloquence, total empathy with authors, and gentle but keenly persuasive suggestions, these letters stand alone as lasting beacons to those who would follow. In writing of Thomas Wolfe and Perkins, the English critic Cyril Connolly, talking about editors, generously found it "unnecessary to point out that American publishers are a dedicated group: they are loyal, generous and infinitely painstaking; they live for their authors and not for social climbing, or the books they want to write themselves; they know how to be confessors, solicitors, auditors and witch doctors. . . ."* So be it.

The future, as Mort Sahl says, lies ahead, and the role of editors, like everything else, is bound to change. Corporate pressures for economies in overhead and benefits are likely to lead to more outside free-lance editing and diminished house staffs. It's a toss-up question as to whether more or less editing in general will be needed. On the one hand, entropic degeneration of the language, diminished devotion to accuracy, and word processor bloat all cry out for increased editorial ministrations. On the other hand, the legions crying "Who cares?" show no signs of fading away either.

Technology, ever the burr under the saddle of stasis, is bound to invade the editorial sanctum, a process long overdue according to recent jeremiads by Jonathan Yardley, Jacob Weisberg, and others who cannot see why editors have not turned en masse to the computer. The trouble is that so long as editing remains a suggestive rather than a coercive procedure, editing *must always leave its clear tracks.* The word processor itself is an inarguable blessing when it comes to writing or rewriting one's own copy, but when someone else's is on the operating table, seamless alteration would both insult and confuse. In that sense, until economical and user-friendly hardware and software for marginal comment, visible deletions, and the like are invented, the Post-it will remain a more significant aid to working editors than the computer. And editors themselves will remain subject to the "joy, fulfillment, grief, and frustration" of their craft, hoping that their ultimately invisible labors will make a real and positive difference.

*Quoted by William Jovanovich in *Now, Barrabas* (New York: Harper & Row, 1964), pp. 79–80.

The Evolution of the American Editor

Marc Aronson

MARC ARONSON *is a senior editor at Henry Holt's Books for Young Readers. As an editor of "multicultural" nonfiction for middle graders and young adults, he has specialized in introducing adult trade authors to children's book publishing. He is also writing a New York University history dissertation on William Crary Brownell and turn-of-the-century publishing. Mr. Aronson created and teaches a course in the history of publishing at NYU's Publishing Institute. Among the authors he has worked with are Bruce Brooks, Coretta Scott King, and Kyoko Mori.*

An examination of the social, cultural, and economic influences on American editors and editing, Marc Aronson's informative, entertaining, often provocative essay takes you from when editing as we know it began—the structural changes editor Ripley Hitchcock made in Edward Noyes West-cott's novel David Harum *(1898)—to a surprising and fascinating look at the innovative ways in which editors will work with writers as the new century approaches. "Editing . . . will enter the twenty-first [century] with an electronic bazaar. . . . We will all be editors when we choose to be, and, I'll bet, that will make us appreciate all the more those teams of hackers, pencil pushers, and typists who take the first crack at shaping our info-glut: the masters of multimedia, the captains of the cyberstream, the editors of the future."*

The Evolution of the American Editor

Editing in America began with an auction. Agents were changing the rules of publishing around 1898 when Edward Noyes Westcott's *David Harum* was published; but the auction that transformed publishing was not *for* that book but *in* it. Westcott, a banker from upstate New York, had written a novel about a shrewd local named David Harum. Cracker-barrel philosophy written in dialect (think of Joel Chandler Harris's *Uncle Remus*) was very popular, and Westcott had every reason to believe he would find a publisher. But he had no luck until his manuscript came across the desk of Ripley Hitchcock at Appleton. Hitchcock, an authority on etchings and the author of a series of popular histories, was an editor who was willing to take a risk. He recognized that the horse swap in chapter 6 of the manuscript was really the first chapter of the book. The editor moved it, transferring five chapters in the process, and made cuts and stylistic revisions throughout. His editing worked miracles. *David Harum* was the number one best-seller for 1899. In March and April of that year up to 1,000 copies a day left bookstore shelves. The book reached a total sale of 727,000 hardcover copies by 1904 and 1,190,000 by 1946, with another 241,000 out in paperback.

The work Hitchcock actually did on the manuscript was not unusual— other editors had also made suggestions for radical cuts and had turned rejected manuscripts into hot sellers—but there were two crucial differences this time: the book sold at a record-breaking pace, and people found out what the editor had done. Hitchcock became known as the man who had "made" *David Harum,* and the book transformed his career. The editor and his wife adapted the book for the stage and shared profits with the house (Westcott died before the book was published); it was then turned into two movies, one of which starred Will Rogers. Forty years after publication, the *New York Times Magazine* was still running features on the book and the editor who was responsible for it. In his long career Hitchcock also edited Stephen Crane and Theodore Dreiser, but his reputation, and modern American editing, turned on *David Harum.*

Following the success of *David Harum* the editor began to become a public personality, and by the 1930s a cultural mythology had formed around editing: the editor as savior, finding the soul of a manuscript; the editor as alchemist, turning lead into gold; the editor as seer, recognizing what others had missed. Another image of the editor was already in place in Hitchcock's day: the editor as friend. Taken together, editor as miner-magician and editor as boon companion, we have the classic image of the "editor of genius" that crystallized around an editor of the twenties, thirties, and forties, William Maxwell Evarts Perkins. But to really understand Perkins we have to start earlier, at least one hundred years earlier.

The first American authors to write best-sellers, men like Washington Irving and James Fenimore Cooper, broke through in the 1820s. Though New York was not yet the publishing mecca it would become, a few proto-agents set up shop in the city and groups of publishers, authors, and critics gathered around bookstores, beer halls, and restaurants to swap ideas and invent books. By the 1830s, recognizable publishing had taken shape in New York, Philadelphia, Boston, and Hartford (home of subscription publishing), and print was available in many formats, from cheap reprints to morocco leather. Twenty years later, in the 1850s, the United States had the largest literate public in history, and publishers put out books that ranged from sentimental love stories and children's textbooks, which sold in the hundreds of thousands, to fiction from sure money losers like Nathaniel Hawthorne, Henry David Thoreau, and (after he stopped writing sea adventures) Herman Melville.

Publishing was growing into an important industry and was contributing to American culture, but there were no editors in the modern sense. In part, this was because, until 1891, British imports had no legal copyright protection. Established houses followed "the courtesy of the trade" and paid English writers a royalty, but many new houses got their start with cheap reprints of Dickens and Thackeray, which required no editorial intervention. At Harper, free-lance house readers helped out on acceptance and rejection. Those called "editors" sometimes steered writers toward more lucrative themes and subjects, but they spent more energy on promoting authors than shaping texts. Robert Bonner, owner and editor of the *New York Ledger,* was a brilliant publicist who paid top dollar for the works of popular female novelists. Bonner's most extravagant move was to decorate a railroad parlor car with a gold wreath emblazoned with the name of one his best-selling authors. The Fanny Fern car rolled across America spreading the author's name far and wide, even after she died. Editors were also expected to write "puff pieces" that would run in the press as objective criticism.

Many houses were small enough that the author and the publisher, whose family name ran on the letterhead, communicated directly on projects. During the Civil War, for example, James T. Fields, editor of *Atlantic Monthly* and a partner in Ticknor & Fields, was forced to suggest that one of his authors make a radical change in an article. "Ticknor and I both think," Fields chided Nathaniel Hawthorne, "it will be politic to alter your phrases with reference to the President, to leave out the description of his awkwardness and general uncouth aspect. England is reading the magazine now and will gloat over the monkey figure of 'Uncle Abe.' " In the heated Civil War debates it fell to the editor/publisher to tell an author not to call the president a monkey. After the failure of *Moby Dick,* Melville wrote a novel about publishing. In *Pierre,* it is the firm of Wonder & Wen that writes to an affluent popular author asking for his next book, and the firm of Steel, Flint & Asbestos that takes up the matter when the author becomes disreputable.

An author's reputation was very important to publishers throughout the nineteenth century and even into the twentieth. Publishers felt it was their duty to ensure that American fiction would be unimpeachably moral in content, tone, and expression. Editing for morals can seem very different from Hitchcock's editing for market, but actually the two were related. American readers wanted moral books; those are the ones that sold. There was no surer way to kill a book than for it to be deemed "objectionable." The editor who could monitor an author's moral tone was also protecting the author's market share. Since many books were serialized in magazines owned by publishing houses before they came out as books, editors used what they presumed to be the virginal sensibility of the typical teenage girl as the gauge for their publications. Like network television a century later, if the magazine couldn't sit out on the coffee table to be enjoyed by the whole family, it could not be published. Houses had two ways of getting this kind of moral imprimatur, by hiring editors in-house who held those values, or by engaging a wide network of free-lance readers who were in touch with the sensibilities of many different groups of tastemakers. Charles Scribner's Sons followed the first approach and eventually made a home for Max Perkins; Macmillan used the second and gave a lot of editorial assignments to well-read or socially prominent women. In both cases these editors remained largely invisible to the general public.

Monitoring morals involved more than just selecting authors and supervising plots. During the nineteenth century, language inspired some heated controversies. Conflicts over proper usage, vocabulary, and spelling were fought out in the development and sales of new dictionaries, grammar books, and especially translations of the Bible. At issue were the claims of tradition (say, the King James Bible) against those of academic experts (who had duller but more accurate translations to offer), the language of the street versus the language of society, but also how, and toward what ends, language would be shaped in America. What kind of society should America be? An ordered one in which language follows tradition and so, it is hoped, do people's lives? Or an open-ended society in which language and behavior change from year to year? Similar conflicts came up in the 1960s as people raised the claims of Black English and debated which four-letter words should be included in dictionaries. We still have some traces of these imbroglios in discussions about gender and language. But the earlier debate was front-page news and had a direct impact on publishing houses, which had to choose who their readers, advisers, editors, and authors would be. Surprisingly, many houses chose the liberal academics or their allies over the elitist traditionalists.

By Hitchcock's day one last wrinkle had been added to the editorial mix. New magazines, financed by an explosion of consumer advertising, built their readership to record levels by publishing authors who employed a more "realistic" prose style. Some book editors who had been trained as journalists went after the same market. These new editors were more like corporate middle managers than moral monitors. They wanted American authors and they followed the latest fashions in public taste. These editors paid for authors who could deliver hard-hitting, lively prose on deadline. Turn-of-the-century writers' magazines recognized this trend and started to print articles on how to write to sell, and to issue profiles of leading editors and what they would buy. Authors complained that editors would take only well-known authors, how-to pieces, or human interest stories, while editors rejoined that they would be happy to publish great literature if only someone would write it. Between morals and market, people began to develop the idea that a house needed editors as well as publishers and that editing was a craft that could contribute to the success of a book. According to some publishers, like Alfred A. Knopf, this was a terrible mistake and led directly to the decline of publishing.

.   .   .

Max Perkins arrived at Charles Scribner's Sons in 1910 to work in the advertising department. William Crary Brownell, the literary adviser to the house, wrote books with titles like *Criticism, Standards,* and *Victorian Prose Masters* and was one of the fifty Americans who are periodically elected to the American Academy of Arts and Letters in recognition of their cultural prominence. Authors felt that approaching him was like entering a church, and Brownell saw editing as a form of cultural mission as well as a hard-headed business. Perkins shared Brownell's sense of the importance of books but made a major shift by decreeing that "the book belongs to the author." The young editor believed that editing involved a sort of compact to uncover and shape an author's talent, no matter what that took. This tireless, even heroic, devotion to the author and to the book was the hallmark of elite editing from the twenties to the forties.

Starting with F. Scott Fitzgerald, whose first novel he acquired over

Brownell's objection, Perkins worked with a memorable sequence of important authors such as Ernest Hemingway, Ring Lardner, Marjorie Kinnan Rawlings, Taylor Caldwell, and, especially, Thomas Wolfe. There is no more resonant image of American editing than the story of how Perkins crafted *Of Time and the River* out of the four-hundred-thousand-word tangle of unnumbered pages packed into three cartons that Wolfe submitted to him. Wolfe acknowledged his help in the book's dedication to "a great editor and a brave and honest man, who stuck to the writer of this book through times of bitter hopelessness and doubt and would not let him give in to his own despair." Perkins was not eager for the publicity, but his role in editing Wolfe's books became so well known that critics began to question how much Wolfe had actually written. Bernard De Voto accused "Mr. Perkins and the assembly line at Scribner's" of essentially creating Wolfe's books. Wolfe himself helped to shape the Perkins legend by turning the editor into Foxhall Edwards, a character in *You Can't Go Home Again.*

Perkins, and other "heroic" editors like Pascal Covici and Saxe Commins, pushed editing to (or even past) the line where it became necessary to an author's success. Did they go too far? These editors took on mammoth editing chores single-handedly while conducting intense, even melodramatic friendships with their brilliant but often self-destructive authors. And, all the while, they had to try to make the books commercial successes. In the mix of what we might now call genius and alcoholism, absolute devotion and codependency, hard work and burnout some of America's greatest fiction was published. But the editors did at times become too attached to their own importance, altering works without the author's permission and distorting the writer's text.

In the thirties, editing was expanded in other ways by women, many of whom were agents. Elizabeth Nowell, for example, did as much for Wolfe's magazine pieces as Perkins did for his novels—or even more: she selected, cut, and revised sections of his sprawling manuscripts to fit magazine word limits, negotiated fees, and even advised him on contraception so that he wouldn't have to worry about getting his lovers pregnant. Simon & Schuster was notorious for hiring secretaries on the basis of their appearance, but women became crucial to the industry as a result of their (often unacknowledged) intellectual merits. Female "executive assistants" often did much of the copy editing and detail work for their better-known bosses. Women also began to carve out a territory of their own as in-house editors of children's books. The most dramatic expansion of the editing pool, though, had to do with religion, not gender.

Starting in the teens, a series of new publishing houses appeared founded by young Jewish men, most of whom had graduated from Columbia University. These included houses that were founded as, or later became, Alfred

A. Knopf, Simon & Schuster, Random House, Viking, and Farrar, Straus, Giroux. The new Jewish houses moved editing in two directions: toward an expansion of free speech and toward a wider public that had been disdained or ignored by the Protestant elite. The new houses were not likely to sign up the stalwarts of mainstream America, who were already aligned with older houses like Appleton, Harper, or Scribner's. Instead, they looked to Europe and to the radicals of Greenwich Village for authors. This led to a series of censorship battles, including one turning point in 1923, when the New York State Assembly actually passed a censorship law only to have the Senate defeat it, and another in 1933, when the Supreme Court ruled in favor of James Joyce's *Ulysses*.

Other houses found new books by expanding their lists. The first books that S & S issued (albeit under a dummy name) were crossword puzzle books. Though tax guides had first appeared during the Civil War, and how-to manuals have existed in various forms since colonial days, S & S transformed that category of publishing with all-time best-sellers like *How to Win Friends and Influence People.* The company's approach was summarized in its motto, "Give the Reader a Break." While for some houses editing for morals was giving way to a search for avant-garde authors, for others the old sense of cultural mission was being supplanted by a well-organized effort to address more pragmatic needs. Either way, the new houses brought new editing styles to the industry.

. . .

Max Perkins died in 1947; while the myth of the heroic editor persisted, it no longer described the day-to-day reality of trade publishing. Perkins himself had grown discouraged, feeling that materialism was ruling America and that some book people were choosing expediency over literary values. Others sensed this as well. According to one character in Dawn Powell's 1942 novel, *A Time to Be Born* (reissued in 1991 by Yarrow Press), "the test of a publishing genius . . . is the ability to keep ahead of the times, to change your whole set of standards, overnight, if needs be." If we can believe this savvy, if cynical, author, the real values of the old-line houses and the herculean efforts of the great editors were also being mimicked by clever hypocrites with their eyes on the market. While Perkins remained the model for eager young entry-level editors until very close to the present day, a whole new brand of publishing began before he died that more frankly courted sales and changed the rules of the game entirely: paperbacks.

Paperbacks had been a part of American publishing at least since the 1840s, but the houses that issued them were disdained and fiercely opposed by the hardcover houses. "Story papers," dime novels, and "pirate" reprints were never treated as mainstream books. It took a more widespread acceptance of "middlebrow" culture, as well as the persistence and market research of Robert Fair de Graff, to make possible the advent of modern paperbacks in 1939. While changes in American society helped to give a new respectability to cheap books, the houses themselves made room for a new type of editor. Frankly seeking a mass readership, some houses hired editors from lower-class backgrounds, and even a few who had not gone to college. Market wisdom began to compete with the old school tie as a reason for hiring an editor.

At first these paperbacks were cheap reprints of hardcovers that were sold in new locations like drugstores and newsstands. Genre fiction, such as detective stories, westerns, romances, and later science fiction, was a natural for paperback since it could be put out cheaply in large numbers with relatively predictable sales. By the early fifties, though, NAL's Mentor list, Penguin, and most famously the Anchor list Jason Epstein founded at Doubleday added trade paperback lines that were sold through regular bookstores and included more "serious" titles. In all cases, paperback houses had to play by hardcover rules, stressing their literary interests, their respect for the main and original publisher, and their deep concern for an author's welfare. Paperback editing involved knowing who was publishing what and how they could be approached.

In the sixties, NAL moved publishing another step when it started to commission books with built-in movie tie-ins, but editors were already well aware of other media. As early as 1944 S & S was bought by Marshall Field, who also owned television and radio stations. Editors first realized the importance of author appearances on television in 1958, when Alexander King's monologues on Jack Paar's *Tonight* show made two of his books number one best-sellers. By the early sixties a hardcover editor had to be concerned not only with the merits of an author's work but with the other lives it might lead: would it go into paperback, could it be made into a movie, might the author (or, in the case of Bennett Cerf, the publisher) appear on television? Mass-market paperback editors began not only to buy books from hardcover houses but also to invent entirely new kinds of fiction, like gothic mystery and romance and later bodice rippers, that might never appear in hardcover.

In some houses the income from these new paperbacks helped to support smaller sellers, allowing upscale editors to concentrate their attention on literary value. Trade paperback editors were especially favored by this trade-off. In the fifties, for example, NAL was very proud that it could call Erskine Caldwell, and later Mickey Spillane, "the world's best-selling author," but it also gave a forum to new black writers like James Baldwin, Richard Wright, and Ralph Ellison. This balance, however, went only so far. At one point, Victor Weybright, copublisher of NAL, regretfully in-

formed the house literary adviser that he could not publish a book unless
it would have a minimum sale of 75,000 copies.

According to Ted Solotaroff, who worked there at the time, NAL still
balanced trade and mass market successfully in the mid-sixties. If this was
so, part of the credit must go to the mood of the much-maligned sixties.
Great Society spending on libraries, as well as the entry of the baby boomers into high school and then college, increased the market for serious and
challenging works. The counterculture may have been a product of television news and rock records, but every self-respecting radical had a shelf full
of well-thumbed paperbacks including everyone from Herbert Marcuse and
Eldridge Cleaver to Carlos Castaneda and Wilhelm Reich. The editor who
acquired and published radicals had risked court challenges in the 1920s; by
the 1960s he or she had a good chance of buying a best-seller.

Civil rights even entered publishing itself in the sixties and seventies as
houses made their first, short-lived efforts to hire nonwhite editors. However, because editing requires a college education yet offers very low entry-
level salaries, most intelligent, motivated people from low-income
backgrounds wisely pursued more lucrative professions. To this day editing
remains one of America's least integrated professions. On the other hand,
women have come near to, or have even broken through, the very highest
glass ceilings in publishing. Not only are many, perhaps most editors female, but women are frequently in very senior roles, such as editors-in-chief
or publishers. While this is particularly true in children's books, publishing
is one of the few industries in which the profile of the typical customer (for
fiction, a college-educated, middle-class woman from the Midwest) matches
that of a typical manager. You might say that, in publishing, women have
come close to controlling the means of production of their own reading. In
that sense, editors may be more in touch with the sensibilities of their
readers today than they have ever been.

• • •

The very success of paperbacks in the sixties and seventies, along with the
increased visibility of all forms of media, made publishing houses attractive
to Wall Street. Many prestigious hardcover houses, faced with the power of
paperbacks and the overtures of potential buyers, had to find new money
to stay independent, merge with other houses, or go out of business. As a
wave of takeovers washed over publishing, the lifetime job security that
old-line houses had offered to editors and authors gave way to a free market
in which both jumped from house to house seeking a better deal. Agents,
recognizing that houses needed bankable names, became more adroit at
using the old technique of an auction to get top dollar for their authors. Big
advances, which often did not earn out, only increased the financial pres-

sures on publishing houses, which were now often small units in large, cost-conscious organizations. "Return on investment" went from being an unfamiliar term in a book, which an editor might query, to being the crucial fiscal marker that could determine whether he or she even had a job.

In the eighties, as many publishing houses were subsumed into a new group of international conglomerates, the individual editor became less and less familiar to the public. Editors who were known at all gained fame more for their own novels, their social lives, or their media appearances than for their labors on texts. With millions of dollars riding on big-name authors, it became more important to a house that a book appear on a list than that it be in perfect shape. Editors simply had less time to edit and had to concentrate on hot new acquisitions. The actual work of line editing then fell to a variety of people, including assistants, agents, copy editors, writers' groups, book doctors, packagers, and well-meaning friends. In some respects this diffusion of editing to many out-of-house helpers was similar to the turn-of-the-century networks of free-lance readers. Today the editor is asked to think like a publisher, taking on many other tasks in addition to editing; as a result, authors and agents are pressured to turn in more polished work. Editing in the day of the media conglomerate looks more like antebellum "puffery," or the "reading" of the late nineteenth century, than the "heroic" labors of the middle twentieth.

· · ·

What is the future of editing? The skills of identifying authors, negotiating with agents, recognizing the strengths and weaknesses of texts, guiding a manuscript through the politics and perils of a house, and adding body English to its passage into the marketplace will continue to be important to publishing. The distinct image of the editor as the one person who discharges all of these functions out of some combination of professional pride and personal passion may not survive. Publishing, it has been said, goes through a standard twenty-year cycle including an initial phase, in which there are many small houses; a middle period, when these upstarts collapse, merge, or are bought out by larger houses; and a final stage, when the large houses falter, breaking apart once again into many small units. Today's large conglomerates may be about to break up, but there is another alternative that would create new possibilities for editors.

· · ·

The Japanese model of commercial organization—many small, often-competitive units working within a loose larger structure—is gaining popularity as a way to organize former nations like what was once the Soviet Union, as well as large corporations like IBM. This structure is especially attractive for publishing now because computer networks make it increasingly possible for authors to share and edit each other's texts, while the design capabilities of work stations blur the boundaries between editors and designers. Some publishers already mate editor, author, designer, and computer as a team entirely devoted to one project. The image of a house as made of distinct departments that report "up" to publishers and CEOs may give way to congeries of teams that share jobs and are responsible only for what they produce. In that loose structure groups of authors, such as a consortium of MFA students and faculty, or the members of a writers' group, might craft their texts electronically and function as a sort of allied imprint of a major house. Taking the current idea of an imprint to an extreme, a house would offer only technical support, distribution, and marketing, while the acquisition and editing of books would take place entirely in these semiautonomous teams whose only responsibility would be to meet some agreed-upon fiscal goal.

Instead of integrated hierarchies, publishing houses would be archipelagoes of diverse units, each with its own strategy and agenda. As multimedia options, including cybertexts, interactive home computers, and electronic books, become more prevalent, houses would offer the expertise, capital, and access to a broad band of media options that creative people will need. In exchange, the creative teams would be the avenue through which houses would keep in touch with the rapidly changing tastes of a public increasingly attached to the electronic media. Under these conditions, editing would come to mean anything that could be done for a book on a computer, including turning it into a multimedia extravaganza.

In the electronic-networked world of future publishing there will be as many editing styles as the distinct units require. Fully computerized editing programs could take quantified focus-group studies, mix them with marketing figures, and generate genre paperbacks from text through bound books untouched by human hands. On the other hand, small literary lines that rely on the taste and devotion of motivated individuals will be able to revive the editing of Perkins's day for those authors who require it and those readers who enjoy the results.

If editing ended the nineteenth century with an auction, it will enter the twenty-first with an electronic bazaar. As the tenth edition of this book is transmitted to your hand-held electronic page, you, the reader/editor, will have the option to compare all of the editions and edit the raw text for morals, language, market, art, mass taste, or some future alternative, and to clip in whatever art you like. The electronic editor will give you those selections, like rhythm buttons on electronic keyboards, and then offer you what some team has chosen as its own, time-saving best choice. We will all be editors when we choose to be, and, I'll bet, that will make us appreciate all the more those teams of hackers, pencil pushers, and typists who take the first crack at shaping our info-glut: the masters of multimedia, the captains of the cyberstream, the editors of the future.

An Open Letter to a Would-be Editor

M. Lincoln Schuster

M. LINCOLN SCHUSTER, *along with Richard L. Simon, founded Simon &
Schuster in 1924. They gambled everything on their first book—Margaret
Petherbridge's first compilation of crossword puzzles—and won! That kind
of imagination and innovation was typical of Mr. Schuster during his long
reign at Simon & Schuster (1924–66).*

*"An Open Letter to a Would-be Editor" was written for the first edition of
this anthology, in 1962. It is really a collection of* pensées, *their sum total
being a distillation of Mr. Schuster's many years as one of trade publishing's most creative and unconventional editors. In just twenty-four trenchant comments, he offers a lifetime of advice to any young editor ready to
read them, remember them, and, when possible, act upon them.*

*Since their first appearance over thirty years ago, I have heard many of
these comments quoted at publishing seminars, sales meetings, editors'
symposia, and wherever publishing people meet to discuss the latest metamorphosis of the publishing industry. Except for a reference to "the moment of truth . . . when you ask yourself the $64 question,"* they have not
dated; they could have been written this year, this month, or this week. Even
in our current age of bigness and emphasis on the bottom line, some things
in publishing just don't change—things like editorial integrity, taste, and
dedication. And I hope they never will!*

*A reference to a popular 1940s radio quiz show, upon which *The $64,000
Question* television show of the 1950s was based.—ED.

An Open Letter to a Would-be Editor

I

The great danger in applying for a job is that you might get it. If you are willing to take that as a calculated risk, I will set down some possibly helpful suggestions in the form of a few *short sentences* based on *long experience.*

II

You ask for the distinction between the terms "editor" and "publisher": An editor selects manuscripts; a publisher selects editors.

III

An editor's function doesn't begin with a *complete* manuscript formally submitted to him, all neatly packaged and ready to go to press. Almost the first lesson you must learn is that authors (or their agents) frequently submit not manuscripts, but ideas for manuscripts, and give you the privilege of "bidding blind." You are lucky if you can see an outline and a sample chapter first. Sometimes you *don't even see a single word.*

IV

A good editor must think and plan and decide as if he were a publisher, and conversely a good publisher must function as if he were an editor; to his "sense of literature" he must add a sense of arithmetic. He cannot afford the luxury of being color-blind. He must be able to distinguish between black ink and red.

V

It is not enough to "like" or "dislike" a manuscript, or an idea or a blueprint for a book. You must know and be able to tell convincingly and persuasively *why* you feel as you do about a submission.

VI

Don't pass judgment on a manuscript *as it is,* but *as it can be made to be.*

VII

Forget all clichés and myths about a "balanced list." If you think in such terms you will soon be stricken with *hardening of the categories.*

VIII

The greatest joy and the highest privilege of a creative editor is to touch life at all points and discover needs *still unmet*—and find the best authors to meet them.

IX

There are times when you must finally say: "Although this is a bad idea, it is also badly written."

X

Learn patience—sympathetic patience, creative patience—so that you will not be dismayed when you ask an author how his new book is coming along, and he tells you: "It's finished—all I have to do now is write it."

XI

Master the art of skimming, skipping, scanning, and sampling—the technique of reading part of a manuscript all the way through. You will have to learn when you can safely use this technique, and when you *must* read every single line, every single word.

XII

Learn to read with a pencil—not simply to note possible revisions and corrections, but to indicate both to yourself and to your colleagues ideas for promotion and advertising that may be activated many months later. Such ideas will be infinitely better if you spell them out while you are excited and inspired with the thrill of discovering the author or the book.

XIII

Deliberately practice the art of reducing to a short sentence or two the basic theme or impact of a book. You will have to learn to put the quintessence of the book on the back of a visiting card. This will later give you the nucleus for your editorial report, your jacket copy, your publisher's preview, your letters to reviewers, opinion-makers, salesmen, and booksellers.

XIV

Don't worry too much about mistakes you make deliberately; that is, disappointments and failures that may come from taking a calculated risk. Editing and publishing are risk-taking professions—sometimes they are wild gambles.

XV

Don't follow current vogues and fads, and never think of doing "another" book imitating the best-seller of the moment. Start trends, don't follow them.

XVI

Give great weight to an author's potential for growth—and to the long-life "survival value" of a given book for your backlist—a criterion far more crucial than immediate sales appeal.

XVII

If you are prepared to cast your affirmative vote for a book because of its prestige value—treating it realistically as a *succès de fiasco* or a *flop d'estime*—spell out the *reasons* for your enthusiasm, and calculate the fiscal arithmetic, so that you know just how much you are willing or prepared to lose.

XVIII

If you feel you must enlist the aid and advice of a recognized authority or specialist on a given subject, remember that an expert frequently avoids all the small errors as he sweeps on to the grand fallacy. A truly creative editor must become an expert on experts.

XIX

Don't be dismayed or disheartened if you learn that another publisher is getting out another book on the same subject. Far more important than being the first, be willing to settle for the best.

XX

Welcome suggestions and recommendations from your sales staff and your promotion and advertising colleagues, but resist any pressures that will be exerted by them for "sure things" and easy compromises.

XXI

Forget or disregard any glib oversimplifications about "the reading public." There is no such thing as one reading public.

XXII

Learn to win the confidence of your authors *before* the book is published, *during* the publication process, and *after* the book is released. Unless you inspire and enlist such confidence and cooperation, you will find yourself going back to the early days when the booksellers were also publishers, and the relationship between an author and a publisher was a relationship between a knife and a throat.

XXIII

For an editor the moment of truth comes when you ask yourself the $64 question: Would you buy this book if it were published by some other firm? This challenge, this test, can be expressed in many rule-of-thumb formulas, such as these: Stab any page and see if it bleeds. Do you feel that if you skip a paragraph you will miss an experience? Does it make the hair on the back of your neck stand on end (this test was suggested by A. E. Housman). But all these criteria come back to the two basic questions: Would you put your own money on the line to buy the book you are considering and, even more important, would you want to keep it in your own library—so much so that you will be happy to find it there years later, and look forward to the joy not only of reading it but of rereading it?

Always remember that you are being watched and judged by your colleagues and by your publisher, by authors, agents, booksellers, critics, and reviewers. They will rate you not on any single success or failure, but on your overall batting average. Babe Ruth, Ty Cobb, Mickey Mantle, and Roger Maris became world-famous champions by batting between .300 and .400—or somewhere between three and four hits for every ten times at bat. Therefore, within reasonable limits, you can luxuriate in integrity by acting with courage, with imagination, and above all, with the creative motivation that means fulfillment.

XXIV

Editing can, and should be, not only a life-enhancing profession but also a liberal education in itself, for it gives you the privilege of working with the most creative people of your time: authors and educators, world-movers and world-shakers. For taking a lifetime course for which you would be willing to pay tuition, you are paid, not merely with dollars, but with intellectual and spiritual satisfactions immeasurable.

Are Editors Necessary?

Richard Curtis

RICHARD CURTIS *has been a successful literary agent for over thirty years. His monthly column has appeared in* Locus, *a science-fiction trade publication, for over a dozen years. It has served as the basis for two books,* How to be Your Own Literary Agent *and* Beyond the Bestseller. *He is also the author of some fifty other books of fiction and nonfiction. He has received an Edgar Award nomination for his first mystery novel and two awards from* Playboy *for his humor pieces.*

"It takes as much courage to love a book, in many ways, as it does to love a person, and sometimes there is as much at stake. But there can be no love without responsibility, and no responsibility without fortitude," says Richard Curtis in this revision of his controversial, trenchant essay, which is every bit as challenging as its provocative title. Noting that today the trade book editor spends more time acquiring than line editing, he finds that "whether we like it or not, the responsibility for well-edited books is shifting to authors." Mr. Curtis recognizes that the multiple roles editors must play in today's complex publishing industry make them "professional company men and women" but urges them to maintain their editorial integrity and convictions by fighting hard for the writers they believe in, for the books they feel must be published. "If editors are to remain more than entertaining luncheon hosts, if they are to be not merely necessary but indispensable, they will have to continue resisting the pressures toward homogeneity and mediocrity that are arrayed against them by the monolith of Big Publishing."

Are Editors Necessary?

There's been a lot of talk lately about the decline of editing. These are fighting words.

The problem with evaluating this allegation is that everything editors do today is invidiously compared to the accomplishments of that quintessential master, Maxwell Perkins. Perkins practiced his art at the offices of Charles Scribner's Sons from 1914 until late in the 1940s and midwifed the masterpieces of such immortals as Hemingway, Fitzgerald, and Wolfe. "Where are today's Maxwell Perkinses?" is the plaintive cry of authors who discover horrifying grammatical, syntactical, factual, and typographical errors in their freshly minted books, or, worse, have them gleefully pointed out by friends and critics. Every such erratum is a rebuke to the hallowed memory of that figure who has been depicted as gracious, patient, erudite, nurturing, precise, demanding, polite, and modest, a man whose love of authors was exceeded only by his love of good and well-made books. Let's assume that he truly did possess all of the virtues ascribed to him, and more if you wish.

I have no desire to desecrate either his memory or his achievements. I just don't happen to think that "Where are today's Maxwell Perkinses?" is a very good question. It oversimplifies editing both then and now, and fails to take into account the fact that today's editors simply don't perform the same tasks that their forebears did. I know a number of great editors working today, but they're great in many significantly different ways from the great editors of yesteryear.

Just about every aspect of publishing has changed since Perkins's era. The types of books published are different. Agents exert far more influence. The paperback industry has revolutionized the marketing of books. Computers and word processors have been created and refined. Bookstore chains have become a dominant force in the marketplace. Printing technology has improved immensely. Books today are not acquired, edited, produced, printed, or distributed the same way they were earlier in this century. They are not even written the same way.

We must also define "editors" before we apply the word irresponsibly. Editing is a highly complex set of functions, and no single individual is capable of exercising them with equal aplomb. The editor who wines and dines agents and charms authors may be a clumsy negotiator; the brilliant dealmaker may have no patience for the tedious and demanding word-by-word task of copy editing; the copy editor who brilliantly brings a book to life word by word, line by line, may be completely at sixes and sevens when it comes to handling authors.

It is certainly easy to wax nostalgic about editing in the Good Old Days (which really ended only about twenty or twenty-five years ago). If accounts and memoirs of that era can be trusted, editors then were steeped in fine arts, philosophy, languages, and the classics. They were a breed of compulsively orderly and fanatically precise individuals who ruthlessly stalked and destroyed typos, solecisms, and factual inaccuracies, and who conducted prodigious debates with authors about linguistic nuances. Their pride in their labors matched—and sometimes exceeded—that of the authors themselves. And when it came to money—well, they placed literature high above crass commerce, and discussed author compensation with the same delicacy they reserved for childbearing.

Christopher Lehmann-Haupt, a book critic for the *New York Times,* in an article about the vanishing breed of editors, quoted Harper and Row editor Dolores Simon as observing that ". . . there simply isn't the old interest in grammatical precision among young people any more." And Joseph Smith, an editor at Simon & Schuster, said that although good editors are still coming into our business, they are not "fastidious" in that "quaint way" we associate with oak-paneled editorial offices of yore. Lehmann-Haupt, himself a former editor, described strolls through Times Square in which he obsessively edited billboards, neon signs, the printing on the sides of trucks, and even sidewalk graffiti. David Leavitt, in his novel *The Lost Language of Cranes,* captured the ideal editor's profile, describing her as driven by the instinct "to put the world in order" and "possessed of the rare capacity to sit all day in a small cubicle, like a monk in a cell, and read with an almost penitential rigor."

Trumbull Rogers, a free-lance technical copy editor writing in the "My Say" opinion column of *Publishers Weekly,* observed:

> When I landed my first job in publishing in 1970, my boss sat me down at a desk and told me to spend the first day learning the house style. The style was important because all the articles I would copyedit had to conform to it—no exceptions. The emphasis of my training was on economy and clarity of marking . . . , accuracy and attention to details. Although the journals were set in hot metal, we still made punctuation corrections in page proof, a very expensive process, but we felt it was worth it to create a product we could be proud of.

Today's editor, industry critics claim, no longer has that pride and painstaking compulsiveness. Indeed, it has been contended, editors today do everything but edit. The nurturing of authors has given way to the acquisition of properties. Editorial taste and judgment have been replaced by the application of success formulas devised by editorial committees. Risk taking, hunches, and commercial instincts have yielded to the conservative application of bottom-line buying policies dictated by bookstore chain managers and implemented by rigid computer programs. The new breed of editorial animal, it is asserted, looks down his or her nose at line editing and production details. The time and money pressures of today's monolithic and highly competitive publishing business have devalued good bookmaking. The result is books that fall apart, prematurely yellow with age, and are scandalously rife with typos. "Years ago," Rogers wrote (his "My Say" piece was entitled "On the Road to Mediocrity"), "you rarely saw a typo in a book; now you rarely pick up *any* book that isn't riddled with every imaginable kind of error."

Invited to comment on the transformation of the editing profession over the last few decades, author Harlan Ellison had this to say:

In large measure because of the niggardly wages paid to entry-level personnel, the caliber of daring, intelligence, and expertise has decreased alarmingly over the past twenty-five years, in my opinion. With the takeover of this "gentleman's sport" by multinational corporations obsessed by the bottom line, those rare urbane individuals who looked on editing as a holy calling have vanished. Priced out of the market. The Maxwell Perkinses, Walter Fultzes, Ben Hibbses and others are no longer with us, nor will the arena permit their sort to reappear. Now, with editors being drawn from a pool of business school graduates, we find entry-level editorial personnel who are semiliterate and understand debentures better than declensions.

Editorial success today means climbing the corporate ladder, passing through the sweaty environs of editorial responsibility. But it is, sadly, a case of the lame leading the halt; because most of the people with whom these arrivistes must work are already working writers. So where is the guiding intelligence a writer looks to in his or her editor? In my view, with modern technology overtaking the scutwork of editorial responsibility, virtually the only value an editor has for a professional writer (first novelists are another matter) is in the generation of "in-house interest," the ramrodding and championing of a book through the labyrinth of publishing house indifference, ineptitude, and chance. And when the editor hasn't the in-house rep or clout to get that enthusiasm translated into promotional and advertising dollars his/her value is damned near zero.

Ellison's criticisms go true to the mark, as they usually do. But they must also be evaluated in a larger context.

Unquestionably, a shift has taken place in the role of trade book editors from what is generally characterized as line functions to that of acquisitions. The earlier role, the one that we most sentimentalize, combined nurturing parent and stern taskmaster, a person who could get a great book out of an author, then groom and curry the text until it virtually sparkled. Although editors then, as now, worked for publishers whose profit agenda seldom coincided with that of their authors, the editor was thought of as the author's friend, protector, and advocate.

The emphasis today on the acquisition role of editors places them in a more adversarial role with authors. Negotiation often pits them against each other, and the residue of resentment and distrust that remains after the bargain is sealed makes it difficult for authors to feel completely comfortable with their editors.

The paternalistic treatment of authors by editors in earlier times, however, produced its own set of inequities, for publishers took advantage of many authors who were too ignorant, shy, or well bred to demand good terms of their editors. Knowing that most authors write for love, publishers tended to assume that they didn't need to write for money.

Resentment toward publishers over their exploitation of authors created the conditions for the rise to power of literary agents, and though new authors today are still at a disadvantage, the balance eventually shifts when they engage agents and become more successful. Good agents often insist on a large measure of control over the author-editor relationship, holding authors at arm's length from their editors to protect them from being taken advantage of. And what has happened in the four or five decades since this transformation occurred is that the agents have begun to take over the role formerly played by editors. Today's agents nurture authors, work closely with them in the development of their work, perform a great many editorial tasks, and lend strong emotional and psychological support. And, perhaps most important of all, in a turbulent world of publishing mergers and takeovers and editorial musical chairs, agents have become the islands of stability and reliability that were once the province of editors. So, if the importance of editors in this respect has diminished, the loss has not necessarily affected authors for the worse.

Or, take the tasks of copyediting manuscripts and proofreading galleys. Although these still fall upon the employees of publishing companies, the high costs of running businesses have caused a shift from in-house line editing to free-lance work done at home. Many copy editors are former employees of publishers who have managed to adapt their responsibilities to their domestic schedules. But the pressures of producing large numbers of books annually have forced publishers to overload editors with work or to seek less-experienced people to do these highly demanding jobs. Some publishers just can't afford the time or expense to train copy editors, supervise them closely, review their work, and instill in them a grasp of house style, a knowledge of company tradition, and a sense of pride. English is not even the first language for many copy editors. And those who are fluent in English may not have the patience, precision, and skill to be good editors.

Whether we like it or not, the responsibility for well-edited books is shifting to authors. Actually, they have always borne much of that burden. In hardcover publishing particularly, most authors are given the opportunity (if not the contractual right) to review copyedited manuscripts and to proofread galleys, and if an author doesn't care enough to double-check every fact, even dubious grammatical construction and spelling, indeed every word of his manuscript and galleys, he has no one to blame but himself for a flawed product.

It is harder for authors to control errors in paperback originals and reprints, however, because tight publication schedules make it prohibitive for publishers to furnish galleys for review by authors in many cases. Also, authors rarely get to see galleys of paperback reprints of their hardcover books. But authors and their agents can and often do demand the right to examine galleys in exchange for a promise to turn them around promptly. Thus, even paperback authors have a chance to bring out unblemished books.

The development of computerized editing and word processing hardware and software promises to eliminate many problems for authors and editors. Although numerous technical, financial, labor, and other obstacles have impeded the automation of some important editorial functions, I'm reasonably certain that these will be overcome in the foreseeable future, making clean copy in both manuscript and galley an everyday occurrence. The same is true for style, design, composition, and other aspects of the publishing process that are now in the hands of a diminishing number of expert craftspeople. In short, emerging technology will replace a good deal of the mental and manual labor involved in producing books.

What do all these changes leave for editors to do? The answer is, just about everything. Unlike those of the older generation, today's editors must master an entire gamut of disciplines including production, marketing, negotiation, promotion, advertising, publicity, accounting, salesmanship, psychology, politics, diplomacy, and—well, editing. But into that last designation goes a bewildering variety of activities, many only remotely connected with the stereotyped one of sitting in a monastic office hunting for typos. "I don't know what *you* mean by editing," one editor said to me, "but among the responsibilities found in *my* job description are proposing ideas and subjects to authors, soliciting authors and experts for projects I'm developing, dealmaking, line editing, packaging, lobbying in the house for books I love, boosting those books to anybody in the trade who will listen, preparing profit and loss projections, and . . . well, how many hours do you have to listen to what else I do?"

The dizzying pace and complexity of modern publishing make it neither possible nor desirable for editors to sit all day reading or conversing with authors. They must be worldly and sophisticated, capable of shepherding the projects they sponsor through a gauntlet of technical, financial, political, and other hazards. Though editors are often criticized for being corporate animals, in this respect at least we should thank our stars that they are. For they and they alone understand how to work their systems, to maneuver, coax, and sometimes ram their beloved books—*our* beloved books!—through the corporate obstacle course. Today's editors are professional company men and women, and if they don't have a problem with that characterization, I don't see why we should.

Jennifer Brehl, a young editor known for her ardent advocacy of the projects she sponsors, expressed what she believes an editor's role today must be. "I don't care how many editorial functions agents have assumed, authors still need someone in the house to see their books through at every stage. We must work, and work well, with every department. Among the many things we are, we are expediters and facilitators." When I asked her if she thought her attitude was typical of her generation of editors, she nodded vigorously. "Lord knows we're not in it for the money. You can't be a disinterested party when it comes to writers. You have to love books; a writer needs someone in the house who loves his or her work."

I believe she has identified the critical factor in the makeup of all good editors, and though her style of dealing with books and authors may be light-years apart from that of Maxwell Perkins, he undoubtedly would recognize the underlying passion.

There are many editorial qualities that are irreplaceable. Among them are taste, discrimination, personal emotional response, a sense of order and organization, determination, devotion, and tender loving care. In these respects, no one has discovered anyone or anything that can remotely take the place of an editor. Agents can't do it because they're outsiders. Computers can't do it because they're heartless.

But none of those virtues means anything if editors are lacking in courage. The biggest threat to the health of our industry is not mergers and acquisitions. It is failure of nerve on the part of its editors. The evolution of publishing from a profession run by individuals to a business managed by committees has created a population of editors preoccupied with holding their jobs. The pressures they live under are constantly forcing them to lower the common denominator when selecting the projects they wish to sponsor. This means that it is easier to say no than yes.

The way that this attitude manifests itself for me is editors' resistance to acquiring books that are even slightly flawed. It was not long ago that the prevailing attitude among editors was, "This book has some problems, but the author is so talented that I'd like to buy it and work with him." Today such words are rarely heard. A book with problems is a book rejected, and more and more one hears editors say, "Let the author revise it, then we'll decide if we want to buy it." Many of them have confided in me that they would love to buy the book, but the prospect of bucking the system is simply too daunting.

"In order to acquire a book I love," another editor told me, "I have to fight. I have to fight with my colleagues, my bosses, with a battery of naysayers telling me, 'This will never work,' 'That will never work,' 'This doesn't fit our formula,' 'That's too hard to do.' A person can get weary and beaten down. Sometimes we all wonder if it isn't easier to say the hell with it and turn the damned thing down."

Also, editors have a tendency to shrink from editing the work of established, and in particular prominent, writers. Their timidity may be exacerbated by the bullying of egotistical authors and their agents, who feel they have outgrown the need for criticism by publishers. Once a writer has "arrived," editors may assume that he has mastered his craft and that their role is simply one of messenger between author and printer. The assumption is often reinforced by publishing executives eager to get the book out in order to start recovering their investment as soon as possible. It takes courage for an editor to resist this trap and point out the deficiencies in the "emperor's new clothes."

It takes as much courage to love a book, in many ways, as it does to love a person, and sometimes there is as much at stake. But there can be no love without responsibility, and no responsibility without fortitude. "I'm responsible for my books," editor David Wolff, formerly with Macmillan, proudly declared to me. "And I *want* to be responsible for them."

When I asked an agent colleague of mine, Betty Marks, whether she thought editors were necessary, she quipped, "Of course they are. Who else can take agents to lunch?" If editors are to remain more than entertaining luncheon hosts, if they are to be not merely necessary but indispensable, they will have to continue resisting the pressures toward homogeneity and mediocrity that are arrayed against them by the monolith of Big Publishing.

I sincerely wish them luck.

Putting his tongue firmly in his cheek, Mr. Curtis answered his own question, "Are Editors Necessary?," in this spoof of the work habits of editors he wrote for Publishers Weekly *around April Fool's Day several years ago.*

On the Decline of Western Literature

Why aren't good books published anymore? Critics know *when* the last good book was published (1978) but they simply do not know why. Some say the answer lies in the eclipsing of creativity by television. Others say the flower of our youth was decimated by war, drugs, and general messing around. Still others attribute the problem to the siphoning off of literary talent by the advertising business, and still others blame our teachers. None of this is true.

The answer is simply that editors no longer work.

Shocking though this statement may seem at first, it has been amply demonstrated in a recent exit survey undertaken by a literary agent outside the Grill Room of the Four Seasons, who offers the following data:

How Editors Spend Their Time Per Year

Total number of days in year 365

From which are subtracted:

Weekend days 104
Legal and religious holidays 20
Thursdays, Fridays, and Mondays taken off for long holiday
    weekends 6
Vacation days, not including weekends 15
Fridays during summer, Memorial Day through Labor Day 14
Jury duty 10
Preparation for American Booksellers Association Convention 5
American Booksellers Convention 5
Recovery from American Booksellers Convention 5
Preparation for Frankfurt Book Fair 5
Frankfurt Book Fair 5
Recovery from Frankfurt Book Fair 5

Preparation for, attendance at, and recovery from Jerusalem,
   Canadian, Third World, Latin American, Moscow Copyright and
   other fairs and conventions 30
Business trips to London, Milan, Paris, and the Coast 30
Preparation for, attendance at, and recovery from two semiannual
   sales conferences 30
Illness 10
Personal emergencies 5
Funerals 3
                                                                                —

Total days out of office annually 307

Leaving:

Total days actually at office 58

We have demonstrated that editors actually spend only 58 days out of
any given year (except leap year) working in their offices. But—do they
really *work* there? A second survey, this one a poll of 460 former editors-in-
chief of major publishing companies, taken at the Midtown branch of the
New York State Unemployment Office, revealed something that most authors have always suspected but never until now had confirmed:

How Editors Spend Their Time Per Day

Total number of hours in working day (9 A.M. to 5 P.M.) 8.00

From which are subtracted:

Time trapped in traffic 0.15
Lunch (including travel time) 2.15
Editorial board meetings, publication board meetings, staff and
   other meetings 2.00
Just going into a meeting 0.05
Just getting off a call 0.10
Just running out the door 0.10
Just down the hall 0.15
Coffee breaks 0.20
Personal phone calls 0.25
Industry gossip 0.20
Keeping up with the industry (reading *Publishers Weekly, Variety,
   New York Times, Newsweek, Playboy*) 0.15
Taking things up with the powers that be 0.10
Noodling with the figures 0.05

Seeing what the sub rights people say 0.05
Checking with legal 0.05
Running down one last figure from production 0.05
Locating the check 0.15
Locating the manuscript 0.15
Typing up, photocopying, and mailing résumés to other publishers. 0.30

Total hours occupied in not editing anything 8.00

Leaving:

Total hours devoted to advancing the cause of literature 0.00

Lunch with a
Favorite Agent

John F. Thornton

In his last full year as a trade book acquisition editor, JOHN THORNTON purchased breakfast, lunch, drinks, and dinner for, by his count, 107 literary agents. It is all the more lamentable that, within a year of his departure for the Book-of-the-Month Club, where he is now editorial director, the publishing division that employed him was dismantled, Lego fashion, and redistributed. His fond hope is that the many best-seller proposals he was promised will eventually come into his purview as finished books to purchase for his club members.

April Fool's jest or not, Mr. Thornton, then associate publisher for Facts on File, rose to the defense of his editorial colleagues, put his own tongue firmly in his own cheek, and sent off to the "Letters" column of Publishers Weekly the following satiric parry to Mr. Curtis's satiric thrust.

Lunch with a
Favorite Agent

"An outrage, nothing less," is what my favorite agent, G. Gordon Bidding, called Richard Curtis's April Fool's Day attack on editors ("News of the Week," Mar. 30). "Relations are tense enough these days without having to throw a sucker punch like that, don't you think?" he asked in a tone of genuine concern.

"Hardly," I said. "The wonder is that editors haven't gotten a proper skewering long ago. And what a pack of smug, supercilious parasites they are, too!" Bidding professed shock and promptly suggested, after coyly asserting that I owed him lunch ("and none of your local third-world bistros, either," he chided), that we discuss it further.

By the time we met (in the Gull Room of the Four Caesars), Bidding's ardor had cooled to a mild amnesia, and he suggested, between mouthfuls of foie gras washed down by chaste Perrier, that we get business out of the way first, to wit:

1) He'd been forced, much against his will, to take a $150K floor on the exclusive he'd given me for Judith Danielle's hot new *roman à clef* on the aerobics industry. ("Michael Cordwood at Ransom House simply seduced me.")
2) If I could just pry loose an extra $5K in advance money, my long-awaited ms. on the Iranian hostage crisis would almost certainly be delivered in time for the Inauguration.
3) He was fairly champing at the bit to get the first serial action rolling on the exciting designer sunglasses exposé we'd signed; in fact, as soon as I could messenger over some finished copies he'd make it a top priority.
4) He was as disappointed as we were about the ghosted John Mitchell autobiography. ("I was certain that once he'd actually *read* it, he'd fall in love with it.")
5) Finally, if I could trust his instincts, he had this offbeat but wonderful little ms. on the history of sewage, which, to be sure, had been around the block a few times, but . . .

By now Bidding was toying with the last of his Grand Marnier soufflé. The effort seemed to exhaust him. He rallied for a moment to rail against a culture that rewarded guile and censored art, then jumped up, said he was off to an early drinks date, expressed his unshakable loyalty to me and my kind, and flitted into the gathering twilight. Would that all my agents were such sterling fellows, I mused, as the waiter took my credit card offstage for a melting.

John F. Thornton

Associate Publisher, Facts on File

New York, NY

April 27, 1984

Breaking Faith

A Publishing Parable

Maxwell Gherkin

"MAXWELL GHERKIN" is the pseudonym of one of America's most distinguished editors.

"The bottom line at Concord Press these days was the bottom line." So how
energetically should a dedicated editor like Martha G. fight the powers that
be at Concord to get behind the new novel by her talented, serious (but
seriously uncommercial) author, David R.? Should she put her in-house
reputation, maybe even her job, at risk to push for more advertising for a
well-reviewed novel she knows will sell less than four thousand copies? Or
should she abandon David and his career and bask in the glory and the
credit for her work on a mediocre, glitzy, sexy novel that is literarily under-
whelming but is already a best-seller?

Veteran publishing insider Maxwell Gherkin's dissection of how Martha
G. solved her professional and personal moral dilemma stirred great controversy when it appeared in the pages of Publishers Weekly. And it is still
being discussed passionately. Is it a piece of fiction about the amorality of
contemporary publishing written by a cynical, embittered editor? Or is it a
brutally candid, shrewdly observed piece of reportage by an unflinchingly
honest editor offering a completely realistic look at a typical, practical
problem faced by editors and writers in many publishing houses today?
Your opinion may be colored by whether you are a successful or unsuccessful, commercial or uncommercial editor or writer. But wherever your career
is at, you'll want to learn what Martha's decision was, and what economic,
cultural, and publishing pressures influenced her decision. You might even
look inside yourself and ask what you would have done if you were faced
with her problem.

Breaking Faith
A Publishing Parable

David R. is a gifted novelist in his forties. His first book, a strongly drawn account of an auto worker's family that is torn apart by the conflicts of the 1960s, had been successful—glowing reviews, a $50,000 paperback sale, a National Book Award nomination, an immediate place in the sun. His next two were shorter, more experimental novels, one about a surreal commune in northern California, the other a metafictional treatment of people trapped inside a detective novel, and there was a sharp tailing off in review interest and sales. He wrote short stories for several years, trying unsuccessfully to find a way to score again.

David had taken all of this hard. He'd wanted to explore the different ways of telling a story, of imagining the world. But coming from a working-class background, he was particularly motivated to get ahead, to make his writing pay, and his attempts to develop his powers had made him lose ground; his career seemed to be going backwards, from modest riches to rags. He was also very conscious of the new generation of novelists, the so-called Brat Pack, who were getting so much attention and astonishing advances for what he dismissed as "go-go writing" but by whom he felt eclipsed. Stuck in a teaching job at a small university in Ohio, where he ran the writing program, burdened by family responsibilities, and bored spitless by the small-time community where he had been living for twelve years— the sort of town that novelists of previous generations had fled from— David felt himself sinking into the excuses and cynicism that he had seen mark the end of the line for a number of writers.

But then an NEA grant came through, and soon after he hit upon a story idea that was rich in possibilities, maybe even commercial ones. Spurred on by his returning powers, he wrote a three-hundred-page novel in eighteen months. Thinking it both the best book he had written and the riskiest, he sent it off to New York, and in the weeks that followed felt like a man awaiting a jury verdict.

Martha G., a veteran editor, was anticipating David's manuscript with mixed feelings. She loved most of his work, was glad that he had come out of his malaise, but was apprehensive about how a new novel by him would fly at Concord Press, where the success of his first book had worn thin. From what he had indicated to her, the new one was much more "main-stream" than his last two, but novelists usually tended to believe that, particularly the more experimental ones. She admired his desire to keep exploring, but she found herself hoping that he had come back to a broadly interesting subject and the common touch that had launched him. Also, she could use a success herself.

For the bottom line at Concord Press these days was the bottom line. A house that had been small and venturesome in the arts, political and social thought, and children's literature, Concord was now trying to find a new, broader identity as the hardcover house in a publishing group owned by INCOM, an international communications empire. Having acquired Concord, one of the last of the independent houses, for several times its value, the new management had dealt with it as a real-estate developer deals with a venerable town house he has bought mainly for its location and then carves up into condos. Under the mandate to spend what was necessary to increase profits by 10 percent each year, Concord had acquired a number of "brand name" authors, doubled its marketing operations, and pruned and diversified its editorial staff to provide more product for the shopping mall market: i.e., books that "meet a need or a trend," as Dot B.—the chic, hard-driving marketing whiz whom INCOM had recently brought in as publisher—put it. The weekend after David's book arrived Martha pushed aside a manuscript called *The Adult Parent* that she was editing and a hot project for a Romanian cookbook, and settled into her reading chair with *Remembering Angie.*

David had found his subject: she could tell that after two pages by the simple, unmistakable feeling of expectant pleasure that fiction that was right on the money gave her. "My first impression of Angie Annaseri was of a pretty, glum-faced girl you might come across in a high school yearbook with one activity underneath her name." The first chapter was in the words of Dwight Jay, a U.S. attorney, who twenty years ago had picked Angie up at a softball game in Dearborn, Michigan, where he was working that summer as a draft resistance counselor. In the next chapter Angie took up the story, prompted by a letter she had received from Dwight, who had been approached for help by her brother, Jimmy, an indicted drug dealer. "Dwight was like a lottery ticket in which you got Peter Fonda. Spectacular but foolish to believe in. Yet she had. People were believing all sorts of craziness back then. Like Jimmy had believed Dwight and ended up in prison."

· · ·

Told in alternate chapters and letters by the two of them—Dwight in Chicago, Angie in San Jose, California—the novel became a political parable of the past three decades, a drama of moral responsibility, and most of all a riveting study of a contemporary working-class woman. Ballsy, full-hearted, resolute, Angie has raised three children by herself; she had also become addicted to the amphetamines that got her through the days and to the Manhattans that got her to sleep. When Dwight contacted her, she was an assistant manager at a Sizzler restaurant, a fixture of her AA group, and thinking of marrying an older man, another recovering alcoholic. But the summer she had spent with Dwight was still the homing device of her heart, and the novel left her in limbo as a more or less emblematic figure of cultural betrayal like her brother.

Martha sensed that David hadn't fully grasped Angie's present life, which weakened the ending. She phoned David late Sunday night, sang the book's praises for several minutes, and then entered her reservations. He didn't agree with her about the ending. "You want some uplift that just isn't in their cards," he said.

A few days later she wrote to David, saying that since this was finally Angie's story, she wondered if there could be an epilogue and some prior indication that registered where Angie had come out. David wrote back that that kind of ending had gone out with Dickens, that he didn't know what decision she would make and didn't want to have to rewrite the last third of the book to find out.

Shortly thereafter, David's agent, Al V., phoned to say that unless Martha made a substantial offer they wanted to show the book elsewhere. "We feel that this is David's breakout book," he said. "We're looking for six figures."

Martha said that she'd been thinking in the $25,000 area if David agreed to find a way to pull the novel together.

"No way. We need much more of a commitment."

"Commitment? We published David's last two books, which didn't earn twenty-five thousand between them. Be reasonable, Al."

"Martha, things are crazy out there. I sold a first novel last month for a hundred sixty-five thousand that doesn't have half the legs David's book does."

There was little else to say. Martha wrote David a wish-you-well letter and thought that was that. Another close, long-standing relationship down the tubes of what publishing had become.

•   •   •

A few months later David called Martha, said he was in New York and needed to see her. When he arrived, his normally sturdy bearing was visibly shaken. He told her of the other houses' responses. Several had passed; one had offered a $7,500 advance; two others had mentioned considerably more, but one wanted "a big dramatic scene at the end in which they meet again" and the other wanted the story to focus more on the romance: "less telling, more showing; less talk, more sex." David banged his big hands together and grinned for the first time. "Less your book, baby, and more mine." The outcome of their meeting was that he decided to take a crack at revising it along the lines Martha had suggested.

At first he reported that it was "like digging into frozen ground," but the more he imagined his way into Angie's recent life and state of mind, the more he found the material opening up again and coming alive. When he was finished, they both saw that his new accession of consciousness about Angie needed to be pieced into the earlier sections of her story.

When the revisions began to click, Martha submitted the first fifty pages and a description of the rest to the publishing committee in order to acquire the book. Believing that *Remembering Angie* now stood a good chance of selling a minimum of 10,000 in hardcover and again in paperback, she asked for an advance of $25,000.

But at the publishing committee meeting she ran into solid resistance. Dot B., looking more harried than stylish these days (Concord had just lost its top thriller writer to another house and its nonfiction leader, a "juicy" account of the Reagans' social circle, was taking heavy returns on a 250,000-copy first printing), said she hadn't gotten very far with *Remembering Angie*. "Half the time I didn't know where I was," she snapped. "Past or present. Chicago or California. Also, a tony lawyer and a hash slinger? Give me a break."

Mac S., the editorial director, liked the writing of the sample chapters but thought that the character of Angie was too blue-collar for many hardcover readers, particularly women, to identify with.

"Such things happen," Martha said as calmly as she could. "Even in fiction. For example, *Love Story*."

"This isn't *Love Story*," Dot said. "It's much less emotional and accessible. Also it's a downer, from what I can see."

Martha said that the book became more moving as it went along, particularly with the revisions the author was making. "I think it can succeed. Also I'm not asking for us to invest a ton of money."

"Who's going to buy this book?" marketing manager Lance L. asked.

Martha reminded herself that he was only doing his job. Gone were the days when a novel like *Remembering Angie* was perceived as an opportunity rather than a problem, when a book this promising by a Concord author created enthusiasm and affection, which was communicated inside the house and which then emanated from it, paving the book's way to the review media and from there to the reading public. Now what was called for was a pseudosociology that reduced the book to some slot in the market. So, trying to keep her tongue out of her cheek, she gave them one. "This will appeal to the *Big Chill* audience. Also the educated reader who likes Bruce Springsteen . . ."

"But those people buy paperbacks," said Lance.

"Well, what about doing it as a quality paperback and take a strong position on it, really break it out?"

"We've been down that road before," Mac said. "If it doesn't work, you get killed."

Martha tried again. "You have to see it for what it is: a finely written love story that evokes an era that meant a lot to a lot of people. People who read books."

"Novels about the sixties just don't sell," said Lance. "Look what happened to his second book about the hippies."

"Well, where do we stand?" Martha then asked. When there was no immediate answer she played her last card. "I really want us to do this book. Also two other houses are after it at about that advance."

"I don't get it," said Dot. "I thought he was working on it with you."

"His agent has been showing it around, but he'd like to stay."

Dot wanted to know who the competition was. When Martha told her, she said, "Offer twelve-five. I wouldn't mind putting Al's feet to the fire for trying to move one of our authors."

"I've been talking in the neighborhood of twenty-five, and that was before he began improving it."

"Well, now you have a captive author so take advantage of it," Dot said. "I want people to know that we play hardball too."

With Mac's support Martha was able to get permission to settle at seventeen-five, with two-thirds of it paid right away. Even so, she left the meeting feeling thoroughly undermined. In her previous career as a senior editor, her estimate of the value of a book like David's would have been more or less taken for granted. Also her first offer would have been honored.

Needless to say, neither David nor Al was happy about the new terms. But now David was mainly bent on finishing the book, and Al was content to let her off the hook with a little dig. "I'm getting used to the fact that editors are powerless these days," he said.

· · ·

While the book was in production, Martha sent out the usual bound galleys for quotes, and the book's luck began to change—or rather its class began to tell. Though most well-known authors are glutted with advance copies and seldom respond, Martha received several enthusiastic quotes, including one of ringing praise from a famous critic, Victor P., which began, "At last a new American novel with a social conscience and a cultural vision. *Remembering Angie* does for the sixties what *The Great Gatsby* did for the twenties by encoding a chapter of the Romantic movement in America in a love story."

"My cup runneth over," David said as Martha read the letter to him. When she was finished, he said, "If nothing else happens, this makes it all worthwhile."

Martha shared the critic's comment with Mac, her one ally, discussing with him how best to make use of it. They decided to shorten it to "It does for the sixties what *The Great Gatsby* did for the twenties." She sent it around with the other quotes in a memo to the key marketing executives that also invoked the success of David's first book. She wrote a similar letter to the field force and added a personal note and a copy of the bound galleys for each of the reps who she thought would cotton to *Remembering Angie* and might speak up for it at the coming sales conference.

At a marketing meeting a book's initial position is established: its tentative first printing and the quota that the sales reps are asked to meet; its advertising and promotion budget, its space in the catalog. Even with the quotes, Martha hadn't been able to drum up interest, much less enthusiasm, from her editorial colleagues, none of whom read the book. That, too, was very different from the Concord she had known. Under the "lean and mean" edict of INCOM the editors were handling almost twice as many books as before and hardly had time for their own projects. And she had observed the ethos of the staff shifting from a collegial to an entrepreneurial one, in keeping with the pressures and rewards of meeting their individual acquisition quotas, which were reckoned on a scale that reflected the amount of the advance paid for a book.

·   ·   ·

Martha had two novels on the fall list: *Remembering Angie* and *The Limelight Café* by Melissa Rogers. The latter, which she was handling for Dot B., was a kind of contemporary version of Arthur Schnitzler's *La Ronde* in which a serial string of amorous relationships in all three flavors connects the odd lives and plenteous life-styles of nine youngish people in the Newport Beach/Laguna strip.

Dot had paid $550,000 for world rights to *The Limelight Café* and the author's next book, the idea being to make her into a "brand name" and publish her books throughout the English-speaking world through INCOM's houses in New York, Toronto, and London.

Much of Martha's stint at the marketing meeting was taken up with the plans to advertise *The Limelight Café* and to tour Rogers. Martha, who felt that her colleagues were being carried away by their enthusiasm for the promotability of both the book and the author, pointed out that there was often a critical backlash to a novel by an author whose first one had gone to the races, and perhaps they might take a more conservative position both in advancing and in flogging the book until the reviewers were heard from.

Dot, the publisher, thought that the house should take an even stronger position: a first printing of 100,000 and an ad budget of $125,000 to give the book "more credibility, particularly with the chains." The publicity, sales, and advertising people around the table began to think of further ways to reach the figure that Dot had proposed. Since Martha felt the matter was out of her hands and that her views would be taken as another example of her not being "on board" at the new Concord, she kept silent.

. . .

Why all the enthusiasm for this soufflé of a novel—tasty but pretty empty? Martha had her ideas about it. The typical big-time publisher today was someone like Dot, whose expertise was high-volume marketing but who still took a certain pride in publishing quality books. Thus the particular feather in their caps was the classy writer like Melissa Rogers who allowed them to keep their heads high all the way to the bank and the management meeting. Also, in an era of publishing of information, advice, and entertainment, one list was pretty much like another, so that the presence of this or that "real writer" was about all that remained to distinguish one house from another. Then, too, there were the status drives of the new breed of publishers like Dot, their need to position themselves in the industry as "major players," their house as a "hot shop." All of which meant that the competition for the quality writer with a significant following had become as fierce and often as exorbitant as that for the tried-and-true authors of best-sellers. The inflated advances led directly to the excessive printings and advertising/ promotion budgets that she was witnessing with Melissa Rogers's book. Martha figured that given the mixed reviews that *The Limelight Café* was likely to receive, they would do well to sell 30,000 copies. With a sensible first printing of 40,000 and an equivalent budget the book would then be a success. She feared that unfolding in the room was a scenario for a failure that was bound to adversely affect Melissa Rogers's relations with the house.

That morning, though, she was much more concerned about the fate of David's book. The marketing manager rattled off the numbers: a first printing of 6,000 copies, a minuscule budget that would drop it into a house ad with three other books, and a half page in the catalog. Martha girded herself to do battle.

"I'm more confident about the reviews for this book than I am for Melissa's," she said. "Look at the quotes it's been getting."

"They're impressive," said Dot. "But so are most quotes. That's why we use them."

"Review editors don't care that much," said Jackie L., the publicity director. "They just figure that the quotes are from the author's friend. Or the editor's."

"It depends how you present them," said Martha. "With the right copy . . ." She could sense that eyes were already glazing over. "Look," she said, "the quotes are indicative of the book's quality and of the seriousness with which other writers and critics will take it. That's all I'm saying. This book warrants our taking a stronger position."

"We can take any position we want," said Bernie T., the sales director. "I'm still only going to get out four thousand copies based on his track record."

"If it starts to get the attention and to move, we can reprint," said Lance, the marketing manager.

Martha realized that she was already down to her last shot. "All right," she said. "This is a book that the reviews will have to make. But if you give it only a half page in the catalog, you're sending a message to the review editors that we think it's a small, run-of-the-mill novel and they'll pass it by."

"Every editor wants a full page," growled Bernie.

At this point Mac intervened. "I've been reading *Remembering Angie,* and it's got real possibilities. Let's give it a page and get on with things."

．　．　．

The two novels were published within a month of each other, though most readers wouldn't have known that. Because of the publicity and industry buzz generated by the advance paid for *The Limelight Café,* as well as the success of Melissa Rogers's first book, it was prominently and widely reviewed, particularly in the book media that emanates from New York, where, generally speaking, the reputation of a book is established. It shared a front-page review in the *New York Times Book Review* with the work of another rising woman novelist, was praised in *Newsweek* and panned in *Time,* made most of the slick monthlies, and was even included in an omnibus review of "trendy" fiction in the *New York Review of Books.* The review in the *New Republic* titled "Trivial Pursuit" summed up much of the negative response. But the book's combination of "the latest in life-styles" *(Washington Post)* and "suave kinkiness" *(Vanity Fair)* carried the day, and soon the novel was making its way up the best-seller list.

Martha found herself being almost as swept away by the reception as Melissa was. As her author's stock soared, so did hers: she felt herself being treated no longer like an old-fashioned family retainer who was out of step with the ambitious and lavish new master and mistress, but instead like a shrewd woman of the world who knew how to make things happen. Her judgment about promoting Melissa and the book was taken seriously, her initial reservations forgotten in the heat of success. Dot invited her to a getting-to-know-you lunch, asked her opinion of a prominent writer who was being "moved" by his agent, then wanted to know whom Martha was "cruising."

Martha said she now and then expressed an interest in an author to his or her agent but didn't like to go further than that. "If the author's worth stealing," she said, "the other publisher must have been doing something right. All you're offering is more money and getting an author who has become committed to the highest bidder."

"I don't see it that way. I'm concerned about the next three years. Also, there's nothing like money for building an author. As you've seen with Melissa. I'll bet she's feeling great about Concord these days."

Which was true. Martha's mind turned to David, who was her unhappy author. *Remembering Angie* had been published a month ago and the reviews so far hadn't amounted to a hill of beans. Though bitterly disappointed, Martha could not honestly say she was surprised. In her mind, editing a book like David's was somewhat like raising her two children. While they were growing up, the world was full of possibilities for them; now that they were out in the world—one a painter, the other an actress— they faced intense struggles and slender prospects of making their ways. So too with a book like David's, which had been nurtured by hope, hers as well as his, but was now at the mercy of chance and conditions.

The main condition was a glutted market. Each month four thousand or five thousand books poured from the presses; most of them sold a few thousand copies and were dead a year later. It was as though books had become as precarious and perishable as fish eggs, so that so many had to be spawned in order for a few to live. The colleges and universities seemed to be producing more writers of literary fiction and poetry than readers of them. Caught in the overflow, book review editors and writers, like readers, latched onto reputation and fashion and hype. Sometimes an unheralded book, like David's first one, hit a public nerve of topicality or taste, got a few breaks from the media, and went to the head of the line. But the culture's memory was short, almost amnesiac, and ten years later, the author had fallen back into the pack of so-called midlist writers.

At his end, David was telling himself some of the same things in a more despairing way. The early quotes from other writers and then an enthusiastic advance notice in *Publishers Weekly* had confirmed the feeling that he had broken out of his long slump, and visions of glowing reviews, even of best-seller lists and choice teaching positions, danced in his head. But then the publication week of the book came and went with a resounding silence, and the weeks that followed brought only a handful of perfunctory reviews.

Something had to be done. He made up a list of demands and phoned Martha. She began to commiserate with him about the "shopping-guide state of book reviewing" but he was through with ironic detachment. He wanted some action. "Have you called the *Times Book Review*?"

"The book has been out only a little more than a month. Let's give it another week or two."

"How about *Time*? You said you had a friend there?"

"It'd be too late for them to review it now."

"What about Washington, Chicago, Los Angeles?"

"I'll ask the publicity director what she knows."

"You sure your friend at *Time* saw the book? You thought we had a good chance there. That it was his kind of book."

"David, I sent him one myself."

"How about calling him, then?"

"I've just told you it's too late now."

"One place it's too soon, the other it's too late, the others you don't know about."

"I'm doing what I can, David. I know it's disappointing but it can still turn around."

But David now had the bit of frustration between his teeth and he continued to grind away. In the ensuing weeks he wanted to know why they weren't pushing his book in Detroit, where he had grown up, and in Ann Arbor, where he had gone to the university, or elsewhere in the state. He wanted to know why the one ad scheduled hadn't even appeared yet. He arranged for the local campus bookstore to do a window display, but the books didn't arrive for three weeks.

· · ·

Around this time two major reviews finally appeared. The one in the *Chicago Tribune* concluded: "With this book he moves into the front rank of midwestern novelists," and the *Village Voice Literary Supplement* sang its praises as "a high-class class novel that will stay in your mind's eye like a piece of grit." Two days later David was on the phone. What were they doing to get more books in the Chicago and New York stores? Could he finally get a decent ad? "Give me just a small fraction of the money and attention you're throwing after the Rogers book."

"That's not my decision, kiddo," Martha said, trying to keep her cool. "I happen to agree with you."

"That's not doing me much good, is it?"

Though aggrieved by David's words, Martha went to Lance to make a case for an ad that could draw on the two impressive reviews as well as the authors' quotes to make a formidable presentation. Lance looked up the marketing figures. "Forty-two hundred copies," he said. He held up empty hands. "Besides, we're cutting our ad budget by 20 percent."

"You mean that he's not even getting that lousy group ad?"

"What can I tell you? I don't make these decisions. Go talk to Dot."

Her gorge rising and her heart sinking, Martha asked to see Dot. Only a few minutes later she was called to her office. Dot was beaming. "Next week, *Limelight* goes to No. 6 and we're going back for another twenty-five thousand copies."

"That's great." Martha let the good news calm her and also permeate the atmosphere with good will. Then she said, "I've got a problem," and laid it out.

Dot's expression went from jovial to impassive to impatient. "So you'll lose this author. What have you lost? Someone whose books sell five thousand copies!"

"He asked me why we published his book if we're not going to support it. I didn't have an answer for him."

"We're not meeting our profit targets, so we have to cut overhead. It's as simple as that."

"Not to an author, it isn't."

"What's this author?" Dot snapped, her dark, pretty face hardening, her words moving toward the side of her mouth. "I'll tell you what this author is. He's a chip in a roulette game, like most authors. Most literary fiction is going to lose money, right? It's a fact of life. But we go on publishing it because you never know. Now and then one of them comes up a winner. If it doesn't we're not going to throw good money after bad. How long have you been in this business?"

"I've been in it long enough to remember when a book got ten percent of the cover price to advertise and promote it. Okay, I'm not asking for that. I'm just asking that we don't abandon David completely."

"Do you know how many editors are going to tell me that if we cut the ad budget this or that author is going to leave?"

"If this was your typical first novel, with little enough to put in an ad, I could live with it. But we've published four of David's books, one of them has made money, and this one has gotten fabulous quotes and is starting to get some major attention. We've got a stake in him." She paused, weighed her next words, and decided to use them. "Also a responsibility. We're building reputations, careers, not only publishing books. Even a small ad with the right quotes in the *New York Review of Books* puts this book on the literary map and maybe helps him to get a better teaching job. I'm asking for fifteen hundred, two thousand tops."

"I'm already five minutes late for a meeting. I'll think it over. But, there's other editors to consider."

Martha stood up. "I think the house owes me one. And this is the one I want."

"Put it in a memo. I'll see what I can do."

Two days later a copy of a memo came to her authorizing the group ad that included David's book. She called advertising and learned there would be room for one quote. Then she called David. As she explained the situation, in the teeth of his silence, she felt like a Soviet bureaucrat talking to a Lithuanian.

When she was finished, he said, "What are the publicity people doing? Any action there?"

"There's not much they can do yet."

"You said they were waiting for reviews. Now they've got them, right?"

"Come on, David. You know that a review in the *Voice* doesn't get you on *Letterman.*"

"It should get me on something. The one in the *Chicago Tribune* could get me on the *Studs Terkel* show. I'm only asking for a little effort from you."

"From me? I'm the one who's neglecting you and your . . . book?"

"Go ahead. Say it. My damn book? My lousy book? Which one?"

"I think we both need to cool off and see things in perspective."

"Which perspective? From Old Bottom-line Moneybags's perspective, I'm a nothing who's being a pain in the ass. From my perspective, I'm an author fighting for his book, maybe his career. And I'm not getting what other authors in my position are getting. I see what Knopf does for Jane Smiley or Harpers for James Wilcox or Seymour Lawrence for Jayne Anne Phillips."

"Seymour Lawrence has his own imprint. And I'm sure that there are authors at Knopf and Harpers who are in your position and are just as unhappy. It's not any one house. It's the way publishing is now."

"What am I supposed to do? Everyone tells me you have to hustle for your book these days, but I can't get to first base with you guys or even get to bat. I'm looking at a major failure."

Martha took a deep breath and interrupted him. "David, listen to me. You remember when you said that getting Victor's words made it all worthwhile, even if nothing else happens. That's what matters finally. The judgment of your peers, of the real critics and writers you've been hearing from. All the rest is just fashion, hype, and luck."

.   .   .

After he hung up, David sat at his desk, his mind still churning with anger and resentment. He tried to shift his thinking, to find consolation in Martha's words, which were ones he had often told himself. Why had he

stopped believing them? It was as though the premise of the literary vocation had shifted from exploring your imagination to marketing it. It was in
the air: the big money, the publicity hunting, the careerism. The brightest
of the young writers he taught or met took it for granted and acted accordingly. He remembered a remark of Louis Kronenberger's some years ago:
"It used to be writers sold out at forty. Today they sign on at twenty-five."
But it had affected him too. Like other writers of the middle generation, he
saw through the higher commercialism, its wanton conversion of fame (still
the "Spur," as Milton called it) into stupid celebrity; and yet felt left out of
the action. He had had his chance after his first book and hadn't exploited
it, and now he was condemned to this third-rate job in Nowheresville and
to struggle for nominal advances, a lousy ad, scraps of recognition. He felt
like a fool.

A week later Martha sent him a copy of the ad, two clips of short reviews
that were six weeks old, and the news that the *Times Book Review* had killed
the review of his book. Several fruitless conversations followed with his
agent and Martha. The fact that his book had still only netted some 4,300
copies and that returns were already coming in to reduce that figure loomed
like a wall that bounced back any suggestions or requests that cost money.
Finally, David wrote a long letter to the publisher that wired all of his
complaints and grievances to set off the explosive conclusion: "Being published by Concord has proved to be the worst form of rejection: another
publisher who had as little interest in the book as you would merely have
turned it down; instead you took it on and then through your indifference
and incompetence killed it."

Enraged, Dot summoned Martha and handed her the letter. "Who does
this bastard think he is?"

Martha read it through, her own anger, frustration, and sense of betrayal
rising finally to match David's. "He's a difficult author whose book will sell
less than four thousand copies," she said. "Forget him."

Mistah Perkins—He Dead

Publishing Today

Gerald Howard

GERALD HOWARD *has worked as an assistant editor in the educational department of New American Library and as a Viking hardcover and Penguin paperback editor at Penguin USA, where he eventually became an executive editor. He is currently an editor in the trade department of W. W. Norton.*

Much admired since its appearance in the American Scholar *in the summer of 1989, and reprinted here with a "Postscript" especially written for this edition of* Editors on Editing, *Mr. Howard's incisive overview of the state of contemporary editing, writing, and publishing, "Mistah Perkins—He Dead: Publishing Today," is still discussed and debated with undiminished interest among editors, writers, and publishers.*

Exploring "the forces that are reshaping the landscape of American publishing, particularly as they affect the function of the book editor, be he the accomplice or victim (or both) of these forces . . . , and matters of taste and judgment in writing that aspires to the status of literature," Mr. Howard ruminates on how the patron saint of American editors, Maxwell Perkins, would fare in today's publishing world.

After a vividly detailed examination of how the pressures of the market-place, the media, and publishing tend to tempt writer and editor away from dedication to the highest ideals of their callings, Mr. Howard decides that "it is impossible to imagine that august figure Max Perkins working happily or even successfully in this world, for his values—loyalty, honesty, taste, proportion, Olympian standards—are not always negotiable currency these days. . . . The heart of darkness at the center of today's publishing world is not a jungle. Rather, it is a flashy, disorienting environment, a combination hall of mirrors, MTV video, commodities pit, cocktail party, soap opera, circus, fun house, and three-card monte game. The message one emerges with, stunned and shaken by what one has witnessed, is: 'Mistah Perkins—he dead.' "

Mistah Perkins—He Dead

Publishing Today

Each year our institutions of higher learning churn out thousands of liberal arts graduates who would just about kill to have my job: book editor for an established trade publisher. I know just how they feel, for in the early seventies I was one of their yearning number, and as pathetically ill-formed and ill-informed as my aspirations were, I can't say that in any essential respect the profession has let me and my dreams down. I am paid a good dollar to read manuscripts and proposals that represent a nice slice of the best that is currently being thought and said, to select and then often help shape some of them for publication, and to engage the various publishing mechanisms so that those manuscripts make their way successfully into book form, into the bookstores, and finally into the hands of readers. The authors and colleagues with whom I work are about as pleasant and cultured and sharp and dedicated a group of folks as this civilization produces, and it is a joy to be associated with them. As a commissioned officer in the forward march of culture, I have something like a universal passport to pursue my personal enthusiasms, be they literary or intellectual or pop cultural. My daily work puts me in possession of the sort of inside skinny on events of the day that makes for interesting conversation at cocktail parties. As for those editorial lunches, well—they're everything you think they are.

So what's the beef? Why do book editors often end the workday with the white-collar equivalent of the thousand-yard stare? Why do so many of us adopt the armor of cynicism as protection against . . . against *what?* Well, each editor will have his own set of gripes, but for me it's a faster, huger, rougher, *dumber* publishing world than I could have anticipated.

The American publishing business today is in a tremendous state of confusion between its two classic functions: the higher-minded and more vocally trumpeted *mission civilisatrice* to instruct and edify and uplift the reading public and the less loudly advertised but, in the nature of things, more consistently compelling *mission commerciale* to separate the consumer from his cash. Happy the publisher (and happy the author) who can manage to make a single book fulfill both functions! The real art of publishing consists not in reconciling what are, in a capitalist system, quite simply irreconcilable imperatives but in orchestrating the built-in tensions in a harmonious fashion. However, the two-way road in publishing from the bottom line to Mount Olympus travels right across a fault line, and that is where the serious editor lives and plies his trade. To put it bluntly, the tectonic plates are shifting, there's an earthquake going on, and all that moving and shaking you've read about is making it hard to attend to business—or even to be certain, from day to day, just what our business is. The delicate task of orchestrating tensions becomes more difficult still when the walls threaten to collapse about you.

I overstate the situation, of course, but not by much. It may be that since book editors stand at the very center of the publishing process and also mediate between what the culture is offering up and what the firm is putting out, they register crises earlier and more severely, like canaries in coal mines. They certainly operate in highly contested, tremendously tricky terrain. Lionel Trilling famously referred to the "bloody crossroads" where literature and politics meet; the intersection between culture and commerce where editors do their work is no less sanguine a piece of ground. In this essay I'd like to explore the forces that are reshaping the landscape of American publishing, particularly as they affect the function of the book editor, be he the accomplice or the victim (or both) of those forces. This exploration will of necessity touch on matters of taste and judgment in writing that aspires to the status of literature. Indeed, it may illuminate the question of whether such writing is likely to be produced at all in the coming decades, and if so, what form it will take. I hope to be able to demonstrate that, first, matters are more hopeful in this respect than the conventional critics of American publishing are telling us; but, second, for many of the same reasons, things are in a parlous state. Our particular bloody crossroads is especially fertile ground for contradictions and ironies.

· · ·

Most essays on book editing begin by attempting to dispel the mystery surrounding just what it is that a book editor *does*. In the mind of the educated public, the figure of Maxwell Perkins, editor of F. Scott Fitzgerald, Ernest Hemingway, Ring Lardner, and Thomas Wolfe, stands forth as the only widely recognized member of the tribe. This is largely a result of an extended fictional portrait of Perkins in Wolfe's *You Can't Go Home Again,* Malcolm Cowley's *New Yorker* profile of him in 1944, and A. Scott Berg's popular 1978 biography. As any reader of *Editor to Author,* a collation of Perkins's superb editorial letters, may attest, Perkins was a giant and a virtuoso of his craft. He was also an eccentric, driven, and somehow *premodern* man in his tastes and working habits, a hero of culture, but one seemingly displaced from the nineteenth century. The equation of Maxwell Perkins with book editing has led to endless misconceptions about the proper function of the book editor, especially in regard to the editor's role as the writer's collaborator and literary conscience. Even today most book editors do somewhat the same job as Maxwell Perkins, but in the same sense that most basketball players are doing something similar to what Michael Jordan is doing. Still, it is an interesting thought experiment to imagine Perkins working (or trying to work) in today's publishing world. It is hard to feature.

Certainly visions of Perkins-esque exploits danced in my head as I prepared to enter my first editorial meeting as a green and poignantly eager and idealistic assistant editor at age twenty-eight. (Nobody above the age of twenty-five should ever care as much about a new job as I did.) Largely by fast talking I had weaseled my way into a position with a very large mass-market paperback publisher, one with a deep and highly profitable backlist of paperback literary classics and highbrow nonfiction works aimed at the high school and college markets. These were the books I was meant to work on and augment. My bookshelves were riddled with books bearing this publisher's colophon, many of them by real live American authors, and so I anticipated at least some involvement with the hot, steaming literary and intellectual material I read about so eagerly in the *New York Times Book Review.* That anticipation was confirmed when I was given Susan Sontag's *Illness as Metaphor* and William Gass's *The World within the Word,* a collection of critical essays, to read for paperback reprint consideration in the week before I was to begin work. I fairly swooned with delight when handed these books, which were by two figures I then regarded as demigods of American criticism. This was even better than I had dared hope. Oh boy oh boy oh boy. . . .

As it happened, the weekly editorial meeting was held on each Monday at 9:30 A.M. So, with no preparation whatsoever, I was tossed into it in my first hour on the job like an infant into the drink. Suddenly I was in a large room with some fifteen other people around a table, a long log of submissions to be discussed, and barely a clue about the real rules of the proceedings about to take place here. With startling swiftness there began a bewildering discourse, understood intimately by everybody but me, a kind of verbal publishing shorthand compounded of first names and a semitechnical vocabulary (first prints, early look, floor bid, closing date) and a collegial back-room air. Largely absent from the discussion was much reference at all to the actual contents of the books, let alone their cultural significance, their contributions, if any, to the world of literature and ideas. By the time *Illness as Metaphor* came up for discussion I was thoroughly disoriented, and whatever fine insights I may have mentally prepared myself to deliver had evaporated under an onslaught of anxiety. I stammered out a few jumbled and perfectly ineffective sentences and then, sensing my utter failure to communicate the book's importance, played what I felt was my only card left: "It will probably be nominated for the National Book Award." (Her previous book, *On Photography,* had won the award some months earlier.)

The reaction was swift, but not what I had anticipated: an editor on the other side of the table snorted sarcastically, "Well, *that* will sell a lot of books."

My performance on behalf of Gass's book was little better. I did say, somewhat apologetically this time, that I thought that it, too, would be nominated for an NBA, a remark that carried the same absence of force in that forum. Needless to say, my employer declined to offer a red cent to reprint either of the books.

There is something to be said for having the stuffing knocked out of you on your first entry into the ring, I suppose. Since that time I've attended several hundred editorial meetings and run quite a few myself, and I now know just what I say under the same circumstances. (Gass's book was nominated for the National Book Critics Circle Award for criticism, and Sontag's book went nominationless, incidentally, but contrary to my new colleague's disdainful remark, an astute publisher, hardcover or paperback, can most certainly use the aroma of prestige such a citation imparts as a tool to sell books.) But I had not fallen into a pit of philistinism; I had simply encountered the world of commercial publishing as a quiveringly unprepared naïf. The shorthand did not necessarily imply disdain for content; it was just a way of cutting to the business heart of the matter. What I heard at that big paperback house did not differ radically from what I have later encountered at the editorial meetings of two distinguished hardcover imprints. That the publishing process can very well chill the blood of the uninitiated does not imply an absence of seriousness on the part of the participants, editors emphatically included. To paraphrase Bismarck's *mot* about the law, it is with books as it is with sausage: if you like the stuff, it's best not to watch it being made.

The point I wish to make is that book editing is not now and never has been a pursuit that permits a narrow purism. F. Scott Fitzgerald characterizes his film producer hero Monroe Stahr in *The Last Tycoon* as one of the few people who can hold the whole complex equation of filmmaking in his head at once; it might be said that good editors do something similar with the publishing equation. Their ministrations extend equally to the narrow compass of the page of text where the reader will experience the book and the wide cultural and commercial arena where the book itself must find its way; their fealty is equally to the spiritual, emotional, and financial well-being of the authors they publish and the firms that employ them. One might say that the effective editor is on comfortable terms with God and with Mammon. The great Max Perkins also published Taylor Caldwell and Marjorie Kinnan Rawlings. Probably the most remunerative book ever published by Alfred A. Knopf was Kahlil Gibran's *The Prophet* (over eight million copies sold in this country alone, and climbing still), and the ultra-prestigious firm that bears Knopf's name is known in the book trade for its top-of-the-culinary-line cookbooks and for the commercial éclat with which it publishes glossy show business memoirs. The firm of Farrar, Straus, Giroux, publisher of several Nobel Prize winners and generally regarded as the most purely literary house in the country, pulled itself out of the red in 1950 after four financially lackluster years by publishing Gayelord Hauser's best-selling *Look Younger, Live Longer;* it is currently happily awash in the incredible revenues generated by Scott Turow's *Presumed Innocent* and Tom Wolfe's *Bonfire of the Vanities.* I could cite dozens of similar examples with ease.

I perhaps overemphasize the point about book editing, even at the highest level of practice, having a lot to do with money and promotion and gamesmanship and overall business sense because these are the aspects of the craft that the public least understands or cares to recognize. The other part, the priesthood-of-literature aspect, well, that certainly exists; that is the star by which the serious editor sets his course, but it is also something primary and largely irreducible and unsusceptible to explanation. The code is simple, really. Be loyal to your authors. Nurture the best that is in them and give them the best that is in you—including sticking by them in lean times. Publish the best writing that you can find or that finds you. Don't send books to the printer that you know can be made better. Be proud of the firm and give it books that the firm can be proud to publish. If you have to or want to publish some junk or sheer product (it happens), don't represent your dross as gold. Honor the past while remaining alert to what is new and interesting and valuable and maybe upsetting to conventional taste—and have the guts to publish it. Don't fall into the all-too-available smugness about who and what will sell—and about your own infallibility. Strive to be the kind of editor your younger, hopelessly literary self wanted to be. Book editing, like politics, at its most fulfilling engages the participant at a very deep, test-of-character level, and that is what makes it worth doing.

On the good days (and for me most of them are good), I believe all that. On the bad days, I feel like a self-victimizing chump for believing it. On the bad days, the days when another venerable American house is neutron-bombed by the mindless conglomerate that enfolded it, or a Big Name in the Lit Biz has deserted his longtime publisher for a big fat check from Long Green and Gotrocks, or an agent has slammed the wind out of me with a punishing demand for money on a book my soul cries out to publish, on those days I decide that literature is the very last thing that publishing is about. I decide that publishing is about power and money and ego and sharp practice and staying ahead of the unearned advances while fanning the flames of memory under your successes. On the bad days I seriously ask myself why I should care so much about a totally uncodified and thoroughly outmoded set of standards and ethics when so many others appear to be doing so well without them—and all of it in the service of a form of cultural transmission unlikely to be in existence much beyond my lifespan. As Bugs Bunny says, What a maroon.

I usually get over it fairly quickly. A sense of humor helps. There are, however, more and more of those bad days for editors to get over. The shape of the publishing landscape changes, sometimes drastically, almost every week. The players change partners with the frequency of a square dance; the houses change ownership with the indignity of a bankruptcy sale. The prevailing atmosphere is very much one of high capitalism characteristic of the late Reagan era: all of a sudden there seems to be this incredible amount of money around, sales are going up and up, but nobody feels secure because it all might go bust tomorrow, because we might very well all be living beyond our means. You know, that homeless-in–Trump Tower feeling. The precious basics of the editor's craft—time, security, loyalty, a shared understanding of literary and intellectual values and financial *value*—become less and less dependably available as stronger and stronger gusts of change sweep through the business. The forward march of culture begins to feel like a rear-guard action, and purely literary values begin to look entirely beside the point of a larger, colder, scarily expensive game. When one reaches the point, as I have on numerous occasions, of having to decide during an auction whether the paperback rights to a first collection of short stories or a first novel are worth many, many tens or several hundreds of thousands of dollars, one's fine discriminations tend to feel awfully fussy and irrelevant. But then, when a van Gogh or Monet or Gauguin is going right through the roof at Sotheby's, the curator doesn't interrupt the proceedings to remind the crowd that the work in question is not from the artist's strongest period.

I've spent a good deal of time brooding over the possible reasons why things seem so badly out of whack—why, to put it bluntly, publishers are behaving so stupidly and self-destructively in some instances, and so peculiarly shortsightedly overall. There is no one primal cause for the transformations all have witnessed and many question and deplore (it suits others just fine, of course), any more than one can explain simply why mergers and acquisitions became the major-league sport of Wall Street. World historical forces are clearly at work. From my point of view down in the editorial trenches, however, I think I can isolate a few broad developments, all working in concert to reinforce one another, that have caused huge distortions and discontinuities in the way publishers in general and editors in particular go about their business.

Pride of place must of course go to the by-now almost exclusively *corporate* nature of American publishing (I exclude from this discussion the university presses and the hundreds of small presses, whose nature, influence, and problems require a totally separate inquiry). Not very long ago, publishing houses tended to be family-owned and family-run businesses, with the founder or the founder's descendants at the helm. Scribner's was run by a Scribner, Putnam's by a Putnam, Doubleday by a Doubleday, Simon & Schuster by a Simon and a Schuster. Even where a specifically family connection to management no longer existed, as in the case of Little, Brown, Harper & Row, and Houghton Mifflin, the houses remained closely held entities, and trade publishing itself formed something of a peculiar archipelago off the continent of corporate America, subject to the same economic weather but governed by its own insular rules. Do not imagine this island nation as paradise, by any means, only as a reasonably stable confederation where change came slowly and business proceeded at a comparatively stately pace.

The philosophers tell us that man has fallen into the quotidian; it may be said that publishing at some point fell into the fiscal—the early-to-mid sixties is the likely starting date. One by one the great trade houses sold themselves to the conglomerates and the huge communications concerns, and so ceded, whether they recognized it or not, the control of their own destiny. On the side of the houses, the impetus for the sale varied. In some cases the founders or their heirs found themselves getting on in years and no longer vigorous enough or committed enough to handle the business of the firm properly. So in effect they cashed out their interests for a handsome price. In other instances the independent houses believed that allying themselves with powerful corporate owners would solve the perennial problems of modest concerns—cash flow and capital shortage—and allow them to ride out the inevitable lean seasons cushioned by the corporation's substantial assets against the squeeze of high inflation and interest rates. Better to go to the friendly corporate owner than the possibly unfriendly banker or the impersonal capital markets for the necessary funds, the logic went. On the conglomerates' side, these houses, controlling as they did substantial literary properties and themselves brand names of widespread recognition, offered a highly cost-effective entry into what everybody saw as a growth industry, now that a vast new generation of Americans was in the process of becoming college-educated and thus, it was assumed, lifelong readers.

At the heart of these sales lay a terrible misunderstanding. The trade houses thought they would run their business as they had before, with similar independence of taste and action, safely cocooned within their conglomerates. The corporations, however, with far less naïveté, expected and insisted that their new assets adopt the same financial lockstep as their other assets, show quarterly growth, institute strict managerial controls—the shareholders expected no less. God, as usual, was with the big battalions, and today almost all the houses bearing the great names in American publishing are either huge corporations themselves or smoothly integrated into vast corporate combines. They now dance to the tune of big-time finance, and it's not a fox-trot; it's a bruising slam dance.

From down here on the shop floor, the results often look ludicrous and disastrous. Publishers are playing a big-money game with comparatively minuscule resources. On the map of corporate America as a whole, trade publishing commands such a small portion of the consumer dollar that it is barely visible. Let me illustrate the point. The January 1989 issue of *Manhattan, inc.* reports that Nintendo Video Entertainment was the toy industry's top-selling product in 1988, grossing $2.3 billion. The net income to Nintendo from that one toy (assume 50 percent of gross) amounts to more than a quarter of the income of the entire trade book industry, which was $4.4 billion last year. What conceivable clout can even a $100 million company wield in such an environment? On the southern tip of Manhattan, twenty-five-year-olds in bright red suspenders buy and sell such concerns the way kids trade baseball cards—and with less feeling for the object in question.

No wonder, then, that publishers are demonstrating an almost inexorable tendency to huddle together in self-protective combinations, to weather the financial storms and preserve some autonomy of action. No wonder they are reaching out to create global publishing empires. Simon & Schuster, under the capacious Gulf and Western umbrella, now includes the Simon & Schuster imprint, Pocket Books, Poseidon, Prentice-Hall, Fireside, Touchstone, and a long list of subsidiaries. Random House, itself owned by the Newhouse family, which also owns the *New Yorker* and the Condé Nast magazine empire, controls Random House Trade, Alfred A. Knopf, Pantheon (which includes Schocken), Villard, the paperback imprints Ballantine, Vintage, and Fawcett, and recently concluded the purchase of one of the few remaining owner-run houses, Crown Publishing—itself a considerable nest of imprints and divisions and a highly profitable concern. On the other side of the pond, Random House has established a substantial presence in British publishing by purchasing the venerable houses of Jonathan Cape, Chatto and Windus, and The Bodley Head, thereby making feasible the purchase and implementation of worldwide publishing rights in the English language. The latter is a special strength of my old employer, Penguin Books, which doth bestride the globe like a colossus and which, in this country, controls Viking, New American Library, E. P. Dutton . . . I can't go on.

I'll learn from the example of King Canute and spare myself a plea that all this merger activity stop. But even when such major reshufflings are handled sensitively and efficiently, there must of necessity be a disquieting interregnum of new managers, shifts in publishing philosophy, rerouting of the lines of communication and hierarchies of authority. At its worst a blind corporate stupidity descends upon a house, a reign of chaos in the putative name of profit and rationalization that in very swift order leads to the demoralization of the staff and the final destruction of its publishing identity and mission. Some of these latter cases are willful, others the simple result of putting the management of the finely tuned entity that is a top-flight publishing house in the hands of apes in suits. (One of the finest literary editors in American publishing was given his walking papers with the contemptuous remark, "You're a six-thousand-copy editor," six thousand being about the lowest feasible printing for the average book. O sweetest of ironies, though, his first acquisition for his next employer sold about a million copies in hardcover!) The effect of all this on serious book editors scarcely needs spelling out. Suffice it to say that they move around a lot these days from house to house, hoping to stay a few steps ahead of the whirlwind, searching for the diminishing solid and stable places where they can hang out their shingles for a few years and do some good publishing.

The loss of an editor is almost always a shock to the writer, for it is the rare writer indeed who can write a book in splendid isolation and autonomy; and once the book is done, the writer must depend on the editor to guide the book through the course of its preparation for publication. The Brownian motion among the editorial class has resulted in a situation where many fine writers no longer feel they can *afford* any particular loyalty to a single publishing house. They've been taught the core lesson in modern corporate American life: expendability. Lately they've been learning another lesson as well, one writ large in the massive prices paid for corporate buyouts and objets d'art alike: that value is an exceedingly variable quality, its assessment highly dependent upon circumstance and subject to all manner of manipulation. The loss of heart suffered by many editors is paralleled by a similar decline of faith on the part of the writers that the writing itself will be enough, that the artistic act will suffice, without assiduous attention to literary politics, public presentation, and publishing strategy.

We enter here into highly ironic territory. The conventional wisdom of the early eighties was that the rise of corporate publishing and the mirror-image growth of the huge book retailing chains could spell the end of serious writing and publishing—that so much time and money and effort would be expended in putting under contract and marketing the sure commercial thing the accountants demanded that nothing would be left over for the risky, the new, the demanding work. (See Thomas Whiteside's *The Blockbuster Complex* for this argument in its purest form.) Oddly enough, something quite the opposite has happened: these days nothing is hotter, nothing more sought after than the prestige property, the fresh new face and voice. For that let us thank God, for a world full of Ludlums and Kings and Steels and Sheldons alone is not a world worth living in.

There are a variety of reasons behind this development. I would first cite a saving conservatism in the book business and in book culture, a saving remnant of people at all levels and in all areas of publishing whose commitment to quality has never flagged and whose energy on behalf of good books (and inventiveness) knows no bounds. Then there was the at-first bewildering and later inspiriting best-selling success of such unlikely books as Umberto Eco's *The Name of the Rose* and Allan Bloom's *The Closing of the American Mind,* which demonstrated the heretofore unsuspected existence of a genuinely mass market willing to purchase, if not finish reading, works of obvious difficulty. Apparently the same vast distribution mechanism that channels oceans of schlock can be used to deliver the better class of goods in heroic numbers. Lastly, a crop of new writers of quality and freshness arose whose first books managed to find an audience sufficient to put their books on the best-seller lists and to indicate the rise, among writers and readers alike, of something like a new generation. These books include Jay McInerney's *Bright Lights, Big City,* Ethan Canin's *Emperor of the Air,* David Leavitt's *Family Dancing,* Tama Janowitz's *Slaves of New York,* Mona Simpson's *Anywhere But Here,* Bret Easton Ellis's *Less Than Zero,* and Michael Chabon's *The Mysteries of Pittsburgh.* Each of these books was a legitimate best-seller; each of these authors was under the age of thirty-five when he or she published his or her first book, and a couple of them were barely past twenty-one; and two of these books were short-story collections, utterly confounding conventional publishing wisdom about the commercial difficulties such books should face.

This is all very fine, in that it gives serious writers and their editors confidence and heart and clout as they write and publish. The world will not end with a five-part miniseries, at least not yet. But there is a palpable Faustian element to the bargain: the huge distribution mechanism and the celebrity-hungry media machine that function to make these splashy successes possible extract their own costs and compromises and create much confusion of literary values and financial value.

Among the younger writers these days one can observe a great deal more career ambition—an itchiness to get it now—than purely literary ambition. Far from offering any resistance to the mighty engines and subtle strategies of contemporary success, they eagerly embrace and employ them. In this regard they are only mirroring the behavior of their contemporaries in business and financial services who reportedly sense failure if they haven't made their first million by the age of twenty-seven. The eighties have not been a decade noted for patience. The proliferation of creative writing programs has made possible *ab ovo* a career-management approach to literature. Go to the right college, get into the right MFA program, make the right contacts among established writers and book and magazine editors, find the right literary agent, who'll sell your book to the right publisher, who'll give your book the right cover and shake down the right writers (some of whom you already know, of course) for the right blurbs, and you're off! You get the good review from Michiko Kakutani in the *New York Times,* the paperback reprinters and Hollywood producers begin throwing money at your book, the hip nightclubs beckon, the galleys begin to arrive asking *you* for blurbs, you guest-teach at the right creative writing program, you summer at Yaddo or McDowell . . . everything is on track and on time.

And, very possibly, out of scale. What nobody will tell the hot young writers, least of all their editors, is that however fresh or unusual their first books were, they may have a long way to travel before they develop mastery of their craft. (That news may be delivered, brutally, by reviewers of the second book.) The system that helps make these talented young people also exploits them and can possibly destroy them. They may be living in a flashy Potemkin village of their agents' and publishers' construction. What the showy early success removes is the possibility of a slow, even fitful progress toward artistic maturity, well away from the harsh spotlight and the demands of an impersonal star system. The Muse does not speak on the Bitch Goddess's schedule, and for many writers the most precious gift of all is not a big fat book contract, but the space and time to find their unique style and subject, to learn from an honorable failure, perhaps, without being tossed on the ash heap for it.

What also seems to have departed from the world for the moment is the desire among young writers to create the masterpiece, the total work that, whether gorgeously compressed or encyclopedically vast, seems to say all that must or can be said at its particular moment. Once upon a time (1944)

Cyril Connolly could write, to general agreement: "The more books we read, the clearer it becomes that the true function of a writer is to produce a masterpiece and that no other task is of any consequence." To live by such words is to cultivate an imperial contempt for the mundane, for the world and its shabby workings. It is impossible, I believe, for an attitude of proud self-sufficiency such as cultivated by a Lawrence or a Joyce or a Beckett to coexist with an eagerness to play ball with the literary star search. It is certainly impossible for an editor to expect his young author to make the complete spiritual and artistic commitment the creation of a masterpiece demands when he has previously ascribed cultural authority to the system of hype. The masterpiece, almost by definition, is written outside this system.

Implicit in the above remarks, of course, is the assumption that the main event happens on the page, not in the gossip columns and on the celebrity circuit. This assumption is not one shared universally by writers and publishers. At the baroque end of the spectrum of literary decay stands Tama Janowitz, a figure one could find poignantly pathetic if she were not so annoying. Having gone to school on Andy Warhol, Janowitz proceeded to promote her genuinely fresh collection of stories, *Slaves of New York,* with shrewd shamelessness—the writer as photo opportunity, the self-huckster as literary waif. Her publishers were delighted to play along: as her publicist averred, "Tama's too fabulous to waste on the book pages." The so-called promotability of an author—one with an interesting personal story, a mediagenic profile, a set of powerful friends, a snappy line of patter—is routinely taken into consideration by publishers these days and may well obscure certain literary failings in the work even as it enhances its dollar value. Shall we call these young writers Capote's Children?

The itch for the big score, the Faustian willingness to strike a bargain with the devil, does not confine itself to the younger set; it is common as well among older writers, even those who have tried to live by Connolly's dictate. This is very understandable, for such writers will have seen on the one hand staggering sums paid over to the hacks of the best-seller list, and on the other disproportionate praise and attention (and money) lavished on the upstart of the moment. Meanwhile, they must labor away, it seems, in prestigious obscurity, and it is all very galling. Little wonder, then, that some of these writers decide that writing well is insufficient revenge, that a system so manifestly incapable of matching reward to merit deserves to be subverted and manipulated. I believe that a number of important American writers have made some such conscious internal decision to maneuver cold-bloodedly for the big time, and I cannot say that I blame them. Their publishers are most likely parts of huge corporations, they've probably had too many editors in their careers to depend on them very much, the faith that art can save your soul is a quaint and dying creed, the surrounding literary culture is thin and fragmented and unsustaining—why subsist on such thin gruel as a prestigious literary career? So off these writers go with their work into the open market, a move usually orchestrated by a shrewd and powerful agent (about whom more in a moment), and sure enough, the classy scent these authors give off proves to be a powerful financial aphrodisiac. The rupture, in some cases, of publishing relationships of long standing can seem a small price to pay for such largesse.

Let me be specific. Up until fairly recently, William Gaddis was known to a pretty small circle of cognoscenti as the author of two massive, dense, and demanding masterpieces, *The Recognitions* and *JR*. These works make absolutely no compromise with the reader as they attack the question of authenticity in the modern age, and they have sold over the years in modest numbers at best. Last year, after publication by Viking of a relatively short and, by Gaddis's standards, accessible novel, *Carpenter's Gothic,* Gaddis and his agent put on the block a proposal for his next and probably last novel, *The Last Act,* a work about the American legal system—and everything else. I know, because I read it for Viking and offered on it. As reported in *Publishers Weekly* (and much discussed on the Rialto), the work was knocked down to Simon & Schuster for $275,000, an amount that makes no sense whatsoever unless you understand that Simon & Schuster was simply purchasing the prestige of publishing one of the few certifiable geniuses (in my view) in current American fiction. The book that Gaddis will write will, I am quite certain, be brilliant, and Gaddis deserves the money and more. But save for some kind of miracle, Simon & Schuster will be quite deeply in the red at the end of the day. It indicates how thoroughly unmoored ends have become from means in the corporate era of publishing.

Other writers of stature have grasped the essence of celebrity culture, none more egregiously than the novelist Harold Brodkey. He has so adroitly broadcast the unbounded ambition behind his long-awaited and long-undelivered magnum opus, *A Party of Animals,* and the angst of his life and its creation that respected critics proclaim the work a masterpiece and Brodkey a presiding genius of twentieth-century American fiction *before they have even read it.* The mixed reviews that Brodkey's recent collection, *Stories in an Almost Classical Mode,* has received did not deter *New York* and *People* from profiling Brodkey and his unhappy childhood and his peculiar adulthood. Meanwhile, *A Party of Animals* has over its twenty-five-year gestation period accumulated an ever thicker layer of advance payments from various publishers; his current one, Knopf, has sunk well over half a million dollars into it. Whatever one makes of Brodkey's talent on the basis of what has already seen print (I find him hard, obsessive going for the most part), a *reductio ad absurdum* of the cult of tortured literary creation has been reached here, possibly the most handsomely rewarded instance of writer's block in literary history. Brodkey has made his very inability to create a sign of his genius; what he is selling is not literature so much as the *idea* of literature. Here is the notion of artistic struggle retooled for the age of intellectual property. Somewhere out there Andy Warhol is applauding.

Little wonder, then, that, in a situation where the writers are so eager to receive and the publishers so eager to give, the literary agents have moved to the center stage of what Ted Solotaroff calls "the literary-industrial complex." Only agents intimately familiar with the territory can orchestrate the complex and often expensive courtship dance between writer and publisher. Only agents who have behind them the clout of their own lists of blockbusting authors can hope to counterbalance the immense power of conglomerate publishers on their clients' behalf. Only agents with a network of well-established connections and years of professional experience can maximize for an author the potentially enormous income to be realized from the complex web of subsidiary rights—foreign, film, dramatic, audiovisual, information retrieval, and so on. Finally, in a culture where the idea of the art object often substitutes for or takes precedence over the object itself, agents serve as the spin doctors of literature, shaping the idea of the book and the author for public consumption. These are the facts, and there is no arguing against them.

For the editor, however, the centrality of the agent in the writer's life has come in part at his expense. It is the rare agent who will become as intimately involved as the editor in the crafting of the work, and that seems a structural feature of the business. But with the ceaseless movement in the corporate ownership of houses and in editorial staff, the agent becomes by default the still point of the turning world for the writer as well as the source of his financial salvation or triumph. Most writers these days are glad to forgo 10 or 15 percent of their income in exchange for the agent's going to the mat with the publishers and wrestling out of them the last dollar of advance money. The agents are quite good at this, of course, and it allows the writer and publisher to live within the convenient fiction that the lethal street fight masquerading as a contract negotiation never took place.

What very few people say explicitly is that publishers are scared stiff of the powerful agents—that the million-dollar contracts you read about are paid over with silent screams. Agents are the direct beneficiaries of the decline of understanding among corporate-owned publishers of financial cause and effect, for the checks always clear but the returns and the losses stay with the publisher. In almost every book negotiation these days is the spoken or unspoken threat that if the terms are not satisfactory, there is some other publisher who would be delighted to pay the asking price—and there usually is. A superb publication of the author's previous work is often used *against* you: every editor has had the experience of an agent reminding him in a negotiation that "there are a lot of people out there interested in ———'s work" when it is the sweat equity and promotional money and publishing smarts you and your firm have applied to ———'s last book, as much as the literary quality of the work itself, that created the interest.

The editor occupies a diminishing space in the midst of these developments. The writer may feel great personal loyalty and gratitude for the editor's intimate understanding and stalwart sponsorship of his work, but such bonds are divisible. The writer's life is a precarious one, the vagaries of taste and talent and the marketplace impossible to predict. If the writer finds himself in the happy (and still relatively rare) position of being a highly sought-after commodity, well, the agent is there to do the nasty work, with the writer in effect saying, "I'm sorry that things have worked out this way, but I'll always be grateful for your help." After all, Thomas Wolfe left Scribner's and Max Perkins and broke the great man's heart, but he did write him that nice valentine in *You Can't Go Home Again*.

This is what it looks like from here, the editor's uneasy chair. It is damned peculiar out there, and damned Hobbesian—what used to be known as a gentlemen's profession has been transformed into a war of all against all. It is impossible to imagine that august figure Max Perkins working happily or even successfully in this world, for *his* values—loyalty, honesty, taste, proportion, Olympian standards—are not always negotiable currency these days. They have not disappeared from publishing—after all, Robert Giroux still shows up for work at Farrar, Straus, Giroux on Union Square—but they surely do not mean what they once did. Editors of my generation and younger (I'm thirty-eight) are resigned to and cynically humorous about the departure of a particular sort of grace from our world, intensely grateful when we encounter instances of it, and determined to emulate it to the extent that conditions will allow. We've learned the rules of the rough new games being played—or rather, the absence of rules—but a lot of us don't like the lessons we're being taught.

The heart of darkness at the center of today's publishing world is not a jungle. Rather, it is a flashy, disorienting environment, a combination hall of mirrors, MTV video, commodities pit, cocktail party, soap opera, circus, fun house, and three-card monte game. The message one emerges with, stunned and shaken by what one has witnessed, is: "Mistah Perkins—he dead."

Postscript

"Mistah Perkins—He Dead" was written in late 1988 and published in the *American Scholar* in the summer of 1989. In rereading it now, three years later, I am struck by its tone of angst, which reflected a certain anguish over what the go-go eighties did to the trade publishing business. We are now well into the nineties, and the giddy, go-for-broke atmosphere has down-shifted into a low-grade, we-may-be-broke depression—and not in publishing alone, of course. On September 2, 1991, Roger Cohen, the publishing reporter for the *New York Times,* headlined his *tour d'horizon* of the state of the business "An Ailing, Murky Industry Looks for Signs of Change." In the midst of a stubborn recession he reported that "Sales are very weak. Even the most die-hard optimists concede that the notion of publishing's being recession-proof has been shown to be nonsense. . . . So a profound change, it seems, has taken place. After a decade of rapid sales growth, which fueled a rapid rise in the money that authors were able to command for their books, a period of retrenchment has begun."

And yet. . . . Cohen takes note of the inveterately optimistic nature of publishers, a quality reflected in the oversized advances still being paid for the hot property ($6 million for the Norman Schwarzkopf autobiography being an egregious case in point) and the highly desirable prestige item. So right at this moment I'm choosing to accentuate the positive as far as book editing is concerned. Yes, the corporate shenanigans described in my piece still go on, the agents call the tune, the culture is decaying, nobody reads anymore, the universe will eventually suffer heat death. . . . Meanwhile, the good editor's task—and there are *plenty* of good editors out there, many of them my friends—*is simply to ignore all this* and go about the business of bringing the best books he or she can to market, at a price that makes turning a profit possible. This may mean any number of personal and business compromises with a commercial culture capable of the most stupe-fying inanition. But victories, however difficult to win, are the lifeblood of editors, and they come more often than one might expect. And such victo-ries are what make publishing mean infinitely more than the simple sum of x thousands of units shipped at y cover price with a profit margin of z percent. It means that the soul of publishing, and to a certain extent of American literary and intellectual culture, if that's not too grandiose, re-sides in the stewardship of editors who care deeply about quality and excellence.

And so we soldier on. And so we'd better.

Doing Good—And Doing It Right

The Ethical and Moral Dimensions of Editing

James O'Shea Wade

JAMES O'SHEA WADE *graduated from Harvard College in 1962 and initially worked in sales and editorial in college and professional publishing. He switched over to trade in the late sixties as a senior editor at Macmillan. He was subsequently editor-in-chief of World Publishing and then editorial director and vice-president of David McKay. He founded his own publishing operation and then joined forces with Kennett and Eleanor Rawson to form Rawson, Wade Publishers. He is presently executive editor and vice-president of Crown Publishers and editorial director of Orion Books.*

Not only editors but writers, too, can profit greatly from Mr. Wade's expert advice to editors on how to conduct themselves according to the highest moral and ethical standards of publishing. In a situation where the interests of author and publisher do not coincide, he asks "how one reconciles the obligations of friendship [with an author] with those of an editor who is expected to contribute to the corporate interests of his or her publisher." His answer is that "the only workable way to reconcile what may seem to be conflicting obligations and interests is to stay with one essential truth: the editor's primary obligation is to the book. *If you fail in that you are no friend to the author and you are not doing what a publisher pays you to do."*

Mr. Wade offers illuminating insights into the editor's moral and ethical role in such areas as censorship, responsibility for the authenticity of a manuscript, the decision to reject a manuscript deemed to be unpublishable, the necessity for honesty between editor and agent, and many other problems and procedures that plague and often perplex the working editor.

Ultimately, Mr. Wade declares that "if you have done your job properly,
if you have really served the book, *you will have served your employer* and
your author and behaved both morally and ethically."

Doing Good—And Doing It Right

The Ethical and Moral Dimensions of Editing

It is not surprising that most editors feel a very strong personal commitment
to the authors with whom they work. Some of the writers I work with today
have become very dear friends over the course of more than twenty years
in harness together. Long ago I had to ask myself how one reconciles the
obligations of friendship with those of an editor who is expected to contribute to the corporate interests of his or her publisher. Under ideal conditions,
the interests of author and publisher coincide. But, alas, not always. And
what about the obligation one has to readers?

The only workable way to reconcile what may seem to be conflicting
obligations and interests is to stay with one essential truth: the editor's
primary obligation is to the *book.* If you fail in that you are no friend to the
author and you are not doing what a publisher pays you to do.

It all begins with acquisition of a book. If you have some strong personal
belief or bias that goes against the argument of a book, if you find the
subject matter or writing or point of view distasteful or even repugnant,
then you should be very hesitant to involve yourself, even if—or especially
if—you think "it might sell a lot of copies." The editor should not play the
role of either expert or censor. If you suspect you are going to distort, even
unwittingly, the author's ideas and expressions for whatever reason (your
"expertise" or your moral evaluation or even hazy issues like taste), then
you have no business editing that book. All of us would like to claim, with
Voltaire, that we might disagree with someone but defend his right to say
what we disagree with—but professionalism demands that an editor not get
involved if there is any likelihood of crossing the line that separates objective, supportive work on the book from trespassing on the author's right of
expression.

Declining to work on such a book is not personal indulgence; you should
not serve as its editor unless you can approach it with a certain degree of
objectivity and the enthusiasm and support it needs to be successfully edited

and published. It is, after all, not *your* book. On behalf of your publisher you will be acquiring certain rights to it but, unless it is employee-for-hire material, the author owns the work he or she has created. That's why every publisher's contract has a warranty clause. In that clause the author-creator of the work "warrants and represents" things that must be taken with unreserved seriousness by both publisher and author—that the work is original, doesn't violate someone else's copyright (i.e., the author is not a plagiarist, the worst nightmare of publishing), that it does not invade the rights of privacy of others, and a great deal more.

That clause gives the editor some very important fundamental guidelines about what an editor is *not*. An editor is neither an author nor a collaborator; he or she does not participate in the creation or the ownership of the book.

This does not mean that you are inhibited from giving your opinion to an author. In fact, you would be remiss if you did not express your opinions, reactions, thoughts; you're paid to offer your author your advice as well as to be the reader's advocate. But you offer opinions; you don't have any right to issue orders. The author listens to what you say—and then accepts or rejects your suggestions. If you and your author have widely divergent opinions about the quality and content of the manuscript, you may well reach a point on the book where another rather important clause in the contract comes to bear: Is the work acceptable?

Publishers fight constantly to keep the definition of what is acceptable rather broad. But if a publisher and its representative—you, the editor— have this wide discretion, you also have a very heavy responsibility. I have, in nearly thirty years as an editor, worked on only a tiny number of books that were ultimately not accepted. Most of the time this happens when a book was acquired on the basis of an outline or some other form of brief presentation; if you acquire a manuscript that is substantially complete, you ought to know what you will have to publish. How and when does an editor come to this unhappy standoff with an author? It should not happen until you are sure that you have exhausted all of the resources at your command to assist the author in making the book say what the author wants it to say, including detailed editorial advice and time to revise the manuscript.

Your conscience has told you that you've done your best. What now? There is no rulebook, no set of specifications to guide you. You may fear that "the book won't sell." First of all, humility reminds us that publishing is a fundamentally unpredictable business. Often the only way to find out what will sell or not is by publishing the book. If you believe that the book represents the best that the author, with whatever help you have given, can achieve, then you have done your job. But this is a complex determination. You've probably read previous books by the author. The outline said clearly that certain things would be covered. Has the author demonstrated that he or she has done the work with a level of skill and commitment commensurate with previous work? Did the book keep the promises that the outline made?

Other considerations may enter in: the legal review of a manuscript may reveal large areas of possible legal trouble that entail considerable business risk. You work with the author to resolve those problems but it may come to a point where the author says, "Here I stand," and you must say, "Good-bye and good luck." But you may also decide, with the approval of your house and counsel, to take a business risk.

Bearing in mind that the author has made certain undertakings in the warranty clause, you may have certain apprehensions, based on experience, that something isn't quite right. At this point you do one of the hardest jobs facing an editor; you go to the maximum lengths to determine if your apprehensions are grounded in fact. While you are not an expert, and while you can't vet or check out every book, you do have an obligation to check out the credentials of an author. And if that author is recommending something that *might* be injurious to the health or other vital interests of readers, you are obliged to seek out experts and determine the degree of risk that might be involved—and advise the reader of these risks, usually in the form of a notice placed prominently in the front of the book.

What you can't guard against is, as I have previously mentioned, that dreadful nightmare of plagiarism. Whether unconscious or deliberate, stealing the work of another brings down horrendous and punitive damages if the case is proved. Fortunately this is a rare outcome. I have been involved in cases where such a taking was claimed but, thank heaven, the claims were proved groundless or withdrawn in every case. So plagiarism is both the greatest and the least of your worries; your only defense against it is the integrity of the author. But there are many other vexing issues that you will face, most of them related to the acceptability of a book.

What then do you do if, all remedies exhausted, you have a book that is a turkey, a dud, an absolute nonstarter? The author has cooperated and done his or her best; so have you. Well, you admit that it is, *in your best judgment,* a book that your house is not going to be able to sell. You have fulfilled your responsibility to the book; in the words of the nineteenth-century poet Arthur Hugh Clough: "Thou shalt not kill; but needst not strive / Officiously to keep alive." It is not a question of your being right or wrong; it is a matter of your honest evaluation. You do no favor to the book to "give it the benefit of the doubt"; that doubt of yours will taint everything you do in the course of publishing the book. You can't present it with full and professional enthusiasm. You will, in effect, have failed your responsibility to the book as well as to the author and your house.

If this decision to cut the book loose sounds simple, it is not. It is the most unpleasant and most morally demanding decision an editor makes. There is some small measure of comfort in the fact that your "wrong" may well turn out to be someone else's "right"—the publisher just down the road that takes on the book after you have rejected it. Both parties turn out to be right. You are right in saying no because you are, given your response, not the right editor for the book.

There is, of course, that limitation of freedom of speech and expression that Holmes set forth: the (false) cry of fire in a crowded theater. Ought you to be, as editor, the one who decides if there's a fire or not? I think not—unless you feel that you can't keep your fundamental vow to the book. In the extreme case, are you (and is your house) ready to go to court? Counsel has warned you of potential legal problems—you take a "business risk." Reporters, newspapers, even television and radio, face this decision more often than we do because they *report* and are shielded by a presumption that their reporting, in which timeliness is essential, gives them a wider latitude than we have in books. That goes to the heart of the lengthy dialogue between editor and author and what you bring to the process: absolute honesty and forthrightness, of course, but also experience and good judgment. And remember that you are not some isolated moral agonizer; you are part of a collegial body that is your publishing house—you have other experienced people to go to when you want to try out your opinion.

But this should be done, if possible, *before* the book is sent on its way to the press, preferably when it is still in manuscript. Once you have signed off on it, barring unforeseen developments, you are responsible for that book. On the basis of your judgment, your house has made a commitment and ultimately its imprint appears on the book. The public has the right to expect that the publisher (and that means, effectively, you) has published a book after reasonable deliberation, with judgment and care that match the advertising claims and promotional sizzle. This does not mean you or your house *approves* of the book; it means only that you and your house have behaved in a responsible way. There is no NIHIL OBSTAT or IMPRIMATUR stamped on the book by you or your house. Still, there is no absolute guarantee that a book won't come back and bite you! Some will. That is what makes publishing and editing such a damnably interesting business.

. . .

No matter how "scientific" we try to make publishing, it is essentially a business of experiment. It needs passion and enthusiasm to drive it—and the strong reins of experience and prudence (yes, and more than a dash of humility) to keep it on the road. While our relationships with authors are formalized in written contracts, the heart of what we do takes place in phone calls and conversations, in the human friction of brief and hasty interchanges. Clarity in communicating in such informal ways can stave off a lot of grief for author and editor. It is desirable to be clear and make sure you are understood—and that you understand. One's colleagues in subsidiary rights are all too aware of this; every day over the phone they conduct paperback and book club auctions involving many thousands of dollars. The obligation to be truthful and accurate is what makes this possible.

This is not a question of moral delicacy; clarity and truthfulness make it possible to carry on a business that depends on mutual trust. If someone is caught lying in an auction, for example, that auctioneer will be badly damaged. Repetition leads to professional ruin. We don't have the time to be dishonest; in most cases chicanery isn't worth it. So let this pragmatic consideration rule your relations with authors. What you mistakenly conceal or withhold from them or their agents will, more often than not, come out sooner or later. As quick as any editor is to pass on good news, so must he or she be prompt and unreserved in conveying the bad news. You, the editor, are generally the author's main conduit of information; you represent your house. But you are not quite a press secretary or cheerleader; you are the person who owes his first loyalty to the book. Once you've done your work with pencil and persuasion, you are the book's chief advocate in the house. You steer it through production, launch—the whole process.

Yet authors have just one thing to think about; you have many things. All books are not equal—in quality or the way they are published. But the author wants to feel that he or she has your undivided commitment and attention. (The same might be said of what the author would like from the publicist or the advertising director or the jacket artist. But the editor is expected to give the best approximation of total and constant attention. While awake, anyway.) Much is made of the kind of hand-holding expected by authors. But my experience is that authors really depend on editors for one thing: the truth. Yes, you can sugarcoat it if you want, but sooner or later you have to come forth with it.

When someone in the house says, "Let's not mention this or that to Author X," your initial response should be to ask if it is really necessary to keep this back. What will it really accomplish? Publishers, editors, and spies have two things (at least) in common; they love to gossip and they love to keep secrets. But publishing is a business of so much detail that it is hard to keep much buried forever. Misinformation (a polite term for lies) does so much harm to publishers that it just isn't worth it. Sometimes we hold things back for good reason; maybe the situation is complicated and we don't have all the facts. But more often than not we are reluctant to tell an author or an agent something he or she has a right to know because we mistakenly think it will cause us problems if we do divulge it. The real motive behind it all, truthfully, is that we fear our case is a bit shaky or that we have something to hide. If you have screwed up, the first thing to do is admit it. If the author wants to know what the first printing is, tell him. If the author wants to know why there weren't any books in the stores in San Francisco when your house sent her there on tour, find out why and explain it. In the process you will educate the author in your realities, the way your business works. It is, in fact, the author's business too. We are locked in a symbiotic relationship; trust and full disclosure are necessities, not luxuries, and they go far in building an enduring, productive, and creative relationship between editors and authors.

Why do we delight in keeping things secret from our authors? So as to keep them secret from the competition? After all, given the fact that our survival depends on greater efficiency in the distribution and sale of books, such efficiency depends heavily on open access to information. Your competitor can get a pretty good idea of how many copies of a book you are selling by extrapolating from widely disseminated information: the sell-through reports of electronic cash registers. With the cash register mated to a computer, when the sale is rung up, the book is automatically deducted from the inventory carried in the store computer. One knows that the book is sold. In an age of electronic ubiquity, closed-information societies are rather hard to maintain, as witness what has become of the Soviet Union. Publishers don't try to "cook" their royalty reports—it would probably lead to horrendous inventory control problems. Misinformation and concealment are inefficient.

But to educate your author, so that the full and correct answer makes sense, demands quite a bit of self-education. Editors have to learn a little about every area of the business. How, exactly, does the entire fulfillment process work? What are the usual terms and conditions of premium and special or bulk sales? What it comes down to is that you must know the basics about how other people in your business do their jobs. What are their problems, their realities? This is an endless process, this self-education. But it makes you a truly effective and capable editor. It not only informs your relationships with authors, it gives you better information on which to make acquisition and other business decisions.

All of this begs a large question: Is it necessary—ever—to lie for "good reasons"? We face the same question in our lives outside of business; we respond according to circumstance and conscience. At an early age we learn that truth prospers and untruth does not. Or some of us learn otherwise. If you find yourself in a publishing situation where there is a willful pattern of duplicity and misinformation, you will save your reputation (and much of your value as an editor) by getting out of it. My experience in publishing is that most lies told are small ones. Big ones lead promptly to disaster.

We sometimes withhold information because authors or agents don't have "a need to know." Generally this is another way of saying that we don't want to open things up for fear that authors or agents will be telling us how to do our business. Open and clear communication doesn't mean you have to give up control over decisions and judgments that are properly the publisher's to make. Publishers are quite right to guard those rights; heavy responsibilities come with them. (After all, it's always our fault that the book didn't sell.) Educating the author, informing him or her fully, doesn't always lead to agreement. But you are morally and ethically obliged to make your best efforts and to stand by what you think is right.

If, after you have heard what author or agent has to say, and you have explained your position, then stand by it. I say "your" position, when in reality it is often a house decision, reached after deliberations by many concerned people or handed down by management. Often you may not be in total agreement with that decision. But your obligation as an editor was to do everything you could, given your understanding and opinion, to shape that decision, preferably in collegial, rational fashion. You may feel it necessary to tell your author you don't agree with that decision. But if you find yourself in that position too frequently, consider that you might not be 100 percent right. You should also give some thought to the possibility that you are marching to a different drummer and maybe ought to march off elsewhere. (Before marching off, make sure the trip is necessary!)

If you are being honest about the book inside the house and with the author (a certain leeway for hype and flattery is human and allowable), then you are living up to your primary obligation—to the book. You are the best (usually) and often the only advocate the book has; and your clout is as good as your reputation for being realistic and honest. Your relationship with the author, based on full disclosure, has some things in common with a lawyer-client relationship. Confidentiality, for instance, is something that authors and agents have a right to expect. This is particularly important in a business that deals with intellectual property—ideas and the form in which they are expressed. Editors are frequently confided in, by authors and agents, with ideas, plots, and various notions, sometimes in written form, more often in conversation. You have an absolute obligation to respect the ownership of that idea.

Confidentiality involves your respecting the author's rights in many ways; authors use the sympathetic ears of editors to sort out problems (often ones that have nothing to do with the book), and there are necessarily certain details of authors' personal and financial affairs that editors are aware of. Because the author is often quite open with his or her editor, that editor has a grave responsibility not to use such confidential information in any way. An editor who talks indiscreetly about one of his or her authors to another author is generally wrong to do so and invariably foolish.

The nature of the friendship that grows between author and editor allows for many abuses—on both sides. Authors have agents for good reason; to use your friendship with the author to influence the business discussions that properly should take place between agent and editor is always wrong. An editor must always be alert to situations where friendship must stop and professional responsibility begin: when you are "doing the author a favor," more often than not you are doing him or her and yourself a disfavor. You should not make promises that your house won't keep. You cannot suddenly become a collaborator—you are on one side of the desk and the author is on the other. The agent represents the author; you represent the book.

It sometimes becomes necessary that you recuse yourself (i.e., step out of the line of fire) when you feel that you are not in a position to speak for the author. That's the moment when an agent becomes a blessing. Agents can say things to publishers that would be awkward for authors to say to editors. Good cop, bad cop? Yes, that's part of the negotiating game. But nothing relieves you of your responsibility for the book. The old Chinese proverb is not always right: "Victory has a thousand fathers; defeat is an orphan." No, win or lose, the editor and the author and the book have enduring family ties!

. . .

I have elected to concentrate on certain general principles that should govern the conduct and attitude of an editor. The ethical and moral problems that can and do arise would require a book rather than an essay to give attention in any detail. But most problems stem from a lack of clarity about responsibility. The author entrusts his or her book to you in part because of your reputation and that of your house. You have a right to expect certain things of an author—and a duty to ascertain, insofar as is possible, that the author is capable of writing a book that you will be able to speak for, honestly and passionately. That doesn't mean you are searching for authors of stellar integrity and character. (What would become of editors if *they* had to meet such high standards!?) But it does mean you are looking for certain professional "virtues." That warranty clause in the contract does not absolve you from being sure that, while you may not believe and trust the author in all things, you can and do trust him or her in the things needful for this book. One can't make a Solomon-like distinction, in many cases, between the author and his or her book. Your house rightly expects you to protect it against frauds, lunatics, and con men, even when they come with seemingly the most angelic credentials. *You* want to be as sure as you can of whom you are dealing with; you can't hope for transcendent goodness, but you had certainly better find competence. You, more than anyone else, are in a position to make this essential judgment as prelude to committing your house to publish any work.

If you are deceived, profit from the experience and hope it will not be repeated. If you fall into it too often, seek another profession. Beware, too, of thinking that your skills can make the book something it is not. If you wish to be a writer, be one. Never tell an author that you can somehow inspirit a book with qualities and essences that will somehow transform it. Be careful to keep a clear idea of your role; you are not the expert, not the creator. You are there to assist.

Remember whence your paycheck cometh—and why. If you have done your job properly, if you have really served the *book,* you will have served your employer *and* your author and behaved both morally and ethically. Remember: no matter how it sells, that book remains in your care until death or other employment do you part.

How Books Are Chosen

What Goes into Making an Editorial Decision

Richard Marek

RICHARD MAREK *started as the "backlist editor" at Macmillan, then became a senior editor there, in charge of the backlist but bringing in new titles. At Macmillan he worked with Bruno Bettelheim on* The Children of the Dream. *Moving to World Publishing, he first published Robert Ludlum, then went to Dial and published James Baldwin and Mira Rothenberg. Leaving Dial, he had his own imprint, first at Putnam's, where he continued to publish Ludlum, then at St. Martin's, where he acquired* The Silence of the Lambs. *In 1985 he became president and publisher of E. P. Dutton, where he published Peter Straub, Judith Rapoport, and James Carroll. When Dutton was folded into NAL/Viking, he assumed his present position, that of editor-at-large at Crown Publishers, a division of Random House.*

"When I'm asked by writers what I, as an editor, am looking for, my answer is, 'Something I haven't seen before.' The reply may infuriate the writer— it is of little help to him—but it is true. The new idea, the new voice, the jolt one feels at the unexpected are what most stimulate the editor and the reading public," says Richard Marek in his shrewd anatomy of the factors that make an editor buy—or reject—a manuscript.

Mr. Marek discusses the favorable impact on the editor of such important factors as the fiction writer's unique voice or vision, pacing, plotting, verisimilitude, gift for characterization, style, and dialogue. For the nonfiction writer, the way to tempt an editor is to display skills in the organization and presentation of original, relevant, interesting material in an entertaining, accessible way.

Mr. Marek concludes his eminently practical essay with two pieces of

*advice for editors that, if followed, will surely enhance their careers. They
will also benefit writers seeking to work with editors who are intuitively
empathetic with their work. The first recommendation is that "an editor
must develop a sense for commercial books even if he might not read them
on his vacation," and the second is that an editor should not publish in
fields he knows nothing about but should "go for what you know. Trust
your instincts and your passions. And the readers will come—and they will
buy."*

How Books Are Chosen

What Goes into Making an
Editorial Decision

Acquiring editors are hired for one primary reason: that the books they buy
make money for the publishing company that employs them.

This somewhat oversimplified assertion does not reflect a new conspiracy
on the part of money-hungry conglomerates; it was just as true thirty years
ago, when I entered the business, as it is now, and historians of publishing
report that it was true from the creation of the printing press.

Nor does the linking of profits and books imply that the editor is hired
to buy "bad" books, junk. I am told that the biggest money-maker in the
history of Random House is James Joyce's *Ulysses,* and numbers one and
two at Macmillan are *Gone with the Wind* and *The Complete Poems of
William Butler Yeats.* Yes, some junk sells, but much does not; best-seller
lists are strange amalgams of down- and upmarket volumes that speak only
of the diversity of American taste.

No matter, the first consideration that goes into making an editorial
decision is a marketing one: whether the book will sell enough to make back
its costs, including the advance to the author, and turn a profit.

In most cases, the answer is unclear; one doesn't *know.* It is probable that
a biography of Cher will sell more copies than a biography of Madame de
Sévigné, that a novel with violent action and steamy sex will outperform a
roman à clef about an adolescent's slow progress toward maturity. But one
must be careful in trying to generalize: perhaps the Sévigné biography will
win the National Book Award and become a staple backlist book selling
steadily over the years. Perhaps the *roman à clef* is by J. D. Salinger.

It's a truism that "brand names" sell, and it is indeed true that the public
is loyal to authors, particularly in the area of fiction. Thus the next book by
Stephen King is likely to outsell his current one, even if it is not quite as

good, and Agatha Christie's sales continued to grow and grow, though her skills in plotting diminished as she went on. One reason is that most hardcover fiction is bought as a gift for someone else, and the buyer does not want to take a chance on an unknown. But more important, the brand name author is *good*. He or she tells a story better than the competition, is more inventive, cleverer at surprise, more insightful in characterization, etc. It is generally true that the better a writer is at what he does, the better the sales.

So it's certainly true that editors go after name authors. But they also remember that the fact that some writers are proven quantities does not necessarily negate the risk in acquiring them. Other publishers daily try to woo them as well, and since the lure is almost invariably money, brand name authors come high, even to the house that published them so well the last time. Eventually the money the publisher must pay in advance may exceed the author's earning power, and a book that sells one million copies may turn out to be a terrific disappointment. It isn't the number of copies the book sells that determines its success; it is the bottom-line profit the book generates.

. . .

There are, I believe, three kinds of books. First, there is the "sales department" book, the profitability of which is better determined by the sales manager than the editor. These books are always nonfiction, fill a market need, are easily explained. The sales manager need only describe the book to a few chains and independent stores to determine whether a market exists.

At The Dial Press, for example, I received a huge manuscript on magic. Our sales manager learned that there were a few expensive books on the subject, and many inexpensive pamphlets on how to do the most common tricks. Nothing existed, however, in a midprice range, so I went back to the author and asked him if he wanted to cut his book in half. He agreed, and Dial published a moderately priced, relatively substantial book that went on to sell twenty thousand copies—it was the only book of its kind. (Sales departments can be useful, too, in discovering the past record of authors whose previous books have been published by other houses. The editor who believes an agent on a past book's record does so at his peril; often, the agent will give as sales the number of copies *shipped,* without taking returns into account.)

Second, there is the "subsidiary rights" book. Much fiction, for example, is genre fiction—mysteries, romances, thrillers, "women's novels," gothics, historicals. It is the subsidiary rights manager's job to know which of these genres the paperback houses are buying, and within the genres what plots, situations, kinds of detectives, locales, etc., are no longer viable. When I first entered publishing, two paperback houses were devoted primarily to science fiction; then the market faded, and one house folded while the other changed its direction completely. Soon after, science fiction returned, more popular than ever.

Since a hardcover novel's greatest chance for profit comes in its sale to a mass-market paperback house (or through sales *by* the conglomerate's paperback arm if the book was bought hard-soft), the editor who does not consult with his subsidiary rights manager before deciding on whether or not to buy a genre book is being derelict not only to his house, but to himself.

Finally, there is the "editor's" book, one that does not fall into a genre, fill a known niche, or remind a sales staff or book buyer of anything seen before. It is the editor's instinct for these books, bought on individual feel and passion, then explained (convincingly) to sales force and/or subsidiary rights departments, that will in the long run dictate the editor's chance for stardom. If his instinct is good, the books will sell. But it is essential to realize that such books come along *rarely*. In the short run, the more an editor seeks advice and follows it, the better off he is.

Jonathan Livingston Seagull was, I understand, turned down by over a dozen houses before it was bought by Macmillan ("a book about a talking *bird?*"), as was Lampedusa's *The Leopard* ("a novel by a *dead Sicilian?*") before Pantheon "took a chance" on one of the great books of the twentieth century. Sure, you and I would never have rejected them (especially in hindsight); there were just dumber editors in those days. The point is that these were surely editor's books; no sales department or rights manager could be expected to predict their success; no precedent existed by which to chart their futures.

•   •   •

Many books are bought on outlines and sample chapters and are years away from completion at the time of purchase; even a book offered as a finished manuscript will take nine months to produce. Thus, currently hot subjects, ones covered in newspapers and magazines, are generally bad bets for books. Yes, there were vastly successful Watergate books months (or even years) after the notorious break-in. But there were vastly unsuccessful Watergate books as well (the majority, I suspect), and publishers lost a lot of money thinking the public's interest in the subject would continue unabated. A book by the only reporter in Jonestown at the time of the famous massacre-suicide, which was published less than a year after the grisly events, sold fewer than ten thousand copies. Other grisly events had superseded Jonestown in the public's consciousness. It is far better to look to "timeless" subjects and give them new slants (relationships, love, child-rearing, natural history, personal finances, etc.) than to try to derive books from material already covered in the press.

Ironically, though, that most immediate of all media, television, has a huge bearing on the decision of whether or not to buy a book. "Is (s)he good on the tube?" is one of the questions most frequently asked about the author; it often seems that articulateness in person (to say nothing of good looks) is more important than articulateness in writing, and for good reason. There is no question that a strong appearance on a talk show like *Oprah* or *Donahue* will influence sales far more than the writer's skill in organizing his material or presenting a logically written case. Still, the writer with new, exciting ideas who has presented them logically and enthusiastically stands a better chance of getting on talk shows than the glamorous hack. So the editor is still better off judging the words rather than their author.

. . .

When I'm asked by writers what I, as an editor, am looking for, my answer is, "Something I haven't seen before." The reply may infuriate the writer—it is of little help to him—but it is true. The new idea, the new voice, the jolt one feels at the unexpected are what most stimulate the editor and the reading public. The great naturalist Loren Eiseley once said that what characterizes great art is that it so renders an idea, an object, or an emotion that it is impossible to encounter it again without thinking of the artist's conception of it. He used as an example a van Gogh sunflower, but he could just as well have used a Melville whale or a Salinger preadolescent.

When a writer comes along with a new voice or vision, something unique, editors scramble after it as though it were gold. Sometimes the voice or vision is *so* new that it is difficult to comprehend, and then only a few editors might go after it (I think of James Joyce, for example—or Charles Darwin). Sometimes, too, the voice takes a while to become familiar, and the sales of an author's early books are small (Faulkner, or John Irving). But my colleagues and I are convinced that no truly original voice goes undiscovered, that no masterpiece lies unpublished in the writer's attic. In his lifetime, a writer is always recognized by his peers, and while not precisely writers' peers, editors at least are people of words, and our hunger virtually guarantees that at least one or two of us, when presented with combinations of words we have not read before, will find them exciting.

. . .

My answer to what we specifically look for in judging a manuscript is one to which most editors would subscribe. (I will take up fiction and nonfiction separately.)

In fiction, above all else, there is voice. Do I want to spend the next several hours with the author? Do I *trust* him? Is he entertaining? Does he render familiar scenes in ways that are new, or unfamiliar ones in ways that make me see them clearly? Does he reveal enough of himself to make me like his company?

The thriller writer who begins his novel with a description of snow falling over Washington or the telephone call that interrupts the general in the middle of a sexual act with a buxom blond had better follow with a terrific tale if he wants me to buy his book (chances are he won't; the author who writes in clichés generally plots in clichés). But if I get in a manuscript with the equivalent of the marching words "Stately, plump Buck Mulligan" as its opening, the author has me won immediately, and his book will have to deteriorate before I turn it down.

Please note that by voice I do not mean *style*. Robert Ludlum, for one, is an infelicitous stylist, yet his impassioned, breathless, extravagant prose is perfectly suited to his melodramas. One never doubts his sincerity and his commitment; his ability to convey his own feelings is what sweeps his readers along.

Following voice there is pace, and for this the test is simple: After I finish one page, do I want to read the next? Ludlum, of course, is a master of pace—events move with something like the speed of a bullet—but the pace of great language drawing its reader deeper and deeper into thought and feeling is also irresistible. I've found that for writers, pace is instinctive (as it seems to be in movies and the theater). If the writer (or director) can make his story move in an appropriate rhythm, then the pace works.

Then comes character. I used to think that plot superseded character on this list, but despite several examples to the contrary, plot *does* come out of characters in conflict, as we're told in our first creative writing classes. So: Do we *like* the characters; do we care about their fates? Do we have an emotional investment in whether they marry or divorce, revenge themselves on those who did them wrong? Do they *live?* Are they complicated, surprising, *real?* If the answers are yes, the editor will be strongly influenced to buy the book.

Fourth, there is plot. Some writers (Ludlum again) can tell such a riveting story that it doesn't matter that his characters are one-dimensional. Others, the majority, develop their plots out of their characters' development. But in any case, here we are looking for the story that draws us along because we want to know what happens next—and if what happens next convincingly surprises us, then so much the better. Arbitrary surprises won't do. Logical ones are glorious.

Next—and there is a gulf between this category and the one above it—comes style. Good writing is a lovely thing in and of itself, but it isn't enough to make me want to take on a book. Indeed, the manuscript I most fear is the one so beautifully written I must go on reading, yet in the end says nothing, reveals nothing, is without impact or astonishment.

Finally, there is verisimilitude. It helps (and it's fun) if the author gets his details right, but accuracy pales before invention if the invention is convincing. The author who tells me that "it's the way it happened in real life" or "it's the way the room actually looked" is not convincing me of a book's quality. The insistence on accuracy rather than verisimilitude is probably the reason so many journalists can't write good novels. If the author convinces me it's true, then I don't care if it's actually true or not.

In reading a nonfiction book or proposal, a similar but different list applies. Here, too, we start out with voice, for, even more than in fiction, the reader must trust the author. A self-assured, enthusiastic writer who seems sure of where his book is heading, and who presents his material with a distinctive voice, has a far better chance than the hack who tells me already known facts to make his case for the book or who presents his "groundbreaking" conclusions without the logic to back them up.

Perhaps more important (although I list it second) is, of course, subject matter. It's foolhardy to discuss what the best subjects are for commercial books, for tastes change, public issues change, categories once considered surefire (self-help, for example) get overcrowded and lose their potency. A big hit in one subject area often spawns so many imitations that books on the same subject, no matter how cogent, will have trouble finding an audience. As a general rule, readers want to read about things that affect their own lives. The sensational subjects—sex, money, murder, bizarre relationships, the kinks of the rich and famous—tend to be perennially popular, if only because the common man can find titillations and balm in the success or misfortunes of others. Other people's lives, provided they are exciting, have always fascinated us; if there is one category to back, that is it.

Third comes organization, the marshaling of material. A logical narrative, as in fiction, going persuasively from one point to the next, building to a climax, is a pleasure to read. Such an achievement suggests that the author knows more than he can put into his book, that he is in control of his material. This aptitude is extremely comforting to the reader. One wants to be led by an expert, and the author sure of his facts, and selecting them wisely, is likely to convince us of his expertise.

Fourth, style. The author who writes really well can make even an unlikely subject seem interesting. I've read pieces by John McPhee, for example, that have persuaded me that Alaska is a fascinating place, and that have told me more about oranges than I thought I wanted to know. On the other hand, dull writers can make fascinating subjects boring. A hack can make the most sensational murder seem soporific; the author who writes with enthusiasm and verve can make us feel virtually any subject is exciting.

Finally, as in fiction, there is verisimilitude. The writer who can take even preposterous subjects and make them convincing—generally through the use of detail and the ability to communicate his own passion and belief— is one to venerate. Recently I read a book on something I simply don't believe in: reincarnation. Yet the author made me believe that *he* believed, and I read the book avidly, troubled and confused. He didn't convince me—a few days later I had dismissed his ideas as poppycock. But he took me with him and, briefly at least, shook my soul.

One last word. Writers are always told to write from experience, and editors should follow the same advice. Your problems, concerns, your passions are not unique—they are mirrored by others, and therefore there is an audience for books about them. The young single editor with relationship problems is far better off looking for writers who share his concerns than for books on marriage. An editor with an expertise in science might be advised to turn over a book on ballet to a colleague better read in the existing books in the field.

There is a difference between personal taste and professional taste; an editor must develop a sense for commercial books even if he might not read them on his vacation. But the editor who tries to publish in fields that do not interest him, just *because* he knows books in those fields have been successful, is likely to fail. Go for what you know. Trust your instincts and your passions. And the readers will come—and they will buy.

Practice

What Editors Look for in a Query Letter, Proposal, and Manuscript

Jane von Mehren

JANE VON MEHREN *is a senior editor at Ticknor & Fields, a division of Houghton Mifflin. She spent six years at Crown Publishers, where she began her career working with James O'Shea Wade and rose to the rank of editor. In addition, she has been a recipient of the Tony Godwin Award, which allows a young American editor to work in Britain. Among the books she has edited and acquired are* Backlash: The Undeclared War against American Women *by Susan Faludi and* Catwatching *and* Dogwatching *by Desmond Morris.*

Submitting a query letter, proposal, or a manuscript to an editor is like going out on a job interview: First impressions count! A lot! Jane von Mehren recommends that "the first thing you, the writer, can do is to make sure that no matter what you submit, it follows the correct format." She then proceeds to offer six basic rules for making your material look professional in the editor's eyes, and goes on to list vital dos and don'ts specific to preparing a query letter, proposal, and manuscript so that they become effective tools and business plans for selling your work, whether fiction or nonfiction. Editors sometimes seem too jaded or busy to pay attention to what you have eagerly, anxiously submitted; but, Ms. von Mehren concludes, "despite their being overworked, remember that editors are always looking for new material. There is nothing quite so thrilling for an editor than coming upon an original, exciting, and thoroughly professional author. Your expertly prepared and presented query letter, proposal, or manuscript can convince her that you are that author."

What Editors Look for in a Query Letter, Proposal, and Manuscript

One of the many myths that exists about editors is that we spend our days sitting quietly in our offices, reading the voluminous numbers of query letters, proposals, and manuscripts we receive. This utopian vision fails to take into account the phone that never stops ringing, the weekly meetings that must be attended, and the numerous stages of the books we oversee. In fact, we almost never consider our submissions in the office between nine and five. We do our reading at home during the evenings or on weekends and because our time is limited we simply cannot afford to read every single word of every single submission.

Then how on earth can an author hope to make an impression or catch an editor's attention, you ask?

The first thing you, the writer, can do is to make sure that no matter what you submit, it follows the correct format. Before sending in your material, make sure it conforms to these six very basic rules:

1. Never send anything that is not typed. If you work on a computer, use a high-quality printer; try not to employ a dot-matrix printer for anything longer than ten pages or so.

2. Always use 8½-by-11-inch white paper. It need not be expensive, top-quality bond paper, but don't use onionskin, erasable typing paper, or any other type of very thin paper that will tear and smudge easily. If you use computer paper, make sure to tear apart and separate each sheet; expecting an editor to do this for you will only irritate this very busy reader and make him or her less inclined to even consider your work. Keep your margins approximately 1½ inches on the top and to the left, and 1 inch at the right and on the bottom.

3. Except in the case of a short query letter, always double-space your manuscript. Many editors won't consider proposals or manuscripts that are single-spaced and will return the material to you unread.

4. Number the pages consecutively from beginning to end, preferably in the same place on every page. Do not begin each chapter with a new page 1; should a reader lose his or her place in the manuscript, it can be impossible to find again.

5. Carefully proofread the material you submit. A typo here or there in a completed manuscript will be forgiven; in a query letter or proposal, however, such mistakes will only make you look unprofessional.

6. Always include a stamped, self-addressed return envelope for an editor to return your work. A business-size envelope is sufficient for a query letter. In the case of a proposal or manuscript, send the packaging appropriate to the size and weight of your material; padded envelopes are recommended for anything longer than one hundred pages.

Neatness counts. Nothing will turn an editor off faster than a manuscript that is sloppy, poorly typed, or single-spaced. The goal is to make your query letter, proposal, or manuscript as editor-friendly as possible—if your reader has to squint, turn the page to an odd angle, or wade through illegible material, you've already given him or her reason to reject your work. While this may sound harsh, it is a realistic reflection of the enormous amount of material an editor must read—besides, you want the editor who buys your work to retain his eyesight, don't you?

In order to make sure that your submission will not be wasted, you need to consider carefully where to send your material. A writer should never send anything to a publisher addressed solely to "Editor," whether it be the "Managing Editor," "Fiction Editor," or even "Cookbook Editor." It's unprofessional. Most editors work on numerous kinds of books, usually both fiction and nonfiction, and these generic labels have little meaning as they often apply to most of the editors on staff. Neglecting to use a specific editor's name will relegate your submission to the slush pile—the equivalent of the lost and found at a major international airport.

Figuring out which editor and which publishing house to submit your material to is not as hard as you might think. The first question to consider is: Which houses publish books similar to what you have written or are planning to write? If you don't have any idea which companies might be appropriate, go to your local library or bookstore and scan the shelves. Jot down the names of several titles from different publishers; then call the editorial department of each house to find out the names of the editors of those books. While you are at it, make sure that you ask for the correct spelling of the editor's name.

Of course, these guidelines will only help you to *present* your material in the best light possible to the most appropriate person within a particular house. Ultimately, it is the submission's *content* and the *style* of your writing that will determine whether an editor responds favorably to your work.

The Query Letter

Ranging from one to five pages in length, the query letter should pique an editor's curiosity about your project to such a great extent that you will be asked to send in more material. Query letters are appropriate for all sorts of fiction and nonfiction, ranging from travel books and cookbooks to biography and how-to. Sending a query letter as opposed to a proposal or a manuscript permits the author to test the waters while allowing an editor to quickly see whether or not the project is right for his or her list. You will usually also get a much faster response to your inquiry than if you had sent more material.

Your query letter is a piece of advertising copy that should sell both you and your book to the editor. It should showcase the concept of the work you wish to sell to the publisher; it is, in a sense, a miniproposal. Because a query is so brief, it is also vital that not a single word be wasted. Give your letter a definite focus, a clear-cut slant. Pack it with information about what your book is about, what credentials you have for writing the book, who you think the audience is for the book, and how you can help the editor reach that audience. Describe its main features, making sure to emphasize what makes it different from other books available on the same subject. This will attest to your book's salability. On the other hand, don't ever tell an editor your book is a "guaranteed best-seller"; it probably isn't and saying so will immediately mark you as an amateur.

When presenting a work of fiction, do not describe the entire plot of your novel; instead, create a paragraph or two that depicts your story in a manner that will tantalize your reader and have her wanting to read more. Characterize your manuscript in terms of its genre. You might compare your novel to that of another writer; is your work like Stephen King's or Anne Tyler's, Amy Tan's or Clyde Edgerton's? If you decided to submit to this particular house and editor because of having read one of their books, say so; it will indicate that you have done some research and aren't sending out your material blindly. Since fiction is often dependent on a successful narrative, you might also send in a chapter of the novel; always include the first chapter rather than a section from the middle of the book, which will be more confusing than helpful. It is particularly important to convey your credits as a fiction writer in your query letter. There are so many people trying to write fiction, that if you have been published, even if it's only one short story, you will have already elevated yourself above the rest of the crowd.

In submitting a query about a nonfiction project, first give an overall description of your project. The next, crucial step is to distinguish it from the other books available in your field. Describe how your book is different from the other books currently available; this will show that you have done your homework, making you look more professional as well. If you have access to new and provocative information that has never been published before, and that presents a whole new perspective on your subject, make sure to mention it in your letter; you might send some examples of this material as a part of your query. Although it is not necessary, you can include either a table of contents or an introduction that succinctly and provocatively sums up what you wish to achieve in your book.

Remember that a query letter is like a fishing expedition; don't put too much bait on your hook or you'll lose your quarry. Be brief, be succinct, be enthusiastic, and be tantalizing!

The Proposal

A strong proposal is both a sales tool and a business plan. It should persuade an editor to offer you a contract for the book you plan to write, and it should estimate the length, cost, competition, investment in time and money, as well as potential profit. Like a query letter, the proposal should make an editor want to know more about your project—and excite him or her enough so that the publishing house will offer you an advance that will subsidize you while you finish the book.

Writing proposals for novels is extremely difficult and they are equally hard for editors to evaluate. A strong outline or proposal doesn't necessarily translate into a good novel; on the other hand, a bad outline will not interest an editor though you might write a wonderful novel given the chance. Unfortunately, unless you have a solid track record as a novelist, you will almost certainly not be given a contract on the basis of a proposal or outline. Your only real option is to sit down and write the whole novel; that is indeed a huge investment, but this is a basic fact of publishing life and ignoring it may mean that you never even begin your career as a fiction writer. This does not mean that an outline of a novel is never useful; in fact, editors will often respond to a query letter about a work of fiction by asking to see the first three chapters and an outline of the rest of the book. This is a means of seeing what an author is up to; if an editor likes what he or she reads, he will ask to see the rest of the manuscript. While this may sound inefficient, it actually speeds up the process and lowers your postage costs.

Proposals are, however, extremely useful for nonfiction works; in fact, most nonfiction is sold on the basis of a proposal as opposed to a completed manuscript. While proposals range in length from a very few pages, sometimes even less than 10, to as many as 125, they tend to contain the following six elements:

1. A proposal begins with a statement a few pages long that explains the concept of the book you plan to write. This section often starts with an anecdote or some provocative set of facts that hooks the editor on your book idea. Writing in the active voice, you should use this section to explain why your idea is unique, why it is the right book at the right time, and why you are the right author for this project.

2. Most proposals have some sort of marketing section in them. This section includes a full discussion of the competition your product will face in the bookstores. Check what is available in your local bookstores—doing research in a variety of stores—and in *Books in Print.* Describe what other books are available on the subject you plan to write about, emphasizing how and why your book will be different. Obviously, you need to limit the number of titles you discuss, so pick the best-sellers in the genre, citing impressive sales figures where you can. The point here is to show how your book will be as successful, if not more so, than these proven competitors in your field.

   The second purpose of the marketing section is to define your audience and ways in which the publisher might reach it. Cite statistics to show how many people will be interested in your book's subject matter; when writing a travel guidebook proposal, for example, include the number of Americans who travel to that destination each year. If you know of professional organizations that might want to buy copies of your book or whose newsletter might be a way to advertise directly to your core audience, say so. Make sure to be realistic in your assessment of the marketplace, as editors, who constantly make their own evaluations, will not be impressed by inflated numbers or wild generalizations. Do not tell an editor that your family and friends think that this book has huge potential, as this is the quickest way to make yourself look like an amateur.

3. A table of contents usually follows next. This will give an editor a sense of how you envision the organization of your book. It will give your reader an indication of the scope and depth of your material.

   While you may not choose to have a separate table of contents, you should make sure to include a chapter-by-chapter breakdown of the contents of the book you plan to write. For each chapter of the book, write a miniature essay, usually no more than a few pages in length and often no longer than a few paragraphs, that describes what material will be covered and how it will be handled. Your aim is to show the depth and detail of your approach and how the themes of your book will evolve from one chapter to the next. You want your chapter summaries to be complete enough to convince an editor that you can write the book you propose, and that it will contain interesting, fresh, valuable material and yet also leave the reader wanting to know more.

4. Provide a section of production details. Approximate how many pages your book will have and how long it will take to research and write it. What kinds of costs will you be incurring? Will you have to travel to do research? Will there be extensive fees for permissions or artwork? Indicate what additional kinds of materials you envision including in the book: are you planning to use photos, charts, diagrams, etc.? Here your goal is to realistically assess what will be entailed in writing this book—and how much money you will need to do the job adequately.

5. The author bio, written in the third person, should establish your credentials for writing the book you propose. Your previous writing credits, if any, should be listed first; enclose any material you have written on the subject. Then give a description of your qualifications; this includes academic degrees, career highlights, or a lifelong study of the subject as an avocation. If you can get or have already gotten endorsements or blurbs from prominent people in the field, cite them. Include videotapes of any TV or other public appearances you have made. Give a rundown of what media, if any, you have already done. Since more often than not it is the author who is at the center of any publicity or promotion a book gets, it is a tremendous asset to a publisher to have a mediagenic author to work with.

6. Finally, you should provide one or two sample chapters from your book. This will prove to an editor that you can write, and although no one will assume that this is the finished product, these pages should show off your writing skills to their best advantage. Each chapter should be twenty to twenty-five pages in length and display the writing style you plan to use throughout the text and contain the kinds of information that will appear in the book. Remember to choose chapters that will suggest all the possibilities for the full-length work and still whet your reader's appetite!

Keep in mind that a proposal is not the same thing as an outline you would use to write your book. The best proposals are those that elicit the fewest questions. Why? Because you've anticipated an answered them all. Remember, your aim is to write a proposal so gripping that after reading it an editor will get on the phone and offer you a contract for your book.

The Manuscript

There is a certain irony in the fact that an editor can tell a writer quite a bit less about what she looks for in a completed manuscript than what she'd like to see in a query letter or proposal. In part this is because editors are not writers and do not know how to write a book; we soon learn that every single writer approaches his or her task in a different fashion. And when a completed manuscript is submitted to an editor, it is quite close to being finished and should persuade an editor of its value on its merits: the content and style of the work. You should, however, make sure that your manuscript, whether fiction or nonfiction, does not indulge in sloppy thinking or careless writing. Ask yourself: Is my plot or argument persuasive; is it well executed; does each scene, character, conversation, and idea make an important and effective contribution to the work; is it original; will it keep people outside of my family and closest friends reading through the last page?

. . .

It may take a while, but a well-written and -conceived manuscript, proposal, or query letter presented with enthusiasm and professionalism *will* find a publisher. In the meantime, consider carefully the responses you are getting from editors and use them to continue honing and sharpening your work for future submissions. Keep in mind how difficult your task is. After all, you're trying to catch the attention of extremely busy individuals who read enormous amounts of material daily while they try to balance acquisitions with their editorial, production, and marketing responsibilities.

But despite their being overworked, remember that editors are always looking for new material. There is nothing quite so thrilling for an editor than coming upon an original, exciting, and thoroughly professional author. Your expertly prepared and presented query letter, proposal, or manuscript can convince her that you are that author.

The Editor and the Author at the Writers' Conference

Why They Go, What They Do

Michael Seidman

MICHAEL SEIDMAN, *the mystery editor of Walker & Company, has more than thirty years of experience in all aspects of the publishing industry. A winner of the American Mystery Award as Best Book Editor, Mr. Seidman is the author of* From Printout to Published: A Guide to the Publishing Process. *His latest book,* Living the Dream: Writing as a Way of Life, *was published in November 1992. Mr. Seidman attends at least ten writers' conferences a year.*

Are you looking for "a large and varied support group waiting not only to ensure that you are not lonely, but to provide the kind of help and lessons the writer needs in order to grow"? According to Michael Seidman, "All you need to do to make contact is attend a writers' conference."

There are hundreds of different writers' conferences held during the year in every part of the country. Mr. Seidman's fact-filled, hands-on essay recommends practical guidelines for choosing the right one for you and tells you how to get the most out of attending it in terms of value for your time and money. He shows you how to make every moment there count, how to select a workshop, how to gauge which ones to avoid, and how to network effectively with the editors who attend the conference in ways that can enhance your career. For it's important to remember that the editors who attend these conferences are there to discover new authors for their list. They're as eager to meet you as you are to meet them. That's what writers' conferences are all about. So turn off your word processor (or, if you just can't stop writing, take along your laptop) and recharge your creative

*batteries at a writers' conference and just possibly change the course of your
career!*

The Editor and the Author
at the Writers' Conference
Why They Go, What They Do

The pundits say that we teach most that which we most have to learn. After
more than a decade of being invited to conferences as a speaker and managing to attend as a writer, I'm not about to start arguing with the pundits.
They've got it right.

They also say that you're supposed to write, write, and write, that time
taken away from the writing is time wasted, that the only way to learn how
to write is by writing. Right?

They say that writing is the loneliest profession, something done alone,
just the writer and the words. Right?

"They." Ambiguous, amorphous, and always quoted. But what they say
is not always right.

If you sit alone and write, with your only feedback coming in the form
of noncommittal rejection slips (". . . not right for our list at the present
time"), you will find yourself repeating the same mistakes. You learn from
your mistakes, after all, only if you know they are errors of some kind.
Unfortunately, reading and attempting to emulate the writers you enjoy is
not the answer; the work you produce that way is simply an echo of
someone else's ability.

As for the loneliness—well, at the very worst you always have the company of your characters, coming to life on the page, telling you what they're
going to do, and to hell with your outline. At best, though, there is a large
and varied support group waiting not only to ensure that you are not lonely,
but to provide the kind of help and lessons the writer needs in order to grow.
You'll have to take a couple of days away from the typewriter (perhaps;
after all, there *are* portables), but the time is not wasted.

All you need to do to make contact is attend a writers' conference.

There are hundreds of writers' conferences held every year. Some of
them, like the Golden Triangle Fiction Writers Conference in Beaumont,
Texas, or the Rocky Mountain Fiction Writers Conference in Denver,
Colorado, are sponsored by writing groups and workshops; others, like the
University of Oklahoma Short Course on Professional Writing in Norman,

Oklahoma, are presented with the direct support of university writing programs. Some are seminars, offered by various experts in the field; Gary Provost, for instance, presents a series of programs around the country.

There are conferences designed for writers in a particular field: satellite organizations of the Romance Writers of America sponsor meetings (most of which, these days, deal with all forms of writing); the Chicago chapter of the Mystery Writers of America offers a program called "Dark and Stormy Nights"; there are conferences for those who want to write children's fiction and for those who want to write for the Christian inspirational market. If you want to do it, there's someone out there ready to help you.

How do you choose the right one, then, from this abundance of riches? Every spring, *Writer's Digest* publishes a list of upcoming conferences, as well as ads announcing the speakers scheduled to attend and participate. It's a good place to begin.

Friends can also provide information that's useful. If they've attended a particular conference, and pronounced it good, that recommendation should be taken seriously.

Finally, librarians—either at a local branch or at a local school or college—are often aware of upcoming conferences and can put you in touch with the organizers.

Having found several conferences that are convenient—travel expenses won't be prohibitive, you can attend without losing too much time from your day job—your next task is to find the one that is most suitable for you. The answer there lies in who will be attending and what will be discussed. If you are specializing in science fiction and none of the speakers (editors, agents, or writers) is going to deal with the subject, you might decide to pass. Of course, there may be someone there who will be of help: a writer whose work you've admired, an editor known to you by reputation for publishing insights—you have to make that decision based on your needs and what you want to gain.

Find out whether there will be an opportunity to arrange individual appointments with the editor or agent you want to meet. Some conferences arrange ten-minute meetings as part of the program; others offer a roundtable at which a speaker will meet with a group of people at one time. At some, you are expected to arrange the meetings on your own. Most of the people speaking at a conference go out of their way to make themselves available, so even if you can't get an appointment, it doesn't mean you won't have a chance to talk with a guest.

Most of the conferences at which I speak (and I try to do eight to ten a year) also offer the opportunity for critiquing. At some, this is in the form of a contest (generally with an extra charge per submission). Following the organizers' guidelines, you submit material that is read and judged by professionals and prizes are awarded. Even if you don't win, however, you receive a sheet of comments pointing out your strengths and weaknesses.

Once you arrive at a writers' conference, you may find as many as three hundred people waiting to check in and receive their conference packets (schedules, speaker bios, publishers' guidelines, meal tickets—if meals are part of the program—and an evaluation sheet for your comments at the end of the meeting). Or there may only be seventy-five. Some may be regulars, people who attend this conference every year, or they will be people who attend two or three different ones as their schedule permits. And there will be those for whom this is a trip into uncharted waters. No matter their particular writing interests and needs, they're all there for the same reason: to learn, to meet other writers and exchange information and experiences, and to become part of a network with its heart in the offices of publishers and agents. That's right: they're there for exactly the same reason you've shown up.

Bring notebooks and pencils and, if it is appropriate, three or four copies of your proposal, partial manuscript, or other materials. Most editors and agents don't want to take manuscripts home with them and they don't have the time to read at the conference. That's most; there are exceptions, and if you meet one of them you want to be ready to reel that fish in right away.

If you'll be staying at the conference, and you've brought that portable typewriter or computer I mentioned earlier, all well and good: conferences have a way of being energizing. You don't need a keyboard, though. Most of what we call literature wasn't created on a machine and the old-fashioned way still works perfectly well.

And don't forget comfortable clothes. Those meeting rooms have a way of getting very warm over the course of a day. If there's an awards banquet you may want something "dressy," though that's by no means any more necessary than a typewriter—even if you're lucky enough to be one of the finalists.

There's little that bothers me more, at a conference, than seeing someone sitting alone in a corner, watching groups of people but never approaching them. (Editors get lonely, too.) Shy's okay, but don't ever think that the other people aren't interested in what you have to say. So, once you arrive at the conference, start making friends. Go up to people and say hello, ask questions. Participate. Yes, you'll get something from the meeting if you just sit back and listen; you'll gain infinitely more by giving as well as receiving.

And there's lots to receive. Maybe too much. Take a look at the schedule: there might be nine or ten panels going on at the same time! Before you arrived you probably received a program; if not, check your registration package and start planning your day.

You've come because of a particular need or because you want to hear a particular speaker; find those panels on the schedule first, so that you don't miss the events that mean most to you. Then, find other sessions of interest and mark them. Uh-oh, a conflict, two at the same time. What will you do?

Many of today's conferences provide recordings of all the sessions at a nominal charge. So, you can begin by picking the session you want to attend (because it is the one in which you are most likely to have questions . . . and ask them) and buy the cassette of a panel you can't attend. Or, you can ask someone who is going to the one you'll miss to share his notes and insights with you later.

Bring your own cassette recorder if you own one. I've never heard of them being banned from a meeting room, even at the conferences that provide recordings. Before you use one, though, make sure that they're permitted and that the speaker doesn't object. Simple courtesy dictates that you get permission: the speaker has no idea what use the tape will be put to; the speaker may want—or need—to sign a release; the speaker may not want his or her words recorded for any number of reasons. It's rarely a problem (though there are times I've worried about exactly what it *was* I said), but there's no reason to cause one when asking beforehand can prevent it.

Between sessions, or at any time during the day, you'll undoubtedly meet one or another of the guest speakers in the hall or in a lounge area. Respect her privacy to the extent that you don't interrupt her if she's deep in conversation with someone else; otherwise, always feel free to come up, introduce yourself, ask if she might have a moment, and let things develop naturally. If the speaker is a mystery editor, don't go on at great length about your horror novel; tell her what you're working on, say something about enjoying one of her sessions (you do write fiction, don't you?), ask if she's enjoying herself (not every conversation has to be about work), and, if appropriate, ask if you might submit something for consideration.

You may be asked for some details—how long is the manuscript, does it fit into a particular subgenre, or any one of the hundreds of other questions editors ask about any submission—and then invited to send the manuscript or a partial. When you do—as quickly as possible (I've had some arrive on my desk the same day I got back to the office)—mention the meeting you had in your cover letter, thank the editor for her attention and consideration, and keep your fingers crossed. (As long as that doesn't interfere with your writing.)

If she says no, don't try to change her mind. Agents and editors aren't always right, but we always have reasons for our decisions. We know our needs, what we can do something with in the marketplace, and what will work for us. You can't "sell" us anything. You can, though, ensure that we'll remember your name if we find you difficult. This business is hard enough without antagonizing the people who can help you.

The speakers are there for you. Some of us are going to be easier to approach, to speak with, to get along with, than others, and only rarely will you meet someone who ignores you. If you do have that misfortune, make a note of it on the evaluation form that was in your packet of materials. Every conference provides one, asking what you thought of the meeting, of the speakers, of the panels; what you liked best and least—questions that will help them produce an even better meeting next year. Answer honestly, and if someone was arrogant, unhelpful, curt, or otherwise didn't live up to your expectations, mention it. And if something or someone was particularly helpful, worthwhile, or otherwise enhanced your time, make sure to mention that, too.

The speakers aren't your only source of help. You'll be meeting writers not only from your area but, possibly, from around the country. Like you, they're there to learn, to gain those insights that are going to help in their careers. Like you, they've had disappointments, downtimes, blocks, and successes, accomplishments, and experiences worth sharing. It won't take long for you to discover those who share your particular writing interests, and lifelong friendships can develop out of taking a moment to say hello. The person next to you has less or more experience, different insights, different knowledge, and is just as eager to exchange that information for yours as you are.

There are writers who worry that someone they speak with at a conference is going to steal an idea. But think about it for a minute: these are writers, too; their heads are teeming with ideas they don't have time to work on. The conference should be a place for openness and sharing.

And having shared, having exchanged ideas with people (and addresses), having learned that you're not alone in your efforts, having listened and asked questions, having *participated* at every level, every step of the way, you come home.

But it isn't over: mail the manuscripts that have been invited; send query letters to those editors and agents you weren't able to discuss your work with but who said things that you liked, that made you feel comfortable with them.

If someone was particularly nice in some way or another, send him a thank-you note, let him know how much you enjoyed meeting him. Tell him you're looking forward to seeing him again. (Don't tell him that you're looking forward to submitting something to him someday. But when you do, remind him of how much you enjoyed meeting him once upon a time.)

Keep in touch with the other writers, too. Ask for their advice and offer your help. Exchange ideas about writing, about work habits, editors, publishers, agents, and possible markets.

You may be physically alone at your desk when you are working on a story, but you're not alone in the real sense; there are thousands of us right behind you, ready to help, to lend a hand. All you have to do is ask.

And you can find us easily enough by attending a writers' conference, by taking a few hours off and talking to people about writing and about publishing what you write. Nothing may be created on the page during that time, but the knowledge gained, and the support received, will make the next page you type that much better.

· · ·

Just as you choose carefully before deciding to go to a conference, I do much the same thing with the invitations I receive to speak. There are conferences I particularly enjoy and those to which I will never go again. The first thing I do is find out who is on the program, because when I have the time, I audit other sessions. There's always something for me to learn, either about writing or about publishing.

· If I don't know the conference, I ask other editors or agents whether they've spoken there and whether or not it is well run. By that I generally mean: Do the sessions start on time? Do registrants have access to speakers? Are individual meetings or small roundtable discussion groups held, so that I can talk one-on-one with people who need that kind of contact? Is there a contest or critique service offered? Is there a pleasant bar or lounge in which we can all meet later in the evening, to have the kind of long, rambling conversations I find the most productive because by then all the barriers are down and all the pretensions left behind?

And that's when I remember the pundits and the thought that I teach most the things I most have to learn, as an editor and as a writer.

At one conference I attended recently, I overheard some of the speakers complaining about all the people coming up to them during their "off time." My feeling is that when someone agrees to speak, he commits to giving as much time as possible to the conference. Whether you meet me or one of the others, though, a little common sense and courtesy will make the experience more pleasant and rewarding for everyone. We know—or should— most of your needs. We try to be kinder, gentler people, but we also tell the truth. We won't encourage you to submit something that isn't ready; we will—or should—give you the kind of feedback in a critique that you don't receive when you get that cold, informal rejection note.

When you're meeting with an editor, you have every right to expect his full attention. But remember that you have the appointment; there's little that's more frustrating to us, or unfair, than agreeing to a meeting and then finding the writer hasn't shown up. The editor's time is wasted, someone else has lost the opportunity for a meeting, and you haven't done very much for yourself, either. If you can't keep the appointment, cancel it. Everyone will appreciate it.

Getting the most from a writers' conference is really simple. Acknowledge that you're there to learn; pay attention; be open. And remember that the editors, whether they know it at the time or not, are getting as much from you as they are giving.

That's one of the reasons I enjoy the experience of lecturing as much as I do—because of the things I learn from you. It's easy to get lost in the clouds that surround the towers of New York City and forget that America begins west of the Hudson and north of the Bronx. Meeting with you, seeing the things you're writing, is a way of discovering not only your concerns but the interests of our customers, the folks who never buy enough books to keep any of us happy. I may gain an insight into a category I should exploit as an editor (or as a writer). I may achieve a deeper understanding of the needs of writers (but I'll never be able to read manuscripts any more quickly). Or I may even discover a new writer for my list.

Yes, that happens too, and frequently enough so that you shouldn't discount that possibility when you attend a conference and start talking with editors and agents; picture yourself and them as members of a team looking for the same thing. I've bought ten or eleven manuscripts as a result of meeting writers on a weekend away from my desk and have been able to help unnumbered others make the contacts they need. It is what I hope to do every time I board a plane for somewhere in this country where there's a writer looking for information and answers.

Each of us attends a conference looking for something different. And most of us find what we're looking for. Or, at least, discover a map that is going to lead us to the next stage of our development.

You never know everything. You never know enough. The creative process is always changing. The needs of publishers change with the seasons. New editors come along and begin to leave their mark both on the publishing industry and on the art of writing.

Take time away from writing to learn something *about* writing so that you will not be the only person who reads the words you've so carefully crafted.

And you can gain strength from the knowledge that you're alone no more, that there is a large, vital, and exciting network of people waiting to help you, to welcome you.

Including the editor who will buy your next work.

The Editor as Negotiator

Martha K. Levin

MARTHA K. LEVIN *is currently vice-president and publisher of Anchor Books, the trade paperback imprint of Doubleday. Ms. Levin sold subsidiary rights for ten years, most recently as the director of the subsidiary rights department of Random House. Authors she has worked with include Edward T. Hall, Naguib Mahfouz, Donald Spoto, and Mark Richard.*

Ms. Levin defines a negotiation as "the discussion that takes place between two parties . . . that will result in the drawing up of a contract for the purchase of some type of book rights."

Starting with two basic rules, "(1) in a negotiation, either party has the right to ask for anything—just be aware that the other party has just as much of a right to say no; and (2) don't presume anything—if it hasn't been discussed and it's not written down, it's open to totally different interpretations by either side," Ms. Levin's essay goes on to offer the editor valuable, workable, creative suggestions on how to make that negotiation an equitable, happy, and financially rewarding experience for author, agent, and publisher.

The Editor as Negotiator

Three months after the author had delivered the manuscript and fifteen months after he had signed the contract, I got a call: "You know, I did a lot more work than I expected to do, and I really think you should pay me more money. And, I've been talking to some of my friends and they say you should be paying me a royalty."

I sighed. I knew when I hired this author on a flat-fee arrangement that there was always the possibility that he might eventually feel this way. I had no idea, however, how ugly it would get.

This was not a straightforward deal to begin with. The estate of another author had contacted me about publishing an anthology of her essays. I thought it was a great idea, but felt the project needed an outside editor, one with appropriate credentials to put the work in its literary context. I spent a month making inquiries and finally was given the name of someone who would fit the bill. I phoned him, and he agreed to work on the project. He didn't have an agent, so I very carefully went over the flat-fee deal I wanted to make with him, saying several times in the course of our discussions: "You do understand, don't you, that this means you won't be receiving a royalty, don't you?" Each time he indicated to me that he did understand.

· · ·

Having begun my career working for a literary agent, I tend to favor authors a bit more than my publisher would like me to. So I wasn't withholding royalties from him because I wanted to. I obviously had to pay the author's estate, and when I'd done a profit and loss statement, I saw it wouldn't work if I had to pay royalties to two recipients. I had explained this, I thought, very clearly. I really felt I had gone the distance in trying to convey what it would mean if he made this deal with us. Clearly I hadn't, and the resulting resentment on his part became so great that he stopped speaking to me and immediately took his new project to another publisher.

Could I have done something more to make him understand? I don't know, but it certainly has made me more cautious when I'm talking directly to authors about money and contractual matters. A lot of editors prefer dealing with authors who don't have agents because they can usually buy more rights (world instead of U.S., sometimes movie rights, etc.) for the same advance, but I'm not one of them. No matter how bad an agent is (and there are plenty who are pretty incompetent), it's better to negotiate with them than to talk directly with an author about that most touchy of subjects—money. And, in a broader sense, the experience also brought home—in a particularly painful way—how crucial negotiation is and how important it is to achieve a clear and mutual agreement—one that both parties fully understand and will abide by.

This incident happened rather recently. However, I have been, in some capacity, working as a negotiator since the beginning of my career in publishing. After the literary agency I moved into sub rights, where I remained for ten years. Then I became a publisher/editor and started buying reprint rights and volume rights for hardcover publication. My history has given me a unique opportunity to see negotiations from a number of different perspectives.

There are lots of rules I'll elaborate on as I continue, but there are two that are so basic and so important that I think they need to be said right away: (1) in a negotiation, either party has the right to ask for anything—just be aware that the other party has just as much of a right to say no; and (2) don't presume anything—if it hasn't been discussed and it's not written down, it's open to totally different interpretations by either side.

What is negotiation? It is the discussion that takes place between two parties—editor and agent, editor and author, editor and subsidiary rights director, or subsidiary rights director and any potential licensee—that will result in the drawing up of a contract for the purchase of some type of book rights. Usually, by the time the contract has been signed by both sides, there have been hours of discussion and often heated debates about the language in a particular clause that seems to have no relevance whatsoever for the moment, but that could be crucial four years down the line. I've been party to many such arguments and have enough experience to know why we are bothering; but I've seen enough instances where the future proved there was good cause to have spent that time working out the terms to our best advantage or, for the agent, to the author's advantage. The unlikely and unforeseen do happen. If an agent decides that it's not worth arguing about the translation split on his client's book, he may live to regret it if, four years later, the client's second book becomes a cult classic in Europe and all the foreign publishers are clamoring to buy the first one.

An effective negotiation requires that both parties understand each other's objectives. The author/agent is usually looking for two major components: the best money combined with the best publishing commitment. The editor's job is harder: she needs to achieve several goals: (1) making a deal that, when it's finished, everyone is pleased with (very difficult to achieve); (2) making the most economical deal for her employer—the publisher; and (3) making a deal that will work financially and structurally for the publishing company and in regard to her ongoing relationship with both the author and the agent.

Negotiating is a very personal thing. Everyone has his or her own style, and one hopes that it's an effective one. I'm a pretty straightforward person, so my negotiating style tends to be that way as well. However, there are a few tricks of the trade that everyone can benefit from, regardless of how they go about their negotiations. One thing I've learned is always to leave 'em smiling. By that I mean that the other party should not feel humiliated, taken advantage of, or in any other way debased. This may sound a bit melodramatic, but there's been many an evening after I've hung up the phone, having made a "great deal" (when I sold sub rights, that meant a lot of money; now it means buying a great book), when I have been so exhausted and unsettled by the person with whom I've been negotiating that I felt no pleasure in its conclusion.

How to avoid that? Well, you can't control the behavior of the person with whom you're negotiating, but you can make sure that he feels good about you by making sure you give something up to him in the course of the negotiation. For instance, when we're buying rights for our paperback list, the lower the royalty we pay out, the more potential profit there is for us. So, we always offer as low a royalty as we can. However, we're fully aware that 90 percent of the agents and hardcover publishers with whom we deal aren't going to take the royalty structure we'd like to pay, so we build in room for movement on our side. The agent says, "We can't accept that royalty." And we, after waiting for an hour or so to make it clear that we haven't given in without a fight, concede the point and give in. This isn't lying or even manipulation. If you're able to settle on the lower royalty, then you've done something good for the company. But you always know that you can concede a point to your adversary without damaging the deal from a business perspective.

There are any number of similar instances that can serve as facilitators in a negotiation. A thorough understanding of the parameters and any resulting flexibility or inflexibility they produce comes in handy for those points on which you cannot give in. There are any number of arcane clauses in any publisher's boilerplate on which the legal department will prove immovable. I'm an employee, so my job is to stand firm. Sometimes I don't agree with the terms of the clause, and frequently I don't even understand them—warranties and indemnities are completely beyond my ken—but that doesn't matter. It's my job to stand by the company position, and stand by my employer I do, but I always try to see both sides in any negotiation. It's possible that some people (particularly my boss) might find me a little too sympathetic to my opponent's side; however, I believe the only way to be an effective negotiator is to fully understand the other person's position so that you can express sympathy and still say no.

That's how you play softball. It's easy because the object is to make your negotiating opposite feel good. But there's another side to the art of negotiating. It's a lot tougher and a lot scarier. It's the publishing equivalent of hardball. Sometimes I'm good at it; more often I'm not. I don't play chicken well and need to know that if I take a rigid position, I've got the support of my boss as well as the personal certainty that I can live with the consequences if I don't prevail. The people who play this game best have a lot of guts. I've gone up against some real tough players, and although I don't like their negotiating style, I have to admire their tenacity.

Several years ago, in the sub rights phase of my career, I was handling the paperback reprint auction for a "hot" book on which I had already accepted a floor. We were a little nervous about the auction because the floor was just high enough to be a deterrent to other bidders. So it was with much relief that I answered the phone that morning to discover that I did indeed have another bidder. Unfortunately, the first words out of her mouth cut my relief short. "Okay, here's our offer, these terms are nonnegotiable, and if you don't like them, then we're withdrawing the offer." Well, I didn't like the terms. The payout was terrible and the royalties were so low that they should have been embarrassed to offer them. (A perfect example of someone who played hardball better than I. I could never have brought myself to offer royalties that low. She had no such reluctance.) Well, although she had enough *chutzpah* to make an offer with terrible terms, she really wasn't such a good hardball player after all. She violated two big negotiating rules. First, don't ever make a declarative statement that you don't intend to stand by. This proved to be the case when, after thirty minutes of letting her wait to hear whether I was going to accept her offer (having already indicated my reluctance to do so), I called her back and told her to take her money elsewhere. Unless she improved its terms, I told her I wouldn't accept her offer. She then broke a long-standing rule of mine, namely, always, no matter what, let some time go by before you respond to anything your opponent says. She immediately backed down and improved the royalties. That ended any advantage she could have had over me for the remainder of the auction. I had gotten her and gotten her good. I knew that we would never accept those first royalties and was prepared to walk away from their money. I also suspected that they were bluffing. The combination of standing fast and good old-fashioned intuition was a winning one for me.

You don't often get to employ that kind of negotiating strategy. More frequent are those situations fraught with uncertainty and terror, in which you feel that the wrong move on your part will result in losing the book (if you're the buyer) or losing the sale (if you're the seller). Acting on your trustworthy instinct, long experience, and, most important, knowledge of your opponent can make the difference between a successful negotiation and a disaster.

Negotiating does not always have to be a do-or-die struggle. The most fun I've had negotiating was when I sold book club rights. There being only two major clubs, you get to know the people you work with very well. One time I had submitted a brand-name author's new book to the clubs. None of us thought the book was as good as his earlier ones, but his success with the clubs was phenomenal. I got a call from an editor who was working at one of the clubs, who told me that they didn't think much of the book and weren't sure they were going to make an offer. Knowing how difficult it would be for the club to face its membership without the newest by this important author, this is how I began (and ended) my negotiation: "Oh, come off it. You know you need this guy and his book. Just make me an offer and let's get it over with!" Not exactly your standard (or subtly complex) negotiating technique, but it was the right one for the situation and the person I was dealing with. Keep in mind, this was someone I'd known for years, whom I liked and who liked me. Never underestimate what you can accomplish with someone with whom you have a good relationship. Publishing is particularly prone to the exploitation of friendships in negotiating, but from what I've observed, all businesses are similar in kind if not in degree.

In my dual role now as publisher and editor, I've found it harder to be as effective a negotiator as I think I was when I sold rights. I'm much better at coaching my staff in their negotiations than I am at conducting my own. Quite recently, a very successful and powerful agent sent us a manuscript by a relatively unknown author. She'd also sent the author's first book, which had been very well received by critics and readers alike, and suggested that we buy rights to them both. Her submission came with many exhortations to act quickly and offer a sizable advance. Each time we hung back, she would remind us of all the other publishers who were dying to get their hands on this author. We decided to take that risk, suspecting that perhaps the agent's door wasn't being knocked on quite as hard and as often as she was suggesting. We stuck by our small, but not insulting, offer, and to no one's surprise she accepted. As I said earlier, agents should ask for the world, but they can't always expect to get it. It's up to us to decide what we can afford to or want to give up, and to gauge the real market value of the property being offered.

My experience has been that selling paperback rights is a lot harder than buying paperback rights or buying volume rights from an agent. When I sold rights, I was forever having to reiterate my position, coaxing and prodding, trying for money, making sure the other side understood me so that when they said fifty thousand dollars was their best offer, they understood that I was taking them at their word. Nothing annoyed me more then having someone phone me a few days later—after hearing I'd accepted a better offer from someone else—and tell me he would have paid me more. I won't play those games and frankly didn't believe most of them when they said it.

There's one last—but hardly least—important rule in negotiating, and while it may seem quite obvious, I have seen many an editor brought down by ignoring it: Write down what is being said. I write down every single facet of my offer (including the time of each discussion) and the recipient's response, and as the negotiation proceeds, I continue to take copious notes. Several years ago that rule rescued my staff member and me from a truly hideous dispute with a paperback reprinter who was talking to us about a lot of money. My staff person had always struck me as being a bit on the compulsive side. Coming from me, this means he really was compulsive. He didn't just takes notes, he literally wrote down every word said by both parties when he was in the midst of a negotiation.

During the course of his conversations with the paperback editor there was what I will call a "misunderstanding." However, it was reported back to the paperback editor's boss, and it was not long before this very scary woman was on the phone shouting at me. She reported her editor's version of the negotiation and I explained to her my colleague's version. She called him a liar. Well, I took out his notebook where he had written down every last word of the conversation and read it to her. After five minutes, she calmed down, and after ten minutes, conceded the point. An extreme example on both sides, but the point is, his copious notes had saved us from a very tricky and possibly unpleasant situation. I'm not, by the way, a proponent of tape-recording phone conversations or any other kind of high-tech method of record keeping. I'm still old-fashioned enough to want to believe in the inherent honesty of the people with whom I negotiate—sometimes they just get confused.

Along with my notes, I also have our contract request form in front of me at the time I'm concluding negotiations. I make sure that every question on the form has been answered. That leaves little doubt that every aspect of the contract has been fully covered.

Negotiating isn't easy. And, like so many other aspects of the publishing experience, it's highly personal. That's important to take into account when you find yourself preparing for a negotiation. Negotiating is a serious business and can be an expensive one. Always keep in mind that the end

Editing for the Christian Marketplace

Janet Hoover Thoma

JANET HOOVER THOMA *is vice-president of Janet Thoma Books, a division of Thomas Nelson Publishers. Prior to having her own imprint, she was senior acquisitions editor of Thomas Nelson. Before joining Nelson ten years ago, she was managing editor of David C. Cook Publishing.*

If you edit (or write) for the Christian marketplace, ignore the stereotype of the "Church Lady" as she was caricatured on Saturday Night Live, Ms. *Thoma recommends, and "understand the audience. . . . That means seeing a more divergent audience . . . or being a committed Christian yourself." And if you edit or write for the predominantly homemaker and white-collar workers who make up the two largest groups of Christian readers, you must first decide if the book is intended strictly for the Christian bookstore market (CBA) or for CBA with some secular (ABA) bookstore crossover. "A CBA book will often quote Scripture liberally, and the subject matter will be addressed from a mainly Christian perspective."*

The relationship between the author and the editor in Christian publishing, Ms. Thoma writes, "is the same as it is in some secular publishing companies, a hands-on approach; that means we often work directly with the author to achieve a quality book, from the concept or book proposal stage all the way through the substantive editing process."

Ms. Thoma's essay is highly informative about what fiction and nonfiction themes (particularly in the area of self-help) can be discussed, and how they should be be treated in books aimed at the many and diverse Christian audiences. It is essential for the writer and editor who wishes to successfully reach those audiences with meaningful books without offending readers with deeply held religious beliefs.

Editing for the Christian Marketplace

Mouse brown hair, curled close to the face. Clear plastic glasses. White Peter Pan collar, buttoned tightly around the neck. A cotton flowered no-style dress. Clodhopper, old-lady shoes. And a high-pitched, squeaky voice. In syrupy tones she often says, "Well, isn't that special!" Or comments, "Who could have made us do that? Who could it be? Maybe Satan!" when confronted with behavior she classifies as immoral or bad. Does this woman look and sound familiar? If you watch *Saturday Night Live,* you will recognize her as the "Church Lady."

If you edit (or write) for the Christian marketplace, ignore this stereotype. To edit or write for this marketplace you must understand the audience, and that means seeing a more divergent audience, rather than this caricature, or being a committed Christian yourself.

The Diversified Audience

Right now the audience for Christian books is split into two marketplaces: the Christian bookstore (of which there are 7,267 in the United States) and the secular bookstore. Different types of readers are obviously represented by these distinctive marketplaces.

Yes, you will find a few Church Ladies in Christian bookstores in this country. But according to consumer research conducted by the Christian Booksellers Association (CBA) in 1991, the typical buyer in the Christian bookstore is a woman between the ages of 25 and 54 (60 percent are between 25 and 44; 15 percent between 45 and 54) who attends church once a week or more. And believe me, the 25-year-old women often look more like singer Amy Grant than the Church Lady. Men make up 25 percent of these consumers.

The occupations of these consumers vary, with homemakers and white-collar workers being the two largest individual groups. Twenty-six percent of the women surveyed classified themselves as homemakers and an additional 21 percent classified themselves as white-collar workers. Twenty-six percent of the men classified themselves as white-collar employees, 17 percent as paid church staff, and 14 percent as blue-collar workers. Nearly everyone surveyed had completed high school, and more than one-third had college degrees. About half of the consumers had an income of $20,000 to $40,000 annually, with the other half almost equally split between lower incomes (under $20,000) and higher incomes (over $40,000). The average income was $31,872.

The beliefs of these readers are also quite different from the Church Lady stereotype. Yes, some of them are fundamentalists who with tight-lipped defiance might say, "I would never do this . . . ," but many of them are honest, ordinary people who are trying to live out their beliefs. Many are sophisticated, educated, and sometimes rather liberal people. They are as diverse as Baptists, on the one hand, and on the other Catholic charismatics who shop in Christian bookstores as well as Catholic bookstores, which have been in existence twenty years longer than CBA stores.

More and more Christian publishers are selling effectively in secular bookstores. Here the audience is still Christian, but more likely "mainline" Christians, those who are members of Presbyterian, Episcopalian, and Lutheran churches, for instance.

So if you edit or write for this marketplace you must first decide if the book is intended strictly for CBA (the Christian bookstore) or CBA with some ABA (secular bookstore) crossover. A CBA book will often quote Scripture liberally—and the subject matter will be addressed from a mainly Christian perspective.

Business by the Book: The Complete Guide of Biblical Principles for Business Men and Women (Thomas Nelson, 1990) by Christian financial counselor Larry Burkett is an example. This book proposes a radical approach to business management, as Larry himself admits: using scriptural standards to form company policy. Tough questions like firing employees, fair pay, and borrowing money are discussed from the viewpoint of biblical principles. Can a Christian fire someone? Of course—if he is slothful (Proverbs 22:29) or dishonest (Proverbs 14:2).

However, the Judeo-Christian viewpoint will be only a part of the discussion in a book that is intended to cross over into the secular marketplace. *Love Hunger* (Thomas Nelson, 1990), a book by Dr. Frank Minirth, Dr. Paul Meier, Dr. Robert Hemfelt, and Dr. Sharon Sneed, is an example. The doctors—two psychiatrists, an addictions counselor, and a dietician and nutrition consultant—speak authoritatively about the psychological and physical components of obsessive-compulsive overeating at the same time that they talk about the spiritual aspect. The true answer to a patient's love hunger, which fuels the food addiction, is God's unconditional love, they believe. This book hit the *Publishers Weekly* list when it was published in 1990 because of its three-dimensional approach—body, mind, and soul—which was unique.

A book published by a Christian publisher, destined for either marketplace, will avoid swearing and foul language and graphic sexual scenes, which would be offensive to the Christian community. Yet when Christian authors tackle difficult subjects—like ritual sexual abuse—they do portray enough details that their book is realistic and does not minimize the suffering these victims experience.

Accurate Publishing Decisions

There is no formula answer to the old question, "What books should be a part of our list?" Obviously most Christian publishers look for books that have unique subject matter, just as secular publishers do. We also recognize our own individuality as Christian publishers; the book must have an inspirational or Judeo-Christian message, which is often not found in the secular marketplace.

We have traditionally published self-help books because people who are going through difficult times often look to God for help as well as to books about the Bible and Christian beliefs. It was natural for Christian publishers to include recovery books in our lists for anyone suffering from obsessive-compulsive behavior. (And often the audience for these books is anyone who is searching for "God as we understand Him," many of whom are not associated with any Christian church.) At Nelson we are now looking for books on spirituality since people, whether they are in recovery or not, are searching for spiritual meaning.

Timing is another piece of the puzzle. When we published *Love Hunger,* we knew that a diet book written from the perspective of body, mind, and soul was unique. The book was written in four months so that it could be published on the upcoming winter 1990 list (January, February, and March) to coincide with the traditional season for dieting books. As the turn of the century nears, books on the end of the world (some Christians wonder if Christ will not return around the year 2000) and prophecy are becoming popular. Books on these topics hit the CBA best-seller list any time the conflict in the Middle East between Israel and the Arab countries turns toward war. Sales in 1991 of books on prophecy, for instance, were 157 percent above 1990, according to Spring Arbor, the major book distributor to Christian bookstores. Spring Arbor called this increase in sales activity "a blip created by the Persian Gulf war."

Timing is also important in the publication of celebrity biographies, particularly sports biographies. Books like *Out of the Blue* by Orel Hershiser (Wolgemuth & Hyatt; 165,000 copies sold) and *Comeback* by Dave Dravecky (Zondervan/Harper; 175,000 hardcover and 75,000 mass-market copies sold) were successful because they were published within a year of the apex of the authors' careers. However, biographies by well-known actors or sports figures whose popularity has faded years before the book is published tend to sell less than 50,000 copies. Celebrity biographies published by Christian publishers reveal the subjects' spiritual faith as well as the details of their professional careers. Literary quality is not nearly as important as timing.

Novels have recently become more prevalent in the Christian marketplace. The phenomenal success of *This Present Darkness* and *Piercing the Darkness* by Frank Peretti (Crossway) and of the Janette Oke pioneer series (Bethany House) have led other publishers to add more fiction to their lines. (The two Peretti books together have sold over 3 million copies, while the twenty Oke titles have sold over 9 million.) Crossway Books was a pioneer in this area because they were able to accept low yearly sales to introduce an author's first fiction book and then build his or her reputation from there. (Author Stephen Lawhead's first book, *In the Hall of the Dragon King,* sold in the four-figure realm, but sales of this book and its two sequels, which form the Dragon King trilogy, are now well over 150,000. The Pen Dragon Cycle, his next trilogy, has sold over 200,000 copies.) Bethany House was also in a unique position to build author Janette Oke since they sold numbers of copies to Successful Living, the rack jobber and book party company, which sells books at small parties in the marketing tradition of companies like Tupperware.

Some publishers see fiction as "a story invented to entertain." Some fundamentalist bookstore owners, however, define fiction as "a story invented to educate." These bookstore owners expect one or more of the main characters to accept Christ as Savior in the book. An editor or writer must know the publisher's policy because it obviously affects the story line (crossover publishers like Nelson, Word, and Zondervan are more likely to define fiction as entertainment).

Most Christian publishers also look for reference books for the layperson, and some publishers (such as Moody, Baker, Zondervan, and Eerdmans) publish theological books for pastors and seminary students.

The Editing Process

The relationship between the author and the editor in Christian publishing is the same as it is in some secular publishing companies, a hands-on approach; that means we often work directly with the author to achieve a quality book, from the concept or book proposal stage all the way through the substantive editing process. My authors submit an initial couple of chapters to me so that we can determine together if the book is headed in the right direction and has the proper tone and pace. (I believe this saves time since nothing is a greater waste than months spent writing a complete manuscript that then needs to be entirely rewritten.) The authors then continue to send me three or so chapters throughout the process.

If an author is a professional in the field—a counselor, a pastor, or a celebrity—who has no writing experience or is too busy to write a book, I often hire a ghost writer. Typical pay ranges from $6,000 to $15,000, depending upon the amount of work that must be done (the ghost may be working from a draft manuscript or may be taping the author and writing the draft as well as the final copy) and the expertise of the free-lance writer. Sometimes ghost writers will get a small percentage of the author's royalty and an advance against that royalty, which is always less than the flat-fee payment, since they will benefit from long-range sales. However, some writers prefer a flat fee, which is paid to them regardless of the book's sales. Most acquisitions editors make sure they either have worked with the ghost writer previously or know his or her work.

I always tell my writers to picture the particular audience for their book—a thirty-five-year-old working mother, for instance, or a young corporate executive—sitting across from them. "Instead of the computer screen see that person in flesh and blood. Use words that person understands and include illustrations and anecdotes that are familiar to him or her."

I compare the first chapter of a nonfiction book to the frame of a picture, which unites the details of the landscape or portrait inside; this first chapter, therefore, should include certain specifics. First, it should open with an anecdote or patient illustration with which the reader will identify. For instance, one author opened a book called *The Path to Serenity,* a book on the Twelve Steps of Alcoholics Anonymous, with the story of an alcoholic college professor. That would have been appropriate if the audience for the book had been people with chemical dependencies. However, the purpose of the book was to apply the Twelve Steps to a broader audience, to anyone who was addicted to obsessive-compulsive behaviors. Codependents. Workaholics. Overeaters. If I, as an editor, had allowed the alcoholic story to begin the book, some potential buyers would have glanced at the first page, mistakenly assumed that this was another book aimed only at alcoholics, and put it back on the shelf. In that instant we would have lost 70 percent of the intended readership.

Instead we began with the story of Andy Thomson, a workaholic whose girlfriend had just called it quits because of his preoccupation with his fledgling computer business. The alcoholic, Martin Woodruff, was not introduced until the second chapter, when Andy saw him at an Adult Child of Alcoholics meeting.

Secondly, the first chapter should define the subject matter and tell the reader the reason the book is being written (the extent of the problem). I rarely use introductions in my books because I believe that many readers skip prefaces or introductions and therefore never read this important information. The first chapter, therefore, should also give the author's credentials for writing the book and the promise to the reader: "If you read this book, we will help you with this problem just as we helped the person in the beginning anecdote."

Finally, the first chapter (or possibly the second) should end with a "road map" for the book. Writers need to give the reader an overall view of the book before they walk the reader through the process. Then it is easier for the reader to understand the principles, some of which may be entirely new to the layman and difficult to comprehend without a professional degree.

And writers need to be sure that readers continue to understand the relationships between consecutive chapters in the book and between sections of the book. Often writers forget to make these relationships obvious to the reader. As an editor, I make sure that these road signs are either near the end of a chapter or at the beginning of the next chapter, since the subject matter of a self-help book is so technical that readers often need these transitions or they become lost in the details of so much new information.

I find that writers also need to be reminded to give the reader some "takeaway" as part of every chapter in a nonfiction book. For instance, we published a book called *The Lies We Believe* by Dr. Chris Thurman. Chris had organized the manuscript to present the five types of lies—self-lies, worldly lies, marital lies, distortion lies, and religious lies—in the first seven chapters. As a typical reader (which is really what the editor is) I became very distressed (and bored) as I read lie after lie. Finally, one chapter at the end of the book gave me eight ways to change my fallacious thinking.

My comment to Chris was this: "I cannot believe that you spend the first fifty hours of the counseling process helping people to identify the lies they believe. You must give them some ways to overcome their thinking during some of these sessions—or they'd never come back." And that's what we did in the book. At the end of chapter 2, which presented self-lies like "I must have everyone's love and approval" and "It's somebody else's fault," we began a section, "How to Defeat Your Lies," that gave readers some ways to combat the lies they believed. And that section was repeated throughout the next five chapters. The final two chapters wrapped the book up by talking about truth and about changing our lives (and these chapters led to the publishing of another book, *The Truths We Must Believe*).

The formula I have adopted for most self-help books written by counselors is very simple: "Put the reader in the chair (or on the mythical couch) in your office and walk him or her through the same process—in the same order—that you do your patient." A more commercial way to say this is: "Give the reader the same information in a book, which costs $16.95, that you give your patients for $50.00 to $100.00 an hour."

A Look Ahead

The future for Christian publishing seems to be even brighter than the past. The success of the Twelve Step programs and support groups in helping people to overcome addictive behavior have made it much more obvious to most people that a personal relationship with God is necessary for health and happiness. Yes, we can all laugh at the foibles of the Church Lady and her superior dance—and then reject her judgmental philosophy. But many of us cannot ignore the yearning within us for God and spiritual transcendence. Inspirational books will be companions to the many people who will make a journey toward God in the coming years.

Editing Books for the Jewish Market

A Commitment to Community

Bonny V. Fetterman

BONNY V. FETTERMAN *is senior editor and director of Judaica at Schocken Books, a position she has held since 1982. She previously held editorial positions at Harper & Row and Basic Books. She earned an M.A. in Judaic studies from Brandeis University and also studied at the Hebrew University of Jerusalem. She was a fellow of the Jerusalem Book Fair in 1987 and a fellow of the American Jewish Committee's Moses Mission in Israel in 1990.*

"Sharing the secrets of Jewish publishing is a bit like telling someone the secret of how we really make matzah. Actually, there is no secret," says Ms. Fetterman in her wise, humorous, and often moving essay on publishing books for "the people of the book."

In many ways editing for the Jewish market is like editing for any specialized list—psychology, science, or education. But there is something that makes publishing for the Jewish market "different from all others—and that is community . . . *as opposed to* market, *because there's no way to do this kind of publishing without a sense of commitment and connection to the community you're publishing for.*

"The Judaica editor's reaction to a proposal is often the acid test of a viable book for this community. Unless you can say, 'Yes, we need this!' using the Jewish 'we' as opposed to the editorial 'we,' you'll always be relying on the instincts of others."

Ms. Fetterman believes that her books should be "accessible to anyone who cares enough to open one: books that are true to the tradition they represent. . . . And if they inspire one of those readers to feel, in a personal, heartfelt way, that the Jewish legacy is indeed his or her own, that in itself would validate my commitment to Jewish publishing."

Editing Books for the Jewish Market
A Commitment to Community

Sharing the secrets of Jewish publishing is a bit like telling someone the secret of how we really make matzah. Actually, there is no secret. What I do as an editor of Jewish books is very much like the work of any other editor of a specialized list, such as psychology, science, or education: one needs some formal background of study in the field, networks of friends and colleagues to advise you and send promising authors your way, and the top-notch editorial skills that go with editing serious scholarly works. Like other editors, I spend a lot of time working with my authors, coaxing them into dealing with their readers' questions first, translating academic jargon into readable concepts, getting them to fully digest and spell out the import of their findings.

But there's a fourth element in publishing Jewish books—and one that makes this kind of publishing different from all others—and that is community. Every specialist editor must know his market, in all its diversity, in order to correctly position his books. But I am deliberately saying *community* here, as opposed to *market,* because there's no way to do this kind of publishing without a sense of commitment and connection to the community you're publishing for.

The Judaica editor's reaction to a proposal is often the acid test of a viable book for this community. Unless you can say, "Yes, we need this!" using the Jewish "we" as opposed to the editorial "we," you'll always be relying on the instincts of others. Books can certainly be done like that; they look like books, they smell like books, but they run the risk of being *golems,* bodies without souls, and the Jewish book-buying public knows the difference.

This obviously doesn't apply to the trade best-seller of Jewish interest that, falling into the hands of a competent nonfiction editor, will walk out of the bookstores all by itself. I'm talking about those of us who work in Jewish publishing, building an ongoing program of Jewish books. This always entails a direct relationship with and commitment to the community itself. It is this sense of mission that defines the publisher of Jewish books—not in the sense of having a specific religious agenda to promote (although that's true for some), but rather having an intense desire to serve the needs of contemporary Jews.

How does one serve the needs of a community as diverse as American Jewry? By offering variety, quality, and accessibility—and realizing that different books will appeal to different sectors of this complex and fascinating marketplace.

Every year there are hundreds of books published on every conceivable topic of Jewish interest by a variety of publishers. They range from the religious publishers serving the needs of their respective constituents—Orthodox (Mesorah, Feldheim), Conservative (Rabbinical Assembly), Reform (Central Conference of American Rabbis), and Reconstructionist (Reconstructionist Press)—to a dozen or so university presses that have begun to publish the scholarly monographs and groundbreaking studies of a new generation of Jewish academics now seated in departments of Jewish studies at secular universities. (Some university presses with active lists in Jewish studies are Yale, Indiana, Oxford, Cornell, Harvard, Wayne State, New York University Press, University of California, and the State University of New York Press.) There are educational publishers that provide curricula for Jewish schools and materials for Jewish teachers (Behrman House, Ktav, Torah Aura).

Jewish publishing is not a perfect counterpart to Christian publishing, in that it does not necessarily mean religious books; it includes religion but encompasses much more: namely, the history and civilization of the Jewish people. Several publishers are known for publishing a full range of Judaica for the interested layperson (Schocken Books, Jason Aronson, the Jewish Publication Society). Their lists include books on Jewish life and culture; history, philosophy, and religion; biblical studies, rabbinical literature, and Hebrew and Yiddish classics in translation. I define a Jewish book broadly as any book that serves to bolster a sense of connection to the Jewish people. Judaica editors in general are committed to promoting Jewish learning among a serious and varied readership. Arthur Kurzweil, vice-president of Jason Aronson and director of the Jewish Book Club, describes his list as "timeless rather than topical"; he aims for books that will become "permanent features in one's personal Judaica library."

A few independent houses have developed lists on topics of particular interest to them, such as Holocaust studies (Basil Blackwell, Holmes & Meier) and spirituality (Samuel Weiser, Jewish Lights). Several Christian publishers (Paulist Press, Harper San Francisco, Beacon Press) have also entered the field on subjects of overlapping interest, such as biblical theology, comparative religion, feminism, and mysticism. Commercial trade publishers, both large and small and too numerous to mention here, also publish books intended for the Jewish market, ranging from current interest issues to celebrity biographies and autobiographies, such as Alan Dershowitz's *Chutzpah* (Little, Brown), to popular works of history and "how-to" guides for various aspects of Jewish life, like *Jewish Literacy* by Joseph Telushkin (Morrow). Some focus on Jewish fiction (Farrar, Straus, David Godine, Grove Press, Henry Holt), while others concentrate on nonfiction (Basic Books, Free Press, Schocken Books, Scribner's, Random House, Simon & Schuster, and their respective imprints). A number of publishers also do Jewish children's books (Viking, Kar-Ben Copies, Holiday House, Knopf, the Jewish Publication Society, UAHC [Union of American Hebrew Congregations]).

The list of publishers above is far from complete and meant only to suggest the various types of Jewish publishing. The would-be Judaica editor and the potential author would do well to survey this roster and find his or her niche. Each publisher of Judaica has a very distinctive character of its own and reaches a different sector of the community. When an editor writes that a particular proposal "does not fit our list," he is not just using a stock phrase to politely decline a proposal, but actually saying something practical and realistic. For the author, identifying whom you are writing for is a vital first step in choosing the house best able to distribute your book. It will also be a guiding force in the writing of the book itself.

A little research can save an author a lot of steps in placing a project. Publishers of Jewish books are listed in a reference book called *Literary Market Place* (under "Religion"), but you can get a much clearer picture of the kinds of books various publishers are currently doing from bibliographic periodicals such as *Judaica Book News* (Bookazine) or *Jewish Book World* (Jewish Book Council). Write to publishers for their catalogs, read them, and check out the Judaica and religion sections of bookstores. Note the publishers of books that are intended for the same readers as yours.

For the editor, choosing your niche means finding the kind of book you do best, know how to publish, and is ultimately closest to your heart. My own publishing program evolved partly as a result of the company I've worked for over the past decade, and partly as a result of personal predilection. My own interest in Judaica was sparked by reading Schocken books as an undergraduate in college, and I knew this was the firm I wanted to work for more than anything else in the world. I began as an editorial assistant shortly after graduation. At one point, Professor Nahum N. Glatzer, then the senior consulting editor of Schocken, took me aside and suggested that if I really wanted to be a Judaica editor, I would first have to "learn something." This meant returning to school for graduate work in Jewish Studies, followed by a few years of working as an editor in general trade publishing. I eventually returned to Schocken better equipped for the particular kind of publishing Schocken does.

Schocken has a long tradition of publishing primarily nonfiction Judaica, most particularly works dealing with the basic sources of the Jewish inspiration—the classic texts that speak to both religious and secular Jews seeking access to the sources of their culture. As one of the few Jewish publishers still functioning in Germany under the Nazis until 1938, Schocken played an instrumental role in bolstering the morale of the assimilated German Jewish community by introducing them to their proud cultural legacy, often for the first time. Their list, then as now, included works by Buber, Agnon, Scholem, and Franz Kafka. Upon the reestablishment of the firm in New York in 1945, many of these classics, such as Buber's *Tales of the Hasidim,* were translated and published in English.

This distinguished list chugged along, largely subsidized by the Schocken family, until it met up with a fortunate advent coming out of the American Jewish community itself during the late 1960s—the rise of Jewish studies courses at secular universities. As a leader in the new field of quality-size paperback books intended for course adoption, Schocken Books became the mainstay of many of these courses, and also for the Jewish adult education market that gained momentum at this time.

This impressive history has guided my selection of books from the beginning of my tenure as senior acquisitions editor for Judaica in 1982. The books I publish are all trade books, aimed at the general trade reader in hardcover, but also have a second life in college courses and adult education markets in paperback. Trade books are notoriously ephemeral; I always acquire with an eye toward the paperback backlist; I look for books that I know will have a consistent market for at least a decade.

A major part of my program is translations—translations of classic texts and, equally important, books by contemporary authors that make these sources accessible. (Books like *Everyman's Talmud* by Abraham Cohen, *Understanding Genesis* and *Exploring Exodus* by Nahum Sarna, and *Women and Jewish Law* by Rachel Biale serve this function.) It is no accident that the most important events in Jewish publishing in the last decade were translation projects—the publication of *The Talmud: The Steinsaltz Edition* by Random House and *Tanakh* (the Hebrew Bible with commentaries) by the Jewish Publication Society. American Jews are desperate to educate themselves in a tradition that they can only read in translation. Since our readers come from a variety of backgrounds, there is no substitute for making the sources themselves available. In the fall of 1992, Schocken will publish the first complete English translation of Bialik and Ravnitzky's *The Book of Legends/Sefer Ha-Aggadah*—a giant compendium of legends and parables from the Talmud and Midrash. It's thirty-three hundred pages in manuscript, an incredible job to edit, and I should have my head examined for taking it on. But I feel that making this classic available in English is a service to the Jewish community and one that they will value.

Schocken's Library of Yiddish Classics series, which so far includes newly translated volumes of Sholem Aleichem, Peretz, and Ansky (author of *The Dybbuk*), aims to give a coherent presentation of a secular Yiddish legacy. Each generation needs its own translations of the classics, to keep them vital.

Times change, and so does the community, and we have to keep pace with it. I've noticed some definite changes in tastes and demands over the years, most recently an increasing demand for Jewish books that deal with spirituality, a topic Jews have traditionally shied away from in the past. I've seen it with the success we've had with Aryeh Kaplan's *Jewish Meditation,* a book that developed a grass-roots following largely by word of mouth. I'm seeing more books from other publishers as well that address spiritual needs and concerns, often in highly personal styles.

Numerous books are still published every year on the subjects of contemporary Israel and the Holocaust, but I don't think these two themes are the exclusive foci of the American Jew's Jewish identity the way they were a decade ago. Contemporary Jews seem to be struggling less with issues of identity and more with issues of content, meaning, and relevance. Since the publication of *The Jewish Catalog* by Richard Siegel and Michael and Sharon Strassfeld (Jewish Publication Society) in the early 1970s, which was the first of the do-it-yourself guides for Jewish adult education, there has been an ever-increasing demand for intelligent how-to books for Jewish living and guides for Jewish learning. The latter received an enormous boost from *Back to the Sources,* edited by Barry W. Holtz (Summit). The key word in education generally these days is "empowerment"; these books encourage and equip the reader with the skills to experience parts of this tradition firsthand. These developments have forced me to reassess our backlist and adjust our program to meet current needs. In addition to translations, I find these days that I am doing more of what I call books "for living Jews, by living Jews."

Schocken's acquisition by Random House in 1987, where it now functions as a Judaica imprint, also forced me to reevaluate my editorial policy. When I first entered this large commercial conglomerate I defended every title on the backlist on the grounds of sheer merit; I was the zealous "defender of the faith." Gradually it dawned on me: if no one is reading the heavier works of philosophy and intellectual history written by a former generation, then for whom are we doing them? Some classics are timeless, others are not, and the Jewish public shows us what it wants. I've also seen new books emerge as classics of our own generation, such as Primo Levi's *Periodic Table* (Schocken).

While the books I publish are for laypersons, I need qualified teachers to write them. Most often, the writers I work with are rabbis and professors of Jewish Studies, and the major task is getting them to write for the general reader. Once, as I congratulated an author on a completely revised and quite wonderful manuscript, he told me that a piece of advice I had shared helped him to find his voice. I had reminded him of a maxim from our days teaching Hebrew school: "First they have to like you; then, maybe, they'll let you teach them something." This had alerted him to the fact that he had plunged into his subject without taking his reader along with him. He started the next draft with a personal account of how his own interest in the subject began, allowing the reader to identify with him, share his excitement, and join him on his journey. Our readers are sophisticated adults who are not necessarily versed in Judaica or used to the catchwords used by professionals in the field. Moreover, their questions are different from the ones an academic may find fascinating. Bringing the fruits of contemporary Jewish scholarship to a broader public entails finding a voice other than the one scholars use in writing for their colleagues. Working with these teachers of our own generation is one of the most exciting parts of our program.

My most valuable time is spent outside of the office, at academic and educational conferences, where I get my inspiration, and ideas for new books. I sell books myself—mainly because I want to hear what people are saying about them. Rabbis, teachers, and professors are all eager to tell me what books they've used in courses and whether they'd use them again. They tell me about the books they wish existed, and suggest the authors who might write them. They tell me when to revive, reprint, or replace a book that has become dated. *The Schocken Guide to Jewish Books* is an example of a book born out of such a discussion of contemporary needs, in this case the need for a really useful reader's guide to books on Jewish history, literature, culture, and religion.

Sometimes a book emerges whole from a lecture series I've attended, or an idea for a book arises from an informal post-synagogue discussion. A major part of my job is finding the right author for these unwritten books. A sample chapter quickly tells me, as well as the author, whether this is a match made in heaven or not. It's always worth a try.

A word must be said about the commercial side of this kind of publishing. As a full-time Judaica editor in charge of a small but prestigious imprint at one of the largest commercial publishing houses, I am constantly balancing conflicting imperatives: the need to maintain the caliber of Schocken's list, the profit expectations of its parent company, and serving the Jewish public, which doesn't always know what it needs, especially when we enter the realm of the things that do not yet exist.

For example, I've always dreamed of doing a collection of essays by Berdichevsky—that early Zionist ideologue without whom it is impossible to understand the mentality of the secular Israeli. But I also know the sales potential of a volume by this virtually unknown essayist, and the kind of marketing effort it would take to put such a book on the map. Even with aggressive marketing, I doubt if we would ever make Berdichevsky a household name. Is it worth doing? Of course! Is it worth putting the survival of the Schocken imprint at risk—with accountants running around with calculators on every floor? Definitely not. This is a project for a subsidized press, a university press, or the company I'd start if I wind up with a very rich husband.

Let's get back to "putting the book on the map"—because that's also part of the job as a Judaica editor within a large company. Other departments depend on you for your firsthand knowledge of the community. The Jewish market is a very diverse one, as I mentioned earlier. There are splits not only along denominational lines, but genre ones as well. The passionate fan of secular Yiddish literature is not the same reader as the person who would buy a book on the Bible or biblical theology—or, for that matter, a guide to some aspect of Jewish practice or holiday observance. It's up to the editor to pinpoint the market, select the right journals in which to advertise the book or get it reviewed, and pick the people whose blurbs will matter in that market. I still remember the ambitious young sales rep who got thrown out of an Ultra-Orthodox Jewish bookstore when he tried to sell them a book by Mordecai Kaplan (the founder of Reconstructionism, one of the nontraditional approaches to Jewish practice). I went back with him to show the book buyer which titles were Orthodox enough for his clientele—and distributed that list to the reps as well. I always try to target the book's audience for the sales force. I also do a lot of direct mail, since different sectors of the Jewish market are so well defined, and because interested readers in many parts of the country will never see these books if they depend on chain bookstores. Ultimately, a book sells well if it is *besheret* (destined to)—but *besheret* also means that *your* efforts have already been figured into the equation.

In terms of promotion, nothing compares to what an author can do for his or her own book. Every speaking engagement, every Jewish book fair and Jewish community center appearance that the author can line up helps, and most publishers are delighted to make copies of the book available for sale at these events. Basically, an author can utilize all of his connections to promote his book, and can help his publisher utilize them as well. I am very much aware of the difference an energetic author can make because I also do a lot of classics in translation; with dead authors, you obviously do not have this opportunity.

Before you get the idea that being a Judaica editor is the most enviable job in the world, let me explain why we as a group are characteristically prone to spurts of zeal, depression, and melodrama: it is due to a searing sense of responsibility. Gazing out his window on the Brandeis University campus, Professor Glatzer, my mentor in Jewish publishing whom I mentioned earlier, remarked: "This is a generation that gets its Judaism from *Encyclopedia Judaica*." What a profound and sobering observation! American Jews depend on *books* for their first serious exposure to the culture—the full-blown civilization—that gives content and meaning to their identity as Jews. And those of us involved in Jewish publishing dare not fail them. As a colleague once confided in me, "I'd like to go sailing just one afternoon without the fate of the Jewish people on my shoulders." I know exactly what he means. I myself often identify with the prophet Jeremiah; Jeremiah had his mission, and once he took it up, he couldn't lay it down, although he kvetched about it all the time. I am sure that if Jeremiah came back in the twentieth century, he would be a congregational rabbi or a Judaica editor.

Each year, articles appear in *Publishers Weekly* and *Judaica Book News* surveying the current crop of Jewish books, celebrating the variety and vitality of this field. I've written a few of these upbeat pieces myself. But the flip side of this celebratory air is a much more sobering consciousness of the stakes involved. At the back of all of our minds is what Leslie Fiedler has termed "the silent Holocaust"—the attrition of American Jews from the Jewish community through assimilation. And for most, assimilation is not a deliberate choice, which must be respected, but a de facto occurrence resulting from sheer lack of knowledge and exposure to Jewish life. For those of us who believe that humanity would be poorer—actually frighteningly poorer—without the unique insights of Jewish culture and the Jewish people, this is a source of unbearable pain.

It would be a mistake to gear Jewish publishing to the reader who wouldn't think of buying a Jewish book in the first place. Certainly we have our hands full keeping up with the needs of a high-caliber, Jewishly educated community, both professional and lay, people who love, use, and need Jewish books. But I also feel strongly that our books should be accessible to anyone who cares enough to open one: books that are true to the tradition they represent and provide keys to seekers from many backgrounds. And if they inspire one of those readers to feel, in a personal, heartfelt way, that the Jewish legacy is indeed his or her own, that in itself would validate my commitment to Jewish publishing and the Jewish community.

Developmental Editing
A Creative Collaboration

Paul D. McCarthy

PAUL D. MCCARTHY *has been a senior editor at Pocket Books since 1986, acquiring fiction and nonfiction for publication in hardcover and paperback editions. He is also a book reviewer and a member of the National Book Critics Circle. His reviews have been published by the* Los Angeles Times Book Review *and* Chicago Sun-Times Book Week *among others. Mr. McCarthy previously worked as an editor for Dell Publishing Company/Delacorte Press, which he joined in 1979 after being an agent at the Scott Meredith Literary Agency. He is currently writing a book about the philosophy and art of book editing.*

Long before an editor puts the first marks on a manuscript, the editor and the author have entered into an ongoing creative collaboration. That symbiotic partnership, called "developmental editing," Mr. McCarthy defines as when "writer and editor jointly evolve a concept or story idea, which either or both have contributed, into a strong outline or proposal. They extend that into a manuscript in progress, striving at every stage to make the partial and then complete work as excellent as possible."

This close relationship between editor and author increases the possibility for both conflict and productivity. The exact character of the relationship and the approach editor and author take to developmental editing depends on their temperaments, personalities, work habits, and a clear understanding of each other's respective responsibilities: "the author's is to write the best book possible, the editor's to help the author achieve that goal. The writer should try to keep an open mind and the editor should not be intrusive." Mr. McCarthy also believes that "making the relationship work is much more the editor's responsibility than the author's. It's a tough but critical part of the job."

Believing that there is "a special pleasure and harmony in the joining of forces," Mr. McCarthy presents many valuable and practical suggestions to the editor and writer that will enhance their prospects of working happily and effectively together. Using specific examples of how developmental editing works in practice, he discusses such essential aspects of the editor-author collaboration as: the importance of editorial objectivity to the writer, the efficiency and importance of an early exchange of ideas and concepts, choosing and focusing on the audience for the book, development of a proposal or organizational plan for the work, and creating the structure of the work.

Seeing himself clearly as the writer's partner, Mr. McCarthy states that "one of the reasons I became an editor is because I have great respect for writing talent and revel in my involvement with it. A source of immense pleasure for me over the years has been the increasing extent to which many of my authors involve me ever earlier in the creative process."

Developmental Editing
A Creative Collaboration

As every author and editor who has experienced its creative joy knows, a world of collaborative potential exists before the editor begins the final editing of the entire manuscript.

In approach and purpose, that collaboration, called developmental editing, is quite different from comprehensive, structural, and line editing. The dividing line is the full manuscript.

In *developmental editing,* writer and editor jointly evolve a concept or story idea, which either or both have contributed, into a strong outline or proposal. They extend that into a manuscript in progress, striving at every stage to make the partial and then complete work as excellent as possible.

Once the author has finished the manuscript, the editorial process changes, and the editor, alone, begins the *comprehensive editing,* preparing a detailed set of editorial notes covering every analyzable aspect of the book, and working on the writing line by line.

Not all authors or books require the early, intense involvement of the editor, but many times developmental editing is essential and the most productive and efficient way to proceed.

For example, an editor suggests an idea to an author. Because he originated the concept, initially at least he understands better than the author how it should be developed, and he'll work with the writer until they're both satisfied that the book is on the right track.

Perhaps the editor and author have worked together before and the author prefers that his editor work with him as they refine his ideas and material. Accordingly, he sends pages and chapters to his editor as he writes them so that the editor can provide immediate response and guidance. This allows the writer to revise as he goes and to avoid wasting time by going too far with stuff that won't work.

Because the market for published books changes so rapidly, the author, wanting to write a book that's going to reach as many people as possible, may decide to discuss with her editor whether there's a sufficiently large audience for whatever she has in mind, knowing as she does that the editor is keeping up with those changes on a daily basis.

During the developmental stage there is, of necessity, a greater closeness between writer and editor. And that means the increased possibility of unusual productivity and of conflict. Therefore, it's important to be very clear about the respective responsibilities: the author's is to write the best book possible, the editor's to help the author achieve that goal. The writer should try to keep an open mind and the editor should not be intrusive. Still, because developmental editing requires, by its nature, significant involvement, the editor's courtesy, continuing support, belief in the writer's work and talent, and tactful guidance are imperative and essential. It is also incumbent on the writer to be diplomatic, but it's my conviction, perhaps unfair to editors, that making the relationship work is much more the editor's responsibility than the author's. It's a tough but critical part of the job.

Successful collaboration allows the author to feel sustained and liberated by knowing that she doesn't have to bear the burden of creation, development, and refinement alone, though working independently is her right and her option. I think there's a special pleasure and harmony in the joining of forces. It both eases the loneliness of writing and editing, and multiplies the effectiveness of the creative process in a synergistic way.

Part of the effectiveness derives from editorial objectivity. The author can rely on the editor's slightly distanced judgment as the work progresses, rather than going through the possibly terrifying course of conceiving and writing the entire work in solitude and guessing and hoping that it is what it should be. There's also the advantage of efficiency. It's much easier and faster to make changes in a concept, proposal, or partial manuscript than in a full-length work, and this early labor reduces the amount of revision that will have to be done on the complete manuscript.

A mutual benefit is that authors aren't under the pressure of thinking they are the only source of ideas, and in turn, editors don't have to be totally reliant on writers for book concepts. Imaginative editors with solid ideas can find the right writer and develop the book with her. Another benefit at the conceptual or developmental stage is that the experienced editor, knowing the strengths of the particular writer and publisher, is able to guide the author toward the new or revised idea that will maximize those strengths.

One of the reasons I became an editor is because I have great respect for writing talent and revel in my involvement with it. A source of immense pleasure for me over the years has been the increasing extent to which many of my authors involve me ever earlier in the creative process.

Sometimes, at her request, I'll begin immediately to work closely with an author I haven't edited or published before. If she has been well edited in the past, she's aware of the benefits of editorial involvement and wants me, her new editor, to know how welcome my thoughts are. If despite wanting and needing editorial direction on previous books she's been edited little or not at all, she's going to take advantage right away of my interest in and enthusiasm for developmental editing.

Other times, after I've worked with an author and we've realized the rewards of working together, he'll ask for my thoughts sooner than he did the first time around. Conversely, because writers and editors are always learning, it's often the case that what an author has learned from our work together on a previous book he can apply on his own to the next book and therefore can be more independent in the writing. If the short-term goal of developmental editing is the best current book, the long-term goal is the maximum development of the writer's talent and independence.

It's been my extreme good fortune to have engaged in, through the years, almost every aspect of the editorial process, from the kind of comprehensive editing of a manuscript that verges on the deranged, with my notes running over a hundred double-spaced pages, to having an idea, finding the writer, and then editing and publishing a fine book with a gratifying minimum of developmental, structural, and line editing. Almost always it's been very hard work, and definitely always it's been deeply satisfying. I must admit though that the creative possibilities inherent in conceiving and shaping ideas into books have a special excitement.

A few years ago I wanted to add a new slang dictionary to my publishing house's list, so I approached an author I'd worked with on a couple of language books at another house. He was interested, and agreed to work on speculation, producing sample material to show the publisher, with no guarantee of an offer. It's hard on a writer but was necessary in this situation.

Our next step was focusing the concept and making the book competitive with other dictionaries. We weren't interested in a scholarly work. What we wanted was a lively, popular book that would be a browser's delight as well as a solid, though limited, reference dictionary. That approach was perfect for the author because that was exactly the kind of book he had compiled successfully in the past. We decided to restrict the scope of the book to contemporary American slang and to concentrate on making the entries as colorful and entertaining as possible.

As we went on, the author's research revealed that it had been fifty years since there had been a slang dictionary arranged by categories of words. I agreed that such an arrangement was a critical refinement because it would give us a competitive advantage over the other slang dictionaries, which only listed their words alphabetically. Combining the topical slang focus with the organization by category, the author prepared a brief but delightful and persuasive outline, and I was able to buy the book. We then developed the outline further, wanting it to be a thorough, detailed guide for the author as he wrote the actual manuscript.

Another example of developmental editing involved matching an internationally respected couple working in civilian law enforcement with the right concept and with an author. Each element was a separate editorial challenge. After reading their earlier coauthored books about self-defense and related issues, I met with the couple and suggested a much larger, more popular book than they'd done before. They were giving speeches all over the world, and I thought they could integrate their powerful message with their personal stories to form an anecdotal book that would dramatize their crime prevention ideas.

They liked that approach, and we next had to find a writer who could do justice to their increased potential. My publisher had made it clear that while they were very interested in the new book, they'd have to see something on paper before making a decision.

I talked to one of my authors with whom I had worked successfully and easily before, and she turned out to be perfect. Not only was she excited about the idea and the couple's message, and willing to accept the risks of writing on speculation, but she made some important contributions to my original concept of the book, giving it more substance and greater appeal by suggesting that we move beyond anecdotes to full, explosive autobiography. The couple thought she was wonderful and the four of us decided to work on a proposal that I could present to my publisher. This is a story currently without an ending because the proposal's still being written, but I've enjoyed the year I've spent in developing its possibilities, and I think the other three will also value the experience regardless of outcome.

Another book, which does have an ending, and a happy one at that, required two years of my editorial time. In this case, when I became involved the work was further along than concept because the author had already written a rough draft of most of the manuscript. It was a raw piece of work, and even at its best it wasn't going to be a major or best-selling book. Nevertheless, I thought that in its own modest way it was unique and

would definitely find an audience that it could continue to reach for years. The writer had a lively, colorful style that set the right tone for his book about mercenary soldiers, based on over forty years of personal field experience. Regrettably, however, he had no feel for structuring a manuscript. He knew approximately how to craft the sections and individual chapters, but the book had no unity or direction.

A sense of structure, though, is among the good editor's gifts. And my belief in the book's potential, combined with the author's willingness to accept direction, made it possible for us to go forward. For the next year, with no contract, only hope, I kept making structural suggestions. The writer would rework and revise the manuscript and send it in again. I would make more suggestions. And so it went. My immediate goal was not to get the manuscript in final, polished shape but simply to improve it enough that I would be able to buy it, with the understanding that more editing would follow. We did get it into that kind of shape, and I did buy the book. The additional editing and revising took another year but, very gratifying for us, the book became more successful than either of us had anticipated.

At the other extreme, there's the time when a novelist and I went from the initial idea to a fully developed concept in only six hours. His handling of the material was so assured, comprehensive, and vivid that we skipped the outline, and he began writing immediately. We were able to accomplish this feat because of the marvelously harmonious working relationship we'd had in the past.

Our challenge was to imagine the basic story for a second book in a two-book contract, which meant there wasn't the usual pressure of developing something I was trying to buy. Because the author's suspense novels featured a continuing character, an American submarine commander, the biggest question was what should happen to the hero this time. I had been concerned that he was *too* perfect, handling every situation with unnatural assurance. I thought he'd be more interesting if he were more human, sometimes beset with real doubt, and capable of occasional error. I proposed that we break him down totally in some way, push this paragon of leadership ability to the edge of suicide, shattering his confidence and sense of self so profoundly that it would be a real question whether he'd be able to rebuild himself enough to function at all. This would give the novel an element of psychological suspense that would parallel the ongoing adventure plot.

The writer at first hesitated to do something so radical and potentially dangerous to his traditional heroic protagonist. The risk, of course, was that the hero's fans wouldn't accept him as flawed and very vulnerable. But after further discussion, his wonderful novelist's imagination began to explore the dramatic possibilities. He envisioned a critical U.S./Soviet mission that would get the hero away from the navy's rumors about his stability and would give him a fresh start. The hero would have to take command of a Russian submarine with a hostile, defiant crew. The pressure would be enormous and the price of failure even more so. Both filled with creative excitement, we kept talking that day until the entire story had been outlined in memorable detail. The author went on to write the first three-quarters of the book with only one suggestion from me, and the editing I had to do on the complete manuscript was light.

On another occasion, I began working with an author on a second book, although this one hadn't yet been acquired, nor had the subject been decided on. As I expected, this smart, veteran author had several possibilities in mind. I liked his ideas but thought that, after decades of writing about the intelligence community, it was time for him to take on the biggest fish of all: the modern CIA in its entirety. I wanted him to do what hadn't been done before: explore it from the inside, showing how the whole operation worked from top to bottom, directorate to directorate, and interweave revelations about the ways in which the agency and these directorates had failed and succeeded, modestly and colossally.

Blessed again with an author of generous receptivity, I got a good reaction, we discussed the idea in more detail, and he wrote an outline. Both because we wanted to save editing and revision time later by making the outline as refined, focused, and complete as possible, and because we wanted the proposal to sell itself, we went through numerous revisions of the outline, each time making it tighter, stronger, and more interesting. Because of the author's reputation, it wasn't necessary for him to write sample chapters, but the proposal had to communicate exactly and potently the full vision of the work. After an overview, the book would analyze deeply the CIA's four directorates—Operations, Science and Technology, Intelligence, and Administration—and the Office of the Director of Central Intelligence. Throughout the outline we had to make it evident that these various parts were connected by the major themes of evaluating the agency's performance and explaining as never before its veiled inner workings.

I finally presented it for acquisition at our editorial meeting with great success. Afterward, there wasn't much to change. We had a final discussion and the author went to work on the actual manuscript, sending it to me in chunks as he wrote it. As with the suspense novelist, the developmental work the writer and I had done in the concept and outline stage had been so thorough that the manuscript progressed perfectly, with the author getting—and needing—nothing more from me except appreciation.

I wish it always went so well. There are times when I plain fail. There was a terrific, gentlemanly author whose first two novels I'd edited and published. I had the arrogance to think I knew what would be the best way to help him create the story line for his third novel. We agreed that we should try to imagine a story that was bigger in scope and number of characters than he'd attempted in the past because he was ready for the challenge.

His first plot had American armed forces engaged in a single foreign country. "One country isn't enough," I said decisively. "Let's stretch the military by having them fighting in three countries in various parts of the world. That makes it easier to have more characters too." He struggled nobly to make the expanded story work but the disparate parts wouldn't come together. We kept revising the outline but progress was painful. Understanding finally kicked me in the head. A good thing too, because the author had never complained.

I had forgotten that good creative ideas cause chain reactions, with one idea leading explosively to the next, and the next. The same is true of editorial approaches. If they are what they should be, the author's thinking and writing will be rolling, not dragging. Obviously I'd chosen and stayed with the wrong approach.

I thanked the writer for his thoughtful cooperation, and as we talked about why we weren't getting anywhere, I remembered that one of his greatest strengths was character, and that for him, story and plot flowed from the people, rather than the characters somehow evolving from an overall structure with foreign countries, etc. As soon as we went back to his main character and considered what situations would engage him, the ideas exploded from the author's stimulated imagination. Fortunately for this bedeviled writer, I'd gotten it right at last.

I followed a different path with a potential novelist who presented a difficult double challenge: he had never written a book of any kind before and there was no manuscript. All we had was a brief outline. Potentially catastrophic situations like these are what good editors thrive on. The novelist was riddled with doubt, but fortunately he combined real talent, an open mind, and dedication. We revised and expanded the outline of his semiautobiographical Vietnam novel, and after he began writing, we would discuss every chapter at length before he wrote the next one, weaving in ideas about the characters and the rest of the story.

After about a hundred pages, I felt it was time to edit in depth, so I prepared a set of notes and the author revised. We did the same for the second hundred pages. One of the aspects at which the author worked hardest was simplifying his technical explanations of naval aviation. I try to be representative of the general reader, figuring that if I can't follow it, others won't be able to either. Sometimes the author had to revise passages several times, but as he kept writing, the need for that effort decreased.

After receiving two hundred revised pages, I started all over again. This triple process of discussion, editing, and revision continued to the end of the complete manuscript, which I then edited comprehensively from the first page to the last. A testament to the value of that intense collaboration is that as we work together on the second novel, the author still sends me a chapter at a time, but he's learned so much that, happily, I have little to say.

These stories can only begin to suggest the many possibilities inherent in the development stage of the writing and editorial process. Keen enjoyment, satisfaction, friendly harmony, and a double sense of achievement are among the rewards of creative collaboration. The ultimate accomplishment is that the writer, because of what he has learned, has increased his independence over the long term and realized further the potential of his talent. Equally important, the author-editor partners have produced the most fully formed and finished manuscript possible under the circumstances, requiring the least amount of editing and revision before being published and providing enduring and perhaps best-selling pleasure for its readers.

The Copy Editor and the Author

Gypsy da Silva

GYPSY DA SILVA *is a production editor in the copy editing department at Simon & Schuster, where she began her publishing career twenty-five years ago. She has had the pleasure of working on fiction and nonfiction, both as a copy editor and supervising the work of staff and free-lance copy editors. Although the* Chicago Manual of Style *on her desk more or less falls open to certain sections, she wishes the University of Chicago Press would publish a thumb-indexed edition.*

Ms. da Silva asks and answers the question "What is a copy editor and why do we need them?" in her concise but comprehensive essay on what a copy editor does "to preserve the author's natural voice." She illuminates for the writer the various roles a copy editor plays in perfecting the manuscript first developed and line edited by the acquiring editor. These include, among many more, corrector of spelling errors, grammarian, fact checker, resolver of inconsistencies, fine-tuner of the author's style, sometimes researcher, etc., etc.

Ms. da Silva calms the anxious writer whose work is returned with a blizzard of query flyers by pointing out that "they are a sign that the manuscript has been read closely and with care" and shows how to handle them swiftly and effectively. The query flyer is the way the copy editor communicates with the author, and Ms. da Silva recommends that "the easiest way an author can let a copy editor know about preferences or ask for assistance is to draw up a memo and send it in with the manuscript."

Quite properly proud of the multiplicity of their skills, Ms. da Silva concludes her essay by admitting that "we copy editors know what we contribute—silently, almost always anonymously—to the finished book, but we do not fool ourselves. The author is the hero."

143

The Copy Editor and the Author

(In affectionate remembrance of Vera Schneider and Pat Miller)

What is a copy editor and why do we need them? A copy editor is that person who, after the author has written the manuscript and the editor has edited it, examines that first sentence, thinking: Would it be better as two questions? What is the antecedent of "we"? Should "them" be "him or her"? Or should I make it "copy editors" so the pronoun agrees in number with its antecedent? And does it matter? All these questions cross the copy editor's mind because the sum of the copy editor's task is to help the author (and the editor) shape this book into the best possible expression of the author's ideas. Yet while deciding whether or not to "fix" the author's grammar (et cetera), the copy editor must first take care to preserve the author's natural voice.

The division of labor between editor and copy editor begins with the fact that an editor's first responsibility is finding and bringing under contract books the publisher deems worth presenting to the public. The editor may then help the author with the general shaping of the book, suggesting some pruning here, some expansion there, perhaps some rearranging of the parts into what the editor sees as a more harmonious whole. Some editors may even focus on the details of finding the *mot juste,* fixing spelling errors, tidying up grammar and punctuation. But these last items are often left to the copy editor. Some editors send along covering memos with their manuscripts, detailing any special considerations for the copy editor. "Author overuses 'as a matter of fact.' I've pruned many. Feel free to prune more." "Author very sensitive. Query *all* changes." "This is a British author writing about a British scene. We want American spelling, but stet Britsh idiom unless hopelessly obscure." Other editors call ahead to alert the copy editor to what is wanted or to discuss the best way to proceed. The copy editor will also double-check the author's consistency of detail and style, and accuracy of fact.

But in the beginning, there is the manuscript. And every manuscript should be typed double space. An author preparing a work of nonfiction should bear in mind that even quotations from other books, footnotes (or back matter notes), and the bibliography should be typed double space, regardless of the likelihood that these elements will be set in smaller type than the main text. Copy editors need room to work. Double-spaced manuscripts provide that room. The copy editor's ideal author knows exactly what elements go into a bibliographical entry and how they are assembled, and there's very little marking the copy editor needs to do. But many authors need help getting notes or bibliographical style into shape. In either case, it's a lot easier to read double-spaced copy. The copy editor and the designer of the text will also bless the author who provides generous margins on all four sides of the page. The author will see how the copy editor keys (that is, ranks by means of letters or numbers) the various heads and marks extracts, lists, and other elements. But what the author may not realize is that after the copy editor does the keying, the designer who crafts the interior typography also needs room in the margin to indicate the typeface and width to which the element is to be set. What the copy editor labels "A," the designer translates into, for example, "12/14 Baskerville × 15 pi." More room is needed for the typesetter to insert computer codes that must be keyboarded with the copy so that the specified type size and style appears in the proofs—and the final book.

Copy editing for consistency of detail may be especially helpful to novelists. Does the author absentmindedly describe the heroine's hair as blond in chapter 2 and red in chapter 16? The copy editor will point out the discrepancy on a query flyer attached to the manuscript and ask which color is wanted. Chronology can get scrambled sometimes in a novel that covers many years or several generations. The copy editor keeps notes of dates and ages, querying the author about, for example, the aboriginal who rescues the woman who falls off her horse into the raging river: "Could a nine-year-old boy have lifted a grown woman?" Sometimes a copy editor will notice a detail mentioned early in the story that is never used again and might enhance the story in a later reference. A man is trained in techniques of silently dispatching enemy spies. The knowledge gained by the character was never put to use in the story—until the copy editor suggested that when the character later attempts a murder, he reach into his pocket and finger the piano wire hidden there. A nice addition to the suspense that the author incorporated into the action.

Copy editing for style involves attention to matters of spelling, punctuation, and syntax. That copy editors fix spelling seems almost obsolete to some people equipped with spelling-checker programs on their word processors. But copy editors know that the catch with machines checking spelling is that if it's a legitimate word, the machine smiles, oblivious to whether it's the right word in context. "Lemon aide"? Well sure. "Lemon" and "aide" are both real words. But can one enjoy a cool glass of "lemon aide" in the garden? The homophone-conscious copy editor gently corrects the spelling to "lemonade." Then there are all those bothersome words that are spelled one way in England and another way in the United States. Does the author prefer *traveller* or *traveler*? *Colour* or *color*? *Judgement* or *judgment*? Should the British spellings be Americanized? Punctuation must also be scrutinized. Comma before "and" in a series or not? Omit comma before coordinating conjunction when the subject of the two independent clauses is the same? Cap or lowercase after a colon? Moving to another consideration that must be in the copy editor's mind: Is the author's syntax and vocabulary felicitous? The bishop "took off his ceremonial sack." Does the author mean "his chasuble"? The blond movie star tells us in her memoirs that she was by the pool, lying on her chaise lounge. Should that be "chaise longue"? Whose syntax and vocabulary should be used here? Copy editing involves close attention to detail.

Good copy editors know that when it comes to making sure the author has the facts right, guessing is not good enough. Carry Nation? Or Carrie Nation? Was Trinity Sunday before or after May 1 in 1913? Could the hero have sailed from New York to California to join the Gold Rush on a boat that went through the Panama Canal? The copy editor will want to look up the facts in an authoritative reference. [Change to: Around Cape Horn/? (Panama Canal begun in 1883, per McCullough.)]

When the copy editor has found a source that gives a version of the facts different from what the author has stated, good practice requires tact in pointing out the apparent problem to the author. Copy editors try to bear in mind that the author has done the hardest part of the work. This must be respected. An experienced copy editor knows after checking a dozen or so items whether the author has been careful, and the more mistakes the copy editor finds, the more checking he or she is likely to do. Time permitting. And time is almost always a problem. Now that the manuscript is in hand, author, editor, and publisher are eager to get the finished book into the stores. So couldn't we please hurry?

Copy editors ideally have a broad knowledge of a variety of subjects, but they also have their specialties. Editors know to request someone who has the right stuff for the job at hand. In every case where nonfiction is involved, the author is well advised to supply all the back matter—the appendixes and notes and bibliography—with the text and not wait until later to hand these parts to the editor, because with the back matter in hand the copy editor knows what sources the author has consulted. Copy editors acquire a number of reference books, but they also use libraries to verify information they do not have at hand. It helps the copy editor to know what books or articles the author has used. Copy editors have been known to rent movies from their local video store to check production credits, to call the U.S. Army Office of Information to check the spelling of names of military installations, to hunt down the sheet music to confirm the lyrics of songs, to stand in drugstores jotting down the correct spelling of trade names of sanitary goods, to twist themselves into pretzels to see if the instructions for an exercise can be followed.

Some publishing houses have copy editors on staff who handle at least some of the manuscripts being prepared for publication, but it is also possible that the work of copyediting will be assigned to a free-lance copy editor who works outside the publisher's office. The person who assigns the copy editing work will have the title Production Editor or Manuscript Supervisor or Copy Chief, or some variation on that theme. He or she will examine the manuscript when it comes in and, taking into consideration the subject matter and the schedule, try to find the most suitable person to send the job to. The production editor will instruct the copy editor as needed.

Can the author put in a few words with the copy editor? But of course. The easiest way an author can let a copy editor know about preferences or ask for assistance is to draw up a memo and send it in with the manuscript. Does the dictionary give two acceptable spellings for a word and the author have a strong preference for the second spelling? Let the copy editor know. The copy editor can then not only avoid changing what the author prefers but also make sure that the author's preferred spelling has been used consistently. (This copy editor did, however, find herself puzzling over one author's assertion that "gray" with an *a* was a different color from "grey" with an *e,* and could only humbly ask, "Will your reader understand the distinction?") Prefer "Tehran" to "Teheran"? Let the copy editor know. And how about capitalization of titles? Sometimes authors who are used to reading government documents make the assumption that all titles of office are always done with initial capital letters. *The Chicago Manual of Style,* which is widely used by book publishers, tells copy editors to use caps only when the title appears with the name of the person holding the office. So the copy editor will style thus: Secretary of State Baker, the secretary of state. How about pronouns referring to the Deity? Many people assume that they should be capitalized, and indeed, they often are. Now take a look at a Bible: "Then he called the twelve disciples together" (KJV, Luke 9:1). "Then he called the twelve together" (RSV, Luke 9:1). And at *Chicago:* "God in his mercy," "Jesus and his disciples" (7.77). Another widely used stylebook, *Words into Type,* recommends using initial capital letters in some instances. An author who can't live with standard book styling (which often differs from newspaper style) or prefers one stylebook over another should say so *before* the work begins.

Is there some nagging detail the author tried to track down and couldn't find? Let the copy editor know, and perhaps he can help locate the missing bit. Is the author worried that when she changed a character's name from

George to Frank, she may have missed a George or two? Alert the copy editor. Copy editors are there to help the author.

When the copy editor returns the manuscript, the production editor may review the queries raised before sending the manuscript to the editor. The editor may go over the copy editing, answering some or all of the queries. In most cases the editor will forward the manuscript to the author.

An author going through the process for the first time may be somewhat startled at first to see anywhere from a few to many dozens of query flyers attached to the manuscript. One author wrote saying that when he saw how many flyers the copy editor had attached to his manuscript, he wanted to hire a hit man. But as any author who has had good past experiences with copy editors will be quick to point out, there is reason to feel reassured by those pink or yellow or blue slips of paper. They are a sign that the manuscript has been read closely and with care. (The author who initially wanted to hire a hit man confessed that after he had read through his copy editor's queries, he changed his mind. "I think I'm in love," he concluded.) If something has been phrased a bit awkwardly, the copy editor will have made an attempt to adjust the words for greater clarity and will be asking if the change is OK. In some cases, the copy editor will not have altered the wording on the manuscript but will suggest possible rewordings and ask, on the flyer, if one of the suggestions would better convey the author's meaning. Sometimes the copy editor will be querying a spelling that is inconsistent with the author's previous (or later) version. This kind of query is most likely to crop up where invented or real but obscure names are used. Perhaps it's a fact that doesn't jibe with a previously stated fact—or with the information the copy editor has obtained in a reference book or other source. Did the author guess about the spelling of a brand name? The copy editor may have gone to the supermarket and looked at the package, confirming that it's Reddi-wip, *not* Ready Whip.

Whatever the queries, it's the author's job to read the flyers and answer *on the flyers* the questions raised. If the flyer says, "OK/?" all the author needs to do is put a check mark through the question mark in order to answer "Yes." If two suggestions are made for possible ways of fixing a single problem, the author need only strike out the one not wanted and circle the one that is OK. Or the author may come up with a third solution, in which case the copy editor's suggestions should be struck out and the author's fix written on the flyer. The reason for keeping the dialogue on the flyer is to avoid making the manuscript messy and possibly confusing for the typesetter. If the author wants to make small changes directly on the manuscript, she should use a different color pencil from any used before and let the production editor know what color the new changes are written in.

If a longish passage needs rewriting, the author can type the new version out on a separate piece of 8½-by-11-inch paper and clip it to the original, being sure to put the page number on the new copy. What the author should *not* do, unless specifically given permission to proceed thus, is re-run the manuscript in whole or in part through a word processor. The copy editor—or the production editor—must have the original version of the copyedited script back from the author. And the flyers should be left attached to the manuscript. Whoever does the final cleanup will then go through the manuscript and incorporate the author's answers and changes into it.

If there's not enough room left on the flyer for the author to respond to the query, the author should add flyers of his own on which to answer. Those Post-its available from stationery stores, dime stores, and even some supermarkets are handy for this. Just be sure they are wrapped around the edge of the page and not stuck in the middle of the page, where they might not be noticed by someone looking at the edge of the manuscript instead of turning each page.

If the author has questions about how to deal with queries, he or she should call the editor and ask to speak to the production editor or the copy editor. There is no need to work in a vacuum when help is always available. Has the copy editor made markings the author does not understand? Pick up the phone! Again, what the author should bear in mind is that copy editors are there to help the author.

A word of caution: A few copy editors will write some queries in the margins of the manuscript even though they may have been told that this is not a good idea because the author may miss these queries. Production editors have been heard to sigh over this habit and maybe even remonstrate with the copy editor. But they may have resigned themselves to the situation because a copy editor's work is otherwise so intelligent and helpful. So the careful author will look sharp for these notations in the margins.

When the answers have been incorporated into the manuscript and the flyers removed, the manuscript goes off to the production department for type design and markup, and then to the typesetter for composition.

After several weeks, the author will be sent a set of galleys—or page proofs, when the schedule is tight and going straight to pages is possible. The author should not expect to get the manuscript back with those first proofs. He is expected to read the proofs "cold," that is, without reference to the manuscript. Proofreading the galleys against manuscript is the job of another professional: the proofreader. There's a good reason for this procedure. Eyes that have been over a manuscript a number of times are not as likely to spot typographical errors as those that come to the work for the first time. The copy editor will have read the manuscript two or even three times (unless the book is on a supercrash schedule), the editor will have done the same, and the author . . . So the proofreader's fresh eyes are what is called for.

Some publishers enclose instructions for marking type proofs when they send the galleys to the author. *The Chicago Manual of Style* explains proof-reading, or the author can consult a dictionary for proofreader's marks. The important thing for the author to remember is that changes in proof must be marked in the margin of the galleys. One strikes out the word being replaced and then writes in the margin (very neatly and legibly, of course) the word to be substituted. Where it is a simple substitution of one or more words for the original word or phrase, there's no need to make a delete mark first. Writing the new word in very tiny letters squeezed between the lines of type is *not* how it's done.

When reading galleys without having the manuscript to check against, the author may be concerned about distinguishing PEs (printer's errors) from AAs (author's alterations); the author, after all, knows that AAs in excess of a certain percentage of the composition cost will be charged against her royalty account. Probably the easiest thing for an author to do is mark corrections of what she believes to be printer's errors as PEs and attach a note to the first galley, asking the production editor to double-check those items against manuscript. When the production editor is trans-ferring the author's alterations to the master galleys, he should find that all (or almost all) of the PEs have already been caught by the proofreader.

The best proofreaders do more than read the galleys very carefully, word for word, against the manuscript; they also back up the work of the copy editor. Even the most highly skilled, conscientious, and persnickety copy editor may miss something, whether it's an ordinary spelling error or some mistake of fact. And just as the wise author hopes to be backed up by a good editor and a good copy editor, the wise copy editor earnestly hopes to be backed up by a first-rate proofreader. It's just possible that, after the author has returned his galleys to his editor and the editor has passed them along to the production editor, the author may get a call with a query or two from the production editor. The work involved in bringing a book as near to perfection as human beings can make it is a process that begins with the writing and continues through not only the editing and copy editing stages but also through galleys, page proofs, repro proofs, and even beyond the typesetter's proofs to the printer's blues, a photographic print made from negatives that will be used to make the offset plates from which the book is printed. The author, however, rarely sees any of the later stages of production and must try to remain patient, confident in the professional efforts of the publisher's staff in the weeks or months of work to be done before the finished book comes off press.

One additional element of the book may be something for the author to consider: the index. It is possible for the author to make the index. The idea may even be tempting, because the author will have to pay for the index preparation if a professional indexer does the work. The author should bear in mind, when deciding whether to prepare the index, the necessary skills for the job. Indexing is a professional occupation—and an art form. A good indexer may be able to give the interested reader access to the author's material in ways that would not occur to the author. If the author elects to have his book professionally indexed, he may still ask to see the index manuscript, to be sure it reflects all the most important ideas he is trying to convey to the reader. (Of course an indexer cannot put into the index what isn't in the text!) The author should also take into account that there are constraints of time and space that the indexer has had to deal with.

Is all of this work made obsolete by computerization? Couldn't the author just give her disks to the publisher and have the publisher send them off to the typesetter? Wouldn't that save money? Well, yes, it might save the publisher some money in composition costs. But if the author wanted to make changes in proofs, the money saved could vanish in a flurry of EA (editor's alteration) and AA charges. Does the publisher really want to hire an amateur typesetter (that is, the author) to do the keyboarding? Does the author want to be paid to be a keyboarder or a writer? Is the author certain that he doesn't need the help of an editor or a copy editor? Well, maybe the editor and the copy editor could work on the author's disks. Does anyone want a professional editor or professional copy editor to become an amateur keyboarder? Bear in mind that when the manuscript goes to the typesetter on disk, there are no PEs. If author and publisher find themselves editing and copyediting on type proofs, they may well end up paying more for the composition than if the manuscript had been set from the hard copy in the first place. The examples that can be cited are painful to recall. So far as I know, the copy editors who have been doing the pioneering work in this area have discovered one thing for certain: working on the author's disks does not at present save time. Think twice on the possibility of sending the disks direct to the typesetter. If the disks are sent, send the hard copy too. Let the typesetter decide what makes the best economic sense. We are all facing a path that may be full of potential but is certainly fraught with potential difficulties. The change from hot metal composition by Linotype to computer setting of equal polish took about a decade, but the change has been made. The change from sending hard copy to sending disks only to the typesetter and getting really good results may take that long or longer. Am I a Luddite? No. But I've been in the business long enough to develop a great respect for the professional skills that go into making good books and making books well.

Line Editing
Drawing Out the Best Book Possible

Maron L. Waxman

MARON L. WAXMAN *is the editorial director of HarperReference at Harper-Collins. The former executive director of book development at Book-of-the-Month Club, she has taught editing in the publishing programs at both the City University of New York and New York University and has lectured at many publishing and writers' conferences.*

Ms. Waxman's clear, practical essay is nothing less than a comprehensive short course in the basic, essential principles and skills of line editing (also known as manuscript editing).

A believer in Maxwell Perkins's dictum that "an editor does not add to a book. At best he serves as a handmaiden. . . . In the end an editor can get only as much out of an author as the author has in him," Ms. Waxman offers her own definition of the working relationship between the manuscript editor and the author: ". . . a long and continuing exchange . . . of questions asked and answers given until both author and editor believe they have produced . . . the best book possible . . . the book in which the author says what he has to say as clearly, as forcefully, and as gracefully as he can. It is the goal of all editing, and most particularly manuscript editing, to achieve this end."

In the course of her essay Ms. Waxman offers sound advice on such vital matters as the difference between editing and rewriting, questions of clarity, coverage (providing sufficient information), organization (presentation of material in a way that can be followed), and tone (addressing the readers who will be most interested in the book). In addition she explains how to handle such technical aspects of manuscript editing as the analysis of the

153

manuscript before the editor begins to work on it and the proper and most effective way to query an author.

Ms. Waxman concludes by reminding writers that "editors are not authors, nor do they wish to be. What the best of editors wishes to be is the perceptive, demanding, energetic, and patient prober who can devote his particular talents and skills to the enterprise of working with authors to publish good books."

Line Editing
Drawing Out the Best Book Possible

In many authors' dreams there is an editor who sits at a desk, hunched over a mass of manuscript. The editor leafs through page after page, discarding some, furiously editing and reworking others. Finally, after days of work, a finely wrought book emerges from this mass, much as Michelangelo's *Moses* grew out of a block of marble. This dream picture is the legacy of Maxwell Perkins, Saxe Commins, and a handful of other mighty editors. The harsh truth is that before we can discuss manuscript editing seriously, we must brush aside this dream. Maxwell Perkins's own words give us the reality of manuscript editing. "An editor does not add to a book," Perkins told an editing class at New York University. "At best he serves as a handmaiden. . . . In the end an editor can get only as much out of an author as the author has in him."*

In this process of extraction the editor does not work alone. Manuscript editing is a long and continuing exchange between editor and author of questions asked and answers given until both author and editor believe they have produced a good book—not necessarily the best book ever, but the best book possible. The best book possible is the book in which the author says what he has to say as clearly, as forcefully, and as gracefully as he can. It is the goal of all editing, and most particularly manuscript editing, to achieve this end.

The Editor as Handmaiden

In practice, manuscript editing has very little to do with changing actual words on pages of paper. Weak writing almost always indicates weak

*A. Scott Berg, *Max Perkins: Editor of Genius* (New York: E. P. Dutton, 1978), p. 6.

thinking or weak structure. Thus as the editor reads through the manuscript, the questions he keeps in mind at all times are:

Is the author's purpose evident?

Do the readers have the information they need to follow the narrative or argument or recipe?

Is the narrative or argument or recipe laid out in the clearest manner?

Are the level of information and tone of voice appropriate for the intended readers of the book?

Boiled down, these questions can be stated as clarity, coverage, organization, and tone. They are the principle concerns of the manuscript editor. Once they are right, the problems of language, if any, often resolve themselves.

An interruption

Like all crafts, editing requires some training and discipline. Here are three points to bear in mind as you prepare to begin editing.

First, manuscript editors do not read for pleasure, no matter what their friends may think. The manuscript editor must train himself to read uncomfortably, to nag, to question, to probe, not to give the author the benefit of the doubt. If you ever find yourself reading for pleasure when you are supposed to be editing, put down your pencil—in fact, you probably already have—and enjoy yourself. See how the book comes out. Then go back, pencil in hand, and edit, noting all the little complaints and comments you withheld for the pleasure of reading.

Second, editing is not rewriting. Many times it would be easier for the editor to rewrite tangled and unclear passages, using the author's manuscript as a primary source. But that is not editing; rewriting is an entirely different job. Keep in mind Perkins's words: "An editor does not add to a book." The editor must find a way to draw the words from the author.

Third, remember that you are the first reader of the book. Your response and impressions are the first chance the author has to see how a reader will respond to the book. This is one of your best tools in editing, so sharpen your ability to read like a reader. If you are confused, distracted, or let down, it is likely that other readers may also be. In the politest editorial manner, let the author know.

Now to the principle concerns.

Clarity

Above all the reader must be able to understand what the author is trying to accomplish, what her purpose is in writing the book.

A manila folder is a helpful aid in keeping that purpose firmly in mind. Before I begin editing a nonfiction manuscript, I put all the descriptive information on the book into this folder—the proposal, with cover letter if that has additional information; the table of contents; the introduction or preface; the author's biography or curriculum vitae. This folder stays on my desk throughout the editing, to be referred to when necessary.

I once edited a comprehensive book on attracting birds to the backyard. Each chapter was exhaustive in its detail, but, strangely, all the author's instructions did not seem to add up to anything. I just could not figure out why anyone should be doing all this. Consulting the manila folder, I saw that the author was an active environmentalist. With great force and sense of purpose, her proposal stated that in this book she wanted to alert homeowners, no matter how little land they had, to what they as individuals could do to preserve bird species and protect the environment for both birds and people. Nowhere in the book, however, was this urgent voice heard. I suggested that the author incorporate the assumptions and values of the proposal into the introductory chapter of the book. When she added this material, the book took on a purpose and offered a powerful reason to get out and undertake the time-consuming tasks the author had described.

In novels, particularly those that rely heavily on plot, editors often reverse this manila folder process and while editing compile a diary for the characters. What was the dazzling young actress wearing when she went for her first audition? Was it the same black Lycra miniskirt in which she was found murdered that evening? In biographies some editors keep the subject's vital statistics at hand—birthdate, important milestones, names and ages of family members. In this way the editor can be sure that, through some slip, the subject does not marry at age nine or that her children do not change names in the course of the book.

The editor must always keep the author on track. Here, in miniature, is an example of how an author can go astray.

> *The Sailor* states the two main concerns of the author's body of work, one of only two novels by Mariner to be written in the second person (*The Wave* is the other); a speculation on the meaning of the sea in coastal countries that grows into a full-blown metaphor; and an examination of the life of the sailor, told in numbing day-to-day detail.

In this paragraph the writer had a very clearly stated idea, but she was distracted and wandered off to another thought, which is decorated with a parenthetical phrase. By the time the reader gets to the first semicolon, he has forgotten what he came for—"the two main concerns" of line 1. As an aside, the punctuation here only adds to the confusion. If the editor tries to fix the sentence by fiddling with the words, clarity is unlikely to result. Without changing a word, however, the sentence can be brought into line:

> *The Sailor* states the two main concerns of the author's body of work: a speculation on the meaning of the sea in coastal countries that has grown into a full-blown metaphor and an examination of the life of the sailor, told in numbing day-to-day detail. It is interesting that *The Sailor* is one of only two books by Alice Mariner to be written in the second person, the other being *The Wave*.

In a sentence or two this kind of meandering is fairly apparent, but in a book whole paragraphs and chapters often roam off, abandoning the reader. The editor is the vigilant guide, always urging the author back to the path. This does not mean that there can be no attractive detours, only that they should be clearly recognized as such.

Coverage

Have you ever read a mystery in which a totally unexpected character, with totally unexpected motives, turns out to be the villain? Most readers find this kind of deus ex machina resolution disappointing. By the same token, a cook up to his elbows in the preparation for a dinner party is none too happy if one of the steps in the recipe calls for an ingredient not mentioned on the ingredient list.

Coverage, or sufficient information, is another major concern of the line editor. I have edited two biographies in which the authors neglected to state the birthdates of the subjects. Now I immediately look for this information. Why was I taken by surprise the first time it happened? Because manuscript editors are too often bound up in the text, busy ransacking it for problems. It is much harder to stand back from the text and look for what is not there. This is, however, one of the most important disciplines the manuscript editor can develop. The primary concern is that all people and terms be adequately identified and defined. Sixth-graders tackle this problem by starting many papers, "The dictionary defines 'absolutism' as . . ." More sophisticated writers try to avoid this kind of unimaginative opening, but in so doing often omit basic information. The editor must constantly be on the lookout for these omissions.

Once I edited a draft manuscript that carefully described, step by step, how to build a deck and a patio and never defined either or told the difference between the two. Recently an article on the front page of the *New York Times* was headlined 10 OF 12 [SOVIET REPUBLICS] PLEDGE SUPPORT [FOR AN ECONOMIC UNION] but did not mention the names of either the ten supporting republics or the two opposing ones. Again these are examples writ small. The manuscript editor can be faced with similar omissions spread over the course of a 150,000-word book and must train himself to ask, as he turns each page, "Has anything necessary or important been left out? Has the author covered the most recent developments in the field?"

There is, of course, the other side of the coin—too *much* information. Writing is a selective process in which the author chooses from a mass of material that which best creates the story, whether fiction or nonfiction. However, in gathering material, the author sometimes gets too close to it and cannot part with a scrap. At this point the editor must step in and gently prune so that the reader will not be lost in a thicket of information. This is not to advocate a Bauhaus severity. Obviously there is room for an aside, for a bit of colorful if not vital information, for a graceful description or a humorous allusion, but the reader should not have to track through all the writer's undigested thoughts and research. One editor tells of a striking set piece in a novel he was working on, a jewel that sparkled but distracted rather than illuminated. In the original draft it appeared in the opening chapter. Out of place there, it was moved, at the editor's suggestion, to a later chapter. With each draft the scene shifted to a yet later chapter, until at last both editor and author decided to save it for the next book. What is important in every book is the information needed to complete it or the narrative thrust to keep it moving, not every piece of information, no matter how fascinating, or every beautifully crafted passage.

Two other factors have to be taken into consideration in considering the content of a book: accuracy and balance. The editor must continually test and question what he is reading. Is it complete? Up-to-date? Correct? Does it make sense? Depending on the type of book the editor is working on— textbook, novel, biography, gardening manual, scientific survey—he will have to decide whether he has sufficient knowledge of the subject or whether the book should be vetted by an expert reader. Accuracy is important for fiction as well as nonfiction. Editors of gritty mysteries keep city maps on hand to be sure the detective can zip from one street to another without bogging down in one-way traffic.

Balance also requires concentration, again because imbalance is more likely to be caused by omission than by commission. In a recent collection of firsthand accounts of the Civil War, the anthologist selected memorable pieces that caught the editor up in their power. However, once the editor separated himself from the emotional impact of the proposed selections, he saw that the book heavily favored Southern writers, that there was no mention of black troops, that there was scant attention paid to the home front. Thus the book did not truly portray the impact of the war on the United States, as it purported to; it was necessary to add new entries and delete some repetitious ones to achieve that.

Organization

Not only does the editor need to check for complete, accurate, and balanced information, he must also ensure that the information is presented in a way that can be followed.

As he reads through the manuscript, the editor must be certain that he can always follow the author's train of thought and that he has been told everything he needs to know to be where he is or do what he is doing. An editor tells of working on a gardening manual with detailed instructions for fertilizing and for killing weeds. The last sentence of the lengthy section read: "Be extremely careful in handling these chemicals, for they are poisonous; in fact, it is wise to wear gloves when fertilizing or weeding." As the editor pointed out, it might be a little late for the careless gardener by the time he or she found this out.

There are two helpful tools for reorganizing mixed-up manuscripts: the signpost sentence and the outline.

The editor should always be on the lookout for signpost sentences, sentences that clearly state or reveal the author's intent or direction. Frequently these sentences appear toward the end of sections, as summaries, rather than near the beginning, where they could function as topic sentences that shape the material that follows. When the editor comes across such a sentence, he should use it to the fullest advantage, moving it to where it orders a disorderly passage and guides the reader through the text. Here is an example:

> Working together is hard. An assistant once remarked that until he worked at a publishing house, he had no idea of how badly authors were treated, almost as if they were pests that had to be tolerated if a house had to publish books. It is the editor's primary job, in the demanding process of publishing a book, to maintain a good working relationship.

This is a paragraph that, reworked, appears on page 161 in what I hope is much clearer form. Note that in the original draft, the main idea of the paragraph came at the end, leaving the reader to wonder about the meaning of the paragraph until he came to the end of it.

Another good way to get at poor organization is to strip away the words and go straight to the structure: Outline the material, whether it is an entire book whose chapters follow one another willy-nilly or a single muddled chapter. Occasionally I have had to go through a chapter paragraph by paragraph, noting the subject of each one in the margin; once that was done, I photocopied the original and cut the copy apart, clipping all the paragraphs on the same subject together and then reorganizing the paragraphs. This method is for extreme cases, however, and should not be necessary in the normal course of manuscript editing. A simple outline usually reveals repetition, omission, and poor organization and is an excellent base from which the author can rework the material.

Bad organization can sometimes be fixed with a bold stroke. An editor was working on a rather well-written history of the Vatican. The book opened with an excellent guided tour through the buildings, then it stalled in the second chapter, which was a chronology of popes. The editor fiddled and diddled, trying to make the chapter readable, to no avail. Whatever he did, the chapter remained a catalog, a barrier to the progress of the book. The information was clearly necessary to the book as reference material, but there was no need for it to interrupt the unfolding of Vatican history. The editor picked up the entire chapter and made it an appendix, where a list of factual biographies posed no problem.

Tone

Very few books, despite what their authors hope and believe, will interest everyone. The editor must help the author recognize the readers who will be most interested in the book and address them, whether they are the author's fellow professionals, readers coming to the subject for the first time, or highly knowledgeable amateurs.

Recently a psychiatrist who had usually addressed herself to a professional readership wrote a book for a general audience. Her editor pointed out several ways in which the text had to be reworked. First, the author was warned that general readers might not be familiar with all the terms and concepts that professionals would readily understand; this meant eliminating jargon and glossing necessary technical language. Second, the editor suggested grouping most of the research data and discussion of source material in appendixes at the back of the book where they could provide the scholarly foundation necessary for the book's arguments but not weigh them down; readers could consult the appendixes if they wanted to. Footnotes were used only for direct quotations. Third, the editor lightened the character of the book, making it more informal by eliminating summaries at the end of chapters and illustrating points with a few striking examples rather than numerous case studies couched in psychiatric terminology.

Most authors do not have to shift gears so dramatically from book to book, but editors and authors should always be aware of the reader at the other side of the book and know his level of sophistication. This is brought home to me very clearly whenever I use a relatively straightforward recipe for brownies as a teaching exercise. Any student with some kitchen experience goes right through the recipe, but there are always a few kitchen-shy students who stumble over the opening instruction: "In a medium saucepan . . ."

Drawing the Work Out of the Author

Thus far we have covered what I would call the editor's first reading, or assessment, of the manuscript, which by and large takes place before the editor puts pencil to paper. This does not mean that editors read all manuscripts through twice. I do think, however, that editors read all manuscripts at two levels. The first reading is this assessment, in which the editor views the manuscript from some distance, scanning it for the large-scale issues of clarity and so on. The second reading is the working level, in which the editor gets down to the manuscript and frames the work he will draw out of the author.

In this demanding process it is the editor's job to maintain a good working relationship with the author. An editorial assistant once remarked that until he worked at a publishing house, he had no idea how badly authors were treated; it was almost as if they were mere pests who had to be tolerated if the house were to continue publishing books. But if the editor keeps the author informed, analyzes the editorial issues considerately, and queries the author with care, it is possible to avoid an adversarial situation in which the author or the editor or both see themselves as losers in a contest for the book. It is, after all, the goal of both to publish the best book possible, and with this in mind the editor works gently but firmly.

Information

A meeting just before you begin editing is one of the best ways to let the author know how the editing will proceed, especially if you have not already met. Obviously, a meeting is not always possible, and a letter or phone call may have to substitute, but the effort should be made.

The purpose of the meeting—and it can be lunch if you want a relaxed atmosphere—is to explain to the author what to expect from you as an editor and from your publishing house. You should explain the difference between editing and copy editing and tell the author at what stage the manuscript will be sent back to her; how much editing you think the manuscript will need; whether any additions are necessary—bibliography, list of sources, glossary. You can also give the author some idea of schedule—how long each stage will take and how much time she will have to turn the material around. The author will get good basic working information, and you will have a chance to judge how the author will respond to editing, valuable knowledge when you are about to spend a good deal of time on the manuscript.

Even after laying out the basics, you should proceed with some caution. Unless you are absolutely confident that the author will agree to all your suggestions, it is wise to edit the first chapter, or perhaps two, and send it to the author, complete with a cover letter. Then put the manuscript aside and give the author two to three weeks to go over the edited chapter and send it back. When the author returns the manuscript, you will see immediately how much editing the author is open to. This will be your guide not only to further editing but also to ranking by order of importance.

Analysis

A few preliminaries about editorial marking are in order before the editor goes to work on the manuscript. Some of these notes sound like a kindergarten lesson, but the editor will be writing all over the manuscript and should keep in mind how this will look to the author. Messiness in these basics can get the editorial process off to a bad start.

In general the manuscript editor uses a black lead pencil, typically a No. 2, and queries in the margins. Stick-on flags are usually reserved for copy editors. Write clearly and firmly; many editors make tentative squiggles, so it is hard for the author to read their comments and queries. If you are editing, do it; do not underscore your doubts with lightly penciled jottings. Edit concisely, using the margin for your notes. The fewer marks you make, the easier it is for the author to follow your comments and, as a corollary, sympathize with and understand them. If a comment is too long for a marginal notation, save it for the cover letter.

If you want to try an exercise in editor-author relations, mail a marked-up manuscript, preferably one that has been edited in red pencil, to yourself to see how it would look to an author anticipating his first batch of manuscript from his publisher. "A bloody rag" was one editor's reaction.

Never paste over the author's original. If you must substantially revise a paragraph or two, type them on a separate sheet for the author's consideration.

Always retain a file copy of the manuscript. By contract the author is required to submit two copies, so the second becomes the file copy. Sometimes someone in the house needs this; keep track of it or copy it. By the same token, most houses copy the edited manuscript before it goes to the author; not only does this offer insurance against loss, it also provides a copy for both editor and author should there be a phone consultation.

Preliminaries covered, we can move on to substantive editing. As should be clear by now, the issues that the editor addresses, his suggestions for changes and revision, are necessary for the success of the book; "sounds better" is rarely justification for an editorial change. Because the author has the final say on all changes that are not actual errors—facts, grammar, spelling—the editor must state the case for his suggestions convincingly. This requires analysis of the editorial issues as well as of the author's willingness to accept editing.

The editor has only so many points to play in any given manuscript, and he must decide which are the most important for every book he edits, establishing a hierarchy of changes that he believes the author must go along with. Roughly, I would group these changes as necessary, felicitous, and meticulous. It is not usually possible to work on all three fronts. In a manuscript that needs reorganization, new material, and substantial revision, it is a waste of time to fault the author for somewhat repetitious or awkward phrases; on the other hand, in a well-plotted novel that moves as smoothly as a canoe across a mountain lake, a poorly worded phrase will stick out like a discarded Styrofoam cup floating on the water.

The absolutely necessary changes are always of utmost importance and should not leave much room for discussion. These would include anything that is clearly wrong: omissions; weak organization and logic, factual errors, lack of balance, and the like. These problems weaken the core of the book and, if they are not addressed in the editing, open the book to criticism. In any manuscript with these problems, the editor must focus all his attention on them and may have to forgo some linguistic niceties.

Consider this excerpt from an obituary in the *New York Times* of October 27, 1989:

> His wife, the former Susan J. Ault, died in 1983. They were married for 36 years.
>
> He is survived by two daughters, Shirley Evans of Salem and Barbara Cleaveland of Alexandria, Va.; four grandchildren, and three great-grandchildren.

From the dates given, the subject's older daughter could be no older than forty-two years old, assuming she was born in the first year of his marriage. For her and her sister, two women in their early forties at most, to have

three grandchildren is possible—triplets?—but not likely. This is the kind
of statement that must be queried. Straightening this out is more important
to the obituary than any other possible change.

The felicitous changes include substituting smooth phrasing for awkward
language, heightening narrative thrust, and eliminating overlong citations
that weigh down a popular work. Here the issues are less a matter of right
and wrong than of improving the manuscript and presenting the reader with
a better book. The editor will point out repetition, distracting plot details,
sentences that plod along in a dull subject-predicate-object pattern, paragraphs of dense, thickly worded sentences, paragraphs of rapid-fire five-
word sentences that leave the reader no time to absorb their meaning.
Compare the unedited and edited versions of this passage:

Begin construction by laying out the bottom, Back,

and Top on 1x4 stock. Then cut each piece.

Three holes are drilled in top to hold the baseballs.

The centers of these holes are located 1 1/2" from

front edge and 2 1/2" from each end and in the center of

top. Mark these points and bore a 2" hole through them

for the baseballs to sit in.

An electric drill and hole cutter will make quick

work of making these large holes. If you use a brace

and expandable bit, securely clamp parts to the

table.

n, ~~by~~ lay~~ing~~ out the bottom, ~~B~~back,

~~anu~~ _A_op on 1x4 stock. Then cut each piece.

Next, the piece○ _for_
_A_~~T~~hree holes are drilled in _A_top ~~to hold~~ the baseballs.

two outer
The centers of the~~se~~ holes are located 1 1/2" from

the _the third hole is_
front edge and 2 1/2" from each end~~, and~~ in the center~~, of~~

each of
~~top~~. Mark these points and bore a 2" hole through _A_them

for the baseballs to sit in.

You can use either an electric drill and hole cutter or a brace and expandable bit○

An electric drill and hole cutter will make quick

however
work of ~~making~~ these large holes. If _A_you use a brace

and expandable bit, securely clamp parts to the

table.

Note that there were no technical errors in the original manuscript, nothing that had to be edited. Every editor, however, brings his own judgment and reading to bear on the manuscripts he edits, and this editor believed that readers might have difficulty following these telescopic instructions, especially with the drilling equipment discussed _after_ the drilling instructions. In rewording the passage, the editor has slowed down the pace; in addition, he has moved the information about equipment. How does the editor query these changes to the author? In a marginal note he says, "Instructions a bit brisk for reader to follow. OK to slow down? If not, please recast."

Note that the author's attention is drawn to the change and that she is given the chance to reject the suggestion and reword the passage herself. The editor must query all changes that touch on content—which means everything except grammar, punctuation, spelling, and house style, which by contract the publisher controls—for the content of the book is clearly the author's province. Frequently the query is a simple "OK?" for minor changes.

Fine points of language and phrasing and nuances of characterization are usually achieved only in manuscripts where there are few major revisions and changes. Here the editor can devote himself to making the language as precise and meticulous as possible. Although the editorial suggestions here will probably be the most fastidious, the manuscript will probably be the least heavily edited because there are no major changes.

Querying

Almost all of the editor's work on the manuscript is presented to the author in the form of queries. He formulates these queries from the questions that arise as he reads through the manuscript, questions that usually suggest revisions, cuts, amplifications, and the like. In most cases, the author has the final say over which of these questions she will address, so it is in skillful and persuasive querying that the editor states his case and hopes to draw out of the author the work needed to publish the best book possible.

Querying takes many forms, including face-to-face discussions, but two of the most common are the cover letter and the marginal note, sometimes combined as a letter with an attached page of specific comments. The letter and note serve two different purposes: The letter discusses general or repeated issues, and the note cites specific instances or passages.

In the cover letter the editor can discuss questions too lengthy or complex to be handled in a marginal note or issues that crop up so frequently that the author may be annoyed if the editor calls her attention to them every time they occur. For example, the authors of a rockhounds' manual made several joking references, from their point of view, to inappropriate clothing worn by women on collecting expeditions ("Tell the little lady to leave her high heels home . . ."). Rather than query each potentially offensive passage in the manuscript, the editor used the cover letter:

> I also think you might rework some passages that readers may find dated and possibly insulting; see checked passages on pages 12, 37, 62, 118, 214, 276–277, and 303.

Here is an excerpt from a masterful letter plus notes written by Saxe Commins, one of the formative editors at Random House, to S. N. Behrman, author of a biography of Max Beerbohm.

> Now, less than twenty-four hours after the arrival of the typescript, I must tell you that you are getting closer and closer in mood and selective detail to the impressionist portrait of Max both of us have in mind. Your own charm and unmistakable style are strikingly apparent on every one of the tentative forty-six pages, and the material is indeed rich if, until now, only suggested.
> I still feel very strongly that it cries for expansion. . . .

It's no favor to you to make so generalized a statement. Unless I can particularize you won't be able to guess what I am driving at. So let me offer for whatever they are worth, page-by-page questions and suggestions, some sensible, some captious, to be accepted or vetoed, but at least a sort of agenda for our summit talks. To begin:

Page 1. It seems to me that much more can be made of Max's and Herbert's background by elaborating on Julius, Constantia, and Eliza, more or less as you did with the forebears of Duveen. . . .

Page 2. Would it be possible to convey a little of the prevailing atmosphere in America, particularly in Chicago, when Tree put on *An Enemy of the People.* . . .

Page 4. Would it be out of place to write in a sentence or two about *The Yellow Book*. It had quite a history. On this page you do give a little of the flavor of the essay, but I think it would profit by a few more comments almost in Max's own vein.

Page 5. The references to Scott Fitzgerald and Ned Sheldon are dangling in midair. Unless you specify some of the similarities I'm afraid the comparison will be lost. And why not more about Aubrey Beardsley?

Page 6–7. The cracks at Pater are too good to miss. They make me want more. The gem-like flame should be blown on a little harder.*

Commins's skill in querying could enhance any editor-author relationship. Most important, he begins by reaffirming his own enthusiasm for the book, a vital factor in encouraging the author and thus in drawing the most from him. It is clear at every point that the editor and author are working for the same goal even if it may take a great deal of time and effort to reach it. The overall tone is one of help and interest. General criticism, which calls for expansion, quickly gives way to specific problems—omissions, repetitions, insufficient information—so the author knows exactly what he has to work on.

Note also how Commins takes advantage of his response as first reader and by extension suggests the response of other readers. Many of his page-by-page comments refer to himself or a reader. This approach not only envisions the manuscript as a finished book or article in the hands of its ultimate audience but also points out manuscript difficulties in a meaningful way. Rather than say to the author, "No one will be able to follow

*Dorothy Commins, *What Is an Editor? Saxe Commins at Work* (Chicago: University of Chicago Press, 1978) pp. 90–91.

argument here," the editor can make the same point by saying, "Am having some trouble following argument here; please give example." The difference is subtle, but by taking some of the burden onto himself, the editor is less condemning and illustrates the reader's need.

Note the detail of Commins's comments. A less attentive and considerate editor might dash off marginal exclamations like "vague," "need more," "anticlimactic"; instead Commins gives the author the reasons and arguments for all his suggestions. This leaves the author very little room to ignore or disagree with them, helping Commins get what he wants. I have seen editors scribble "right?" in the margin next to a questionable passage, with no explanation for the query. This seldom yields the response the editor wants. What if the author answers "yes" and gives no further evidence or authority? Worse yet, what if the author, bothered by the question, answers "no"?

Effective querying elicits the response the editor wants, and he must direct the author to it. After all, if the author has been vague or confused in his first draft, there is no reason to believe that, undirected, he will improve substantially the second time around. Thus the query must be carefully worded. Take, for example, this garbled paragraph:

> In the nineteenth century, tuna was strictly chicken feed. This was
> not true of salmon, which was canned and widely available. One
> year the sardine catch fell short, and a sardine canner hit on the
> idea of putting up tuna. Canned tuna caught on immediately.

If the editor queries marginally "confusing; please clarify," how can he guarantee a less confusing rewording? But what if the editor says, "Hard to follow. Do you mean salmon and sardines were both commonly canned and a sardine canner, lacking sardines and salmon, used tuna? Please add explanatory sentence"? Here the editor has laid the groundwork for the author, and if the author answers the query, the editor will probably get enough information to make the passage comprehensible or, at the least, editable.

· · ·

And so, in the end, we return to the author-editor exchange, that long and rewarding process that results in the best book possible. How much work that takes from the editor depends on what kind of manuscript he has received from the author, but the more effective the editor, the less his work will show, no matter how much he has put into the process.

Editors are not authors, nor do they wish to be. What the best of editors wishes to be is the perceptive, demanding, energetic, and patient prober who can devote his particular talents and skills to the enterprise of working with authors to publish good books.

Line Editing
The Art of the Reasonable Suggestion

John K. Paine

JOHN PAINE *is the senior manuscript editor for the NAL/Dutton wing of Penguin USA.*

Ms. Waxman's goal in line editing is "drawing out the best book possible." John Paine describes some of the most effective techniques and principles he uses as a working manuscript editor to achieve that high purpose in his short but sagacious essay.

Believing line editing to be "the art of the reasonable suggestion," Mr. Paine deems it essential that an editor learn yet another art to make the first one work with maximum effectiveness: "the art of communication." He points out "two features in any editorial note that are paramount in building editor-author rapport. One is that an editor state, continually, what she likes about a work. . . . Second, the language employed should be that of a helpmeet."

Mr. Paine details ways in which a helpful manuscript editor can stimulate "a creative response" in an author. "This is what an editor truly wants, that an author consider a point and fashion her own original response. This is what leads to a better book."

Line Editing
The Art of the Reasonable Suggestion

A line editor performs a useful role as an author's critical first reader. Rare is the manuscript that does not profit from the benign shaping and trimming that hands-on editing provides. On the other hand, even an author eager to please his publisher cannot help but be dismayed when a manuscript returns with page after page of marginal notes, sentences reconfigured, lines crossed out, and—who is this guy?—entirely new words or phrases introduced into a work he had considered finished, pristine. Because of this, a line editor has to learn early on an essential asset: the art of communication.

Before proceeding to the different levels of suggestions a line editor makes, I'd like to point out two features in any editorial note that are paramount in building editor-author rapport. One is that an editor state, continually, what she *likes* about a work. This is essential, for any author is going to be sensitive to criticism, and blast after negative blast raises the specter of the editor as arrogant, know-it-all jerk. Second, the language employed should be that of a helpmeet. My suggestions are rife with such phrases as "it seems," "you may want to consider," "perhaps a better tack is," etc. In this way an author does not feel threatened, leading to a wary but open-minded assessment of the note, which is precisely what an editor desires.

Conveying to an author why his material may be better emended takes various forms. Starting at the broadest level, changes of the sweeping structural variety are often best suggested at lunch or over the phone. This gives the author the chance to toss back and forth possible new avenues for larger-scale revisions. Sometimes an editor decides that writing an overall letter will work better, since the full scope of an idea is often better conveyed when written down. In this sort of letter, general observations of perceived problem areas can be followed by open-ended suggestions of remedies. The word *open-ended* is key here, since an author almost invariably is going to have fresher, more creative solutions than her editor.

A more in-depth approach may be better yet. The fact is, sometimes an editorial letter setting forth general ideas has the effect of leaving the author in the lurch. Yes, now I know what you don't like, but you haven't shown me, really, how to go about making it better. An author may go off in a wholly different direction that does not help the original problem. For this reason, I usually adopt a more detailed approach. Problems discussed in general in a cover letter are then supplemented by notes written on specific ms. pages throughout the manuscript. In this way an author can attack an overall problem step by step—if he so chooses. For instance, let's say a political writer uses too much interview material, to the point that the lengthy quotations swamp the narrative's direction. In this case, a series of editorial notes could point out specific places where interviews could be cut to short excerpts backing up a narrator's summary of a point. In this system the author can still disregard any given suggestion. But at least she has the chance to consider if a detailed suggestion will help a larger problem.

This secondary type of note is useful especially for building stronger characters. Brief suggestions—two to four sentences—are typed at the top or bottom of a manuscript page, with arrows drawn to the specific action that has spurred the note. Weakly drawn characters constitute one of the most common failings of fiction writers, and continual notes from an editor can go a long way toward helping the author face what in fact he wants from a character. Egged on by the sheer number of innocuous suggestions, an author can not only insert new material in these places, but go on to recast a better-rounded figure altogether. Seeing an author fly off on his own wing like this is, of course, an editor's ultimate desire.

Such marginal notes also help in trimming a manuscript. Unfortunately for authors, one of a line editor's primary functions is cutting away deadwood. This area ranges from simple trimming of unnecessary adverbs and adjectives all the way to deletions of entire paragraphs and even pages at a stretch. Obviously, an editor had better be ready to supply cogent explanations for such large-scale action. And if a few sentences in a margin won't be enough, a half- or full-page note can be clipped to the ms. page, explaining why the deleted section is hindering the narrative's drive. One genre in which such block cuts are often made is true crime. Most of these authors are newspaper reporters. Their strength is in gathering information (as in "hunter-gatherer," I'm afraid); their weakness is in composing cohesive, well-constructed chapters, let alone parts or the book as a whole. Whole pages of minutia, often courtroom related, have to be stripped away so that the story of the leading detective, say, or murderer, maintains strong forward momentum. Continual editorial suggestions pointing out the need to concentrate on narrative threads help these authors see the forest for the trees.

Another form of suggestion is helpful in a lesser field of line editing, that of large-scale grammatical work. Early on in a manuscript, a series of long notes can pinpoint specific stylistic deficiencies that will be corrected throughout the book. The note could address the first instance of passive construction, say, or redundancy or excess verbiage—to name several common problems. Taking the length needed to inform the author fully, the editor sets forth the principle(s) of stronger style on which she is acting in making these changes continually. After reading such a prefatory note, the author may not agree to this sort of change in every instance, but at least she understands why it is being repeatedly made. For instance, let's say an author is drawn to using participial phrases rather than indicative verbs. The manuscript reads: "He turned his head, lifting the blackjack from the low shelf and slamming it on the counter." With a note—"See attached page"—I would explain why such construction is weaker than the use of active verbs, the engine of strong prose. The stronger sentence is: "Turning, he lifted the blackjack from the low shelf and slammed it on the counter." This relegates the minor introductory business to its place and stresses the tension of the twin pieces of connected action. Such changes don't have to be made inflexibly in the manuscript, but in this case the author went along with 98 percent of these changes—because the reason why was explained up front.

On an even smaller scale, finally, a common notation that lets the author know why an editor is making emendations concerns word or phrase substitution. Even a careful author can fall into a common trap: words and phrases used too often to describe similar actions and especially emotions. If an editor lightly circles the word at the point he feels it is growing stale and then marks "overused" in the margin, then every time this word is substituted for, the author knows why. If he is sloppy enough to use a distinctive word twice within a given section, two light circles and checks in the margin explain a substitution. As always, the purpose is simply to make the author realize that his editor is not interested in rewriting the book.

If a line editor employs enough communication to assure the author that the criticism raised again and again is meant to help, not belittle, her prose, a creative response is stimulated. This is what an editor truly wants, that an author consider a point and fashion her own original response. This is what leads to a better book.

The Role of the Editorial Assistant

Casey Fuetsch

CASEY FUETSCH *began her career as an assistant to three very patient editors at the Literary Guild. She has since become a senior editor in the trade division at Doubleday, where she has acquired and edited a variety of books, including* When Heaven and Earth Changed Places, A Special Kind of Hero, After the Ball, *and* The Sound of a Miracle. *She works with novelists Valerie Sayers, David James Duncan, and Sarah Bird, among others.*

The answer to the question "What does an editorial assistant do?" is "Everything!" Everything from being first reader of almost all submissions to finding shortcuts through the corporate bureaucratic maze, keeping track of production schedules (and telling the authors about them, too), line editing, locating missing unsigned contracts and misplaced manuscripts, requesting payments for authors, and just about anything else a harried editor might need. In return, a wise editor will train the editorial assistant in the intricacies of building a list until one beautiful day the editorial assistant becomes an associate editor with a list of his or her own.

Wise authors who want to advance their careers should realize that working well with an editorial assistant is just about as important as working with the editorial assistant's boss. "The day I began working for [the editor], seventeen authors called to welcome me. They asked about my background, they said they hoped to meet me soon, and generally they showed me so much respect and consideration that I thought for sure they were mistaking me for someone important. These people were awfully *nice.*

"It took me a day to realize (was it really an entire day?) that these authors knew precisely on which side their proverbial bread was buttered. I wasn't simply working for an editor, I was working with him. My job was an entity unto itself, not merely an appendage of his important title."

From this master-and-apprentice relationship comes the next generation of editors. And, as Ms. Fuetsch says so insightfully: "As apprenticeships go, the one that publishing offers is, perhaps, the last of the great equalizers. Since experience counts for everything, virtually everyone begins at the bottom." Ms. Fuetsch instructs the editorial assistant how to rise from that bottom to the loftiest of publishing heights in an essay rich in wit, charm, and great good sense.

The Role of the Editorial Assistant

Typical of most editors in the book world, I began my career in trade publishing as an editorial assistant. My first boss was a hip, energetic senior editor who acquired books about popular culture and rock 'n' roll. Looking like the industry's equivalent of Pigpen in the *Peanuts* cartoon, he was usually attired in an untucked shirt with a badly knotted tie, and traveled in a cloud of creative enthusiasm, leaving laughter and not a little befuddlement in his wake. While some editors were content with publishing fifteen hardcover titles a year, he wasn't remotely satisfied unless he had thirty on his list. If all thirty books had two authors, a free-lance photo researcher, and a foreword written by a major authority (complete with separate contracts for each), so much the better. His was the "fun" office, where ideas were tossed out like coins to be picked up by any colleague or writer who stopped by to chat.

The day I began working for him, seventeen authors called to welcome me. They asked about my background, they said they hoped to meet me soon, and generally they showed me so much respect and consideration that I thought for sure they were mistaking me for someone important. These people were *awfully nice.*

It took me a day to realize (was it really an entire day?) that these authors knew precisely on which side their proverbial bread was buttered. I wasn't simply working *for* an editor, I was working *with* him. My job was an entity unto itself, not merely an appendage of his important title. I was his reader on almost all submissions, as well as office manager, wending through the bureaucracy for the smooth operation of his mini-empire. This included clearing permissions, keeping track of production schedules (and informing the authors of such), knowing the whereabouts of unsigned contracts, line editing various manuscripts, getting coffee, and requesting payments for authors. To his enormous credit, my boss fetched an equal amount of coffee, acknowledged my accomplishments willingly and openly, and, when an author called screaming about a late payment, he never, ever blamed the delay on my inefficiency. He helped me acquire my own projects, too—a time-consuming effort on his part, a veritable boon to my career.

Over time we discovered where our strengths lay, and we shared the labor to the satisfaction of us both. His passion was for photography books and, hence, he cared deeply about each book's "package," the look of the jacket, the quality of the paper. As a consequence, I learned much about paper and binding, the kind of details that are essential even when publishing a novel. *My* favorite task, however, was line editing, and my boss allowed me to tinker with his writers' prose under his vigilant guidance.

The tradition he was employing, and the one his authors so readily accepted, was that of master and apprentice. As apprenticeships go, the one that publishing offers is, perhaps, the last of the great equalizers. Since experience counts for everything, virtually everyone begins at the bottom. The number of university degrees earned, the names of the colleges bestowing the degrees, and the extent of world travels or family lineage are only as valuable as they are applicable to the job at hand. Exactly how much responsibility is given an editorial assistant depends heavily on the talents and experience of the assistant, on the work load and temperament of the supervising editor, and on a particular house's attitude toward grooming its employees for the future. Few entrants into publishing—fresh out of school, idealism intact—aspire to spend their days transcribing their boss's editorial letters to, say, Joan Didion. Most would prefer asking Joan themselves whether nausea is an apt symbol for urban angst. But in order to rise to the level of lofty literary conversation over lunch at the Four Seasons (a common myth among the idealists), an assistant must log a lot of hours at the Xerox machine.

The assistants who make the rise successfully to editor are the ones who make the most of their early working years. As parents always say when the chore seems too tedious to bear, "It's a learning experience." Even a duty as simple as calling the inventory department to obtain sales figures can enhance an assistant's knowledge, especially if the inventory controller says something like, "Of course we shipped a lot of copies last week; it was Father's Day. Too bad Mother's Day doesn't sell books." Bits of information that seem inconsequential one moment may be precious later on, when the assistant becomes an editor and the pub date of the new Tom Clancy novel is being decided.

Authors who enjoy the happiest publishing experience are those who fully realize just how much an editorial assistant can help them. Authors should simply ask the editor and the assistant which of the two handles what domain, and take advantage of the fresh energy coming from two sources. The result, for editors and their assistants, is a dynamic division of labor. An editor must spend an inordinate amount of time acquiring and editing the manuscript and ensuring the proper attention from the publicity, sales, and marketing departments. Assistants . . . well, they handle everything else. One of their chief jobs is to "traffic." It is the assistant who knows the exact location of a contract, manuscript, or schedule at a given moment. Will the author be trekking in Nepal at the time the galleys need reading? The assistant will work with the production department to change the galley date. Did the author just receive a fabulous letter from Fay Weldon containing quotable raves about his new novel? The assistant can call the art director and stop work on the jacket before the editor returns from lunch. Later, the three can decide the blurb's best placement.

An assistant is ordinarily the first reader on any project that arrives in the editor's office. The arrangements vary, but it's not unusual for a manuscript to appear on the editor's desk with the reader's report already attached. This concept scares some first-time writers. Surely, the writer says to himself, the value of my lyrical prose cannot be appreciated by a lowly *assistant*. But remember the theory of the apprentice. The assistant may turn out to be a former Rhodes scholar (great appreciators, traditionally, of lyrical prose) and, in any case, will already have a pretty good idea of what "publishable" means. Also, this is where an agent comes in, calling an advance warning to assistants and editors to pay close attention to a particular novel or nonfiction proposal. Even without an agent's call, however, the better manuscripts will catch an assistant's eye. A great many submissions fall below the mediocre range, or deal with a subject that is not germane to the editor's area of expertise. The assistant separates the bland efforts from the stellar, sometimes dispensing submissions to appropriate colleagues, thus leaving the editor time to consider carefully the best new manuscripts and work on the books already under contract.

Even so, sometimes the novice writer's fears may haunt conscientious assistants. The assistants begin to have nightmares of overlooking the next Pulitzer Prize-winning best-seller, so they knock themselves out reading every page of every bad novel. And then the nightmares really begin, because the same attention can't, and shouldn't, be given to each manuscript. Ironically, the same writers who were worried about having their manuscripts declined by an assistant may be the ones—once their books are under contract—who are unappreciative of the long weekend and night-time reading hours the editor and assistant spend discovering the quality books.

Most writers, however, are respectful of an assistant's job, and it's to both their benefits. Assistants are part of the reading public whose opinions about a particular character or plot line may be invaluable. A writer need not accede to every suggestion given by an early reader of the work, but a measure of consideration is imperative. An editor, in a headlong rush to sign up a new novel, or see a controversial book to a timely publication, might overlook lapses in a narrative voice or weak points in a thesis. The assistant, however, buffered from direct pressure by a publisher or agent, is in a unique position to see where the emperor lacks the appropriate clothes.

An assistant can be the second strongest supporter a book has in-house. An editor's job is to thrust the book into the best possible light against the seemingly dark, cold world of the video-watching public. But between the time the editor demands four-color bound galleys and the author flies off on her sixteen-city tour, smaller, significant events may involve an editorial assistant. Recently, a free-lance reviewer called my office to request a catalog. Answering the phone, my assistant buoyantly lauded a novel we'd been editing. The reviewer was so taken by my assistant's excitement that she placed the book on her "must review" list and, in turn, called a movie producer friend to tell *her* about the novel. Time will tell whether the phone call amounts to a great review or a lucrative movie deal, but the anticipatory "buzz" has begun. And in the meantime, my assistant has established two new contacts of her own.

Every relationship in publishing, be it writer-editor, editor-assistant, or writer-assistant, is similar to a marriage: the parties come together for a common good, with all hopes resting upon the honeymoon lasting a lifetime. As marriages go, these are passionate unions. The book is, after all, a writer's creative baby. It is the book—the third, ever-present, all-important entity in each partnership—that must be championed and somehow made better by every move.

Everyone's career (indeed, everyone's day-to-day experience) can be made more pleasurable by healthy exploitation and large doses of compassion. Assistants are miserably underpaid for the number of hours they spend working. One of their chief joys is talking with an appreciative writer—an author who respects their opinion of the book; an author who understands that assistants won't always have the answers at their fingertips but will do their best to find it; an author who acknowledges that he or she is one of many professionals whom the assistant and editor must work with daily.

It helps, too, for an assistant to be reminded, in quiet, friendly conversations with the editor and authors, that a certain book took five long and torturous years in the writing; that the writer may become anxious and temperamental as the book nears its publication date; that an assistant's job can, eventually, come to a happy conclusion.

The conclusion, of course, is the promotion to associate editor. The associate editor is no longer responsible for typing other people's correspondence or answering a boss's phone. He or she can buy books and shepherd them through publication with a certain degree of autonomy. Although a promotion is terrific public recognition for hard work and talent, it shouldn't be a jarring move. It's a gratifying opportunity to shed annoying duties and take on full responsibility for a vocation the assistant has practiced for years. Suddenly, writers may find that the helpful assistant of yesterday is now their editor. And associate editors discover that they did not slave away for naught: they are now on the receiving end of worthwhile submissions from agents and authors who long ago became their admirers.

With experience comes confidence, and confidence allows publishing neophytes and novice writers to finally displace an oft-held but inaccurate assumption: that there exists a huge literary "club" to which everyone who is anyone should aspire to belong. The encouraging reality is that the imaginary club is only the figment of an outsider's insecurities. Genuine efforts to praise good work, encourage talent, and care about another's well-being—no matter what end of the business you're on; no matter what a person's title is—will always foreshadow a long and fruitful career.

Working with a Free-Lance Editor or Book Doctor

Gerald (Jerry) Gross

JERRY GROSS (as he is known in the publishing industry) graduated the City College of New York in 1953 and began his publishing career in that same year at Simon & Schuster as Henry Simon's first reader. During his years as a paperback and hardcover fiction and nonfiction editor, he created the gothic romance and gothic mystery as mass-market paperback categories and edited Publishers on Publishing *(1961) and* Editors on Editing *(1962 and 1985). In 1987 he became a partner in Gross Associates. From his home in Croton-on-Hudson, New York, he has worked as a fiction and nonfiction free-lance editor/book doctor with authors both published and unpublished, agented and unagented, and with publishers' editors. When he is not editing or critiquing manuscripts, Mr. Gross gives workshops on various aspects of editing and publishing at writers' conferences around the United States.*

When should a writer consult a free-lance editor or book doctor? What can a book doctor really do for an ailing manuscript? Why has the book doctor become an increasingly important editor for author, agent, and publisher? When would a publisher's editor assign a manuscript to be edited by a free-lance editor or critiqued by a book doctor? How can a writer choose and work effectively with a reputable book doctor? Mr. Gross provides practical, realistic answers to these important questions in this comprehensive look at today's new breed of editor—the book doctor—whose skills could help you improve your manuscript and possibly save your career.

Working with a Free-Lance
Editor or Book Doctor

1

Working with a first-rate book doctor can be a creative and rewarding
career experience. A talented book doctor can stir and free your imagination, enabling you to look at your manuscript in a fresh and original way.
Following a book doctor's advice on structure, characterization, dialogue,
plotting, and organization of material can increase your mastery of fiction
and nonfiction techniques, not only for the project you're currently working
on, but for other works to come. But, as with choosing a physician, it's
important to find and select a reputable, experienced one and to establish
a good rapport in your working, professional relationship. It's essential to
understand that the editor-author relationship should be collegial, not adversarial, symbiotic, not parasitic. Writer and editor must respect each
other's talents, values, and goals.

Book doctors are free-lance editors highly skilled in analyzing the problems presented by a manuscript or a proposal and offering solutions to
those problems. These solutions are usually presented in a lengthy, in-depth
report to the client (author, agent, or publisher's editor) that should also
serve as a guide to rethinking and revising the manuscript. These critiques
often run from fifteen to thirty pages or more in length, depending on the
size of the manuscript, the number of problems in the manuscript, and the
insight and skill of the book doctor in solving those problems. Many book
doctors also critique a manuscript line by line and make recommendations
for revision in terms of adding or deleting sections; improving pacing,
plotting, ambiance, characterizations, motivations, and dialogue; supplying
line editing, etc., etc.

Some book doctors, however, begin the editor-client relationship by first
skimming the manuscript to get a sense of it and whatever problems it might
pose, and then calling the client or writing a short note outlining what the
editor believes has to be done to the manuscript to make it more effective.
After the client responds to the editor's recommendations in a follow-up
phone call or note, the book doctor begins the detailed critiquing of the
manuscript. My own feeling is that both book doctor and client are best

served by the former approach—the editor beginning the author-editor relationship by writing a detailed report. The latter approach, a more cursory preliminary reading of the manuscript, risks the possibility of misunderstandings developing between editor and client as to how the manuscript should be revised or edited. The editor could critique the entire manuscript only to discover that the client didn't like his or her approach. This kind of situation often results in the client not paying the editor because of dissatisfaction with the editor's work, and the editor having to take the client to court to be paid his fee.

Many book doctors—myself included—do not do any line editing until the client receives the detailed critique of the manuscript (containing, as I have said, suggestions for line editing) and approves the editorial approach the book doctor wants to take with the manuscript. In point of fact, the suggestions for line editing in a comprehensive, well-written and -organized critique are often so clear that the author can do the line editing, or effect any other of the editor's recommendations, *without* the book doctor's help. In any case, line editing a manuscript should always come *after* the developmental editing (the heart of the critique) is completed and approved by the client. (The actual line editing, revising, restructuring, etc., by the way, are separate editorial services and are not covered by the fee paid by the client to the book doctor to critique the manuscript.)

In some situations, book doctors work from a detailed critique written by the *client* that instructs the editor to do exactly what the client wants done. The editor is not asked for any suggestions or recommendations; he or she is paid only to follow the client's instructions. In this arrangement, clearly the client loses the benefit of the editor's expertise by not soliciting the book doctor's help. And the book doctor's creative talents are frustrated and wasted. The editor can and should be much more than a red or blue pencil for hire, but sometimes that's all that's wanted or needed by the client. Both parties are shortchanged in this kind of arrangement.

Further services a book doctor may offer might include collaborating and even ghostwriting. But if you hire a book doctor for these services, make sure that the editor is also a writer: not every editor is. Editing is very creative, but not in the same way that writing is. The editor's creativity comes from exercising his or her critical faculties. The writer's creativity comes from the exercise of his or her imagination. The two don't always function with equal effectiveness in the same person.

. . .

It is important that client and book doctor know what is expected of each other *before* the actual editing begins.

Most book doctors work on all types of fiction and nonfiction but some edit only fiction, others only nonfiction. Others specialize in specific genres: mystery, self-help, romance, science fiction, espionage, etc. Learn your book doctor's areas of expertise *before* you hire him or her to critique and/or edit your manuscript.

You may want to hire a book doctor for any number of reasons and at various stages of the manuscript—from working on the theme of the project, through the creation, development, and critiquing of a proposal to present to an editor or agent, through completion of the manuscript and even, in some instances, after it has been accepted by a publisher's editor.

If you're a nonfiction writer, a book doctor could help you create your proposal, or critique it *before* you send it to an editor or agent. A proposal is really an "interview" with a prospective editor or agent and so you want to make sure that what you have to sell is in the best possible shape in terms of readability, organization of material, clarity, effectiveness, targeting of the potential audience, and salability. If you've already submitted your proposal to an agent or an editor, he or she might suggest consulting a book doctor to improve it before either taking it on or presenting it at the editorial meeting.

If you're a fiction writer, a book doctor's critique of your novel can offer you a new way of looking at your work. In this way, you can rethink, revise, and rewrite it to put it in the best possible shape before your try to get an agent to represent you or an editor to bring it before the editorial board of the publishing house. If there are specific areas you feel unsure about—dialogue, or pacing, or characterization, or plotting—be sure to ask the book doctor to give special emphasis to these aspects of the novel in the critique.

An agent interested in your work might advise you to work with a book doctor before the manuscript is sent out to potential acquiring editors. The agent makes the referral; you make your own financial arrangement with the book doctor. The agent also realizes that the manuscript is an interview, and that the first impression it makes can be the difference between the editor wanting to take the book and rejecting it. Realizing how pressured for time the editor is, the agent wants to present the editor with a manuscript that requires little or no editing. If an editor perceives your manuscript to be riddled with problems that will take a great deal of editorial time to solve, it will be difficult for the agent to make the sale. As a result, book doctors have become pre-editors, working on the manuscript to make it as effective as possible even before it is seen by the first acquisition editor.

A book doctor can be valuable if you or your agent finds that the manuscript keeps being rejected but that there's no consistency in the reasons for the rejections: some editors loved the plot but hated the charac-

ters; others hated the plot but loved the characters. Some thought the style mannered and overripe; however, several thought the style was too minimalist, too spare. Most editors don't go into much detail about why they reject a book or offer suggestions about how to improve it: they just don't have the time to do so. Also, editors must be very aware of the types of books their house can or cannot sell. Not every publisher can sell every type of fiction and nonfiction book. Accordingly, an editor will often decline work saying that it's not right for _____ (fill in the name of the publisher for whom the editor works). What the book doctor provides is constructive, objective editorial advice from a skilled editor who will take the time to offer a specific "cure" for the ailing manuscript. Being a freelancer, concerned only with critiquing the manuscript at hand, the book doctor does not have to worry about whether a particular publisher could or could not sell it. It's like having the uninterrupted attention of a private doctor as opposed to taking your chances with whatever doctor is available to treat you at a clinic.

Sometimes, too, your book keeps getting rejected for the same reason but you're too close to the manuscript to know how to fix it. A book doctor will have the objectivity to evaluate the book with a fresh perspective and be able to advise you on how to rewrite to eliminate the features of the book that the editors found unacceptable.

Frequently an agent or editor will tell you that your manuscript needs to be cut or line edited or restructured and you don't want to do it or can't do it. Here again the book doctor can do the work that, psychologically or emotionally, you are not able to handle yourself. Many authors don't have a realistic perspective on their manuscript once they've completed it: the process has been too demanding and/or draining. And it can be almost physically painful—in addition to being intellectually and aesthetically impossible—to cut one's manuscript or undertake a radical revision and restructuring of its contents.

Even when a manuscript has been accepted by an editor, authors hire book doctors for a number of reasons. Many editors are mandated just to acquire books; they have an acquisition quota to meet. They just don't have the time to work with the author—either in the developmental or, later on, in the line-editing stage. Sometimes they don't have the experience either: they haven't been trained in the arts of developmental and/or line editing. They are skilled in going after authors, coming up with ideas for books, and intuiting what will sell to what audience and what the size of that audience is, but they don't know how to work with the author to shape the book and line edit it when it comes in. Instead, the manuscript often goes directly to the copy editor, who is an extremely valuable, important, and skilled editor in his or her own right but is not trained to shape and line edit a manuscript.

As a result, authors sometimes don't get the editorial care and attention from editors that they feel they need and deserve. In such a situation, a free-lance editor, a book doctor, is called in by an author who wants to make sure that his or her manuscript is sent to the copy editor in the best shape possible. Good (or bad) editing can affect the critical reception and sales of the book.

Under certain situations, even a highly skilled editor will call in a book doctor. Sometimes, because of contractual stipulations, a manuscript must be published by a certain time. But if the editor cannot meet the deadline, a free-lance editor is hired to prevent the publisher from being in default of contract and thereby open to legal action instituted by the author. Sometimes, too, an in-house editor, who often works on as many as twenty books a year, is just plain overwhelmed by several manuscripts coming in at once and hires a free-lance editor to ease the burden.

A publisher's editor might hire a book doctor when he or she is not happy with a manuscript that has been turned in. The book doctor might be hired to work with the author to improve the manuscript so that the editor will accept it for publication. Sometimes the book doctor's fee is paid all or in part by the publisher; sometimes the fee is taken out of the second half of the advance, which is owed the author upon acceptance of the manuscript. The alternative is drastic: the editor rejects the manuscript and the author not only does not get the second half of the advance but has to pay back the first half. In such a situation, it's clear that all parties—editor, agent, and author—will want an outside editor to save the manuscript from being rejected. After all, everyone wants the book to be published: the author so that the rest of the advance is paid, the agent so that the commission is received, and the editor so that the book gets on the list to fulfill his commitment to author and publisher and create a revenue-generating project for all concerned. Sometimes, though, it takes an outsider—the book doctor—to make it all happen because everyone concerned is too close to the project and relations among all parties may have soured to the point of damaging feelings, reputations, future relationships and, last but certainly not least, the project itself. Indeed, sometimes a book doctor is hired because tensions and hostilities are so great that agent, editor, and author are not returning each other's calls and the project is at a total impasse. The book doctor comes in and takes over the project, under the supervision of the editor, and works with the author and the agent until the manuscript has been revised and edited to everyone's satisfaction.

Finally, a publisher's editor sometimes reads a manuscript once too often. It loses its freshness, its purpose on the list. The editor wonders why it was bought in the first place, and for what audience, but knows it needs work: perhaps a new opening or a new ending or a reorganization of the material or a deletion of maybe fifty or sixty pages (but where?!). The editor also knows that he or she has become jaded with the manuscript and doesn't know how to regain enthusiasm for it. Or what's lost is a clear idea of how to fix what's wrong, or even of what needs fixing. And so the editor turns to a skilled outside editor—a book doctor—to critique the manuscript and come up with a fresh perspective on the book, ideas on what the editor could and should do to make it effective and salable.

2

Now that you know what a book doctor does, how do you find, choose, and work with one once you decide you need that kind of editorial help?

To find a book doctor, solicit the opinions of any authors, friends in publishing, or agents or editors you might know. Talk to people you meet in writing classes or at writers' conferences. Write to the National Writers Union or the Editorial Freelancers Association. They publish directories of their members, listing their specific skills. You'll find the addresses of these organizations in *Literary Market Place* (LMP), which can be found at the reference desk of most libraries in the United States. *Literary Market Place* also lists the names and addresses and services of editorial consultants throughout the country.

Before you hire a book doctor, ask to see one or more of the editor's critiques of a work in a genre or on a theme as close to what you have written as possible. These reports should be comprehensive and should not only point out what's wrong with the manuscript but offer solutions to right those wrongs. You may not agree with the book doctor's approach in these critiques, but you will at least get a sense of the quality of the critique and whether it is the kind of critique that you will find valuable in improving your own work.

Ask for a résumé of the editor's career history, the names of books acquired and edited that are close to your own in theme, and a list of colleagues and authors the editor has worked with to serve as references. By all means, check those references: talk to the book doctor's previous clients to learn if he or she is diligent, creative, qualified, and easy to work with.

If you want a book doctor to line edit, cut, revise, or rewrite, commission a report that will show how the editor would perform these services. The two of you should agree on the thrust of the editing and the content of the final, edited manuscript before the editor begins work. So wait until you have read and discussed the report before you hire the editor to actually work *on* the manuscript. You probably won't agree with every one of the editor's recommendations, but you should feel comfortable with most of what he suggests needs doing; otherwise, don't go ahead and ask that the work be done. Naturally you are obliged to pay the editor for the report whether or not you hire him or her to do the work: after all, time has been spent in reading the manuscript and writing the report.

Before any editorial work is begun on the manuscript, there should be a fully executed letter of agreement between you and your book doctor itemizing what services the book doctor will provide, the delivery date of the services, and how the fee will be paid. The usual method of payment is one-half of the agreed-upon fee on signing the agreement and one-half when the critique is completed and sent to you, along with the manuscript. Do not ask a book doctor to work on spec, agreeing to pay for the report only if the manuscript is taken by a publisher. (Would you ask your medical doctor to treat you on spec, expecting payment for care only if he or she makes you healthy again?)

Book doctors should not reveal the names of their clients unless they have given permission for their names to be used. Generally speaking, if you receive a sample critique, the name of the author should be inked out so that it is unreadable. Book doctor–author confidentiality and privacy should be adhered to as strictly as is confidentiality between medical doctor and patient.

Determine in advance if the editorial work you are contracting for will be done by the highly experienced editor you contacted and who signed the letter of agreement, or whether it will be turned over to an editor with less experience who works with or for the more experienced editor. If it is understood that the manuscript will be turned over to a less experienced editor, the fee should be less than that paid to the senior person.

Beware a book doctor who guarantees that if you work with him or her, an agent will take you on as a client and an editor will buy your manuscript. No free-lance editor can make that promise—not even the most successful book doctors in the country. No agent will take on a writer on the book doctor's say-so, and no publisher's editor will buy a manuscript because the free-lance editor tells him to. These grandiose promises are as unethical as a medical doctor's guarantee that he will cure you of whatever is making you sick. So if you get this kind of pitch from a book doctor, don't fall for it. Just look elsewhere for some honest, ethical editorial help.

Naturally, anyone who has read this far wants to know what it costs to hire a book doctor. Well, as in everything else in life, you get what you pay for. Consulting with a young doctor just out of medical school won't cost anywhere near as much as seeing a brilliant physician of mature years, great prestige, and accomplishment. Accordingly, the fee charged by a relatively young editor is far less than the fee charged by a book doctor with many years of experience and expertise.

Broadly speaking, though, the cost of a twenty- to thirty-five-page critique of a four-hundred-page, double-spaced manuscript can range from as little as $600 to as much as $2,500. Hiring a book doctor to line edit, cut, or revise a manuscript or a proposal can cost between $35 and $150 per hour. Some book doctors take less of a fee up front for their critiquing and editorial services but take a percentage of the book's advance and royalties when and if it is sold. Fees and percentages should be discussed in great detail, and be clearly understood by both parties, before the letter of agreement is sent to the client. Avoid phrases like "fee to be mutually agreed upon." Work on the manuscript should not begin until that letter of agreement is signed by both parties—author and editor—and at least a portion of the critiquing fee is paid to the editor.

Fees for the creation and development of a book proposal vary according to the extent of the book doctor's participation: How much of the idea for the book came from the book doctor? How much of the writing and organization of material will be done by the author and how much by the editor? Will the book doctor be critiquing an already written proposal or creating one from conversations with the author and some rough notes?

Hiring a free-lance editor as a collaborator or ghostwriter involves not only a fee for the editor's services but also agreeing on the percentage of the advance and royalties the editor will receive if the book is sold. Depending on the extent of the editor's participation in the project, the percentage received by the book doctor could vary anywhere from 25 to 50 percent of the advance and royalties earned by the book.

A final caveat: A talented, creative book doctor can help your work achieve critical and commercial success. An ineffective, unimaginative book doctor can be hazardous to your creativity. Take as much care in choosing a doctor for your manuscript as you would a doctor for your body. The life of your career may be at stake!

Editing True Crime

Charles Spicer

CHARLES SPICER *is a senior editor at St. Martin's Press, where he edits both fiction and nonfiction. In addition, he heads the True Crime Library imprint of St. Martin's Paperbacks and was the editor of* Unanswered Cries *by Thomas French,* Beyond Reason *and* Murder in Boston *by Ken Englade, as well as* Sudden Fury *by Leslie Walker and* The Milwaukee Murders *by Don Davis, both* New York Times *best-sellers.*

"There are all sorts of theories about why people buy true crime," but Mr. Spicer contends that "the real reason people are so eager to buy true crime books is that, in the best of them, the reader is guaranteed a terrific story. And story, with all its elements of character, plot, setting, texture, and resolution, is what I look for when I sign up a book."

Defining the difference between two basic types of true crime books, "gut" ("books that affect us at a very primal level") and "glamour" ("books . . . set in the world of the rich or celebrated [that] usually involve a fall from status"), Mr. Spicer then discusses the editorial elements each type needs to make it successful.

Despite predictions of the imminent death by overproduction of true crime as a genre, Mr. Spicer takes heart from the fact that "as long as wives and husbands gleefully kill each other off, and parents and children merrily rub one another out, there will be someone to write about it and someone to read what they write. True crime is here to stay. And for the right writer, true crime can certainly pay!"

Editing True Crime

The *New York Times Book Review* recently called true crime "currently the hottest genre in publishing." Perhaps it is, but it is certainly not the newest genre. True crime has been around since Cain killed Abel and the Bible gave us a bird's-eye view of *that* family's problems. Even its current vogue status can be traced back at least to the sixties, with Truman Capote's *In Cold Blood* (Random House, 1966). Recently there has been an explosion of popularity, particularly in the paperback market. Best-seller lists reflect it with reprints of well-known hardcover books being joined by instant books published sometimes within weeks of a highly publicized case.

There are all sorts of theories about why people buy true crime and certainly there seems to be a voyeuristic element, a kind of morbid fascination with the dark side of human nature. These books permit the average reader to peer into the mind of a psychopath, to look into a world where murder really does happen, without ever leaving the safety provided between the covers of a book. But I still contend that the real reason people are so eager to buy true crime books is that, in the best of them, the reader is guaranteed a terrific story. And story, with all its elements of character, plot, setting, texture, and resolution, is what I look for when I sign up a book.

Frequently I receive news clippings of particularly horrific crimes from aspiring writers with the question, "Wouldn't this make a great book?" And, just as frequently, my answer is, "No." There is a world of difference between a crime that makes a shocking news story and one that makes an exciting book. At the risk of sounding callous, I might be the first to pick up a *New York Post* cover about a man who loses his job, shoots his boss and then himself, but I doubt that I'd want to read 360 pages about it. Now, give me a tale about a beautiful woman who carefully plots the death of her own babies to earn the love of the man with whom she's sexually obsessed, and you'll bring a smile to my face. Reading *that* book will be a weekend editorially well spent!

Okay, the bare facts of the second story are compelling, but there is another, perhaps more important element that makes a successful book—the *telling* of the story. It takes a writer with a novelist's ability to reveal character and create suspense to make a true crime story really take off. It is a big mistake to assume that any reporter, given access to the facts in a case, can deliver a good book. Chilling as it is to contemplate, there are other women besides Diane Downs who have been accused of murdering their own children (remember Alice Crimmins?), but it's because Ann Rule is such a masterful storyteller that *Small Sacrifices* is such a riveting book.

What do I look for in a story? A colleague of mine came up with an excellent description of *types* of true crime books: she calls them "gut" versus "glamour," and by "gut" she does *not* mean more gore! Rather, there are books that affect us at a very primal level: in *Small Sacrifices* (NAL, 1987), a mother kills her children; in *Sudden Fury* (St. Martin's, 1989), an adopted child stabs the couple who gave him a home. We are shocked and deeply disturbed. A mother's love for her children is sacrosanct; the gratitude of an adopted child to those who have rescued him is assumed. And yet the world isn't working as it should and, as readers, we find ourselves profoundly unsettled by the experience of reading about it.

Glamour crime books are set in the world of the rich or celebrated and usually involve a fall from status: in Tommy Thompson's *Blood and Money* (Doubleday, 1976) and William Wright's *The Von Bulow Affair* (Delacorte, 1983), wealthy, privileged husbands are brought to trial for allegedly murdering—or trying to murder—their beautiful, rich wives. The husband's fall is evident as he is dragged into a crowded courtroom, and the victims themselves have suffered the ultimate fall. There's a titillation as the reader is allowed into the halls of the rich and a smug satisfaction at seeing their lives come a cropper. "So the life of the rich is not that great after all!" The glamour ones are my favorites; many is the time I've closed a book after turning the last page, awash in a warm feeling of smug self-satisfaction.

Character is every bit as important in a true crime book as it is in a novel. And, again, the actual story may involve fascinating people, but unless the writer knows how to reveal character, the book will fail. There are heroes, villains, and victims, and each has a crucial role to play, but my own favorites are villains—and the kinkier the better!

Frances Schreuder, the scheming socialite murderess of Shana Alexander's *Nutcracker* (Doubleday, 1985) and Jonathan Coleman's *At Mother's Request* (Atheneum, 1985), is delightfully appalling. What could be worse than a mother who kills her own children? How about a mother who blackmails her own child into killing her own father? And neither Alexander nor Coleman is content merely with *telling* us what a horror Mrs. Schreuder is; they *show* us. And if God is in the details, so is the Devil, because we learn that this pretentious, social-climbing dragoness, so concerned with public appearance, has filthy personal hygiene habits. This woman, who claimed to be a loving mother, ambitious only for her children, was emotionally sadistic, and the authors let her speak for herself as she cruelly abuses her young daughter, a dance student. Character is so important to this story because the catharsis comes at the end with our knowledge that Frances Schreuder will pay for her sins. *Beyond Reason* by

Ken Englade (St. Martin's, 1990) successfully depicts the villainess as a study in contradictions. Englade contrasts the prim, extraordinarily intelligent, boarding school–educated Elizabeth Haysom with the grotesquely spoiled, vindictive girl who helps plan the vicious murder of her own parents. Something is wrong with this picture and we want to know more.

Are there no heroes anymore? Of course there are. In *Small Sacrifices,* Fred Hugi, one of the men who helped put Diane Downs behind bars, is raising two of her surviving children. Unlike the villains, the hero usually achieves his status by dogged determination rather than one showstopper of an act, and the writer's challenge is to make his or her struggle compelling and moving. For me, Joe McGinniss, the author of the classic *Fatal Vision* (Putnam, 1983), turns Freddy Kassab, the stepfather of the murdered Collette MacDonald, into a memorable hero and character. How? By making the reader experience Kassab's anguish as he begins to suspect that the son-in-law he has trusted just may be the monster who destroyed his stepdaughter and grandchildren. By making Kassab a figure with whom we all can identify, the author lets us empathize with Kassab as he begins to think the unthinkable. McGinniss's formidable talent as a writer enables us to enter into the story, rather than just hear the facts.

What about the poor victim? In many ways this role is the pivotal one because, unless the writer can make us care about the victim or find him or her intriguing, why read the book? Again, in *Blind Faith* (Putnam, 1989) Joe McGinniss demonstrates why his books are so unusually successful. It is exactly because Maria Marshall was such a devoted mother and wife, a woman who believed so completely in her role as both, that her death at the hands of her husband's hired killer is so bitterly ironic and emotionally stirring. In the early part of the book, McGinniss takes us into her home to watch her prepare pancakes for her all-American sons, and later we see her attend their sporting events with such happy enthusiasm. She takes such joy in them and they so warmly return her love that later, when they discover that it is their father who has taken her from them and had her murdered brutally, we want to rip him to shreds. In Thomas French's *Unanswered Cries* (St. Martin's, 1991), the victim, Karen Gregory, has already been killed when the book opens. It is a testimony to French's ability as a writer that he makes her so real to us through the carefully selected and presented memories of her friends that by the story's end, she dominates the book. And her haunting absence is almost as achingly painful to us as to her friends.

What do I look for in addition to characterization? Every mystery buff knows that a good investigation is essential, and in true crime, it has the advantage of being real and authentically portrayed. Here is the place for a writer to include what happens when detectives arrive at a crime scene, to explain the fascinating complexities of forensic science and its vital role in proving guilt, to take the reader inside a police task force and show how each person plays a role, to make interesting to readers the grueling legwork that goes into tracking a killer. Of course, it helps if luck plays a role. In *Beyond Reason,* Ken Englade places the reader with the Virginia detectives as they close in on the beautiful Elizabeth and her bizarre lover only to lose them when they flee to England and disappear without a trace. Months later, Englade places us inside an English department store as a young couple is arrested for shoplifting. Smelling something bigger at stake, the British detectives soon discover false identity papers and a connection is made that gives the investigation section of the book real suspense and drama.

Again, it's the author who must judiciously pick and choose the high-lights from mountains of material and then weave them into a riveting story. Anyone who has ever listened to hours of testimony from a medical examiner knows how deadly boring it can be, and the author who tran-scribes it word for word is not telling a story—he's recording. Like a mystery writer, the true crime writer may decide for himself when and how to reveal a piece of information to the reader—even though the writer presumably knows it all before beginning the book. Here's one hypothetical example of how to create tension: "As Detective Smith studied the blood spatters on the wall, a pattern began to emerge and suddenly he understood what happened that terrible night. But, he wondered, could he prove it?" He doesn't tell us what he has discovered—yet. The reader is kept hanging, giving the writer the opportunity to introduce red herrings, keep his audi-ence guessing and suspense churning. How much more interesting than, "As Detective Smith studied the blood spatters on the wall, he realized that John Jones had committed the murder because . . ." And this in the first quarter of the book!

Setting and a sense of place add immeasurably to the texture of any story, but particularly to a true crime book. In McGinniss's *Blind Faith,* the town of Toms River, New Jersey, is described with such clarity (its geography, appearance, and mores), that it assumes the impact of a character; so does the Kansas town in which the Clutter family is murdered in Truman Capote's *In Cold Blood*; Tommy Thompson's *Blood and Money* is almost as much a book about Texas and Texans as it is about Joan Robinson Hill.

A true crime writer is well advised to take a crash course in libel and publishing law. All true crime books are legally vetted at considerable legal expense and time, both of which can be avoided if the author is aware of the kind of documentation needed and knows how to word material to avoid suits and the threat of suits.

A trial, by its very nature, makes a wonderful crucible in which character and plot combine in an explosion of drama, yet it takes a skilled writer to *make* it dramatic. Nothing makes me put down a true crime manuscript faster than coming across endless pages of trial transcripts; if it were transcripts the true crime reader was looking for, we could simply publish the court records and it would be one very dry book. I want to feel as though I'm inside the courtroom as the prosecutor and defense attorney battle it out like gladiators in a Roman arena. Bryna Taubman, in her book *The Preppy Murder Trial* (St. Martin's, 1988), about the Robert Chambers case, re-creates the war of nerves between two brilliant lawyers, Jack Littman and Linda Fairstein. While they spar, the life of a young man hangs in the balance—as well as justice for the killer of a vital young woman. A writer needs to make the reader feel the roller coaster ride of emotion as sympathy swings back and forth, as the families of both victim and accused killer—not to mention the actual defendant—react to events in the courtroom. It is the point toward which most true crime books build and it should be—must be—powerful.

So where's the payoff, where's my reward for reading 360 pages? In an age when true crime books are frequently contracted for before the trial even starts, it's hard to guarantee that payoff. Although it's possible to do a book where the accused is acquitted, it is not as satisfying if the real killer isn't arrested by the book's conclusion. (It's like a mystery without an end.) Clearly, unlike the novelist, the true crime author is helpless in the face of real events, but I usually look for cases in which a guilty verdict seems likely.

What is the future of true crime as a genre? Writers, editors, and publishers have been predicting its demise from the moment this newest wave of popularity hit, and it is probably true that the marketplace will not sustain the number of titles now being published. The weaker books, poorly written accounts of less than fascinating cases, will fail no matter how well packaged. The genuinely good books will rise to the top. But one thing is sure: as long as wives and husbands gleefully kill each other off, and parents and children merrily rub one another out, there will be someone to write about it and someone to read what they write. True crime is here to stay. And for the right writer, true crime can certainly pay!

Editing Crime Fiction

Ruth Cavin

RUTH CAVIN was a writer and a free-lance editor before she joined the staff of Walker & Company in 1979. The house was known for its mysteries, all of them U.S. editions of British books. Cavin began to acquire a number of American authors' works, and bought the first crime novels of, among others, Bill Crider, Aaron Elkins, and Jeremiah Healy. Crime fiction became her specialty, and in 1988 (when she moved to her present position at St. Martin's Press) she was honored by the Mystery Writers of America with the Ellery Queen Award for contributions to the genre.

"No one can give you a formula for writing a good crime novel—and it wouldn't be a good novel if one could," says Ms. Cavin in her informed and informative essay. "Good crime fiction is good fiction with a crime at its center. I use the phrase 'crime fiction' rather than 'mystery fiction' or 'mysteries' because the first phrase allows the inclusion of works that one way or another go beyond the strict limits of the whodunit. But whatever you call it, the day of the pure puzzle with cookie-cutter characters is gone."

Once Ms. Cavin buys the novel, her work with the author begins, and that work can range from just asking the author "to answer a few queries and straighten out a confusing sentence," all the way to suggestions for "rewriting several episodes, rethinking some vital aspect of the plot, or re-creating a character." By phone, fax, and editorial letter, she tries to offer solutions to problems in a manuscript that range from showing the author how to avoid digressions and lumpy exposition to how to increase suspense and build characters (by what they say, do, and what others say about them).

What she looks for, ultimately, is "a first-rate piece of crime fiction . . . [whose] appeal is that it is fresh, different, perhaps even quirky. When a manuscript has these qualities, an editor is willing to work long and hard with an author if necessary in order to make the book what it can ideally be. Indeed, realizing the work's potential is the challenge that makes editing so exciting and so rewarding."

Editing Crime Fiction

Authors sometimes ask me if I have any editorial "guidelines," and with a straight face I tell them I do: Prepare your manuscript on a typewriter or word processor/computer. Double-space it, use one side of the paper only, and don't, please don't, start a new sequence of page numbers with every new chapter. Probably the most extreme instance of the search for a magic formula for writing a crime novel was when a woman cornered me during a writers' conference to ask me on what page the murder should take place.

Oh, dear.

No one can give you a formula for writing a good crime novel—and it wouldn't be a good novel if one could.

Good crime fiction is good fiction with a crime at its center. I use the phrase "crime fiction" rather than "mystery fiction" or "mysteries" because the first phrase allows the inclusion of works that one way or another go beyond the strict limits of the whodunit. But whatever you call it, the day of the pure puzzle with cookie-cutter characters is gone.

As a *crime novel,* a book has a plot that raises ingenious questions about a crime and about the characters involved. It has suspense and a logical conclusion that explains the heretofore mysterious happenings.

As a *novel,* a book has real characters, believable people who are unique human beings, with depth and layers of personality. They may be good or wicked or (cleverly) a bit of both. All of them must be real. How can you care what happens to paper dolls?

As a *novel,* a book has a sense of place. Readers are given not only a description of the setting and its various locations; they are made to feel *that* landscape or *that* room, the peculiar character of that city or town or house. This happens because the author feels it and knows how to bring a place to life on paper. You accomplish this by selecting the details—and they may be very small ones—that form a kind of shorthand of the place, and eliminating all those general descriptions and universal details that tell you really nothing.

As a *novel,* a book is well written. I don't care if the style is as succinct as Hemingway's or as complex as Proust's; I do care if it's clunky and fuzzy. I value the kind of accuracy of language where the words say exactly what the author intends to convey and not some approximation of it.

A good crime novel, therefore, not only is about a crime but has all the attributes of any good so-called mainstream novel. When I take on a novel for publication, it will have at least the potential of developing these characteristics; the aim is that by the time it is published, the potential will have been realized.

Okay. Now we have this manuscript, which I have read, admired, seen promise in, and bought for publication. But my buying the manuscript doesn't necessarily mean that I consider it finished and ready to go to the copy editor to have its commas polished. To extremely varying degrees, the manuscript will need more work. I may just ask the author to answer a few queries and straighten out a confusing sentence, but I could suggest rewriting several episodes, rethinking some vital aspect of the plot, or re-creating a character.

The first phase can be done in person (often over lunch, courtesy of the publisher), by phone, or most often—in my case, at least—with an editorial letter, a usually fairly long exposition of just what I feel is wrong with the manuscript, what needs changing, and what might be done about it. Not every author gets an editorial letter or the equivalent; not every manuscript requires one. If the story works well, I put some penciled notes in the margin and the author can make minor corrections when the copyedited manuscript is sent to him or her.

Remember, we're talking about a manuscript that has been selected (usually from among the fifty to a hundred currently in the office) for publication. This means that basically I am pleased with the writing, the people, the atmosphere. And if those characteristics are okay, but there are problems with the plot, never mind. Plots can be fixed; bad writing, paper-thin characters, blank backgrounds are harder to salvage. Any manuscript I've already bought, unless I was suffering a temporary loss of wits at the time, which is always a possibility, is going to be fixable.

The editorial letter, therefore, almost always deals with matters of plot, action, suspense. If I had to say, "Your people aren't real," I shouldn't have bought the book in the first place.

The author receives the editorial letter and possibly goes into shock. He or she has worked so long over the manuscript, fixing and polishing, maybe showing it to friends for comment, until it seemed perfect. Now it has suddenly become the equivalent of a first draft. It's not quite that drastic, of course, but when we're talking about one's own precious creation, perceptions can be skewed, at least temporarily. So far, all my authors have recovered confidence in their skills and have survived—often to write again and again.

In my letter or conversation or whatever, I not only point out what I don't think works well, I suggest ways of fixing it. "Here he could tell her about the missing file, so that she can have some motivation to look in the walk-in refrigerator." Other editors may simply say, "As written, she goes into the refrigerator without any reason for doing so; you have to find one for her."

Sometimes a structural problem will require rewriting, but often one can easily be dealt with just by switching material around a bit. I had a manuscript recently in which the individual parts were fine, but the sum of those parts was skewed. The book's protagonist was Jan. Yet the story began with Carol, a secondary character not nearly so interesting or important, and for the next thirty pages, Jan was just present at the edge of Carol's thoughts. So Carol took first place in the reader's mind. As the story went on and Carol had no real part to play, the initial emphasis on her became a source of confusion. "Start out with Jan instead," I told the author, "and Carol will sink to her own place." It worked.

Authors—and editors—are subject to what I inelegantly call the "subliminal itch." That's the nagging feeling that there's something wrong with what's on the page; nothing obvious, just *something* not quite right. It's a temptation to leave the knowledge lying there in your subconscious, and authors often give in to that temptation. It's easier for the editor, aware of the itch him or herself, to be firm about acknowledging it and asking the author to revise.

I find that the aspect of a novel that inexperienced authors often have trouble with is exposition. You've got to get certain facts across to your reader about happenings that took place before the story began. If you just relate them, you will probably go on at more length than you need to, and you will probably be pretty boring. Remember, this information isn't part of the action; it's just setting the stage, as it were. You've got to get it across seamlessly and painlessly. There are various ways of accomplishing this, some more effective than others.

Your story opens, say, with the protagonist, Joe, walking around New York's SoHo district, looking in shop windows, greeting friends (which, incidentally, is one way of indicating he's a familiar figure in that neighborhood), stopping to read the For Rent cards in the supermarket entryway. It's important for the reader to know:

1. His marriage has recently broken up, at his wife's instigation;

2. He's been living at a friend's house on the Upper East Side; and

3. He's now looking for a room of his own in SoHo because he wants to
   move out of the friend's place.

You can open the story and then go back . . .

> I had been staying with Barbara in her row house in the East Sev-
> enties since my wife threw me out. Now I was planning to move on.

You can bring up the before-the-story facts in conversation between two
characters, although it is tricky to pull this off without sounding forced and
phony . . .

> "Isn't your brother the one who has been staying with Barbara?"
> "Yes, but there's nothing going on there. He needed a place
> when his wife threw him out. Now he tells me he's moving."
> "Why? I know he's a SoHo type. He doesn't like the Upper East
> Side?"
> "Not at all. It's just that he's a considerate guy and doesn't want
> to impose on Barbara anymore."

If you find yourself writing pages and pages of exposition, stop and consider
whether it might not be best for you to start your story further back in time,
so you can tell all this directly. That may mean putting an earlier date on
the first chapter, but that's acceptable.

What you don't want is for your character to sound like the little maid
with the feather duster who opens a play by hopping around the room
soliloquizing on the fact that the son of the family, who has been in Aus-
tralia for twenty years, after a dispute with an older brother, is expected that
afternoon. Try for some subtlety.

One of the things I can help an author do is increase suspense. It surprises
me how many manuscripts there are in which the detective detects only
because a crime has been committed. "Oh, here is the landlady with her
throat cut. Of course we must call the police, but let's solve the crime
ourselves." Unfortunately, the protagonist's enterprise and curiosity are
not enough to keep a reader's interest.

Suspense comes from the promise of harm. Something must be impend-
ing that will make the main character *have* to solve the mystery in order to
ward off a looming danger. There must be a *threat,* and it must be nigh.
Perhaps another murder is imminent. Perhaps someone we care about is
wrongly accused and must be cleared. Perhaps the protagonist is in serious
jeopardy. The criminal must be found and stopped or . . . or what? Something very bad. It's up to you, the author, to say what, and up to me, as the
editor, to say whether it works or not, or offer another suggestion.

One way to destroy suspense is by digression, and I am always surprised by how often I find even experienced authors committing this blunder. You need momentum in a crime novel even more than in some other kinds of fiction, and you don't dare stop the action for something that doesn't either advance the plot, illuminate the characters, or add to the atmosphere. For example, a lot of authors feel for some reason that they must give their readers the itinerary every time their character gets behind the wheel:

> I went down Montrose two blocks, then swung a left into South Street. The stretch there up to Second Avenue is usually a pleasant one, but this time I hit four red lights before I could make my right turn into Second . . .

And so on, until she reaches the suspect's house or the scene of the crime. Other writers stick in a sex scene or a political harangue, neither integral to the story, that simply stops the action—and the interest—cold. Use any of it—itineraries, sex scenes, political harangues (within reason)—if they have a real place in the story. Otherwise, no.

Well, the author and I hash all that out and usually none of it presents a problem. I've found most authors very willing to consider my comments. They mostly agree with what I suggest and when they don't, they have good reasons. Of course, occasionally there will be some disagreement that we can't resolve; unless the problem I see in the manuscript is especially egregious, I most often go along with the author, even if I don't really feel comfortable doing it. I've never personally had the sort of disagreement over a very important point that ends, as some do, with the editor saying, "It's clear that we can't work together on this book, and I'm going to cancel it and ask for a return of the advance." That's a very drastic thing to do, but it does happen from time to time.

Of course, the editor is not always right. Anyone can exercise bad judgment sometimes. And there may not be only one "right." But if the editor *is* right more often than not, it's partly because he or she has had experience helping to shape books, launching them into the marketplace, taking note of how they are received by bookstore buyers, readers, and critics. And it's partly because just about every writer in the world can benefit from a second pair of eyes and a reaction from a second person, particularly one experienced as an editor. As a onetime writer myself, I know perfectly well that weaknesses I would spot in someone else's manuscript could go unnoticed in one of my own.

With the revised manuscript in front of me, I line edit. This is not copy editing. Copy editors, in addition to looking for infelicities of language that the editor and the author did not catch, must check any facts in the book—dates, numbers, proper names. They must make sure that words that could have more than one form are consistent—proper names are always spelled the same way, titles are always—or never—capitalized, etc. They fix any grammatical or spelling errors that have sneaked by unnoticed.

Line editing involves reading the manuscript over minutely, smoothing out awkward phrases, querying any minor thing that seems unclear or odd, suggesting a better word somewhere. I do this by making notes in the margin. Here are the kinds of things I write:

> It doesn't take two people to cover some exposed roots. Have one of them watch while the other does the work. That's also a good chance to show the difference between the two characters.

> I'm not sure I get what this is supposed to imply. Please clarify.

> Wouldn't she take the bag out of the trunk *before* she hurried to the porch?

> This doesn't work.
> 1. They all swore to remain single.
> 2. They're supposed to give the members patchwork quilts on their 30th birthdays.
> 3. "Most got quilts as wedding presents," you say. Were all of them married at 30? Seems unlikely. And if they did marry, why did they get quilts at all? Please clarify.

> This is the first we learn a fact that seems important and that we should have been told at once—that they got the check the day she disappeared.

Not nitpicking, just an effort to get rid of every ambiguity and tie up every loose end—always desirable but particularly important in mystery fiction.

· · ·

Although the title of this chapter is "Editing Crime Fiction," I can't confine myself to an account of working with the author on an acquired manuscript. Acquisition itself is as important a part of an editor's job as readying the book for publication.

I am often asked a question that I find only marginally less irritating than "Who is your favorite mystery writer?"* It's "What are you looking for?" At least there's a ready answer for that one: I'm looking for a good book.

---

*I have no *favorite* mystery author; how can you choose only one from a universe that includes such disparate wonders as Tony Hillerman, Ross Thomas, Sue Grafton, and Ngaio Marsh, to name just a few of the many?

I really don't care whether it's hard-boiled or traditional, tough or academic or what is annoyingly called "cozy." I don't care whether it's in the third person or the first. (The second person doesn't work; please don't try it.) I admit that I myself have a slight, very personal dislike of books written in the present tense, but that's my quirk, not a condition of sale; every now and then I encounter one that is otherwise so engaging that I'll publish it anyhow. The book can be humorous or serious, literary or whatever the opposite of literary is. It can have a male protagonist or a female one— straight or gay, black or white, old or young—so long as it's believable. I'm sure you get the idea; I'm open to every kind of crime novel as long as it's fresh, compelling, and well written.

My company is one of the few that considers unsolicited manuscripts from nonagented first-time authors. As a result, they pile into the office at a frightening rate. We also, of course, get submissions from a large number of agents and from authors whom we have previously published. There's a lot to choose from. Do I read them all? I *look* at them all. In the majority of cases, I don't have to read very far into a manuscript to know that it's not something I want.

For the most part, the manuscripts I reject (at St. Martin's, we use the kinder, gentler "decline") are not really "bad." Many are at least respectable. But I buy only a few from the pile, perforce. Of the rest, it's impossible to tell an author why I am returning the manuscript—even if there were time to do it, which there isn't. Authors are looking to be told about a distinct flaw that they can then remedy; they'd like me to say, "I am not buying this manuscript because the murder takes place in the boatyard and that's hard to believe." Whereupon they will shift the scene of the murder to the conservatory and have a publishable manuscript. Alas, it doesn't work that way.

The real story is that there's just about nothing to say. When a manuscript is really bad (one of my colleagues, reporting on a submission she had been asked to read, said, "I've read a hundred pages. If I read any more of it I'll break out in a rash"), one can't send a letter saying, "This is awful. You can't write. Get into some other business." So we use some polite, if meaningless, phrase—"It isn't right for us," or "It doesn't fit our list."

About the competently done and ultimately tedious stories, there's also very little to say. There's no distinct flaw to put one's finger on. Everything is set up, thought out, if I can't praise the writing I can't actually fault it, the characters move and walk and talk like human beings (if dull human beings), and nothing is very original. The manuscripts are derivative; there is no freshness, no individuality, no spark. Nothing to make me want to read on. Especially when they are compared to the occasional gem that turns up as I sit reading in a more or less empty office on a gray Sunday afternoon. So—"It isn't right for us," "It doesn't fit our list," says it all, because that's really all there is to say about the merely ordinary.

I frown on an author's trying to tailor a story to fit a trend. Every so often some media person, stuck for a story, calls me (and my counterparts in other houses who are free to take the call) and asks about trends. They are never very imaginative; nine times out of ten they'll ask me to comment on "the new trend for hard-boiled female private eyes." I don't know when a trend stops trending and becomes established, but the hard-boiled female private eye is a result of the changed status of women, was featured by the originators of this kind of book and their many imitators for many years now, and is here to stay. It is no longer a trend; it's as much of an institution as the hard-boiled male private eye, the intellectual university professor sleuth, the put-upon city cop, and so forth.

I do see from time to time more authentic, or more current, trends; elderly sleuths, for example. But it's foolish for you to write about anyone or anything other than what you really have in mind just because you think it's popular with the public. Good books are always popular with the public. From a purely pragmatic point of view, consider how long it will take you to write that trendy book, how long to sell it, how long to edit and revise it, how long it will take to get it into the stores. By that time, your trend may have evaporated. The fickle buying public may have forgotten that last year or two years ago they liked elderly sleuths. Psychiatrist sleuths might be in fashion, or even mimes.

By all means write a book that happens to fit a current trend if that's the kind of book you really *want* to write. But don't write it *because* it fits. Your lack of genuine interest will show through clearly enough to turn off a mystery editor.

Authors with some kind of specialized knowledge are indeed lucky. If they are enterprising or savvy enough, they'll build that specialty into the novel or even use it as the framework of their crime fiction. Among the books I know—either those I've edited or those I've just read—I've encountered sleuths who are, variously, an escape artist à la Houdini, a radiologist, a Navajo policeman, a forensic anthropologist, an astrologer, an arson investigator, an antiques expert, a tarpon fishing guide. And many more. These special elements give your story additional color and interest and help set you off from other crime fiction writers. The cliché "Write about what you know" is good advice, especially if you know something off the beaten path. But it must be authentic knowledge. No cheating. You'll get caught out.

I've said earlier that it's hard to tell an author how to create good characters, but in my view, good characters are so important to a manuscript and so influence me when I read a submission, that I'm going to put down a few things that may be somewhat helpful:

Take a tip from the dramatist: It's always better to show than to tell. A playwright doesn't have the prose writer's option of describing a character to the audience. "He was often moody, and sometimes near deep depression, wondering whether his life had any meaning at all." You can't do that in a drama. A playwright has only three ways to convey character to an audience: by what the character says, by what the character does, and by what the others say about that character. A prose writer is not forced to abide by those limitations, but it doesn't hurt to remember them.

Be observant. I can't overstress the importance of this for any writer. Note how two different people will voice the same thought differently; each person's way of doing it gives an indication of what sort of person the individual is. (You see this if you have a chance to observe jury deliberations.) If possible, keep a journal of sorts, in which you write what you notice about people. Try to figure out how their words and actions define them. Getting back to writing for the theater a moment—it's a very demanding craft and consequently one with valuable lessons for other writers—a very old play by George S. Kaufman and Edna Ferber, *Stage Door,* has a huge number of quite minor characters, young women who have no more than one or two lines in the whole play. In a student production, the director was short of female actors and, as is so often done, he doubled the parts, giving one actor two characters' lines. It was a revelation to discover that the playwrights, pros both of them, had so fashioned each speech to the fictional person, never mind how minor, that it had to be changed before it could be given to a different character.

Some authors find it helpful to base characters on real people they know—or more often, on a kind of composite of several people. This can be effective, but be careful. If you are too conscious of the real-life equivalents of your characters, they will remain at a distance from you, whereas if you have actually created a person on the paper, you know more about him or her than you could about a friend or relative or lover.

What all these tips and suggestions come down to is that the editor aims to get from the author a book that lives up to its potential. Its plot is logical. It has suspense and interest and freshness, and its characters are real and human enough for the reader to care about them, whether "care about them" translates to love or hate or amusement.

A first-rate piece of crime fiction is never ordinary. It has a voice unique to the person who created it. That's admittedly ambiguous, but an editor recognizes the voice right away even though I cannot really define it other than to say it's an individual way of communicating unlike anyone else's;

its appeal is that it is fresh, different, perhaps even quirky. When a manuscript has these qualities, an editor is willing to work long and hard with an author if necessary in order to make the book what it can ideally be. Indeed, realizing the work's potential is the challenge that makes editing so exciting and so rewarding.

The Pleasures and Perils of Editing Mass-Market Paperbacks

Mel Parker

MEL PARKER *is vice-president and publisher of the paperback division of Warner Books, where he oversees a paperback list featuring some of America's most popular authors, such as Scott Turow, Sidney Sheldon, Nelson DeMille, P. D. James, Larry Bond, Sandra Brown, David Morrell, and Alexandra Ripley.*

Before coming to Warner, Mr. Parker was editor-in-chief of the Berkley Publishing Group, where he acquired a number of major paperback bestsellers, including The Hunt for Red October *by Tom Clancy.*

"When I look back at the essay 'Born to Be a Paperback' I wrote for Editors on Editing *nine years ago," writes Mr. Parker, "I realize how much that essay was a product of the 1980s—its point of view was brash, confident, bullish on the business. . . . Let me tell you, mass-market paperback publishing has changed a lot in the last ten years."*

How those changes have affected paperback editors and writers is the theme of Mr. Parker's new essay. Seeing the recession of the early 1990s as "the single overriding factor" in mass-market publishing, he discusses its impact on the editor-author relationship: what kinds of books work in mass-market publishing today, how they are edited and marketed, how and when mass-market writers can make the leap into hardcover, the competition of TV and movies with paperback publishing, the decline of paperback reprint publishing, and the increased editorial emphasis on publishing originals.

Mr. Parker cautions writers who want to start out in paperback "to become savvy trend watchers. They have to know when a trend is growing

*and to capitalize on it, with an eye toward finding what will work . . . as a
lead-title paperback."* ·

*"There's beginning to be no difference in the working relationship" be-
tween working with a paperback or a hardcover editor, Mr. Parker says,
observing that many hardcover houses also publish paperback lines, and
that many of today's best-selling hardcover authors started as writers of
paperback originals. Paperback editors work as closely with their authors
as do hardcover editors, and have the same high standards of quality.
Detailing the crossover of Sandra Brown from best-selling paperback author to best-selling hardcover author, Mr. Parker notes that "Sandra
Brown's paperback editor also served as her hardcover editor. In this case,
as in many others, sometimes paperback editors show us where to begin."*

The Pleasures and Perils of Editing Mass-Market Paperbacks

When I look back at the essay "Born to Be a Paperback" I wrote for *Editors
on Editing* nine years ago, I realize how much that essay was a product of
the 1980s—its point of view was brash, confident, bullish on the business.
Although we were headed toward the end of an era, the mid-1980s still
seemed like the go-go years of paperback publishing. I believed that mass-
market publishing was at the very center of popular culture, and that if the
special job of a paperback editor was to see people on beach blankets all
over the country reading paperbacks, then that made it all worthwhile. Yes,
when books sold in the millions, paperback publishing was fun! But as we
pay off our debts in the 1990s, the job I do now is a bit more difficult. As
Warner's paperback publisher, I'm no longer in charge of only my own
books; my responsibility is to publish and manage an entire paperback list.
And let me tell you, mass-market paperback publishing has changed a lot
in the last ten years.

In the recession of the early 1990s the negative economic climate has been
the single overriding factor in mass-market publishing, as corporate down-
sizing and consolidations, escalating costs, shrinking "markets," and com-
peting media have slowed the momentum of paperback publishing. In a
way, the sins of the 1980s have come to haunt us all, as publishing now
resembles the motion picture industry, with big stars (i.e., best-selling au-

thors) and powerful talent agents (i.e., literary agents) determining the health of the industry. This has had a ripple effect throughout the business as publishers, under pressure to recoup their investments, have published too many titles, escalated print runs on undeserving books, and in general have flooded the distribution network with more titles and copies than retailers (or customers) can handle. And since publishing is one of the only industries that allows its booksellers or distributors to return unsold merchandise (in this case, millions of copies of books), many smaller and less efficient retailers and distributors returned more books than they sold. In essence, we were all greedy in the 1980s, and because we thought the prosperity would never end, publishers also created conditions that have now made it difficult to develop more successful authors and reap corporate profits.

In my earlier essay, I said that "the mass market is made up of many specialized markets," and by that I meant that midlist category publishing still had a chance in those days. It was always clearly preferable for editors to search for lead titles in the big genres of glitzy contemporary women's fiction à la Judith Krantz, Sidney Sheldon, or Danielle Steel, or international intrigue in the manner of Ludlum, Follett, and Clancy. But there was also a place in the middle of the paperback list where aspiring authors could learn their craft and develop as writers by writing romances, mysteries, westerns, and male adventure. An author who dreamt of being the next Clive Cussler could cut his teeth on a category male adventure series, eventually working his way up to, say, a lead paperback original. When midlist category books thrived during the years of strong growth in paperback publishing, when there was a demand for *more* titles, the midlist served as a kind of farm team for future authors. While working on the big paperback lead title, an author could at least support himself as a writer by writing a category series.

But publishers soon learned that they had to shorten their lists. From their point of view it became preferable to try to make more profit with fewer titles—since fewer titles meant less staff, overhead, plant costs, etc. And from a bookseller's or distributor's point of view, fewer titles meant tighter, more manageable inventories and lower costs. The victim of all this was the midlist category book, and the author who was trying to start a career by writing them. Ten years ago, a typical supermarket, for example, featured racks as far as the eye could see filled not only with the top ten *New York Times* best-sellers of the week, but an ample supply of popular mysteries, westerns, male adventure series, and other category books. But as customers threw fewer paperbacks into the shopping cart—simply because in hard times, a box of laundry detergent is far more important than a $2.95 mystery—the accounts responded by displaying fewer mysteries, in turn putting pressure on the publisher to publish fewer titles. Now that same supermarket carries only the top ten best-sellers, in multiple quantities of each. Readers have far less to choose from; writers have fewer opportunities.

So, if the economics of the business have made midlist category publishing far less important than it once was, how do you break into the business if you're a first-time author who wants to write the big commercial book? First of all, think *big*. In my earlier essay I suggested that a book born to be a paperback embraces one of three major markets loosely defined by gender: the women's market, the men's market, and the "crossover" market. And by that I meant—and still mean—that books for women that succeed on a grand scale touch on the issues and feelings that are important to the greatest number of women at the time—whether it be the challenge of succeeding in a man's world, or escaping back to a time when love seemed less complicated. For men, the big books still focus on the big concerns, intrigues, and conspiracies. Men love thrillers—because adventure is a fantasy for them. Books that propel male readers into a world they've never seen before—whether inside Gorky Park or on a submarine in *The Hunt for Red October*—sell in great numbers because that kind of escape is the ultimate reading entertainment for men whose real lives may be far less adventurous. And the monumentally successful epic novels such as *Roots, Exodus,* or *Shogun* are the ultimate crossover books—few and far between these days. Those novels were blockbusters because they "crossed over" to both men and women by incorporating all the elements that appeal to every reader—romance, adventure, and intrigue all in one book. So now, if you're trying to break into the business by writing a paperback book, it's still true that the so-called big books I've just described provide a model for the kinds of books commercial publishers are always looking for, books that are born to be paperbacks.

But while all of us wait for the next Danielle Steel, Tom Clancy, or Alex Haley, and since publishers have fewer opportunities (e.g., categories) in which to publish, it's absolutely critical for authors who want to start out in paperback to become savvy trend watchers. They have to know when a trend is growing and to capitalize on it, with an eye toward finding what will work not as a midlist category book, but as a lead-title paperback. Sometimes a blockbuster novel can create a new trend. *Presumed Innocent* and *The Silence of the Lambs* burst onto the scene with such force that whole new genres seemed to spring forth. *Presumed Innocent* created keen interest in legal thrillers, and *The Silence of the Lambs* made psychological thrillers enormously popular by focusing on a new kind of horror—the serial killer. Add to the publication of those books two blockbuster movie versions starring Harrison Ford and Anthony Hopkins, and it's safe to say that the public expressed its enthusiasm for those genres. Have Scott Turow and

Thomas Harris created future opportunities for authors? Seems to be so.

Sometimes movie tie-ins alone set the cultural pace, stimulating the development of new genres. The impact of Oliver Stone's controversial and successful movie *JFK* touched a chord in the country; the film is now widely regarded as the catalyst behind the government's decision to look into opening the Kennedy assassination files. For enterprising authors looking for the next big lead-title category, is it possible that *JFK* will spark the return of the so-called paranoid political thriller, books in which the enemy may be inside our borders, not outside of them? Certainly Warner's nonfiction paperback, *On the Trail of the Assassins,* one of the books on which the movie was based, showed that this was a *subject* people wanted to read about. The paperback hit the No. 1 spot on the *New York Times* best-seller list, selling nearly 750,000 copies. Perhaps political thrillers, drawing on the public interest in conspiracy books, is a new subject for the big suspense novel of the future. Remember *Seven Days in May* and *The Manchurian Candidate*? Is another great paranoid political thriller waiting to be written?

Television also seems to be a cultural marker. "Tabloid" television, for example, seemed to literally create the public interest in true crime. From programs such as *A Current Affair* and the TV movie of *Fatal Vision,* the mass-market appetite for true crime stories seemed insatiable. It was no wonder, then, that mass-market paperback publishers tried to satisfy this hunger and reaped success from the trend. A flood of true crime paperback originals resulted (published quickly as paperbacks to follow the outcome of specific cases), and many became best-sellers, such as the St. Martin's Press paperback on the Jeffrey Dahmer case, *The Milwaukee Murders.*

Finally, sometimes the trend isn't created by a brilliant new author like Scott Turow, or a blockbuster Hollywood movie or popular TV series, but by the general social and political atmosphere of the country at any given time. Take the enormously popular genre of recent years, the military technothriller. Although Tom Clancy single-handedly created this genre, the mood of the country had already been created to welcome its emergence. In the early 1980s, Americans had finally begun to make their peace with Vietnam, and as patriotism grew during the Reagan years, the military community, largely scorned by many during the Vietnam era, was no longer an outcast. As the wounds of Vietnam healed, soldiers were good guys again, and everything about their lives—including every inside detail about the men and the hardware of military life—fascinated readers. In other words, the mood of the country was already there to make *The Hunt for Red October* a huge best-seller and set the stage for a best-selling trend for new authors.

But just as important as looking for the cultural signposts that signal the emergence of a new trend or genre, you have to know when the market has become glutted with cheap imitations. True crime, for one, has suffered from overexposure, with books on every sordid—and uncompelling—case. True crime books that offer little more than portraits of gratuitous violence without probing the psychological motivations of the killers or following the trail of an intrepid investigator are rip-off books, pure and simple. And the same can be said for the genre of horror, which has already been tarnished by overpublishing. Simply inspect a typical "horror" section in the bookstore. If you see more than a dozen horror/occult novels featuring demonic children, it might be time to worry about that genre. Publishers call this problem title pollution, and even though authors such as Stephen King and Dean Koontz still sell in huge numbers, the horror "trend," so to speak, has been hurt by shoddy, derivative imitations that have flooded the market. Readers, like consumers, want the real Rolex watch, not the street-corner fake.

Spotting the trends that will prevent you from spending a lot of time writing in the wrong genre is half the battle. But another development—the decline of paperback *reprint* publishing—may create additional opportunities for writers who want to start out in paperback. Nine years ago, I spoke of the dual function of the paperback editor as both an editor of original manuscripts and a reprint editor, i.e., an editor who acquires paperback reprint rights to hardcover books published at other houses. I tried to describe the special pleasure of reprint editing—which is not unlike the excitement a journalist experiences when he finds the next scoop—combining a hardcover publisher's catalog for the book that could become, in its reprinted version, a huge paperback best-seller. Many books "born to be a paperback" were acquired via the reprint route, and the reprint side of a paperback editor's job was considered so important that many paperback editors did nothing but acquire reprint rights. Their job was to totally "cover" the hardcover house, to know exactly what was going to be published by each one, and to convince the hardcover subsidiary rights director from whom they would buy the rights that their paperback house was the best paperback publisher for the book. These paperback reprint editors were charged with establishing strong contacts with the hardcover houses they covered so as to be in a position to set the all-important paperback floor bid on a hardcover book, which allowed the paperback house to top the final bid in any future auction for reprint rights. If a paperback editor spent his morning working on an original lead-title manuscript, more than likely in the afternoon he'd be on the phone with a rights director keeping tabs on future reprint possibilities.

But for the past nine years, the reprint market in paperback publishing has gotten smaller, as hardcover publishers work more closely than ever with their own paperback subsidiaries and retain rather than sell paperback rights. Authors and agents gradually decided that it made no economic sense to pursue the traditional reprint agreement, because by contract the hardcover house sold paperback rights but had the benefit of sharing in the author's future paperback royalties. But now, in the so-called hard-soft deal, authors do not have to share their paperback royalties with anyone, since the hardcover and paperback publisher are the same entity. Publishers encourage hard-soft deals because they keep the control of the future paperback publishing in the hands of one house, as opposed to casting the paperback to the winds of fate elsewhere. And authors like them because if one company controls the total publishing plan, there's a sense of continuity in the author-publisher relationship.

. . .

The net effect of all this for paperback editors is to put them largely out of the reprint publishing business. Since there are obviously fewer opportunities to bid on paperback rights (for example, major paperback auctions used to be a weekly occurrence in the mid-1980s; now they hardly occur at all), paperback editors are under greater pressure to develop *original manuscripts,* which is good news for writers looking for more opportunities. In earlier years, a paperback editor had a more balanced work load of originals and reprints—and a deeper pool of potential paperback best-sellers. Now paperback editors spend more time looking for original material, creating the possibility of greater demand for paperback originals.

If this is indeed good news, what can you expect in your dealings with a paperback editor if you choose to go this route? In what respects is working with a paperback editor different from working with a hardcover editor? Is there, in fact, any difference at all? The answer is that there's beginning to be no difference in the working relationship. When hardcover and paperback houses were completely separate—either as different corporate entities or as separate subsidiaries under their own corporate umbrella—the hardcover editor acquired the book, worked with the author, and edited the book. The paperback editor, one floor below, generally had very little editorial input. His responsibility was simply to reprint the book and to map out the paperback publishing and marketing strategy. But this "upstairs/downstairs" relationship is changing at many publishing companies, most notably at houses such as the Putnam Berkley Group, which realized that many of its Putnam hardcover best-selling authors were coming to the house via its Berkley paperback editors, authors like Tom Clancy, LaVyrle Spencer, and W. E. B. Griffin. Paperback editors have helped bridge the traditional gap between hardcover and paperback subsidiaries. In the day-to-day working relationship between a paperback editor and his author, all the traditional steps in editing and publishing take place. And since the book is brought in by the paperback editor, if the author ever goes into hardcover, the author generally stays with his original editor.

Let's look at some examples of how paperback editors work with authors. Say the publisher has decided that the house would like to publish a lead-level paperback original, a historical saga about the opening of the American West by a first-time author who, on the basis of an outline and sample chapters, has convinced the publisher that he has a great story to tell, that the historical detail is just right, and that the author himself is a potentially promotable writer who is an expert on the American West. Once a proposal and sample chapters are bought, the editor would write a preliminary editorial letter suggesting that perhaps one of the main characters needs a stronger role in the story. Say the book is going to be about a man and wife who together form the beginning of a powerful family dynasty, moving westward to make their fame and fortune in Gold Rush California. But the wife in the story—a potentially wonderful character—seems underplayed in the early chapters. In this instance, the paperback editor would alert the author to this in the letter, thereby suggesting an important point about the overall future direction of the book. If the author always suspected that this was a weakness in the story line, having this pointed out to him by the editor is reassuring, since the author now feels that he and the editor share the same vision of the book.

The author then delivers a completed manuscript a year later—and major editorial work would begin, with an extensive revision letter pointing out the larger structural elements that still need attention. Perhaps there is an underdeveloped subplot between rival sons in this family saga; or the overall proportion of the book is slightly off, as the author spends too much time preparing for the family's departure from Independence, Missouri; or there's a notable absence of historical detail in the Indian sections of the book; or characters sometimes talk as if they were in a drawing room in 1876 New York City instead of on the 1876 frontier. All these concerns would be addressed in the revision letter, stating the editor's excitement and enthusiasm for the book, but tactfully suggesting areas that would help the author realize the book's full potential. Buoyed by this constructive advice—and the gut feeling that he is working with a diligent editor who has done his homework and really cares—the author goes back to his word processor, strengthening some characters here, shading in the historical detail there, or speeding up parts of the story as suggested by the editor.

Then the second draft comes in and the excitement begins. A terrific book has been written, and both author and editor know it. Now all that remains to be done is some light line editing on the manuscript itself—perhaps, in this case, on the dialogue, which needs some fine tuning. Here's where some actual blue pencil editing on the manuscript takes place, all of it subject to the author's approval. Then there might still be a few questions from the editor regarding some internal inconsistencies in the book, pointed out to the author often with query tags attached to the margins of the manuscript. And then, after the author has approved the line editing and answered the editor's queries, the book is ready for the copy editor and transmitted to production. What the paperback editor and his author realize is that their constructive, collegial editorial relationship has been focused on one goal— to bring out the best the author can offer. Although they may have disagreed on a few points, the final manuscript is the product of an author's trust in his editor, a solid foundation for the challenges ahead in selling the book not only to the publisher's own sales force, but finally to the fickle customer browsing the paperback racks.

And, needless to say, there are a lot of challenges in launching the marketing campaign for a successful lead title as a paperback original. In my earlier essay, I spoke of the difficulty of getting review attention for paperbacks, and this is still largely true. But I've come to learn that review attention is not totally relevant to the success or failure of a paperback original. The main goal is that the book be taken seriously by the sales reps since they will be selling an unknown quantity, so to speak, a book without any previous sales history in a hardcover edition. One of the ways paperback editors do this is to solicit endorsements for the book from other best-selling authors. Although this practice is sometimes overdone, getting quotes helps position the book. The manuscript itself is another "selling" tool for generating excitement among the sales force. If the book is being described as an epic western saga in the tradition of James Michener and Louis L'Amour, sending sales reps bound galleys or a special reader's edition is very effective, particularly if some advance quotes are emblazoned on the cover. And the cover itself, foiled and embossed for eye-catching appeal, with a beautiful illustration grabbing the reader's attention, becomes another critical selling tool.

Finally, the author himself may be the book's "best seller." One effective method is the paperback solicitation tour, where the publisher sends the author out to meet key accounts around the country. Sometimes this takes the form of brief wholesaler "driver" breakfast meetings in which the author meets the paperback book buyers, the people who will eventually place the orders, as well as the truck drivers who call on individual accounts, checking stock and making sure this new paperback original gets prominent display. If the major accounts and their employees have read the deluxe bound galleys, have gotten a tee shirt with the name of this new saga emblazoned across the front of it, and have enjoyed meeting the author at one of their breakfasts, those buyers and drivers will order the book in substantial quantities, remember when it comes out, and ensure that it is displayed for maximum sales. By this point the editor has been not only editorial manager of the book, but also its in-house impresario, rolling up his sleeves to become a multifaceted marketing expert, well versed in all the methods of selling paperback books, and able to speak to his marketing people so that they, in turn, can successfully make the book a roaring success.

.   .   .

Having read all this, do you still want to be a paperback writer? Isn't there that nagging question, "Won't I be taken more seriously if my first book is published in hardcover?" Well, it's time to lay to rest the notion that authors have to begin their careers in hardcover, or that it's necessarily more desirable to do so. If reviews are the most important thing to you—if critical acclaim is what drives you to write in whatever genre you've chosen—go hardcover first. Even nine years after writing my first essay, paperbacks still have a long way to go before they get the review attention they deserve. So if you've written a novel about a young man's coming of age in the Midwest in the 1950s, and your book will have to be nurtured by the review media and hand sold by independent booksellers, hardcover is the right place for you. That's how Anne Tyler got started; and if she's your literary role model, my words won't convince you to make your publishing debut in paperback. But if you're working the territory of the so-called commercial authors who generally dominate the top ten spots on the best-seller list by writing in the mainstream genres, you can get to where those authors are by starting out in paperback. Best-selling authors such as Danielle Steel, V. C. Andrews, Janet Dailey, and W. E. B. Griffin built their readerships in paperback, and it can be argued that by seeding the market with their successful paperback books they built legions of loyal readers who stayed with them when they finally went to hardcover.

But you still might ask, "Why do I have to take the time to build a readership? Why not go for broke right now with a hardcover? What if I've written a terrific courtroom drama, and I think I could be the next Scott Turow?" Well, the answer is, not much *will* happen if your terrific court-room drama ends up as a midlist 15,000-copy hardcover, with very little advertising, promotion, or publicity support, damaged further by having to compete with other hardcover first novels on a publisher's overcrowded list. But what if, instead, the manuscript of that same book falls into the hands of a paperback editor who tells the literary agent that he loves the book, that the main character, a young prosecutor in Los Angeles, could be a continuing character for future books, and that the editor is so enthusiastic about it that he'd like to publish the book as the No. 1 title on his paperback list. Now the author has to ask, do I want a 15,000-copy midlist hardcover, or an estimated 400,000-copy lead title in paperback? Here are the possible scenarios in greater detail of what might happen if the same book were published differently.

SCENARIO 1	SCENARIO 2
Hardcover	*Paperback*
$19.95 cover price	$5.95 cover price
10% royalty ($2.00 per copy sold)	10% royalty ($.60 per copy sold)
15,000-copy first printing	400,000-copy first printing
$5,000 ad/promo budget	$50,000 ad/promo budget
No author tour	Author tour to presell book to key accounts
Possible reviews in a fair number of major newspapers	Review in paperback pick columns in major newspapers
12,000 copies sold	225,000 copies sold
$25,000 advance	$25,000 advance
$24,000 royalties earned; book needs to earn $1,000 more for author to begin getting additional royalties	$135,000 royalties earned; author makes an additional $110,000

Although the same manuscript was submitted to two different editors, the outcome of the publishing story was very different. The author was proud of having been published in hardcover, but his promising courtroom drama didn't sell more than 12,000 copies. Because of that, the book couldn't really attract a major paperback reprint sale; that level of hardcover sales wasn't considered strong enough to merit publishing the book as a lead title. With the author having already been paid a $25,000 advance against royalties, the book earned only $24,000 in hardcover royalties, so the author earned no additional money. If in this scenario the hardcover house had a paperback subsidiary, the paperback chances would be equally slim, since the book has already been tarnished by its lackluster hardcover performance.

The author who took the paperback route first, however, felt successful about his book. While the hardcover house wondered whether it wanted to take on the next courtroom drama by an author who sold only 12,000 copies, his paperback counterpart in scenario 2 already signed a contract for a second book, since his publisher was happy about the success of having sold 225,000 paperbacks of the first one. While the hardcover author received a fair number of respectful reviews, the paperback author received only a few honorable mentions in paperback columns. As for their futures, the unhappy author who chose hardcover went on to write another solid courtroom drama, but this time for another hardcover house, working with a new editor willing to take a chance on him. Our paperback author, on the other hand, earned the good will of his publisher, and his second paperback original was slated as a lead book for that house with a 500,000-copy first printing. Now, ironically, this paperback author found himself in a better position for hardcover success than the fellow who began in hardcover in the first place. If his second (or third) paperback original hits the best-seller list, editors and publishers will view our paperback author as a major hardcover prospect, unlike the author who took the traditional hardcover route.

At publishing firms such as Warner Books, where hardcover and mass-market paperback publishing literally take place on one floor, the ongoing success story of best-selling contemporary women's fiction author Sandra Brown illustrates how paperback publishing can become the solid foundation of an author's future hardcover career. After Sandra Brown had written many category paperback romances, and had established a solid readership for her books, it was time to publish her in the lead position on Warner's paperback list. Her talented editor, Jeanne Tiedge, became her most intrepid spokesperson, championing her to the management of the company as a major new voice in women's fiction, an author destined to become a star because readers were saying so about her paperbacks. If increased sales book after book is a barometer of how readers feel about an author, it was clear that readers were falling in love with Sandra Brown. Not only were Sandra Brown's heroes and heroines wonderful characters, but the author also displayed a talent for clever plotting, adding a touch of suspense to her stories and showing that she had a real knack for keeping readers turning the pages. According to Jeanne Tiedge, "The charm of Sandra Brown's writing lies in the heartwarming themes of her novels: good always triumphs over evil and love really does conquer all. Whether her heroine is struggling to overcome the horrors of acquaintance rape, or the overzealous attacks of self-serving characters, she succeeds because she believes in herself and in those she loves."

With each wonderful new character building her readership with every book, when her third lead paperback original for Warner appeared, *Mirror Image*, Sandra Brown had her first *New York Times* paperback best-seller, and it stayed on the list for nearly two months. A second paperback best-seller, *Breath of Scandal,* followed roughly a year later, and before long Warner—hard-soft publisher that it is—knew that Sandra Brown had developed a real foundation for future hardcover publication of her books. As Jeanne points out, "Brown's paperback success and appeal grew as her novels became richer. I can honestly say that because every novel got better, and bigger—in terms of sophistication of plot and depth of minor characters and subplots—the decision to publish her in hardcover seemed natural. Her transition from genre writer to mainstream bestsellerdom came from continuously challenging herself to write the best possible book she could."

Clearly confident in the ongoing editorial quality of her books, why did Warner decide to tinker with success? Why not keep Sandra Brown in paperback? Why take the risk of publishing her in hardcover? The answer to that is simple; the publisher made the business decision that, based on the momentum and sales of the author's paperback books, a critical mass of her paperback readers would follow her to hardcover. Bolstered by the paper-back-to-hardcover success stories of authors such as LaVyrle Spencer and Judith McNaught, Warner felt that it too had an author who could make the transition to hardcover. Sandra Brown's sales had grown with each book, the word of mouth got better and better, and she herself became a wonderfully promotable spokesperson for her novels, convincing every major account that she was here to stay. By the time Warner announced that it was going to publish Sandra Brown in hardcover (and that her books would now command a retail cover price of $19.95 as opposed to $5.95), retailers and booksellers were thrilled because they, too, believed that this author's time had come.

Sandra Brown's first Warner hardcover, *French Silk,* was taken as a dual main selection of the Literary Guild and appeared on the *New York Times, Publishers Weekly* and other best-seller lists around the country. Clearly our hardcover launch was successful. But what was special about the entire process was the fact that Sandra Brown's paperback editor also served as her hardcover editor. In this case, and as in many others, sometimes paper-back editors show us where to begin.

Editing Trade Paperbacks in Middle Age—Theirs and Mine

Mark Alan Gompertz

MARK ALAN GOMPERTZ *is vice-president and publisher of Avon Trade Paperbacks, an imprint that had its debut in 1990. Prior to coming to Avon, Mr. Gompertz was a senior editor at Crown Publishers. His first job in publishing was at the Overlook Press, where he spent ten years, becoming vice-president and editorial director. Among the books he has been associated with are:* Don't Know Much about History *by Kenneth Davis,* Into the Woods *by Stephen Sondheim and James Lapine, and* The Music Room *by Dennis McFarland.*

Born when trade paperbacks were first introduced at Anchor Books in the early 1950s, Mr. Gompertz notes that "now, in the last decade of the century, trade paperbacks and those of us who grew up with them begin to face our middle ages. This, then, would seem to be a good time to ask some questions about this unique area of publishing." Mr. Gompertz does indeed ask some very challenging questions and comes up with some iconoclastic answers to them. Along the way he smashes some myths and misconceptions about the appearance, character, and content of trade paperbacks, the editors who work on them, the authors who write them, and the audience for this unique format that has influenced and changed the reading habits of millions.

Written with affection and expertise—and with a youthful vigor that belies its author's middle age—Mr. Gompertz's essay not only reviews the editorial and marketing history of trade paperbacks but also defines the changing nature of their readers—from yesterday's yuppies to today's baby boomers. *Gompertz calls them "the Cultural Literacy Generation" and believes that "trade paperbacks and the editors who have published them for four decades reflect this generation." Admitting that "these books and editors have become less daring and more practical," he contends that, "as always, a new generation of editors and readers will come up from the ranks who will be innovative and bold and will inject new life into trade paperbacks."*

Editing Trade Paperbacks in Middle Age—Theirs and Mine

I inherited this space from a very wise and interesting publisher, John Thornton, who almost ten years ago forecast that—despite a downturn in the national economy and a widespread retrenchment in the publishing industry—trade paperbacks would survive. He ended his essay by saying, "I predict that the next edition of *Editors on Editing* . . . will feature another article telling the latest truths about trade paperbacks."

Clever fellow that Mr. Thornton! Trade paperbacks have survived (even though the same economic gloom and doom is back a decade later) and now I'm here to tell you the latest truths about trade paperbacks. You may be wondering why me. What in my background gives me the right to write this piece?

The truth is that most people who end up working in any job in publishing, including trade paperbacks, do so by accident. Until 1989 I knew very little about the paperback business, having worked in hardcover for fourteen years. Sure, I had edited books that were printed and bound between two soft covers, but that is not the same as editing and *publishing* paperbacks, as I will demonstrate in this chapter.

I was born when trade paperbacks were first introduced at Anchor Books in the early 1950s and we (trade paperbacks and I) came of age in the 1970s when companies like Avon Books, where I work now, pioneered methods of publishing them. For me and many people in my generation, the trade paperback has been the format of choice to read. Some of the highlights of my post–"Wonder Years" were *The Stranger, Waiting for Godot, Growing Up Absurd* (I spent a fair amount of time highlighting passages in this book with a yellow felt tip pen), *Slaughterhouse Five,* and *The Last Whole Earth*

Catalog. An overly intense and deeply romantic young man, I gave a former girlfriend Hugh Prather's *Notes to Myself* and she, in turn, gave me the photographic gift book of our generation, *Family of Man.*

When Thornton wrote his piece, he was describing the *thirtysomething* decade of trade paperbacks. Now, in the last decade of the century, trade paperbacks and those of us who grew up with them begin to face our middle ages. This, then, would seem to be a good time to ask some questions about this unique area of publishing. What is a trade paperback today? What role do editors play in acquiring them and shaping them? Who is the audience for trade paperbacks? How do we reach them? Can trade paperbacks be bold and innovative as they were in their formative years? Or, like many people approaching middle age, have they become distinguished and respectable and, perhaps, a little bland? Finally, will they be around in the next millennium?

Like everything else in life, there are myths and misconceptions about trade paperbacks and editors who work on them. A perennially popular one is that trade paperbacks appeal only to an upscale market. This is just not true. Because Anchor Books, from its inception, dedicated its line to publishing "quality" trade paperbacks, many assume this format to be the class act of the industry, something for a mainly academic, literary, and highbrow audience. They forget the books about Rubik's Cube, Pacman, the New Kids on the Block, Kliban's cats, and some of the genre books like historical romances that have been published in trade paperback.

·   ·   ·

So what do we mean when we talk about trade paperbacks? Strictly speaking, they are larger in format than mass-market or rack-size books. And they cost more. On the other hand, trade paperbacks are often the same size as hardcover books but retail for about half the cover price. In addition to their size and price, trade paperbacks are considered more durable since they are better bound to last longer than the smaller, cheaper paperbacks. And often their covers and designs are more attractive, on the cutting edge, and upscale (but not always). They are generally sold by a direct or trade sales representative who gets them into trade accounts, i.e., bookstores and libraries. But some trade paperback books find their way into wholesale accounts like airports or supermarkets.

From management's point of view, trade paperbacks are a way of maximizing profits. Why not? The margins are higher and, theoretically, the returns are fewer because smart and efficient booksellers order the "right" quantity. They have to because it costs them more for each unit ordered and they can't strip the covers and return them for credit as they do on mass-market books. Instead they have to ship back the whole book, at their own expense, for credit. No wonder, then, that they order conservatively.

Trade paperbacks are a prime vehicle for a publisher's backlist, and they allow many companies to diversify, acquiring and offering a full line of books in any format (shape, size, and distribution of the book). In the case of reprints, publishers have a better idea of how many copies to print based on the hardcover track record.

Trade paperbacks also give publishers more markets to reach. Mass-market books, although sold in many more outlets, are editorially more limited since there are fewer things you can publish in this format: reprints of hardcover best-sellers; genre books like romances, science fiction, thrillers, and westerns; or the work of a category novelist you're developing, such as a mystery writer. Editorially speaking, when we talk of nonfiction trade paperbacks we generally think of a wide range of subjects: history, science, health, psychology, travel, business, reference, mythology, New Age, and child care, to name a few. All these categories offer a lot of information. When we talk of trade fiction, we generally think of literary, or more difficult, books, such as *Lord of the Flies, Paris Trout, The Mambo Kings Play Songs of Love,* and *Possession.*

Depending on the type of book they have written, publishing in trade might give authors a greater window of opportunity. Because space in stores is crucial, the average shelf life for books gets shorter every day. The mass-market shelf life is three to six weeks. The trade paper shelf life is six to eight months, thus giving them more time to find an audience. If the book takes hold and gets established in the stores, booksellers reorder it year in and year out. We call this backlisting, and backlist publishing is the essence of trade paperback publishing. These books are like annuities. Each year they earn royalties for the author and add money to the bottom line of the publisher's balance sheet. Many healthy publishing companies have been built on strong backlist titles.

The distinctions between mass-market and trade paperback are often blurred. Many an editorial meeting is spent discussing whether a book should be published in mass or trade. There is no easy answer. Let's take a diet book. Will the diet appeal to a mass market (like *Fit for Life*)? Will this book be ordered in large enough quantities to justify a mass-market publication? Another way of asking that is, will it get out through the wholesalers into, say, supermarkets, which have very little space for books at all? At what price point are consumers no longer going to buy the book? Is the diet or author a household name? How much did we pay to acquire it? If we paid a lot, we have to put it into mass market. This is always an important consideration. Consider the example of Amy Tan's first novel, *The Joy Luck Club.* The paperback rights were sold for $1.2 million to Vintage, a trade paperback imprint of Random House. Because it is a more literary book, one would have assumed that Vintage would publish it in trade. But executives at Random House realized that in order to earn back the money more quickly, it might make more sense to release the book in mass market first, so it was published by Ballantine, the mass-market division of Random House.

Another enduringly popular misconception is that a trade paperback editor is just a reprinter, someone who reads bound galleys or finished books from a hardcover house and then acquires the paperback rights. WRONG! Buying reprints is just one way that an editor acquires a list. In fact, a trade paperback editor of the nineties finds it is becoming increasingly difficult to buy other companies' hardcovers because the original publishers are now making in-house deals with their own corporate paperback imprints. As a result, the trade paperback editor looks to do more and more originals.

The original is the most creative and fun type of book to do but it is also the one that is most work intensive. As in hardcover publishing, you must begin with a good idea. And then you must be tenacious in following up, developing the idea, finding the best author, going after that writer, negotiating the contract, editing the book, and making sure your sales and marketing people know how the book should be published. Ideas come from many places: while reading magazines or newspapers, talking to a friend or a member of your family, sitting on a bus, or pursuing a hobby. (I once got one standing in the lobby of a theater during intermission.) But with trade paperbacks you must first understand the book's market in order to decide if your idea is best suited for this format. There are no definite rules when you determine whether a book should be published first in hardcover, trade paper, or mass market. Rather, you find yourself asking a lot of questions. Let me give you an example.

We published a book called *Secrets of the Astonishing Executive* by Bill Herz, a businessman with an M.B.A. who also happens to be a magician. His book was an offbeat business manual that taught executives how to perform magic in the workplace using simple everyday objects you might find in any office. The goal of the book was to help you motivate staff and show you how to break the ice with clients. Ordinarily, business books are first published in hardcover because the audience for these books can afford the higher price and because you need to get the books reviewed in periodicals that don't always review paperbacks. But this was a quirky book, practical but sort of humorous, that would appeal, perhaps, to younger middle managers and hip executives; this type of audience is used to buying books in paperback.

The author has speaking engagements all year long at Fortune 500 companies, and he has received many endorsements and was even written up in the *Wall Street Journal.* So two more things became clear: we would have a lot of blurbs that could be put on the cover, and we would have a very large special sales audience who might buy the book in significant quantities at his speaking engagements if the price were right. As significant as we thought the sales might be, we knew that those numbers wouldn't be achieved through wholesale outlets, so we rejected the idea of mass market. Clearly, the trade paperback was the way to go on this title.

Many books sell better right away in paper because that is where the main market is; examples are how-to manuals, parenting guides, volumes on alternative health and culture, and books of humor or about pop music. Sometimes it is merely a function of price. Avon published a big six-hundred-page volume called *The Whole Pop Catalog;* its twenty-dollar price was probably about as much as the market could bear. Its hip package and nostalgic content cried out to be published as a trade paperback original.

But what if the author and/or agent insists that their book come out in hardcover for prestige, for reviews, or for the library market? Or what if the market for this book will pay a hardcover retail price? You certainly don't want to miss out on that opportunity. Or you may decide that the real market is in paperback but you need the hardcover to establish the market. What the editor can do is to find an interested editor at a hardcover house. Usually he turns first to an editor of an imprint within his own corporation, and then together they buy the book hard-soft. How the book is handled from here varies depending on many factors, including the working habits and style of each editor and the chemistry between them. The type of book it is and who has a particular strength with that book, or who has the relationship with the author or agent, are also important determinants. If the project started at Avon, as an example, the paperback editor would probably do the bulk of the editorial work (conceptual and line editing), or both editors might go through the manuscript, confer, and then respond to the author with one, unified letter. The hardcover editor at Morrow, our hardcover imprint, would then see it through the various stages of production, present it at sales conference, and push it though publicity, etc. I would do the same at our paperback sales conference the following year.

Let's suppose an agent sends me a proposal for a history book on America during the Second World War and I think that this is a book that will become a classic in its field, with course adoption possibilities. I will send it up to an editor at Morrow who also understands this type of book and will recognize its hardcover market. Assuming this editor likes it, we will run profit and loss numbers within our companies and then "marry" those numbers so that we can determine how much we can afford to pay to buy it jointly. If we buy the book, the author writes his manuscript and submits it to the editor he feels more comfortable with, perhaps even to both. As a

common courtesy, the editor who received it usually informs the other that
the manuscript is in and makes a copy for the other one. Then, depending
on individual schedules, they set out to edit.

In a perfect world, both editors see eye to eye on the strengths and flaws
of the work. Usually one editor picks up certain things and his counterpart
picks up others. Sometimes they disagree on certain points and both points
of view are presented to the author, who can then decide which opinion he
wants to go with. I always insist on one letter going out to the author so that
he isn't confused. Some editors can get territorial about who should sign the
letter, but usually a compromise can be worked out based on who "found"
the book, who did the most work on it. If I'm dealing with an old-fashioned,
traditionalist hardcover editor, I usually let him write the letter as long as
my comments are passed along and my name is mentioned as the other
editor. This is by no means a perfect method. It can sometimes irritate
people's feelings; overall, however, the advantages outweigh the disadvan-
tages. I genuinely believe that having two pairs of trained editorial eyes
looking at the work is a real plus for any author.

·   ·   ·

A hardcover editor approaches a paperback house for a partnership for
various reasons. Often it is a simple monetary one. If the hardcover editor
wants a book that an agent is selling but that will cost too much money to
acquire, this editor knows that by joining forces with a paperback company
there will be more money to work with and she may be able to beat out her
competition.

Sometimes, though, the introductions go the other way. There are times
when the paperback house has a previous history with an author who either
has never been published in hardcover or is unhappy with his present
hardcover publisher. If the trade paperback editor thinks it is worth it, he
will introduce the author to the hardcover house within his own corporation.

Because the paperback publisher has put up at least half of the acquisition money, he will often have a big say in the way a hardcover house
publishes the book, from title selection to jacket design to marketing plans.
Again, this influence varies from company to company and from project to
project. My experience has been that there really isn't much of a difference
between the way a hardcover editor and a paperback editor would shape the
work, since both are really thinking of the same reader. However, there is
usually a big difference in the way their respective companies would market
the book—everything from title selection to jacket/cover designs to advertising and publicity campaigns.

For instance, when a hardcover editor I know bought a controversial book on relationships by a well-respected sociologist, his company chose to go with a long, serious title that was authoritative, and they put nothing but type on the jacket. His trade paperback partner lobbied for a shorter, punchier title and some sort of illustration that would play up the controversial subject matter. The hardcover editor was going for reviews and prestige. The paperback publisher was going for something that would make people sit up and notice the book—and remember it years later, when the paperback would be the prevailing edition in the stores. Sometimes the two sides can come together. If they can't come up with a solution both sides can live with, sometimes the paperback publisher will have an opportunity to change the title and cover approach one year later.

About the time that Thornton's piece was being read in the early 1980s, something interesting was starting to happen with trade paperback fiction. Young men and women in their early twenties and thirties were writing dynamic, hip novels on the cutting edge, and a large audience responded to their hardcover editions with great enthusiasm. Trade paperback publishers, led by Vintage Books, bought them for reprint and packaged them with bold, modern covers that often looked like record album covers. Reviewers couldn't stop writing about them, so publishers decided to publish some of these novels directly in trade paper, the most popular example of this being Jay McInerney's *Bright Lights, Big City.*

But this turned out to be a relatively short-lived fad. Too many publishers jumped on the bandwagon, the market became glutted, and the audience for this type of "youth fiction" moved on to something else. Another problem is that the price of acquiring a good literary novel has gone up astronomically, which means that publishers need to sell a large quantity of books to earn back the advance paid to the author. When publishers try to publish them right into paperback, most newspapers and magazines don't review them.

When we started up Avon Trade Paperbacks, we saw that many of our competitors were cutting back on all trade fiction titles, so we decided to limit the number of fiction titles to one per month. By doing this we can put a lot of effort into publishing that one title, with more advertising, promotion, and publicity money allocated. This, of course, means we have to be very selective about what we acquire. When we find we have had to pay a lot of money to acquire a trade fiction book, we make that book a lead title and publish it at the top of our list, giving it even more attention. We did this with a first novel called *The Music Room* by Dennis McFarland, and the book was a big success for us. But you can only do this every so often and only with the right book.

Although editors want to publish them, trade fiction titles are very difficult to do now. Unfortunately, there just isn't enough of an audience to support the number of books published in this area. With a few exceptions, most trade fiction reprints don't sell more than what they sold in hardcover despite the lower cost. There seems to be a finite number of readers who can pay the hardcover price for good quality fiction, and then one year later there aren't many left over for the paperback edition. Of course the hardcover benefits from getting the review attention at the time of publication, which gets readers into the stores. One year later and people just don't seem to remember a book they read about in some review. So as a result, most paperback publishers have been cutting back their lists. The exception, in recent years, seems to be books that win the major literary awards like the National Book Award.

Now, in the early 1990s, the majority of hard-soft acquisitions in trade paperback are nonfiction.

Those of us in the industry who are fortunate enough to work on trade paperbacks have discovered ways of combining hardcover and mass-market publishing techniques, from the way we acquire books to the way we get them to the marketplace. A trade paperback editor's life isn't much different from a hardcover editor's life except that he is more likely to be in more meetings during working hours. This is especially true if this editor works inside a mass-market house, where the pace is much quicker and the pressure is greater to keep things on schedule. As if there weren't enough meetings in our company, we added another one just for trade paperbacks. We call it a "target marketing" meeting. Essentially what this does is call the sales and marketing departments' attention to books on the list that warrant special attention because, given the book's subject matter, there are some unusual avenues to explore. These meetings also train editors to think like publishers. Before the meeting the editor is asked to think about why she acquired the book, special markets that sales people might not usually solicit, other books on the subject and how they compare, specialized media where review copies and press releases can be sent, special interest magazines where it might make sense to advertise, and how the author can promote or help us exploit contacts in his/her field. The final question we ask is, who will read this book and how can we best get to that reader?

One of the major things I've learned toiling on trade paperbacks is not to count on the big best-seller reprints. Some of them work, but some of them will bite you on the butt a year later in paperback. I discovered this the hard way with two big hardcover best-sellers that we almost bought for reprint, Kevin Phillips's *Politics of Rich and Poor* and Peggy Noonan's *What I Learned at the Revolution*. Both books were sold at auction for a lot of money and both books didn't sell well in paperback. Most likely, the vast amounts of media attention these books received at the time of hardcover publication helped create a buying frenzy at one concentrated time, which resulted in the bookstores reporting to the people who compile best-seller lists. The reprinters acquired paperback rights in the heat of the moment. The real audience for these books were people who could afford the hardcover and wanted to read them right away. One year later and people were interested in something else.

If you look at paperback best-seller lists you will see books that didn't show up on hardcover best-seller lists and seem to have come out of nowhere. *Don't Know Much about History, What to Expect When You're Expecting,* and *The Road Less Travelled* are examples of this. Since I worked on both the hardcover and the paperback of *Don't Know Much about History* by Ken Davis, I think I know why it succeeded in paperback. This popular Q&A about all the things we should know about American history hit a responsive chord among a generation of Americans who either were bored by what they learned in school, forgot what they learned, or doubted all the myths and misconceptions, like George Washington and his cherry tree. With a slightly humorous tone Davis presented everything in small bites. This appealed to a large group of people who, despite busy lives, still felt they needed to know and learn. The hardcover sold a fair amount of copies. Reviews and word of mouth were strong, but the book was often out of stock, it was expensive, and, although it had a handsome jacket, it looked serious.

When the paperback came out at half the price, it had a tongue-in-cheek cover and didn't look nearly as intimidating as the hardcover. It was portable and it was packaged with wonderful quotes. The booksellers ordered a lot of copies in paperback since they hadn't been able to get the hardcover and there was pent-up demand. The paperback, published in June, was promoted by the stores as a perfect gift for dads and grads, and together with fun advertising and extensive publicity campaigns that revolved around national holidays, the book made it onto best-seller lists and stayed on for months.

An editor also thinks like a publisher when he looks on his company's list of trade paperbacks as a program, searching for ways to build on strengths and looking for opportunities. For instance, if he has done well with a book on the Soviet Union, he looks for other books on the subject. He thinks, too, of series that he can do. After our success with the aforementioned *Don't Know Much about History,* we signed the author to do *Don't Know Much about Geography* and *Don't Know Much about World History.* The possibilities are limited only by our imaginations and by the popularity of the series with the public.

Even if a book didn't do too well at first, the author may be active later on doing speaking engagements or getting attention in the media. It is the editor's responsibility to keep tabs on these opportunities and alert his sales department to go out again with a book that may work the second time around.

Returning for the last time to Mr. Thornton, when he wrote his essay, the nonbook, impulse-buy trade paperback, like the previously mentioned book about Rubik's Cube, was all the rage. Now, with the exception of brand-name humor and a few quirky, trendy, short-lived titles, these disposable books have fallen by the wayside. Personally, I'm trying to stay away from fads; by the time you get the fad-oriented book into the stores, the fickle public is following another fad.

As I write this essay, we're in a recession. As a result we've probably lost the occasional impulse buyer. But I believe it doesn't matter what economic climate we're in: there will always be serious readers going into bookstores to find good books that contain real information and that cost less than the hardcover. This, I am convinced, is the real audience for trade paperbacks, now and in the next millennium—a mere seven years away. If corporate owners learn to be patient they will see what so many have seen before them, that the only way to build up strong companies is with strong backlist titles that contribute to the bottom line every year. Slow and steady *does* win the race. The mission of trade paperback editors is to recognize this but also not to turn their noses up when a rare chance for opportunism comes along (for example, an instant book on a popular rock band).

There is a large audience whom we used to call yuppies, who have aged into what we now sometimes call the baby boomers. I identify them as the Cultural Literacy Generation. This generation is becoming more sedate, turning inward, raising families, and staying at home more. These readers are looking for good serious fiction, a "liberal arts" program of nonfiction titles, and popular books on a wide variety of subjects that are not too dry or academic in content. Trade paperbacks and the editors who have published them for four decades reflect this generation. I suppose these books and editors have become less daring and more practical. But as always, a new generation of editors and readers will come up from the ranks who will be innovative and bold and will inject new life into trade paperbacks. One of these editors will no doubt inherit this space in the next edition of *Editors on Editing*. It will be interesting to see what the latest "truths" about trade paperbacks will be at that time.

Editing Nonfiction
The Question of "Political Correctness"

Wendy M. Wolf

WENDY M. WOLF *is a senior editor at HarperCollins and was previously a senior editor at Pantheon Books. She edits books in history, popular culture, music, sports, biography, science, and humor. The authors she has published include Barry Commoner, Robert Christgau, Vine Deloria, Jr., Tom Lehrer, and Matt Groening, as well as John Cleese, Michael Palin, and the other members of* Monty Python's Flying Circus.

What role should the nonfiction editor play in the current debate over P.C. (political correctness)? Should the editor "otherly label" controversial words, opinions, and political, social, and personal situations and relationships to suit the trend toward using currently fashionable euphemisms for these difficult and problematical aspects of our culture? Or should the editor maintain the traditional role of the facilitator of the author's intent? And what if that intent differs from the political, sexual, or social beliefs of influential areas of the literary or academic establishment, or even those of the editor?

Wendy Wolf approaches these controversial issues by recognizing her editorial responsibility to her author, her publisher, "to some vague notion of the world or Western civilization at large, and to myself. . . . The key to sane survival, to my thinking and in my experience," she writes, "is to focus on the word 'responsibility' and to try to see how the balance of my conflicting obligations affects various major and minor editorial issues."

Eloquently, passionately, and provocatively, Ms. Wolf considers all the ramifications of the pressures and impact of political correctness on her choice of nonfiction books to edit, on her relationships with her authors, her publisher, the reading public, and on her own integrity, conscience, and humanity.

"Difficult ideas," she writes, "have to pass scrutiny so that their arguments hold up against the evidence amassed. But we can't surrender our responsibilities either from fear of the bottom line, fear of associating ourselves with a disturbing thought, or fear of mere dissent from the prevailing wisdom. Writers may owe us a great deal, as their stalwart editors and defenders of their faith, but we owe them something, too."

Editing Nonfiction
The Question of "Political Correctness"

Most of my friends who started out with me as editorial assistants saw the light and went on to something sensible like real estate. A few hardy souls, however, decided to stay in for the long run. Remember that word, "decide." Any editor who doesn't own up to that initial act of free will sooner or later find herself in trouble when she tries to clarify one of the murkier but unavoidable aspects of our work: facing up to the constant query, "How do I choose what to publish?"

My answer is actually simple. As an editor, I have responsibilities in a number of directions: to my author, to my employer, to some vague notion of the world or Western civilization at large, and to myself. Nine times out of ten I don't know or worry about where one begins and the other ends, because the ends of each are jointly served. It's when they fall out of synch, and conflicts of interest and responsibility result, however, that I wonder if the role of the editor is anything more than cultural bureaucrat or literary cipher. The key to sane survival, to my thinking and in my experience, is to focus on the word "responsibility" and to try to see how the balance of my conflicting obligations affects various major and minor editorial issues. It's in this context that I think about the question of "political correctness," now ubiquitously dubbed "P.C."

An editor is an active participant in a great chain of choice. When you take on a book, you have to answer to yourself why you're doing it and be willing to live with the consequences. The chain operates in different ways over time—at the moment you decide to work for a particular company, over the course of your tenure with them, as you generate a track record (and you see which races are counted on that ledger), and over the historical performance of your employer in the long and short run.

I—like, I suspect, most of my colleagues—choose a book after I consider how that book can fulfill one of a myriad of different goals or expectations that I have set for myself. It might be to win a prize, to make the news, to attack an enemy, to uncover a crime, to make money, to amuse, to annoy, to bring down a government, to please the eye, to create an object I can give my mother for Christmas, to present a new argument, to refute an old one, to offer a useful synthesis of a broad topic, or to explain how to fix a broken steam pipe. Not every book starts a revolution, and I'd be the first to list the many, many books I've published over the years that serve no more sophisticated purpose than to give a few laughs. No one can say that, for sure and forever, any one of these reasons is more or less valid than any other. I have my priorities, both for my own list and for the industry as a whole; others have theirs. I wish we all agreed; we don't. At best we can agree to respect each other's decisions, and that no one factor—profitability or current political vogue—is, a priori, a *necessary* element in a book's potential profile.

More often than not it's some quirky combination of several of these categories that encourages me to pursue a book, and I'm often hard-pressed to say precisely toward which one or toward what valence my brain is being drawn. It's a source of delightful frustration to the computer-systems folks who strive valiantly to come up with a data base that would reduce the editorial decision-making process to a set of variables and programs. We sit in conferences gladly urging them to create these informational resources, and then politely add, "But of course that's not really how it works."

I don't entirely accept the increasingly popular argument that editors have been stripped of all responsibility in the decision chain, that their job—the reason they're paid—is just to pump out what sells, content or impact notwithstanding, that we are neutral facilitators, not gatekeepers whose job includes deliberately regulating the flow of ideas. Some would in fact argue that we have no right regulating—who are we, after all, to determine what will and what won't pass into the marketplace of ideas? Shouldn't all views, all writers have unfettered access to the reading public? Publish what the public wants, or what sells; they try to claim it's a neutral, nonjudgmental stance we should be taking. But deciding what the public wants is not as easy as it looks, as we'll see. The rage over cultural disenfranchisement, control of the canon, and that much-debated new hegemonic force, "political correctness," sends off clashing and often contradictory messages about exactly who the "public" is and what they want, or should want. Interestingly, the war over the canon seems to have been waged by armies other than those that fight the battle of the best-sellers.

You can like a book for as many reasons as there are to write one, but to pretend that, as an acquiring editor, you're not standing in judgment and making a choice is a dangerous and self-deluding stance. Even those who claim that they're just providing, as a public service, "what the world wants to read" have in fact judged, this time not just one author, one project, or one's own interest on one day, but a large and usually unknowable broad taste in the world at large. So much for neutrality.

My point here isn't to assign some divine order to which kinds of reasons are better or worse; the point is simply to acknowledge that an editor must, in the end, take responsibility for the decision to take on a book or an idea, to fund it, to see it through execution, to help the publishing company position it in its dual journey through the world of ideas and the world of commodities. Just saying "I'm doing it because it's what the world wants to read" isn't, to me, a satisfying explanation. You've made a conscious calculation. There's a whiny complaint lurking in the comment that the editor is a victim of the marketplace, forced by circumstance to take on a distasteful project against his or her will. I find this rarely borne out in reality. Books don't fall out of the sky and land on you like smelly albatrosses (though many quickly become just that in the process). No one publishes a book utterly against his will and against his better judgment. Somewhere inside, some voice is whispering that there's a reason.

In an ideal world, we work to integrate our own balance sheet into our company's by publishing books that we find both attractive and stimulating intellectually and that, *on the whole,* allow us to function profitably. Remember that italicized phrase. Thomas Boswell, *Washington Post* sports columnist, says that you can't tell anything about a baseball player's abilities from a single week, much less a single game—performance quality shows up only over time. The same is true for an editor or author, and even for a publisher's list. Not every player is expected to get on base at each at bat, and the way I see it, nor should every book be judged solely on the basis of its potential financial profile or its immediate popularity estimation. First of all, our predictive capabilities are just too crude to rely on for long. We know about those durable war-horses of the best-seller lists, but if we publish only in the existing categories and genres, we risk missing out not just on the most interesting new books, but on the greatest profits. Ask me, an early (and doubting) reader, about an Italian manuscript, a dense and difficult historical mystery by a semiologist, of all things. Who was to know what could come of *The Name of the Rose* in the right and able hands? The same pertains in the entertainment industry; ask the A&R guy who first heard Elvis.

Second, books have, since the beginning, served a critical function in the discourse of ideas as well as in the marketplace of goods. We run grave risks when the two parts of books' identities are severed, and we get carried away with our own perceptions of the demands of the marketplace. Even when I'm calculating a small readership for a book, I'm making an implicit assumption about a book's potential readership—what readers it might reach, whom it should reach. As I try to imagine a book's readership, I have to ask how important it is that people agree with said book's content, for giving the public what we think it wants, now as well as in the past, doesn't necessarily mean publishing garbage. But it involves a precise definition of "audience," which all too often conforms for us to the demographics of the suburban mall.

Even an editor who claims to make a judgment entirely in market or money terms has to, at some point, account for his or her failures. We all spend far too little time in postmortems, reviewing our miscalculations and misreadings of the marketplace, but if we did, I suspect we'd find that while there may have been different justifications voiced for a signing decision (I took this on because it's good/it's important/it will sell), in fact all decisions are a mix of value judgments and more or less accurate ideas about potential sales. And in this context, it's not that editors are more or less interested in markets, but that those in pursuit of the mass market probably hold it in more contempt than those who target the various niche audiences. We have to consider the so-called rights of the niche audience to gain access to the mainstream outlets for books, and our complicity in keeping them out by bending to the status quo in book*selling,* an issue I'll elaborate on further.

Part of the challenge of being an editor at a time when many of the old assumptions about history, historiography, and language itself are under fire is to stay honest about the person I imagine as a reader or book buyer. Writers from the disenfranchised minorities claim we discriminate against their potential audience because they aren't "traditional" (white, well-educated, well-heeled book club types). I think we do, in large part because our bookselling outlets service those "other" audiences so poorly. It sounds like a vicious circle of blame, and it is incumbent upon all the participants to take responsibility for breaking the cycle, but as we press toward greater representation of *all* voices through the books we publish, we should be trying not just to expand the rolls of writers, but of readers as well. Opening up the book-buying world, supporting libraries, attending to literacy on a mass level—these are tasks as crucial as finding the new Terry McMillan or Toni Morrison.

. . .

The large majority of the books we all deal with raise little controversy—other than disagreement over sales potential and whether blue or red on the jacket makes the most sense. What happens, then, when I am presented with what we delicately refer to as one of "those difficult projects"—nonfiction books that propose unpopular ideas, that challenge conventionally held

and often widely beloved notions, that upset and are upsetting, that sometimes seem designed to cause trouble and nothing else?

It's simple. I know I have a choice. I have to figure out why I want to
publish this particular work and ally my name with it—what it's going to
do for (or to) the universe, the discourse, the author, my company, and
myself—and go on from there. It's no more than taking responsibility for
your own decisions, and then standing by them. I know that the decision I
make to pursue one project will affect what happens on several others on
my desk at the same time, and that a book that appeals to me one year will
sound like old hat another. No standard formula works for long because the
individual variables in that formula change not just from editor to editor
but from book to book, and change over time, as the demands of keeping
a list functioning create certain other demands. But I personally don't
subscribe to the belief that the money quotient always comes first and last.
Anyway, there just isn't that much money to make. If maximizing profits
at any cost is your interest, go into the shoe business. At least you can wear
the remainders.

Now here's the part that's not quite so simple. What if, in said book, the
argument being presented not only flies in the face of world opinion or taste,
but speaks against your own sensibilities or values. The author presents a
fascinating account of working at the pioneering frontiers of brain biology
and research, but amasses his evidence to prove that there is not only racial
differentiation but limitation in capability or content; you find the lab work
riveting and the conclusions revolting. Or a discredited refugee from a
notorious political scandal comes to you promising that he will name names
(perhaps or perhaps not clearing his own); you know his name will attract
attention—and revenues—but believe the man to be in fact guilty of the
crimes accused. The offense can be launched from anywhere on the political
spectrum—Right attacking the Left; black attacking Jew; female attacking
male; a proponent of "family values" alleging a gay conspiracy; and so on.
The pairs of possible opponents and available controversies are infinite, and
for this argument, the particulars are irrelevant. But what happens when
I'm both attracted to and disturbed by the contents of the proposal or
manuscript at the same time?

One of two other awful considerations usually arises here, too. Either the
book is almost certain to lose money or—sometimes a worse prospect, I
think—we might actually sell large quantities of something readily deemed
hateful; after all, it's what the public wants/believes/is believed to believe.
What do I do?

There is no convincing argument for avoiding controversy or conflict, for
suppressing a minority opinion, for controlling language, for rounding
sharp edges, for censorship. Period. Even if applied under the supposed

"best of humane intentions" in a particular situation, any censoring effort creates a precedent of suppression. But if I don't censor *them,* they won't have that excuse to censor *me.* However—and I think this is crucial in the debate over the tyranny of the marketplace and censorship through commercial choices—this is *not* the same as saying an editor or a house is under *obligation* to publish anything and everything they are presented with, nor does the simple fact of controversial content merit selection and promotion as a trade book. Recognizing that I chose to be in this position not only gives me a responsibility—it gives me protection as well.

Much ink is spilled these days over what is now commonly called "the new McCarthyism of the Left"—the tyrannical rule of "political correctness," which in its extreme form is said to demand that any attempt to write history or to describe the past or future of our society pass through stringent screens designed to filter out discriminatory language, hegemonic cultural assumptions, or any intended or unintended slur against the traditionally disenfranchised special-interest or "ethnic" (read non-Caucasian, usually non-European) people in American society. Writers across the cultural and political spectrum, from Robert Hughes to C. Vann Woodward, have argued in venues from the *New York Review of Books* to the *Village Voice* about the breadth and depth of the P.C. Reign of Terror on campuses today, and I would not presume to venture unarmed into *that* debate. I can only speak about the supposed tyranny of P.C. as witnessed from the acquiring editor's chair, and I merely point to recent best-seller lists as evidence of who's on top, who's selling, and who's getting big bucks. The fury over P.C. may in fact be yet another index of the well-organized, well-connected, highly visible, and voluble Right effectively articulating its paranoia. Chew over the sales figures for Allan Bloom, Camille Paglia, Dinesh D'Souza, E. D. Hirsch. Notice that there's nary a defender of the misbegotten rights of otherly abled Trotskyite Basques of Puerto Rican descent among them. Defending the old regime still seems to be a pretty marketable commodity.

From where I sit, being an O. A. T. B. of P. R. D. neither qualifies nor disqualifies you from publication. On the other hand, neither does being a tenured professor at Yale. It's the same boring story—I gotta like, or at least respect, what you're trying to say, or find a value in it on my own terms. Needless to say, a *balance* of voices from niches large and small should be the ideal.

Books have also become an extension of the celebrity tee shirt–rock video–breakfast cereal-endorsement merchandise package. It's innocuous when it's merely football players and soap opera stars to whom this publishing prerogative is extended. Their books may not save Western civilization or advance the cause of freedom, but they usually don't harm anyone either, and can generate revenues that can be put to good use elsewhere. But consider this more troubling scenario.

What if David Duke were to approach me with a proposal? The celebrity component is certainly there, as is the public recognition, the proven publicity machinery, and the arguably legitimate interest in hearing his arguments, seeing them played out, testing their validity. There's also the point to be considered that such a book could conceivably produce revenues and profits. After all, so they would say, many people agree with him and would want to hear what he has to say. But to take him on, I would have to find my own answers to a series of pointed questions. How would I be serving any community's interest or enlarging the debate about race, the social welfare structure, and the role of government? Would I in fact be contributing to the legitimizing of what I consider a wholly unacceptable position by permitting him this platform to sound off from? Now, an assemblage of Duke documents as evidence could be a usefully frightening object. But my answer, on the packaged offering of Duke *himself,* would be a clear no. I might question the judgment of another publisher who did take him on, but that would be that publisher's prerogative. Yes, that's a personal political and moral decision on my part, but so would be the decision *to* publish him. There is no such thing as an impersonal decision in this realm. This touches on an area I'll elaborate on later, in specific issues of language and terminology. Certain books arrive in more or less fixed shape, due to the odd insistence by the author to have it his way, come hell, high water, or editor armed with sharp pencils. In assessing a book's "worth" and its hazards to me, my house, and the world at large, I try, not always successfully, to stay aware of the distinctions between what I would like a book to be or become, and what its real features and limitations are.

As editors, we more often are presented with less extreme cases of crises of conscience—a well-grounded argument that takes a few uncomfortable turns, throws a few dangerous curves. I don't have a hard-and-fast rule for myself, and I attempt, not always with success, to stop short of the doctrinaire, to keep my own mind open to new persuasions. "It's a mixed bag," I often say, describing a complicated project. But there are usually few surprises; it's rare that, if you take the time to investigate even the skimpiest three-page proposal, you can't suss out where the dark corners are going to be. I know that I have to make a choice whether to throw myself into it, but once I do commit, then my absolute obligation is to help the author get it right.

If only there were a computer program to work this one out—but you're stuck with your own cost-benefit ratio analysis; of course, the definitions of what constitutes a cost—or a benefit—follow no rigid formula. The decision to take on only profitable books is not automatically or a priori more or less defensible than a choice based on "political" principles. It's not a given but a deliberate choice in and of itself, and one with grave ramifications as editors perform the necessary ritual of trying to come to terms with why they do what they do. Unfortunately, we spend little time assessing or accounting for the times we miscalculated the size of the audience, the nature of the book's appeal.

. . .

So I've got this daring work of dissident scholarship on my desk. Now what do I do with it?

There are, to my mind, three stages of influence or intervention for an editor, each with distinct opportunities and requisites. Stage One is the period in which I'm considering signing up a project. Once there might have been a significant portion of a manuscript and a clear profile of the author to back it up. These days I'm lucky if I get three irrelevant magazine articles and a ten-page outline. Still, I've got investigative tools at my disposal to help me determine just what I'm getting into—where this argument might lead, for better or worse, what skeletonic secondary characters might be dancing in the author's closet, what portions of his or her work I know I'll have issues with.

First, I talk to other people I know and trust in the field. As a "general interest" editor, there are a few areas I know a lot about, and many I can't pretend expertise in. One of my talents (or maybe just a trick of the trade) is knowing how to get good advice from people who do know. Second, I try, if possible, to meet with the author in person; I find that if the author-hopeful seems to be calculatingly eyeing the size of my window rather than investigating the contents of my bookshelf, brain, or in-box for clues to my identity and status, that tells me something about our future relationship. Where necessary or appropriate, I also explain where my personal opinion diverges from his or hers, and where I think the potential weaknesses or danger zones of the book's argument might lie. Obviously, if you're only working with an outline, there's much detail to come, but a good free-ranging but directed conversation will reveal most potential bugaboos.

The point isn't to be best friends with each and every author, but if there isn't a common basis of trust, I won't be able to do my job; I can't engage in the necessary dialogue with a writer I don't respect, even as we disagree. I also believe the author has as much right to "discovery" vis-à-vis his or her editor's position as the editor has of the author, because once the decision is made to go ahead—once you do your numbers and decide what to do with your numbers—and you give an author a contract, there's no waffling. Wrestle your angels to the ground here, in Stage One, before commitment, because once you have accepted the book's premise, body, and conclusion, your commitment is to work to make it as perfect a piece as your collective energies and personalities will warrant.

Thus we enter Stage Two, where the editor's role, to my mind, is blindingly clear: to dog, torment, torture, question, challenge, pry, invade, coax, cajole, praise, and attack that work and its creator until its argument is airtight, or until it has reached the goal of acceptability you mutually have determined upon embarkation. This mutuality of assumption is a critical, if weasely, aspect of Stage Two, since it's the vexing decision of whether a work is "acceptable" that has the most profound legal, moral, and financial repercussions; it is, in fact, *the* critical breakpoint for many a controversial or risk-taking book. This is also the stage during which I must constantly keep in the front of the discussion whose book this is—the author's, not mine. Where am I challenging the author to defend his position against my dissenting argument, and where are we agreeing to disagree?

In romantic fashion, I like to imagine all our arguments being over deep political truths, but in fact, the issue is usually not what is said but how it is said—its manner of expression and, in particular, who the readership will be or what it will do in reaction to the writer's choice of words. This can be turned into an issue of ideas and censorship by an aggrieved author, but that's usually self-deception. I think the realm of language, expression, and simply choices in words is one where the sensitively blunt editor can perform the most heroic duty in helping a manuscript toward completion.

I don't subscribe to a fixed lexicon of political correctness; I do think the minutiae of language and rhetoric are hugely significant, and I try to impart a respect and sensitivity about that belief to my authors. But it's been my experience that actual language usually flows from the ideas, that if the thought is sensitive, it's not difficult to make the expression of the thought equally so. I try to help writers, for example, see the impact of words like *mankind* versus *humanity,* or sort out difficult vocabulary decisions—determining whether to use *Native American* or *American Indian*; *Black, African American, people of color,* or a more "retro" form, perhaps in a historical context or to make a specific dramatic statement. I try to explore the political implications of controversial name changes like Kampuchea or Myanmar, where what we (or the *New York Times*) might casually presume to be the currently popular or P.C. choice is in fact the expression of imposed will by a small group of tyrants, and hardly the people's term of choice.

You can tie yourself into linguistic knots trying to accommodate the various needs and demands voiced by special-interest groups regarding how they would like to be described. In many cases I think it's a matter of the disenfranchised, being powerless to control the more substantive issues determining their condition, at least asserting themselves over labeling. We know from the experience of schoolchildren that labels have powerful and enduring social effects, but at some point you've just got to apply some combination of sensitivity to both politics and the language and good old-fashioned common sense. In many cases you can avoid cumbersome labels for groups by simply rewriting the sentence, avoiding those "portmanteau" descriptive phrases and using plain nouns and verbs instead. I think of this as combing the knots out of tangled prose.

The choice of gender in pronouns can be deliberately provocative and can also be alienating. I don't think there's a slide rule of implications that will automatically determine what's right. I do think that author and editor together can discuss why (or even if) a choice has been made, and whether it's been an informed and directed one. Is the author trying to conform to a vocabulary mutually agreed upon by a preselected readership? What if a term is comfortable to the writer or to the person described, but not to readers outside the preselected group? Who should prevail?

I often think of myself as playing the role of Gentle Reader with an author. That is, my job isn't to *correct* his or her words, but to alert the author to the impact of his or her phrases: "This is how I read this sentence; this is what it says to me. Is that what you *want* it to say? Is that the most effective (or most direct, or most evocative, or most provocative) way of accomplishing that end?" The run of issues is usually similar from project to project. Is the argument well documented? Is the evidence there? Is the presentation effective? Is the language sensitive and accurate? Is its effect what you want? It's not always easy to listen with an open mind to the author's answers to my questions when I still may profoundly disagree with aspects of his argument, assumptions, or conclusions, but my job isn't to impose my will and worldview on every book I publish, just to give them the benefit of my skepticism.

When are we through? Obviously, every book takes a different course, but they all wind up in somewhat the same place. A book is done when the author can say to me with absolute conviction: "This is how I want to say it, damn it, and I stand by my words!" (Or sometimes, "This is the best I can do, and I think it's good enough.") In a reasonable world, that is also the place where I believe the manuscript does what I wanted it to do in the beginning, and I stand by it as well.

At this point, I (perhaps in conjunction with a battery of attorneys, expert readers, and colleagues) must make the decision whether to accept the manuscript or not. This is of course the second key moment in a book's life. Once a book is accepted, the publisher is under legal, contractual responsibility to publish it within a specific period of time, and I firmly believe publishers should be held to that legal obligation, regardless of shifting winds of opinion within or outside the house. The fact that many publishers' contracts already contain language covering the publisher's failure to fulfill that obligation indicates that not everyone agrees. I recognize that the changing contingencies in the fragile marketplace can place a publisher in an awkward bind, but face up to those realities at the moment of acceptance.

Stage Three is the preparation for publication once the manuscript is complete. With potentially noisy manuscripts, I believe it's part of my job to pave the way for the book in-house by preparing the sales and marketing staff; this might include alerting them to the nature and extent of the controversies in which the book engages, what kinds of reactions we might expect from reviewers, and whether the author belongs to one camp or another in a particular academic or political battle. Forewarned is forearmed; if I can keep a publicist from being caught by surprise by a hostile interviewer, or give the sales department the essential context from which a book was written, there are likely to be fewer unpleasant surprises or unmet expectations. This is as important a part of "positioning" the book as is trying to predict the size of a book's audience. While, as I've said before, it's the unanticipated breakouts and breakthrough books that in the long run generate the greatest profits, I don't think you do anyone—author or publisher—a favor by unrealistically overselling a book. The clearer we can all be on why a book is important, and what our expectations are, the happier we'll be when the book goes on to exceed them wildly.

• • •

The assumed neutrality—that supposed value-free stance that publishers like to claim they are taking when publishing controversial materials—is worth examining closely. It works in two directions—when we're asked to publish works that, in all likelihood, the larger part of the book-buying audience will find disturbing (and therefore not buy), and when we're asked to publish works that we ourselves find disturbing, but that we believe people "out there" will agree with, will embrace, and will buy. The argument is generally made that publishers are not complicit in any crime simply by "giving the world what it wants," that in fact they are under obligation to provide books across the board or spectrum. Therefore, publishing the distasteful-but-popular is seen as a neutral position, with the editor as a mere cipher passing along public taste. In fact, no part of a book's publication is neutral. Choosing to publish, at least the way books are published today, confers an inescapable kind of legitimacy on a writer or public figure by the act of a commercial presentation of his or her argument.

I think we are, more often than not, disguising our moral responsibility with market-oriented camouflage. We do not just present undigested documents to the world for the world at large to read, analyze, and respond to.

In every aspect of the packaging, presentation, and in the language with which we describe books, we are attempting to influence and control the reception of that book, by reviewers and critics, by booksellers, and by readers. We aren't saying, "Read these words, judge for yourselves," but "This is the truth." We grant authenticity and legitimacy by our imprimatur and, equally important, by advertising, author tours, and the other usual mechanisms of the marketing apparatus. We deliberately attempt to control the debate or reception with our labels, covers, copy, promotion efforts, and even with our name and logo on the spine.

The book was once (and sometimes still can be) a source of celebritydom, but book publishing is increasingly embedded within a vast network of media events and exploitation of material—star in a movie, do the talk shows, film an exercise video, endorse a spaghetti sauce or perfume, write a book. Publishers would be fools not to cash in on their portion of this exploitable market, but we should also not let what was once a *by-product* of publication (fame) become a necessary *prerequisite* for a book contract. While not everyone agrees with me, I believe that in fact it's part of a publisher's obligation to give voice to just those people who don't qualify for the nine-city tour, that balancing big and little books is a sign of a publisher's healthy recognition that we, in fact, are not mere merchants of cultural artifacts.

. . .

Naturally, I'm attracted to writing that already reflects my own set of beliefs, but I've had my mind changed many a time, just as I think I've changed the mind or at least the temporary orientation of some of my writers. Sometimes I come across a book that I know will play a key role in moving a debate along because of its extreme position. I might find that the argument, be it about feminist psychology, national drug policy, black capitalism, or colonial Indian policy, strays much further than I personally find acceptable. But if I feel confident that giving voice to this extreme point of view will make a concrete and positive contribution to a debate, then publishing the book is a responsible act. Is this imposing on the world my will, my prejudices, through the act of selection? Of course. But so is signing up a book because you think it will make money.

The powers of persuasion of a book, and of a publisher, are large and terrible, and none of us should ever lose sight of that. If you truly believed numbers tell the only truth, then compared to the awesome audience draw of a single television show or movie, our impact on the world should be almost undetectable; instead we influence debate, thought, individual self-image, public policy, national conscience and consciousness. With that influence comes an inescapable obligation to attend to the unpopular as well as popular, the troubling as well as the conventional, to give voice to those who would be silenced by the majority of opinion-makers or by purveyors of fame. I know I have an obligation to those who pay my salary to give them a return on their investment in me. I like to believe that they understand this return can come in more forms than hard currency, and I try to confirm for them that it's true. Changing the way we think has its value, and books have proved a durable vehicle for such social change.

This does not mean I advocate the indiscriminate publication of provocative materials just *because* they are unpopular. Difficult ideas have to pass scrutiny so that their arguments hold up against the evidence amassed. But we can't surrender our responsibilities either from fear of the bottom line, fear of associating ourselves with a disturbing thought, or fear of mere dissent from the prevailing wisdom. Writers may owe us a great deal, as their stalwart editors and defenders of their faith, but we owe them something, too.

Editing Fiction
The Question of "Political Correctness"

Michael Denneny

MICHAEL DENNENY *is a senior editor at St. Martin's Press and the general editor of the Stonewall Inn Editions, a line of trade paperbacks devoted to gay and lesbian literature. He is the author of* Lovers: The Story of Two Men *and* Decent Passions: Real Stories about Love. *He has edited* First Love/Last Love: Fiction from Christopher Street *and* The Christopher Street Reader, *and is currently preparing a collection of his essays for publication. He was one of the founders of* Christopher Street *magazine and worked at the University of Chicago Press and Macmillan before joining St. Martin's Press.*

In this eloquently outspoken essay on political correctness and its relevance to fiction, Michael Denneny considers whether P.C. exerts a benign or malign effect on the writer and editor's freedom of expression.

Observing what he calls "The Supreme Rule of Editing: Always remember that this is not your book but the author's," Mr. Denneny recognizes the sensitivity of minorities—particularly African Americans, gays, and lesbians—to their portrayal in fiction. But he cautions editors to bow to no pressure in the effort to bring out the best of what the author has to say—however unpopular it may be with the currently influential literary, academic, and mass-media establishments. "The truth of the matter is that serious works of art can be neither propaganda nor public relations efforts, no matter how urgently needed or how well intentioned."

Following a stimulating discussion of the ethical and aesthetic quandaries faced by an editor dealing with a question of P.C., Mr. Denneny concludes that *"in general, the attempt to make any fiction politically correct is a misguided one; it is an attempt to police the imagination. This inclination has been quite prominent among the politically committed since Plato first banished poets from his ideal republic; its resurgence today is merely an unfortunate but quite predictable by-product of a valuable surge in political activism, the dangers of which have always been self-righteousness and intolerance. . . .*

"As an editor, my loyalties lie with the freedom of the individual imagination, the fruits of which have done very little harm in the real world. Unfortunately, the same cannot be said of political action. Until the politically correct can actually produce a better world in fact rather than in theory, I for one am not willing to grant them control—or even veto power—over the realm of imaginative literature."

Editing Fiction
The Question of "Political Correctness"

The recent squalls over politically correct speech that have swept through various college campuses and on into some of our national news magazines give some indication of the turbulence generated when a culture undergoes profound realignment. In the case of the P.C. debate, we see some of the strains attendant on the quite remarkable social changes occurring in American culture in the last few decades. For most of our history, American culture was dominated, defined, and evaluated by a relatively small segment of the population: English-speaking male persons with a deep grounding in and loyalty to the Anglo-Saxon literary and cultural tradition. Although there has always been some tension between the dominance of this so-called genteel tradition and various nativist, regional, or immigrant self-assertions, the main line of American culture has been emphatically Anglo, as has been the case with other countries that began their history as British colonies.

However, since World War II this country has witnessed seismic shifts in both the culture—consider the emergence of urban male Jewish writers in the fifties, African-American women writers in the seventies, and gay and lesbian writers today—and in the demographic and social substratum upon which that culture rests. For instance, on the Berkeley campus in 1960, only 3 percent of the students were nonwhite, whereas in the autumn of '91, over 50 percent of the incoming class came from non-Anglo traditions. This opening up of the educational and cultural establishment to hitherto disenfranchised groups, the emergence of what is known as pluralism, appears today to be an irreversible trend. If it is indeed irreversible, this would mark a profound—and in my opinion a highly desirable—shift not only in the composition but perhaps even in the basic nature of that culture.

Times of such basic transitions naturally generate confusion, conflict, and trouble for those of us who work in cultural fields such as publishing. The recent insistence on politically correct speech, or more precisely the attacks on writers found guilty of being politically incorrect, i.e., offending members of one or another minority group, is a case in point. Its effects are felt on both ends of the publishing process, as a pressure on the individual author and as an influence on the opinion of the reviewer as well as the response of the reader, and they raise nice questions of judgment for the working editor.

.   .   .

When an author from a hitherto marginalized group succeeds in raising her voice in the public space, she feels not only the weight an author feels—the dreadfully public nature of publication—but also the burden of being a spokesperson for her community. While attempting to speak in her own unique and authentic voice, she is constrained by the realization that she will be heard and read as a representative of her group. This is a dilemma that is inherent in the historical situation and cannot be avoided; each author must negotiate her way through these dangerous waters, finding a balance between the claims of her own voice and her responsibility to the community. There are in my opinion no flat rules here, and the responsibility of the editor is to be sensitive to the issue while acting as a sounding board for the writer. The decisions taken are so basic that they must be thrashed out by the author rather than imposed by the editor, who in this instance, as in so many others, plays a part oddly reminiscent of the non-judgmental but supportive therapist. At times this can be a rather tedious role—editor as echo chamber—but it does have the great advantage of adhering to The Supreme Rule of Editing: Always remember that this is not your book but the author's.

The truth of the matter is that serious works of art can be neither propaganda nor public relations efforts, no matter how urgently needed or how well intentioned. It is curious that this is not abundantly clear to everyone today, given the dismal results of the fifty-year literary experiment with socialist realism in the USSR. I mean "Man meets tractor, man falls in love with tractor, man marries tractor" just doesn't cut the mustard. If we want art—and whether or not we want art has indeed been a serious question to political thinkers since Plato—we must give up this absurd notion that art can provide role models for anyone. It is beyond me how this idea ever achieved currency, since a moment's reflection blows it away.

Homer's Achilles, whatever else he was, was certainly no role model for the ancient Greeks, as he rejected all counsel of moderation and stormed against the limits of mortality, which for the Greeks defined the human condition. Nor was Madame Bovary intended to be a guide for the lives of provincial French women. This role model theory of literature boils down to a simplistic notion of monkey see, monkey do, which reveals a profound misunderstanding of the relation between literature and life.

Nevertheless, there is an understandable tendency on the part of social groups who have not previously achieved visibility in the culture or who have suffered under negative public images generated by others to feel intensely possessive about how they are portrayed, especially by their own. Ever since the furor over Philip Roth's *Portnoy's Complaint,* various communities have shown a tendency to judge works of fiction by the impact they assume such works will have on the community's public reputation. This is both a remarkably shortsighted and a remarkably persistent tendency, as can be seen in the initial reaction to Ntozake Shange's *for colored girls who have considered suicide / when the rainbow is enuf* or Larry Kramer's *Faggots,* both of which were attacked most bitterly by members of each author's own community. As far as I can see, the author has no choice but to endure such emotional buffeting and critical riptides, while preserving the authentic honesty of her own vision; the editor's job is to support the author against all comers. This can sometimes be a bruising experience for an editor—though nowhere near as bruising as it is for the author—but it comes with the territory, as my mother would say. To my mind, the most apt response to such a situation was that of Spike Lee after the storm of advice and criticism unleashed by the announcement that he intended to make a movie about the life of Malcolm X: "If you don't like the movie I make about Malcolm, go make your own."

In such situations both the author and the editor will constantly feel the pressure to conform and be politically correct. But this is merely another expression of the essential dialectic of the creative imagination, the tension between the author and society, between individual talent and the tradition. Society, tradition, and the currently politically correct always have the advantage, both of weight of opinion and of numbers. It seems reasonable to me that the editor do what he or she can to redress the balance by standing behind the author's individual talent and unique vision.

．　．　．

In addition to protecting the author from the demands for political correctness emanting from her own community—"Is it good for the Jews?"—there are other, more subtle issues that arise when publishing writers from a community different from one's own. As Joan Pinkvoss of Aunt Lute

Books has pointed out, the great danger when, for instance, a white editor is working with a writer of color is the sometimes almost unconscious temptation to make the writer's voice more intelligible or acceptable (the one sliding into the other) to white readers. This temptation must be resisted absolutely. It is the integrity of the writer's voice and vision *alone* that can provide the editor with a true standard for the editing process. The goal of editing is to make the book better, not different. From the history of black music in this country, we know fairly well the mechanics of producing a white "cover" for a black song. This is essentially a commercial and cultural rip-off, which to my mind would be a serious crime if committed by an editor. Even if the writer is willing—or eager—to make such changes in an effort to be more commercially successful (which we used to call selling out), it seems to me that such pandering to the marketplace negates the reason you would sign up such a book in the first place—your delight in the power and freshness of a voice and message that expand your own horizon.

The temptation to make a black author more acceptable to white readers, far from making the work more "universally" available is a subtle but serious betrayal of the author, for it masks the attempt, however innocent, to change the audience the writer intended to the readers the editor has in mind. This truly negates the purpose of engaging in pluralistic publishing in the first place and is reminiscent of the early explorers and anthropologists who brought back samples of the "exotic" humanity they encountered around the globe for the amusement or edification of Europeans. This is abhorrent since it would ultimately turn literature into a zoo. The purpose of pluralistic publishing is to open the realm of the written word to hitherto excluded groups while at the same time letting people from other communities hear these new voices. Of course, the first time you listen to someone who speaks in a dialect or accent new to you, it takes some time to get the hang of it. But the editor's job is never to make everyone speak in the same way, but to rejoice in the richness that a variety of different voices offers us.

. . .

Although most of the conflicts over political correctness emerge from differences between the writer's vision and the convictions of the more vocal members of her own community regarding how members of that community should be portrayed publicly, there is also the question of writers characterizing members of "other" groups in what could be considered a negative way. In fact, one gets the impression from public discussions of the topic that this is the major problem, for instance the presentation of African American men in the media mainly as criminals or drug addicts, thus slandering a whole group. Whether or not this is still true of the media in general is another question; however, in my experience it comes up remarkably rarely in publishing. Negative stereotypes of African Americans are now unusual and generally arise from clichéd thinking and lack of imagination (the signs of a poor writer of fiction) rather than from racism. And, except for an occasional British book, one simply doesn't come across casual anti-Semitism in novels today.

One does still see unthinking homophobic comments now and then, in which case the editor's job is to point these out to the author. If there is no justification for such comments in either the plot or the portrayal of the character, the author should be made aware of the possible impact on the reader. (Obviously portraying a homophobic character or a homophobic act does not make the author homophobic.) Recently I was working on a mystery in which one character asserted, "I'm not queer," and I flagged it for the author. In context the use of the word "queer" instead of "gay" would to my ear indicate one of the following: *(a)* this is a bad guy because bad guys use bad language (which he was, but at this point in the plot the reader should not have been tipped off to that), *(b)* this character is homophobic and that will somehow be relevant to the plot, or *(c)* this character protests too much, which means he's uncertain or conflicted about his sexuality and this fact will somehow be relevant to the plot. Since the second and third explanations did not seem to me to fit the plot, I thought the author had made the mistake of tipping the reader off to this man's character too early in the mystery. However, after some discussion the author realized that he did mean to indicate some severe sexual repression in this man; it was a theme that he had intended to bring out more but that had gotten lost in the writing, and a few further changes in the manuscript made it fit smoothly (without giving the plot away).

The fact that such words are today freighted with more significance in fiction than they may carry in real life *is* a fact, and the author has to take it into account. A woman executive swearing in the office is common; a woman executive swearing in a novel will probably signal things to the reader that the author might not intend. As always, the editor's primary task is to clarify the author's intentions.

It is certainly possible that one would come across an author who was actually homophobic, racist, or anti-Semitic, in which case you have the option of simply not publishing him. But let us be clear: the option of *my* not publishing a given author can *not* be called censorship. Censorship is a general prohibition against publication, usually requiring the power of the state or a similar social institution, such as the church. As specific editors, or even specific publishers, a disinclination to publish a certain book is a matter of taste, of whom we choose to be associated with, not of censorship. As long as the author has the option of taking the book elsewhere, or of publishing it himself if all else fails, there is not a question of censorship, only of commercial or social success, which is a different matter entirely.

There is, of course, also the possibility that one might find a homophobic, racist, or anti-Semitic author who was a truly great writer—consider the cases of T. S. Eliot or Ezra Pound. I have always wondered what I would do if I came across a fiction writer whom I believed to be truly excellent who was also, say, homophobic; but since this has never happened, I honestly don't know how I would react, although I'm very curious. I could certainly imagine publishing a nonfiction book by an author I thought was significant although he was homophobic—the essays of Louis Farrakhan, for instance.

. . .

As a rule, I firmly believe that an editor's own politics, opinions, and prejudices have no place in the editing process, which can lead to some strange situations. While editing G. Gordon Liddy's autobiography, *Will,* I found myself in the odd situation of helping Gordon rewrite his attack on the student radicals who had converged on the Democratic convention in Chicago in '68. There we were, sitting at my dining room table as I urged Gordon to cut the rhetoric and hone his comments on the antiwar demonstrators into a substantive attack, an irony not lost on either of us since Gordon knew well I had been there myself rioting in Grant Park. Luckily, we had become good friends despite differences in some of our political opinions, and in return for my editorial help I extracted a promise that he would read Hannah Arendt's *On Revolution,* which salved my noneditorial conscience somewhat.

In some respects it is easier to edit someone whose experience in the world or political convictions are widely different from my own than it is to edit someone who stands closer to me. The very distance creates a discipline and an alertness: you can feel yourself making the effort of imagination and empathy required by the task; the discipline is palpable, indeed sometimes mind-wrenching. When dealing with a closely allied sensibility or political orientation, the temptation to slide oneself into the text is more subtle. Before signing a contract with Dennis Altman for *The Homosexualization of America; The Americanization of the Homosexual,* Dennis and I had to have long and frank discussions, for this was an area I was actively involved in, had in fact written about, and Dennis was understandably nervous that precisely this closeness could represent a danger to the integrity of his views, the individuality of his opinions. Thus prepared, we managed the process quite well and, while I do not agree with everything written in that book either, I was proud of the fact that in the end Dennis assured me that he felt the book had remained totally his.

Perhaps the tenderest area of P.C. sensitivity in gay fiction today concerns the portrayal of unsafe sex in gay novels set in the era of AIDS. On the one hand, there is the strong stand taken by Sasha Alyson, who will not allow any descriptions of unsafe sexual practices in any fiction published by Alyson Publications. On the other hand is the position taken by Warren Singer, an old friend of mine who had AIDS and with whom I discussed Sasha's position: "Lord, the only place we ought not to have to practice safe sex is in our imagination!" This quandary could lead to endless philosophic discussion, but the question is best addressed on a concrete basis, case by case.

Recently I read a story of gay romance between an HIV-positive and an HIV-negative person—their antibody status clearly established in the text—in which the protagonist who is positive realizes after withdrawal that the condom he was using had broken. Neither the protagonist nor the author made any comment about this, and the story simply went on, but I didn't. I had been brought to a full stop because I didn't know how to interpret this incident. It would certainly be a significant event if it happened to you in the course of a romance and it must be significant in the course of this story, but the author had left unclear what that significance was supposed to be. This is a bit like saying offhandedly that there is an elephant in the living room and not mentioning it again. This will not do. As Chekhov informed us: if you introduce a gun in the first act of a play, it had better go off before the end of the last act, otherwise it shouldn't have been there in the first place. If a character practices unsafe sex in a contemporary gay novel, that fact carries an interpretive weight that the author has to take into account, because the reader certainly will. Times have changed. Similarly, if a character casually uses words like "Jew boy" or "nigger" today, the reader will inevitably feel the author is making a rather strong point about that character, whereas we would not necessarily assume that if the text were written sixty years ago.

The point, I think, is not to have general rules, which never work very well in editing anyway, but to point out to the author in each case what implications the reader will likely draw from the incident and to make sure that the author does not inadvertently create an effect that was not desired. The author may well intend a character to be obnoxious, but authors seldom intend to present themselves as obnoxious. As always, the editor's role is to help the author achieve her aim, not to ensure that the writer is politically correct.

In general, the attempt to make any fiction politically correct is a misguided one; it is an attempt to police the imagination. This inclination has been quite prominent among the politically committed since Plato first banished poets from his ideal republic; its resurgence today is merely an unfortunate but quite predictable by-product of a valuable surge in political activism, the dangers of which have always been self-righteousness and intolerance.

The political activist and the poet have always marched to different drummers. As an editor, my loyalties lie with the freedom of the individual imagination, the fruits of which have done very little harm in the real world. Unfortunately, the same cannot be said of political action. Until the politically correct can actually produce a better world in fact rather than in theory, I for one am not willing to grant them control—or even veto power—over the realm of imaginative literature.

Editing Scholars in Three Modes for Three Audiences

Jane Isay

JANE ISAY *began her career in publishing in 1963 as first reader for Harcourt, Brace. Beginning in 1964 she spent fifteen years at the Yale University Press, leaving in 1979 as executive editor. Since then Ms. Isay has held executive editorial and publishing positions at Basic Books, Harper & Row, Simon & Schuster, and Addison-Wesley. She left Addison-Wesley in 1991 to become publisher of Grosset Books, an imprint of G. P. Putnam's that she is reviving.*

Ms. Isay's enlightening essay discusses the "special strains and special opportunities" inherent in the editor-author relationship when the author is a scholar. When there is a "built-in inequality between the authority who is writing the book and the editor who is trying to make it the best possible work," Ms. Isay writes, "a special kind of alliance needs to be formed between the authority, who knows more about her subject than anybody, and the editor, whose task is to help bring forth the very best book of which the scholar is capable."

Citing specific editorial examples and experiences, Ms. Isay's advice is practical, direct, and candid on every aspect of this relationship, whether the scholar is writing for a peer group, attempting to interest a wider range of scholars, or hoping to interest the general reading public.

"Scholars are not always trusting of people who know less than they do," Ms. Isay writes. And so she advises that the editor's attitude be one of "informed interest and respect," and that "being genuinely knowledgeable

252

about the author's field is a great boon because it makes the editor a sophisticated reader and because it provides a common language."

Editing Scholars in Three Modes for Three Audiences

Books written by scholars, whether they are simply academic, reaching the writer's peers, or somewhat broader, intended to interest a wide range of scholars, or most general, trying to interest the general reading public, all benefit from the relationship between editor and expert. But this alliance, a fundamental element of success in any of these publishing quests, is a delicate one, subject to special strains and special opportunities. I'll talk about that relationship first. Then I'll sketch the differences in editing the different kinds of books and offer some tips.

Editors in trade houses publishing general nonfiction are often working with professional writers, many of them journalists whose professional experience includes rewriting on the basis of an editor's suggestion. But when there is a built-in inequality between the authority who is writing the book and the editor who is trying to make it the best possible work, a special kind of alliance needs to be formed between the authority, who knows more about her subject than anybody, and the editor, whose task is to help bring forth the very best book of which the scholar is capable. The editor's attitude, therefore, should be one of informed interest and respect for the author's subject, and of course for the author.

Being genuinely knowledgeable about the author's field is a great boon because it makes the editor a sophisticated reader and because it provides a common language. Scholars are not always trusting of people who know less than they do, and they can be premature in thinking that an editor's ignorance of the field may signal ignorance of what to do for the book. Sometimes an editor's canny ignorance or naïveté can help a scholar understand how much needs to be explained and can push an author into clarity, but with scholars writing for other scholars, sophistication is generally best. A good grasp of the field, and even having strong opinions about the subject, can be crucial to your success. A knowledgeable and tactful editor can sometimes embolden the author or help the author anticipate criticism, and thereby make the book stronger.

It was once editing a book written by a distinguished psychiatrist who was writing about psychiatry and philosophy, a field I had studied and about which I knew more than he. In the course of editing the manuscript,

I was able to point out the arguments that were going to get him unnecessarily into trouble with the philosophers. The author was able to strengthen his arguments, not take them back, because I offered him dissent in the form of helpful advice. This wasn't easy, though, because this author, like all experts, wanted to be in charge of the content of his book. In another situation, I was working with a superb literary critic of the Bible, whose book needed a final chapter. In trying to tell him what I wanted in that chapter, I compared it to the service that closes Yom Kippur, the Jewish Day of Atonement—he understood what I wanted immediately and wrote the final chapter to one of the most influential books of biblical criticism of the era. On the other hand, editors need to know when to admit ignorance. Herbert Simon, the Nobel laureate in economics who is also a computer genius, was queried about a word in his essay. "It's not in Webster III," I wrote. "The editors promise me it will be in the Fourth Edition," replied Simon. Touché.

It takes time for the mutual trust to grow as the dialogue between an editor and the author continues. Even when the book itself is not the subject, it is important to chat, to listen, and even to gossip about the scholar's world. The editor picks up lots of information about what is going on in the discipline, and can become more sophisticated about the readership for the book. The author may discover a genuine comrade-in-arms in his or her editor, easing the experience of going public. I'm sorry to say that it is not so easy or natural for a scholar to listen to somebody who doesn't know as much about the subject as he or she, especially when the editor is young. And authors are perpetually told horror stories about the perils of publication. An open mind as to the value of what the editor has to say can speed the process of successful editing.

It is true that a good editor can see the problems in argument, order, language, and clarity no matter what the subject. I think the main problem scholars have to overcome is the attitude that if they understand the manuscript, and it has received good peer readings, it is ready to publish. Nobody likes to be told there is more work to do, especially by a nonexpert. In my experience, the truly great scholar is more likely to be open to honest criticism and to be ready to pitch in and make the sensible changes. Defensiveness doesn't pay.

In the course of conversations about the field, the manuscript, and the world at large, the relationship of trust that underlies any satisfactory author-editor relationship is slowly built. You cannot overestimate the importance of that trust, especially when the author is a great expert and has no particular reason to listen to the editor's suggestions or to take them seriously. It is extremely difficult to get a point across to an author who thinks the editor doesn't understand or appreciate her or his discipline, and infinitely easier to make suggestions to a scholar who can tell that you respect the field. I once had a manuscript in the social sciences that was almost entirely written in jargon. It was clearly exciting research, and an important book, so I had it rewritten for the author. The book was well reviewed and sold much better than anyone expected, but the author never forgave me. My being put off by the jargon alerted him to the fact that I was not a proponent of his discipline. He was right about that, so not only his writer's pride, but also his scholar's pride was hurt. Authors can smell out a silent dissenter, so it's best to stay away from editing scholarly books whose discipline you don't respect. The look on a scholar's face when I've struck just the wrong note isn't a happy sight. But there's plenty of good work to be done with scholars in the fields you enjoy, so let's get on to that.

The Purely Scholarly Book

The scholarly book aimed to the academic audience presents a narrower range of challenges and opportunities for creative editing, but there are many things that can be done to help. You need to have a pretty good idea of where the research stands vis-à-vis the prevailing scholarship so that you can help the author to figure out in advance what aspects of the book are vulnerable to unfair criticism and strengthen those areas. In disciplines that are full of contention, authors need to explain in the early chapters what the book intends, and what it doesn't. Scholars who take chances, for instance by moving into subjects that are truly interdisciplinary, need help to be certain that they are as powerful in dealing with the new discipline as they are in their own.

Then there are some simple rules of scholarly writing and editing. I call them the three freedoms:

Free the author from the overhang of dissertation style: long introductions, reviews of the literature, needless footnoting, and reiteration of goals at every stage.

Free the author from the agony of reference. Younger scholars who are insecure, or authors with bold theses, tend to footnote, and then to footnote some more, bolstering their nerve by demonstrating to themselves and the reader that they have read—and can comment on—every paper and book of any relevance at all. Convince the author that the book is a strong, even bold one, well argued and well defended, and the footnotes for effect will evaporate.

Free the author from fear of attack. A well-argued work of scholarship is its own best defense. A work that is defensive in tone never is convincing. Telling the author how good the book is (when you believe it), or how bold, can really make the difference, creating an atmosphere in which the writer really takes off and becomes emboldened to say what she or he really wants to say.

The Midway Book

This second kind of scholarly book, the "midway book," calls out to a wider readership and more can be undertaken, though its main audience will consist of academics and other experts. It could be an interdisciplinary book, or it might present material of significance to experts in tangential fields, or it could be so original that it will have a major impact on other disciplines. Midway books adorn the lists of university presses and distinguished houses like Basic Books, W. W. Norton, and the Free Press. These houses have published such works well, and over the years have amassed enough cachet to make sure that their midway books receive wide review attention in more general media, such as the *New York Times Book Review* and the *New York Review of Books*. The author and editor can do a number of things to increase readability. And it makes sense to take the time, since the subject matter is a bit broader, the ramifications are a little wider, and the author might well desire a larger readership. Here are some suggestions:

Make sure that the author places the work in its widest context at the start. The introductory chapter is key in the exposition, and it should not be written until the rest of the book is done. Only then can the author really come to understand the breadth and importance of what she or he has written.

Convince the author that the manuscript isn't a mystery, that the outcome—or in the case of scholarship, the conclusion—needn't come as a surprise at the end of the book. The early chapters should contain clear and forceful statements of what the author believes. A forewarned reader can appreciate how evidence is being marshaled only when the author's direction is clear.

Make sure that the introductory chapter and the conclusion are parallel in force and tone. In doing these two parts of the book in concert, the author is often helped to clarify the point of view of the book and to recognize its importance anew, which makes for more exciting writing—and reading.

Keep the early chapters the most general, getting more specific as the book continues. Leave the most detailed information, wherever possible, for the appendixes. Here again, if you are hoping to reach readers who aren't as expert as the author, then the most general information will keep them reading, while the most erudite is likely to turn them off.

Keep the organization of the book, and of every chapter, as lucid as possible so that the reader doesn't get lost. I find that subheadings are useful elements, not only for the sake of the reader, but also for the sake of the author: you'd be amazed how going through the exercise of putting in subheadings can clarify the order of the argument and help to point out its confusions.

Paying special attention to chapter openings is very important. The time spent devising good ways to introduce the new material, while keeping the reader alert to the movement of the book, can really be a boon.

Imaginative chapter titles can be of great help to the reader. And make sure that the order of chapters is logical and sensible.

Finally, the title: titles don't make the book any more than clothes make the man, but boy can a great title make a difference! One of my two favorite stories comes from my days at Yale University Press, when I was privileged to edit one of the great scholars of the ancient Near East, Thorkild Jacobsen. At the time his masterwork was to be called *Four Millennia of Mesopotamian Religion.* Shakespeare and the Bible are the first places an editor goes to get inspiration for titles, and I was browsing through the Old Testament, appropriately, I thought, looking for a title to another book I was publishing that season, written by Father Theodore Hesburgh. I didn't find Hesburgh's title there, but a phrase in Isaiah leapt off the page at me. The prophet was upbraiding the Israelites for worshiping idols, which he called *The Treasures of Darkness*—a perfect title for a work. The other incident was at Basic Books, where I was lucky enough to work with Howard Gardner on his pathbreaking book on multiple intelligences, then called *A Theory of Multiple Intelligences*—until one day I phoned Howard with *Frames of Mind,* a title that really stands out. In both cases, the original title became the subtitle. And both books had a profound effect on a large readership.

None of these tricks of the trade guarantees that the book will succeed beyond the expectable readership—the work's originality and importance make the difference. But the attention paid to these elements makes it easier for the truly important book to make its way into the consciousness of the serious reading public.

The Scholar's Popular Book

But what about the popular book? What causes a scholarly book to hit the public imagination and sell to the nonexpert reader? We really don't know much about this, but I believe that in order to appeal to the general readership, a scholarly book must have one of these two attributes: either it tells a great story, or it presents an original and important argument.

History, of course, if well told, has always captured a general readership. The string of successful academic retellings of the Civil War is a good example. It has always seemed to me that the novelist's techniques can help the scholar trying to tell a good story. I wouldn't be surprised if James McPherson had *War and Peace* in the back of his mind when he was writing *Battle Cry of Freedom;* I don't know Simon Schama, but his novelist's sense of pace and timing are crucial to the pleasure of reading his scholarship. The ability to stop the story and focus on an individual or a moment is the stock-in-trade of a novelist, but it is also appreciated by the readers of good history. The dramatic use of a telling detail that illuminates a larger question is a novelist's tool that can be imported into scholarly writing (Robert Darnton's *The Great Cat Massacre* does this brilliantly). The ability to create full-blown personalities on the page can enhance a scholar's work immeasurably. (Peter Gay is very good at this.) When the structures of a novel don't apply, it's always a good idea to point out the contemporary relevance of the approach of the ideas in a book. It is widely known that Paul Kennedy's editor suggested that he add the last chapter of *The Rise and Fall of the Great Powers.* There Kennedy made the connection between his subject and the present situation in Europe. That chapter caught the eye of reviewers and commentators and put what was essentially a work of scholarship onto the best-seller lists.

The other way to capture the public imagination is to have an argument. Allan Bloom's *The Closing of the American Mind* is a case in point. Nobody expected that book to sell hundreds of thousands of copies, but the writer had a strong point of view, went out on a limb, the time was right, and the rest is history.

I have found that when intellectuals want to reach a general readership, they sometimes underrate the general reader, so they think they should oversimplify, write down, and to some extent vulgarize. These tactics never work. Readers looking for serious books—and there are lots of them—want new ideas, something to think and talk about. They are prepared to stretch, so long as the writer doesn't try to confuse them. A sophisticated argument, clearly proposed and elegantly argued, has a much better chance in the marketplace. Lester Thurow's *The Zero-Sum Society* is a superb example of the success that sophisticated arguments, clearly stated, can bring. And sometimes even a good dose of obscurity helps. This isn't something I recommend working toward, but we have all seen books such as *Gödel, Escher, Bach* and *The Emperor's New Mind* sell and sell. Just being able to read a bit of those books makes readers feel smart, and even if they give up the struggle before finishing the book, they feel that they have come a far distance.

Of course not all scholars' books directed toward the general public succeed. Much has to happen, beyond the efforts of the author and editor, to make a best-seller. There has to be a buzz in the academic community about the emergence of the book; many reviewers have to be knocked out by the book simultaneously; news of its publication has to seep into the world at large; and the god of bookselling, that old scamp, has to smile on the book. But you can be sure that reviewers and readers alike won't sit still for a scholarly book that is aimed to the broad readership and lacks a story or an argument. Let the scholarly surveys of important subjects be written and well published, but don't expect them to break out. Let the evenhanded analyses be well written and edited, but don't look for unparalleled success. Let the lucid retelling of the known be well written, but don't look for outstanding success.

Of the three modes of scholarly editing, which is the most fun? Over the years I've enjoyed every one of them. Today I find the last most exciting, because it is so tough to stay true to the scholar's research and also make the book accessible to the widest readership. It's the most challenging, and the most perilous, journey. But if you are lucky enough to find the kind of scholar and writer who is up for it, then good luck to both of you, and fortunate indeed will be the readers who will benefit from the book you create together.

Editing for a Small Press
Publishing the Way It Used to Be

Scott Walker

SCOTT WALKER *is the founder, editorial director, and publisher of Graywolf Press, a company that has published poetry, fiction, and literary nonfiction since 1974. He has taught at the Radcliffe Publishing Procedures Course and at the Denver Publishing Institute, and lectures and consults regularly on publishing issues.*

When should an author seek to be published by a small press, rather than a huge one? What can a small press offer a writer that a huge one can't? Why, when, and for what kind of writer is it preferable to accept a small advance but receive a lot of tender, loving care from a small press rather than bank a big advance but suffer indifference and outright neglect at the hands of a giant-sized publisher? These are just a few of the questions asked and answered in this reasoned and affectionate guide to the dedicated, idealistic world of the small publisher "for whom the notion of 'midlist' is meaningless." As Mr. Walker puts it so clearly and correctly: "To a smaller house, all its books are equally important; every title must sell well."

Mr. Walker outlines what could be, for the right writer, the very real advantages of being published by a small press. Among them a greater receptivity to literary writing, innovative marketing techniques that engage publishers' "hearts and minds rather than their checkbooks" to target the writer's audience effectively, a deeper and more long-lasting involvement between editor and author, and a greater willingness to keep books in print than is the practice of larger houses.

"Ten or even five years ago," Mr. Walker writes, "the small press might

have been the last resort for some authors; now it is often the first and best option. . . .

"This is publishing the way it used to be: good books published well. And it is yet another case of small being not just beautiful but more effective, too, for the right author with the right book."

Editing for a Small Press
Publishing the Way It Used to Be

Authors should consider publishing with a smaller press if they are concerned about their book being lost on a massive list, of which only three or four command most of the publisher's attention; if their book is likely to reach a narrower-than-mass audience; if they prefer a nurturing, ongoing relationship with a publisher and editor; and if they want their book kept in print. Or if they want to be sure the book is published—edited, designed, produced, and marketed—with care and enthusiasm along every step of the way.

Graywolf Press has published literary fiction, nonfiction, and poetry, for what is obviously a narrower-than-mass audience, for nearly twenty years. Graywolf authors are known for their adept use of language and their artful sense of the proper shape of a good piece of writing. Graywolf books often use good literature to take on important cultural issues: *The Graywolf Annual Five: Multi-Cultural Literacy* is a seminal work in a much-debated field. We've also published anthologies of short fiction centered on the topics of aging, alcoholism, and the family. The books are beautifully designed. They are marketed not only to the bookstores but to places most publishers never think of: the aging anthology sells to state and county offices on aging and to doctors' offices; the anthologies on the family are sold widely to therapists; we've sold novels and books of poetry to environmental organizations, who offer them as membership premiums.

Graywolf Press is cited here because I know it best, but it is similar to dozens of smaller, independent houses for whom the notion of "midlist" is meaningless. To a smaller house, all its books are *equally* important; *every* title must sell well. A smaller house is unlikely to divert its human and financial resources entirely to the aid of a potential best-seller, nor is it likely to concentrate only on one part (say, chain stores) of the book market—the small publisher will chase down every nook and cranny of a book's potential audience, because it must.

Ten or even five years ago, the small press might have been the last resort for some authors; now it is often the first and best option.

. . .

Graywolf Press is one of many hundreds of smaller publishers who have in the past fifteen years emerged to publish books and genres abandoned by larger, aggressively commercial houses. As larger houses have been taken over by conglomerates, their management has become more oriented to the bottom line than to the finely wrought sentence, and other economic pressures have forced them to concentrate resources on "big" books. They have stopped publishing books that fail to offer quick return on investment— midlist fiction, poetry, essays, philosophy, natural history, how-to books in areas that have yet to become broadly established. In the 1990s, this process has accelerated.

At the same time, the smaller, independent presses have both greatly improved their ability to publish books of all types and seized the opportunity presented to them by changes in the publishing industry. Nowadays, the smaller house is likely to have national sales representation, good sales to chain stores, more varied publishing list, better design, and usually can offer all of the ancillary services—imaginative publicity efforts, author tours, foreign and domestic subsidiary rights sales, and accurate and on-time royalty reports and payments—that were once solely in the domain of the larger houses. As the larger houses, catering to the chain stores, began to cut their lists to concentrate on publishing best-sellers, the independent bookstores needed to find some way to distinguish themselves. The small houses began not only to publish better and higher-profile books, but simultaneously to supply the independent stores with just what they needed: a diverse stock.

There are still many good reasons to publish with one of the six or seven large, often foreign-owned companies responsible for the publication of 85 percent of the books we are likely to find in the local Waldenbooks. If your book is one of the few able to reach a large audience, an audience large enough to be called a "mass," the bigger houses offer a big advance on royalties and the marketing muscle to *make* a best-seller. You can be taken to lunch at the Four Seasons, stay in the best hotels as you are flown from city to city on a promotion tour, and toast in the warm glow of a full-page advertisement in the *Times Book Review*.

There are for most authors and books some downsides to publishing with a larger house. Authors are often left with the following questions:

What happened to my editor? Books are most often acquired rather than edited. (Enjoy that lunch—it may be the last time you see or hear from your editor.) At any gathering of writers you will hear about the musical-chairs world of big-time publishing, in which an author's book is liable to have three or four editors as one after another leaves the company between the times the book is accepted and published. Since the editor is a book's main in-house advocate, and since received enthusiasm is diminished enthusiasm, the book seems abandoned even if it is finally published.

Where is everybody? A Graywolf author had one of her books, published by Graywolf in hardcover, brought out in paperback by one of the largest mass-market houses. She heard absolutely nothing from anyone employed by the mass-market publisher from the time the contract was signed until she managed to corral the company's head publicist at a PEN meeting. She was told that her book was one of eighty-five scheduled for publication that July, and that the company could afford to promote only two of them. Most books are published seemingly without thought, into an awful silence.

Where's the book? Most mass-market books have an average shelf life of ten days, after which their covers are ripped off and returned to the publisher for credit and their innards are "recycled." Most books receive at tops three months of active promotion and then are either declared out of print or relegated to the deep backlist.

For some authors, the big check makes up for most of this misery, but many others have begun to regard smaller houses as a wonderful alternative, as publishing the way it used to be.

．　．　．

Editing for the small publisher is in some respects no different from editing for a large commercial house. Manuscripts are sought and acquired and prepared for publication. But for the author, the difference in attitude and commitment at a small press can turn publishing a book from an isolating to an involving and very pleasant experience.

Editors for smaller houses are much more likely to read and even to encourage "over the transom," unagented submissions rather than rely on a select group of agents to provide prescreening. A small-press editor may not respond as quickly to submissions because he or she must read so many more manuscripts than do the editors at larger houses, but each manuscript is given a fair reading by a senior editor.

The author won't receive an exorbitant advance from a smaller house (though a fair amount of money may change hands), but is more likely to receive substantial and ongoing praise and support. The publisher of only twenty books a year doesn't have cracks for books to slip through: the publisher must care deeply about every book published, and is more likely to be thorough, attentive to details, and communicative with the book's author. The small-press editor is in some respects more like the author, in that they both are, in the old sense, amateurs, engaged in an effort for the love of it rather than for the money. More than one small-press editor has likened the acceptance of a manuscript to the decision to get married; the editor is not only taking on a book, but committing to an author's work in the future. Authors are likely to be treated respectfully, with the extra care one takes in any long relationship. The editor can be relied on to be the author's chief advocate, career counselor, and cheerleader—and to be there for the next book and the next.

Many authors and literary agents have realized that even though the small-press advance may be smaller, since small presses market midlist books longer, more carefully and energetically, and because they are more likely to keep the book in print, authors can often earn more in royalties over the long run. For the first three years after North Point Press published Beryl Markham's *West with the Night,* total sales were about 5,000 copies; the next year North Point sold 29,000 copies; and for the next three years the book was on top of the paperback best-seller lists. Because North Point was committed to the book, able to keep it in print and continue to advocate for it, the audience finally discovered *West with the Night.* It is likely that at a larger house the book wouldn't have stayed in print more than a year.

A small press has no bureaucratic superstructure in which books and authors can become entangled and lost. Most small-press editors not only acquire books but serve as line editor, managing editor (coordinating scheduling and the work of copy editors and proofreaders), legal department, receptionist, and administrative assistant—i.e., as the entire editor half of the old-fashioned author-editor relationship. The small-press editor's acquisition won't get shot down in an editorial or marketing committee meeting. To be sure, an editor must be able to position the book in such a way that other members of the publishing team will share in his or her enthusiasm, but in the more intimate surroundings of a smaller house the editor is more likely to succeed. The editor will be leading the charge when the book is published, on the phone with an author as the reviews come in, and leading the cheers as the author composes his or her next book.

The small-press editor also is intimately involved in the marketing and design of an author's book, and the author is likely to be, to the extent desired, a full-fledged partner in the entire publishing process. Smaller houses are more likely to recognize how powerful an ally an interested author can be, and to encourage ideas and enthusiasm and involvement. An author is likely to be asked to contribute ideas for cover art, to participate in the writing of sympathetic jacket and advertising copy, to suggest stores receptive to hosting a signing, etc. You can be sure that a small-press publisher will take very seriously an author's list of towns he or she has lived in—notices will go to libraries, stores, newspapers, and magazines in all the "hometowns" an author can think of.

Small presses market books in a manner that can be just as effective as, though quieter than, the ways of the larger houses. Because they publish so many books, the large commercial publishers can, at best, throw books into the standard book pipeline (chain stores and the larger independent stores), take out a couple of ads, and rush on to the next season's list. A smaller house, because it needs each book to produce more, is more likely to delve deeper and more imaginatively for a book's audience.

Smaller houses focus their trade marketing efforts on actions that build enthusiasm among the community of reviewers and booksellers who care deeply for good books. Trade marketing efforts are likely to rest on advance galleys that are sent with personal letters from the editor to key booksellers nationally; on a marketing director who knows the reading interests of each store's clerks and book buyers, and who can pique those interests with a well-timed letter or phone call; on carefully placing in-store promotions for individual titles and carefully touring the author. A good small-press publisher will make use of the many low-cost and very effective vehicles for obtaining publicity for a title, both in and outside normal book trade channels.

Most smaller publishers will market not only into traditional trade accounts, but will take the time (for the small house, time and imagination can replace the large publisher's capital) to explore other markets for books. Globe Pequot Press does a fine job marketing to the book trade, but also sells books in many other imaginative ways: their bicycling books are sold through bike shops; their bed-and-breakfast inn books sell as many copies in the inns as in bookstores. Seal Press has a thriving nontrade business, selling their superb titles on women coming to terms with abusive relationships to women's shelters nationally. Graywolf Press once published a book of Caribbean folk tales that was marketed as a short-story collection, as folklore, as "prose poetry," as a children's book, to Caribbean studies departments, and to storytelling guilds. That effort wasn't terribly successful, but the effort was made. We were much more successful marketing anthologies of short stories on aging not only to the trade as good literary collections, but to doctors with an elderly clientele and to retirement centers.

      ·   ·   ·

As the market for authors' works shrinks, with more of the larger houses swallowing portions of other, formerly large houses, authors would be well served to look outside of New York to one of the many fine, smaller, independent houses dedicated to publishing good books well.

Check the best-seller lists and the review sections of your newspaper: you are likely to find books there published by houses like Thunder's Mouth Press, Algonquin Press, Workman Publishing, Chronicle Books, and the more notable university presses. Even the more literary Graywolf Press has one title (*If You Want to Write,* by Brenda Ueland) that has to date sold over 120,000 copies. The smaller houses are marketers, not mass marketers; they care about the books they publish, and their readers and authors care about them. They all have to make a profit, but because of lower overhead, an unwillingness (and inability) to pay huge advances, and the tendency to solve marketing problems through the more effective means of using their hearts and minds rather than their checkbooks, they are able to turn a good midlist book into a profitable one.

This is publishing the way it used to be: good books published well. And it is yet another case of small being not just beautiful but more effective, too, for the right author with the right book.

Editing Fiction as an Act of Love

Faith Sale

FAITH SALE is vice-president and executive editor of G. P. Putnam's Sons, where she has been since December 1979. Before that she was a senior editor at E. P. Dutton for two years, after more than a decade as a free-lance editor. She is a member of PEN American Center's Executive Board and cochair of its Freedom-to-Write Committee.

"My devotion to fiction," Ms. Sale writes, "is born more out of instinct than intellect, based more on emotional response than calculated judgment. The moment of connection is the moment I become a book's (or an author's) advocate—its nurturer, defender, supporter, mouthpiece, bodyguard."

Ms. Sale dramatically demonstrates her passionate commitment to her authors and to her editorial art and craft in this illuminating essay.

She begins with some deeply perceptive comments on the role of the editor: "The process of helping to shape and polish the work of a writer I admire can be a form of an act of love"; "I remind the author as often as I can that any remark I utter or any mark I make on the manuscript is to be taken only as a suggestion"; "What I try to be for the author is the smartest, most sympathetic reader of the manuscript (at least until it becomes a book)."

Ms. Sale then takes us along with her on a typically atypical editorial experience: the discovery, editing, and publication of a novel. The novel she discusses is Sugar Cage *by Connie May Fowler. We share everything about the way Ms. Sale guides the work from manuscript to published book, beginning with learning her first impression of the work ("I did find it immediately readable and I felt compelled to keep reading . . ."). We accompany Ms. Sale through her negotiations and discussions about the book with the author's agent, a telephone and then personal meeting with the author, detailed editorial suggestions, and reading the author's revisions.*

We are there as she discusses the book's jacket with the art director, the design of the book with the book designer, as she writes the jacket copy, alerts and solicits reviewer attention, and energizes the sales reps and subsidiary rights people with her enthusiasm for the novel.

Reading Ms. Sale's essay is to be in the company of an extraordinarily sensitive and creative editor at work, witnessing the creation of a novel and learning just how productive and deeply rewarding an editor-author relationship can be.

We leave Ms. Sale as she awaits with interest and enthusiasm Ms. Fowler's next novel, aware that the agent will want a lot of money for it. "And no doubt we'll go through the same process . . . all over again. But that's what an editor does. And it's what I love to do."

Editing Fiction as an Act of Love

It is very hard for me to write about editing fiction (as the editor of this volume will readily confirm) because it is something I do differently with each author and even with each book by the same author. But more than that, for me editing fiction is extremely personal . . . and pleasureful. It is true that much of what I have to do in the position of editor (with whatever adjective precedes that title) at a publishing house is drudgery or routine. But the process of helping to shape and polish the work of a writer I admire can be a form of an act of love.

Good writing—interesting use of language, evocation of genuine emotion, revelation of unrecognized truths—is, in my estimation, the highest form of art. And I (as one who could never accomplish it) am proud to be in service to it. So, when I choose to approach a work of fiction, I do so in that spirit. And I remind the author as often as I can that any remark I utter or any mark I make on the manuscript is to be taken only as a suggestion. For I believe unequivocally that the work must end up exactly as the author wishes—"It's your book," I insist, even as I beg and plead for a change that I am absolutely certain will enhance the work; "Thank you. I know I'm exposing myself," I've had an author say, "but this is the way I want it"— after having the benefit of my insight or intuition.

What I try to be for an author is the smartest, most sympathetic reader of the manuscript (at least until it becomes a book). This means I must earn the author's trust, make the author feel comfortable with me and my perceptions, which may be why I find myself taking on various roles, often unconsciously, with the four or five writers I work with in an average year. I have seen myself behaving as mother, sister, niece; as teacher or disciple; as prison matron or nursemaid; as shrink or best friend. And because I regard the relationship between writer and editor as privileged, I do not intend to let on in these pages which of these roles I have assumed with which writers.

For me, "editing fiction" begins with the selection of a piece of writing. If the writer is a first novelist, this is generally a full manuscript; if the writer has been published, it might be a partial manuscript, perhaps a synopsis; a well-known writer can get by with a wispy promise. But my intention always is to enter into a long-term arrangement, as I believe in writers' careers more than in any one book. I have published eight of Alice Hoffman's nine novels, seven books of fiction by Lee Smith, four of the late Donald Barthelme's; I'm working with Amy Tan on her third; and so on. Once I have been captivated by the voice of a novel, I am prepared to do whatever I can to escort that novel to its maximum readership, whether that means simply walking it through successive stages of the publishing process or presiding over total reconstruction and banging heads in-house to get attention for it. When I'm hooked, I'm unshakably committed for the long haul, regardless of obstacles. But I can't fake it: my devotion to fiction is born more out of instinct than intellect, based more on emotional response than calculated judgment. The moment of connection is the moment I become a book's (or an author's) advocate—its nurturer, defender, supporter, mouthpiece, bodyguard. Not infrequently, my dogged protection causes consternation among publicists or sales people or others in the house whose outlook must take in the big picture. They balance and measure, playing give-and-take with the whole list, while I hold out for individual treatment of the one book. I don't enjoy being in this position with my colleagues, but I feel the book has to be my primary concern.

Having made the decision to take a book on, I must figure out how to convey to the author what I think could or should be done to make the book the best it can be. It never is—because I think it never should be—making the book into anything other than what the author has envisioned. In my role of the author's best reader, I will express my reaction to the whole or any part of a book and ask, "Is this the way you want your readers to feel? If not, let's figure out how to make it so they'll feel the way you want them to." In other words, what I mean to do is help the author to realize the *author's* intention.

This necessarily involves considerable discussion, in person or on the phone, if only to confirm that I have correctly understood that intention. I do not write one of those famous "editorial letters" at this (and rarely at any) point. I hear editors say, "Whew, I just finished a twelve-page editorial letter." And I wonder how they were even able to frame a second question without hearing the answer to the first. A writer I met not long ago (I hasten to admit that this is a writer who gave up books for a lucrative career in Hollywood) reminisced about the wonderful editor who would do up ten single-spaced pages of maybe three hundred suggested changes but who would then cheerfully accept the writer's making only four of these: "What a good editor!" he said. I don't regard the editor-author dialogue as a competition or a test or a report card. If I'm doing my job properly, every point I make should cause the author at least to think, if not to act.

To me, the editing of fiction is an organic process, a back-and-forth exchange, in which both author and editor benefit from listening as well as speaking/writing. It becomes a building process, often deepening or enriching what already exists, in the best case making sublime what had been merely adequate, when an author is led to reimagine or create anew, rather than just make repairs. The author and I might come up with a number of possibilities for the shape of a book or a chapter or a scene, for the behavior of a character, for the turns of a plot. But in the end neither of us may remember—or care—which one suggested the solution that appears in the final version.

My concern (beyond being the show-don't-tell police) may be broadly described as assuring a kind of believability within the fictional setting of a character's speech—the rhythm, the diction, even the content. Or it might be the order of events or their nature—making sure that nothing is stuck in to make a date come out right, say, or to have two characters end up in the same place at the same time that couldn't logically occur in the world the author has imagined for this book.

I can't count the number of times authors have said to me, "But this scene is based on a real accident I once had," or "My mother and father did in fact meet in that improbable way," or "I really know someone with that outlandish name who's a mild-mannered bank clerk," and so on. I've said, "It doesn't matter if it happened in real life, if it doesn't work in fiction." We have all experienced any number of coincidences that couldn't be used in fiction because they would look like cheap contrivances. "But it's true" just won't hold up: the best fiction must be truer than true.

Sometimes just raising an issue will inspire a writer to come up with an improvement neither of us would have thought of if we hadn't talked about it. This reminds me of John Irving's description of how the late, beloved

Henry Robbins edited *The World According to Garp* and the early parts of *The Hotel New Hampshire.* "This spot feels a little soft," Henry might say, and John would go off and dig back in to strengthen the passage—his own way. And that, he claimed (at least at the time), was the best "editing" he could have. In contrast, one of the most chilling remarks I once heard from an editor went something like this: "Do you believe it? The young author I've been working with just made a hysterical phone call to the agent complaining about the 'horrible damage' I've done to his novel. Well, that's just too bad. All that work had to be done. I'm just glad the call went to the agent instead of me—I'd have had plenty to say: 'Damage' indeed!" This, to me, is unthinkable. I never put pencil to manuscript, except to write questions or comments in the margin, without talking to the author. All of this is a long way of saying that I don't prescribe revision, I simply locate troubles and, if invited, participate in finding cures.

How an author responds to this part of the editing is particularly interesting—sometimes even scary. The first time I was to edit a Joseph Heller manuscript, I could hardly bring myself to speak to him. This was not long years ago. I was unquestionably what we like to call a grownup. But still, who was I to presume to improve anything this world-class writer had put on paper? And he confirmed my worst fears by saying no to every suggestion I made. Little by little, however, in the course of two- or three- or four-hour phone sessions during several days of each of many weeks, he went back and changed every spot I had pointed to. By the end of the process, he was deputizing me to do whatever I thought was necessary if I couldn't reach him. That's the scary part: I didn't make the smallest change without consulting him, and I wouldn't. In fact, I worry sometimes when a new author pounces too readily to accept my suggestions. I always say, "Please don't just do it. It's only a possibility for you to consider. Think about it to be sure it's what *you* really want." I know—and I think I should teach each first-time writer (and remind others)—that there is no such thing as the one right way to fix anything.

The editing process does not end after that first go-round, as far as I'm concerned. I'll keep reading and keep talking until the author is ready to let go (or until I'm ready to persuade the author to let go). I stand by during copy editing to answer general questions the copy editor may have and to consult with the author about responding to queries. I may put pencil back to paper to incorporate these responses into the manuscript if the copy editor does not seem to me to be altogether in tune with the author. Once the work is set in type, I don't usually read it again, but it is not at all rare for me to take down the author's galley corrections, in person or on the telephone, to help make sure that nothing is being done to harm the work in any way. I also look over the proofreader's markings to ensure that the author's style has not fallen victim to a by-the-book grammarian. And I follow along through the further stages of production so that neither the author nor I will discover any surprises in the printed book.

Meanwhile the niggling procedures of publication must be seen to: catalog, marketing, and publicity plans, dust-jacket copy, and so on—all of which I convey to (or in the case of written copy, beg from) the author. Then comes the limbo, the eerie period between the moment when the book is truly out of the author's reach and the dreaded onset of the critics. Even the most hardened of the self-proclaimed geezers—Kurt Vonnegut, say— quake in anticipation of the public airing of a new work. This may well be the time of the author's greatest need for nurture/therapy and the time the editor least remembers to dispense any, having become caught up in the early editing, perhaps, of the next writer or the active publication of the one who came before.

I'd like to be able to illustrate all this generalization with one typical case. In fact, in my experience, no one case is typical. But, anyway, here is the story of *Sugar Cage,* a first novel by Connie May Fowler, which arrived on my desk one day in June 1990, having been sent by an agent I admired very much but had never actually done business with. The agent had very high hopes for this book, hopes that she wanted to see shared by a publisher, and she was prepared to submit the manuscript to a number of publishers at once in order to determine which one would put the most money behind it. Still, she said, she was showing it to me exclusively, on her hunch that I would fall for it and see the same potential she envisioned. That's a bit of weight to put on a prospective editor, I thought, but I started reading the manuscript—which, incidentally, bore the impossible title of *Ave Erzulie* at that time—with my mind as free of dollar signs and other pressures as I could make it. I did find it immediately readable and I felt compelled to keep reading, if only to see what would happen, how the author would resolve a fairly difficult set of circumstances.

Essentially, this was a novel about two families in a small town in northeastern Florida. The two couples are quite plain, everyday folks who just happened to have gotten married the same day in 1945 and were honeymooning at the same beachside motel. Later, they found themselves living next door to each other in Tiama, a town distinguished primarily for having an inordinate number of penitentiaries. These people, the Looneys and the Jewels, have been friends—and enemies—for nearly twenty years during the present time of the novel, when the Looneys' son, Emory, is a teenager who makes his philandering father's life miserable. Each of these characters tells part of the story, and there were five other voices besides. So it shouldn't be hard to imagine that there would be problems with such a novel; indeed, plenty of them jumped out at me as I read. But I did keep on reading.

I should point out that I'm not one of those people who can't put a book down no matter what. I find putting most books, and surely nearly any manuscript, down the easiest thing to do (not to mention that it's probably the only way I can survive). Indeed, it's almost like a scientific test: if I can't stop reading a manuscript, I'm bound to publish (or at least try to publish) it. This novel was pretty mixed up—the prologue didn't fit with the rest of the book; the fields (yes, fields!) were speaking; the lushest character (Soleil Marie, a voodoo-practicing cane-field worker who becomes Emory's beloved when his father exiles him to an uncle's plantation) came in too late and all her passages were lumped together instead of threaded through like the others'—but I was in the hands of a real writer. This Connie May Fowler, this wise and caring and careful person, was not playing out some writing-school exercise; she was not offering up some gee-look-what-I-can-do-to-shock-you stuff. This was the real thing, a writer who creates a world, puts flesh-and-blood, true-sounding characters in it, and, most important, makes the reader care about them.

So, yes, I tell the agent, I would be interested in publishing this book, this writer, presuming my reading of her manuscript does not go against her vision of it. But, in light of all the work that the author (and I) will have to do to make it the book it wants to be, I don't feel comfortable committing to an advance of more than a third of what the agent is hoping for. This meant that the agent had to decide whether to accept my projected offer or to go ahead with her earlier thought of a broad multiple submission. My reasoning was that I didn't feel the novel was in good enough shape to be widely read—by the people inside the house who would have to make the determination of what the various markets would be. Or to tell the real truth, it was not in good enough shape to show to the outside people who might or might not purchase rights for book clubs and reprinters. In other words, it was not yet, to my mind, in a state that would enable us to obtain assurances that this book would earn the kind of revenue in its lifetime that would support the agent's financial hopes. What I did succeed in persuading the agent was that the book that would emerge after my ministrations and, especially, the author's reworking (presuming that she was willing to proceed) would indeed be worth what the agent foresaw. There was a bit of hedging, a tentative foray with another editor, a little limbo time, before the agent agreed. She did trust my impulses about the novel, and she did think that I was the right editor for this novel and that the house was the right house. We negotiated the possibility that some early success would redound immediately to the author's pocket even before the advance was earned out (and the part that was to go to her in the event of a six-figure reprint sale was indeed paid very soon).

But now it was time to talk to the author.

Connie May Fowler turned out to be a woman in her early thirties, although the astonishing wisdom both the agent and I had perceived in her work had led each of us to guess she might be twice that. I was frank with her, telling her what made me uncomfortable as a reader. I told her how the prologue made me think the novel belonged to Rose Looney, how I felt Soleil Marie wasn't being given her due. I said it seemed to me that, because the book had nine actual characters' voices, the fields could be done away with. And, I added, the balance of the voices seemed to be off and the book itself seemed rather unshapely.

The magic of that phone call was that it was obvious that Connie was eager to hear all this, was in fact more responsive than almost any author I've worked with. But she claimed she couldn't talk well over the phone and would instead send me a letter describing her plans for revisions.

The letter came within days. She said she'd thought of opening the novel with Inez, the black maid who knows things she doesn't want to know (such things as that Martin Luther King is going to die). Doing this, we both recognized, would allow Inez to become the framework, as well as a thread throughout the book, instead of a minor presence. Connie responded to the other points, and she knew exactly what I was asking for, exactly where I was having trouble. It was immediately clear to me that we were on the same wavelength and that we could work very well together. We were under way.

Six months later, after the author had done an extensive revision, I sat with her at her dining table in a small house near the beach in St. Augustine. The external shape of the book seemed pretty well controlled by now, but internally there was a lot of "business": each chapter had a number, a title, a date, the speaker's name—information that I thought had to emerge from the story rather than being stuck on at the top. We talked and talked and came up with a plan to divide the book into two (later, four) distinct sections, instead of the string of chapters it had been. We agreed about which parts needed cutting, which needed to be moved about, and where some characterizations still needed tuning up. And so Connie went back to her word processor, and I went back to New York.

In about a month, Connie sent up a complete revision. We were nearly there. It was the book we wanted it to be, but it needed some tinkering, some cutting, and a lot of "line work." For me, line editing—pencil editing—means many things. It is making sure a voice is consistent in tone or inflection or diction—doesn't this young boy sound too old in this exchange of dialogue? is this person really likely to swear? It is recommending cuts or compressions in scenes that seem attenuated and thin, that could gain greater punch with brevity. It is spotting anachronisms, infelicities of language, soggy passages, anything that might pull the reader out of the novel because The Writing is sticking out.

This might sound like a lot of work, but it isn't that at all. It is the most pleasurable part of what I do: working with an author—I emphasize the "with"—and hearing her respond, seeing her come up with fixes and revisions that express what she really wants to say, witnessing the evolution of a work of fiction the way one might watch a sculptor, observing as she makes things deeper and sharper and delves into her characters to draw more out of them.

Connie's response to all my suggestions—and, remember, they are always only questions and suggestions, as far as I'm concerned—was to send another complete revision a couple of weeks later, with a few phone calls in between. At this point (ten months after submission, eight months after contract), I was ready to let other people in the house read the manuscript: it went to publicity, subsidiary rights, sales, other editors, and, at the same time, I sent it into copy editing. The feeling was very high. We sent the manuscript out exclusively to a single reprinter (instead of holding an auction) and, after some negotiating, they made the six-figure offer we were looking for. (There's no way to be sure, but I know in my heart that there'd never have been such an offer for the original manuscript.) Same with the clubs; they were so keen we had several rounds of bidding before it went for a nice five figures. Other departments—and, notably, the publisher—were also enthusiastic, and I know the excitement wouldn't have built nearly as well if I had shown them the original manuscript and the various reworkings. To arouse that essential in-house enthusiasm it was necessary to show people something like the final version.

Copy editing was reasonably routine. We had already caught most of the obvious problems, and the copy editor was painstaking. But when I was going through the manuscript, taking down Connie's changes over the phone, I noticed a few points that had been nagging at me. Each time, Connie would come up with a line or a thought that brought some new emotional resonance. The most striking of these, to me, was the scene in which Emory, as a young man, is preparing to go into the army, to be sent to Vietnam, and must get rid of his father's car. He finds a bobby pin as he cleans out the glove compartment; *he* is sure it is his mother's, left there years before, but I kept wondering how he knew it didn't belong to his father's mistress, or how *we* knew it didn't. Connie was completely persuaded that it was the mother's, but she was adamant about wanting to avoid any ambiguity, as the issue of the mistress had long since been resolved. She hung up and fifteen minutes later called back with a new passage. She was blubbering as she read it to me, and I welled up as I listened:

> I checked the interior for any personal belongings. Nothing—clean as a whistle except for the glove box, which had one of Mama's rose-colored scarves in it. We used to always give her something rose-colored for her birthday. Jesus, that was a long time ago. The scarf must have been in there since before Daddy died. For a second I considered leaving it, but then thought, No, maybe it belongs with me. It was dusty and soft, and there was something so sweet about it I almost wanted to cry, which was stupid, since that scarf had been in there all the while I owned the car and I had never given it a thought until now. But shit, the army was soon going to own my ass—why not take a little bit of my mama with me. I put it in the duffel bag.

"How did you ever think that up?" I asked. "Where does it *come* from?"
"You just ask the right questions," she said.
I could be happy with that as my epitaph.

.   .   .

Editing is only so much about words: the rest of the job is a lot of politics.

First, the book itself. The jacket matters, because it has to be right for the book, has to suggest the character, the tone, the content—at best, to be a visual representation of the emotional quality of the novel. For this book, I wanted something that would convey a feeling of heat, Florida/Caribbean heat, but not be specific to any character or element of time in the book—and it had to be pretty, too. I hired an art researcher to come up with some paintings, and the art director and I spent about a week choosing the most eye-catching and colorful. There was a long process of getting the background colors right, the size of the image on the cover right, the hue and tone of the reproduction right, but after several months, consultations with all departments, and two separate daylong visits to the printer, we had something we were happy with.

For the inside of the book, the designer and I decided on the type, running heads, and all the other elements that, however subliminally, give the reader the sense of being within a special, separate world, the world only of this book. We spent hours selecting ornaments for the beginning of each chapter and assigning a different one to each of the nine characters who narrate.

At the same time, I sought early comments. Each stage of a new book's life—especially a first novel's—requires some tool to help it reach its next audience. Before publication, this means the people who will be selling it— the publisher's representatives, who must persuade bookstore buyers to stock and display it, and the bookstore people, who (the publisher hopes) will recommend it to their customers. A first book has no public notices, no previous reviews, so endorsements from known writers are often the most believable support the book can have, and it is my job to find people who are willing to read the book early and whose names and reputations mean something. At this point, all that was available to read was the typescript, which is the last thing any potential reader wants to be handed by the mailman (or, worse, have to fetch from the post office). Besides, what ruder imposition can there be than to ask a writer to interrupt that precious time, free of touring or teaching or reading for pay, that is most happily spent with a manuscript of one's own? Connie Fowler knew no one whose name would signify on a jacket blurb (how refreshing in this day of anxious "networking" and cultural inbreeding), so it really was up to me alone. I don't like asking the writers I work with to do this for each other. But once in a great while—and only when I think there may be a genuine affinity— do I beg a no-strings, only-if-it's-honest reading from a couple of them. After all, I figure, if we all know we're maintaining our integrity, why should these writers be deprived of each other's comments just because they have the same editor? They do it, when it strikes them to, for writers with other editors. I have to be sure, though, that they're adhering to their own standards. So I went to three authors I thought would be responsive, and they outdid themselves with, they assure me, legitimate blurbs. Now we had quotes from Alice Hoffman, Lee Smith, and Amy Tan, which I circulated in-house and put on the bound galleys.

Next, sales conference, where the editor must persuade the thirty-plus sales representatives who actually go into the bookstores that this book is worth their efforts with the book buyers. As it turns out, they were way ahead of me, having read the galleys, and they asked me to come up with a special personal letter to the bookstores, editor-to-seller, that could accompany early reading copies they would present to their customers. Writing that kind of institutional letter wasn't my favorite idea. I'd never done it, because the ones I'd read always sounded hucksterish, and I can't stand to oversell a book, especially one I have such strong feelings about. I like to present a novel with a message that says, in effect, "I like this and I hope you will too." I can't stand those popular catchwords: brilliant, wonderful, stunning, dazzling, and (save us) unique . . . unless, of course, a *reviewer* uses them in print. But the sales department wanted this letter and I agreed.

Here's how I managed it:

————G. P. PUTNAM'S SONS————
200 MADISON AVENUE • NEW YORK, NEW YORK 10016

FAITH SALE   June 5, 1991
VICE PRESIDENT
EXECUTIVE EDITOR

Dear Bookseller,

    I have never done this before, and I may not
be doing it again soon. But I really believe the
novel that inspires this letter is itself a special
event.

    <u>Sugar</u> <u>Cage</u> is the first work of fiction by
Connie May Fowler, a young woman who lives in St.
Augustine, Florida, and it has already captivated
a wide range of readers--in house (from art to
design to publicity to rights to sales), at the
first reprinter to see the manuscript (Pocket Books,
who came up with a six-figure offer), and throughout our sales force (more than likely including
your rep).

    Still, I am convinced that nothing is as
important in a book's life as what happens when
it arrives in your hands. After all, I know it
was your support that was responsible for the
success of a number of other books I have discovered,
especially Amy Tan's <u>The</u> <u>Joy</u> <u>Luck</u> <u>Club</u>, of course,
but also several books by Alice Hoffman and
Lee Smith.

    Naturally, I hope that you will read and be
pleased by <u>Sugar</u> <u>Cage</u> and that you will urge others
to read it too.

    All good wishes. And many thanks.

                       Sincerely,

The response was heartening and convinced me that I hadn't gone to this extra effort in vain. Booksellers from all over sent notes and—more to the point—orders. Regional book fairs asked to have Connie come to talk. Baker & Taylor, the big wholesaler, asked for special reading copies for its salespeople. Many accounts asked for the in-store promotion piece (a stand-up board with quotes and a beautiful reproduction of the jacket art, prepared with special affection by a young person in the marketing department).

Finally, it was time to apply pressure—careful pressure (the right words to the right people, and only to certain people about certain books)—on potential reviewers, book review editors, likely quote-givers, and people good for word of mouth. This is a job an editor has to grow into, meeting and courting the right people over the years; and the pressure must be applied very carefully, given the sensitive nature of authors and reviewers, the volatile nature of literary opinions. I am known for the books I have published over the last decade, and if I push a new book on someone, it is with the understanding on both sides that I have a record, that I am the same person who has published X and Y and Z that you all admire so much, and that I don't go around lightly making recommendations. I see this as an important part of an editor's job, but there is no shortcut to it; it comes only with the slow, not always steady, compiling of a history of (at least literary if not commercial) success; and it is a well that can be gone to only every so often, and then with care.

And so now the book is out. At this moment I am waiting for the reviews, for the first reports from the bookstores. I know I have done my part, done what an editor can do. The rest is beyond my control at this point, and all in the hands of the fates.

Connie is writing another novel. I'd like to publish it. I haven't seen any of it yet, but I have a lot of trust in this writer. No doubt I'll see the manuscript in a few months; no doubt the agent will want a lot of money for it. And no doubt we'll go through the same process, modified by her first-book achievement, all over again. But that's what an editor does. And it's what I love to do.

On Editing Nonfiction
Multiple Majors in a
University of Subjects

Fredrica S. Friedman

Since 1988, FREDRICA S. FRIEDMAN has served as vice-president, executive editor, and associate publisher of Little, Brown. Before that she was a senior editor at Little, Brown, a senior staff editor at Reader's Digest Condensed Books, a senior editor at Reader's Digest Press, and a magazine editor.

"The editor of nonfiction needs two principle qualities, besides an optimistic personality, to maintain the dynamic between books that probe and books that elucidate: an interest in a range of subjects and expertise in several, and the ability to know which of those subjects, in today's market, will stand out in terms of a provocative nature and/or a contribution to the field, and thus sell," writes Ms. Friedman in this fascinating exploration of the risks and rewards of editing nonfiction.

Ms. Friedman offers valuable insights not only into the intellectual equipment an editor needs to publish nonfiction but also the business sense necessary to publish it successfully. "As an editor I do not buy books because I 'love' them, or even because I think they are important and should be published, although clearly these factors are significant parts of the equation. I buy books that I think will reach a market in some depth so that the author will be read, and the publishing house will make money—the goal of any business, including publishing, which admittedly is unlike other for-profit enterprises." Ms. Friedman discusses what qualities she looks for in selecting books for her nonfiction list—an author in control of his or her material, an element of controversy, and creativity. And she illustrates her approach to editing nonfiction with illuminating and entertaining anecdotes about her editing of her authors, among them Cleveland Amory, Alan Dershowitz, Carl Rowan, and Lionel Tiger.

When editor and author have done everything that could *be done with the material, they await the public's critical and financial reaction. "If the book reaches its potential, then the author's work will be acclaimed. For no matter the extent of an editor's backstage contributions, the book is first, foremost, and always the author's success."*

Editing means long, difficult, often exhausting hours of work. "Is it worth it?" Ms. Friedman asks. "Editing certainly does not make most editors rich or famous. However, when you deal with nonfiction subjects, the material is literally as broad as the world around you, and your reward as an editor is to have the opportunity to continue to learn: every day you are bombarded with stimulating ideas—the luxury of multiple majors in a university of subjects. . . . Above all, you are among the lucky few whose life's work does make a difference: the books you publish will affect their readers."

On Editing Nonfiction

Multiple Majors in a University of Subjects

The number of nonfiction books published in hardcover each year outweighs the number of novels by almost eight to one: 38,500 to 5,500. That tells you something important at once: nonfiction is a large and extremely varied universe. Nonfiction categories can range from political memoirs to literary biography; from true crime to cat books; from scientific frontiers to historical and contemporary issues visited and revisited. In short, everything that has happened, is happening, and may happen is a possible subject for the nonfiction writer and editor. "All books are either dreams or swords," Amy Lowell noted, and the great challenge is to find both that inspiration and that point to publish.

The editor of nonfiction needs two principle qualities, besides an optimistic personality, to maintain the dynamic between books that probe and books that elucidate: an interest in a range of subjects and expertise in several, and the ability to know which of those subjects, in today's market, will stand out in terms of a provocative nature and/or a contribution to the field, and thus *sell*. No editor can afford not to understand what were, in decades past, the business functions of publishing: sales, marketing, accounting. Contrary to romantic notions, an editor does not spend the day in a quiet office reading manuscripts, interrupted only by meeting with authors over a luxurious lunch in a glamorous restaurant (however, more on that later). What an editor does relates first and foremost to the business of book publishing—and that business is, again, to *sell* books. Thus when I acquire nonfiction books, it is always with the understanding that each will sell into a segmented market—buyers interested in presidential memoirs, buyers interested in feminist issues, buyers interested in Hollywood stories. Today's successful editor not only has the basic responsibility to help an author shape and develop his subject to realize his best book; the editor must also understand how to position and market that book to reach the widest audience. As an editor I do not buy books because I "love" them, or even because I think they are important and should be published, although clearly these factors are significant parts of the equation. I buy books that I think will reach a market in some depth so that the author will be read, and the publishing house will make money—the goal of any business, including publishing, which admittedly is unlike other for-profit enterprises.

For each product is distinct, and each must be developed and marketed individually. An editor launching twelve titles a year, the usual base number, is like a twelve-sided figure opening twelve different shops in that period, hoping to find enough customers to make a bottom-line profit despite the substantial start-up costs involved in creating a wholly unique item. Every book is a singular, detached consumer product, yet each must be published with the intention that it will create a continuing demand— for a sequel, for a series, for another book on one segment, at the very least for its subsequent editions in trade paperback and/or mass market if first published in a hardcover edition. In other businesses, the shoe business for example, or even an allied media business such as newspapers or magazines, each article, issue, or shoe manufactured is only part of a collective enterprise, frequently stamped out on the same mold or in the same mode to duplicate success. Each book published is a separate product that sells or not largely on its own merits. That's where optimism comes in, as does the individual editor's motivation, the recognition that a book, always distinctive, is a more interesting product than a shoe. Book editing at its best is intellectually stimulating, and the product connects its purveyor—the editor—to the power, durability, and, yes, even the immortality of the printed word: it is in the Library of Congress forever. Few other products have the power to shape our minds and our lives, and to *last*. Or to drive us as mad. One shoe may be like another shoe. If it sells, you produce more exactly that style—millions perhaps. Now look back at the number I cited of nonfiction books published each year: of that number, perhaps three hundred hit one best-seller list or another; perhaps several thousand sell substantially—that is, in excess of their initial printings and to produce a profit for the author and the house.

An editor to be successful must have more than one specialty—or design—to penetrate the marketplace that season, or the next. In my case, to be quite specific, there is no attempt to be the generalist: I cannot learn enough about the multiplicity of nonfiction topics to make informed judgments about a large range of subjects. Because of my academic training, as a historian and political scientist, and because of my interests in contemporary society, my focus is fivefold. I publish biography and autobiography (of Washington political figures and media people—Robert McNamara, Patrick Buchanan, Richard Goodwin, Larry King, Dan Rather); I publish social and cultural history (the great real-estate dynasties, the R. J. Reynolds family, the Sakowitz-Wyatt feud, Paris in the 1930s); I publish contemporary issue books (on Jerusalem, the failure of feminism, the rivalry between the *New York Times* and the *Washington Post*). I also publish the occasional quirky book that does not fit a defined area but has a crossover market: animal biography became a subspecialty of mine when I was fortunate enough to work with Cleveland Amory on his last two books, *The Cat Who Came for Christmas* and *The Cat and the Curmudgeon.* With over 1.5 million copies sold, those titles are a phenomenon in book publishing. Since they also have nine lives, in hardcover, in trade paperback, in seven foreign languages, they are almost their own mini-publishing line—a continuation every publisher looks for as a way, as noted before, of one discrete product leading to the multiple product. I also publish books on minorities that are controversial arguments. When Carl Rowan decided to do his autobiography, what excited me was that as a black man in America who had achieved establishment success (as a syndicated national columnist and a former ambassador and cabinet officer), he was still as angry at the white majority as an inner-city black kid today. The result, *Breaking Barriers,* is a provocative book on what remains to be done in America for a more equitable life for all citizens of color, and its pronouncements excited enough people to make it a local and a national best-seller. When Alan Dershowitz decided to write *Chutzpah,* what interested me about this book by the Harvard Law School professor and famous appellate lawyer was not so much his account of his legal challenges as his evaluation of the status of Jews in America. Contrary to popular opinion, Jews are not first-class citizens, he claimed, but actually second-class. That controversial thesis, buttressed by exciting and relevant examples, would, I thought, tap into what I call the "Holocaust mentality" market, one driven by the fear that lurks beneath every assimilated Jew: anti-Semitism may rise again, at any moment, with potentially deadly results. The book has sold over 200,000 copies in hardcover, and was the No. 1 nonfiction best-seller on the *New York Times* list this summer.

How do I acquire the books I publish? Most of the time it is as a result of submissions from literary agents. Those nonfiction submissions are usually in the form of a proposal. The proposal presents, in outline, the book the author intends, specifying the chapter contents and theme(s). The smart agent and author will include sample material: a chapter or two, perhaps a partial manuscript; occasionally there is even a videotape of the author to demonstrate his "promotability" on television talk shows. When the author is a prior best-selling and/or critically acclaimed writer, the submission is frequently no more than a two- or three-page letter or description of the next work. Sometimes it may be merely a verbal presentation: the agent brings the author in to meet the editor and publisher to describe his next book. But then the author's record of accomplishment is there, in all its glory, in a previously published work, or several. For those authors not yet well established or at the crest of popularity, the most convincing demonstration of the validity of their topic, and their ability to execute it as they claim, is thorough and convincing sample material. The author needs to be in control of his subject and to demonstrate it: the proposal or sample pages should be clearly written, consistent in the point of view, coherent and concise in the presentation of the subject. There are two other elements I look for in a nonfiction proposal. I touched on one before: controversy. I know that if some potential readers will be outraged, others will be impassioned—and both qualities help sell books. The last element I look for in a nonfiction work is not always applied to it but it is essential in separating out books that will succeed: creativity. However important the documentation of the subject, however substantive the material, if it is not presented in a dramatic and compelling way it will not hold the interest of the reader, or this editor. A savvy agent also will help his client position his book in the initial submission. Among editors there are always two contradictory responses to a proposal: either there is "too much competition out there for books like this," or "we need a book like this on our list." The writer must know the competition for his project and should identify it in terms of a bibliography and of current bookstore stock.

For example, since I published Cleveland Amory's books on his pet, Polar Bear, *The Cat Who Came for Christmas* and *The Cat and the Curmudgeon,* I have learned marketing facts that have applicability to other works. To illustrate, it is useful to know how many Americans own cats (56 million); how many copies of successful books in the field have sold; why the author's book is different from the others in the genre (his talent as a witty stylist and his personality portrait of his pet); what media experience the author has (every major television talk show, and features in leading newspapers and magazines). Of course I also knew the author is president of the Fund for Animals (every animal lover knows him!) and reached 66 million people with his *Parade* magazine articles. When an author includes similar information, that addition to his proposal indicates, to this editor at least, that the author has thought beyond his own material to the market "out there." Thus I know from the start that I will be working with an author who is interested in *selling* his book, and who will be responsive to editorial and other suggestions designed to effect that outcome.

Nonfiction books also result form an editor's pursuing an author, or from finding an author for a particular subject. I may write several short letters each week to writers who interest me—perhaps I admired an article he wrote in a magazine or newspaper; perhaps I liked her last book. Sometimes these are just fan letters; sometimes the article I read may suggest a book on that very subject or one that is related to it. To help my awareness of what a wide range of people are writing and how they write, I "read" (or at least look at) forty to fifty magazines a month and several daily newspapers. To stay current, I also read parts of books that are especially well received or that are on best-seller lists. But because of the exigencies of our business—the number of submissions I receive a year: eight hundred to a thousand; the number of books I edit and publish: twelve to eighteen with perhaps forty others in various stages of delivery—it is difficult to find the time to originate the ideas and locate the appropriate writers (and then to negotiate an advance and contract on terms suitable to all parties).

The one area where this is different—three books this year alone—is developing new books by authors I have already published successfully. With the success of *Breaking Barriers,* Carl Rowan and I talked about how to follow that memoir. As with all good books, there were stories left on the "cutting room floor." But we agreed that those alone would be simply recycled material. Then Carl came up with a new way to reframe those stories, and to build on them in a unique biography. He had had unprecedented access to Justice Thurgood Marshall for two award-winning television interview programs he created for PBS. And since he and the justice were also old friends from the civil rights movement, their lives had intersected at key times. Thus he proposed his new book, *Dream Makers, Dream Breakers: The World of Justice Thurgood Marshall.* Since this will be the first insider's account of the life and times of the first black justice, the marketplace handle for this nonfiction account is immediately apparent. With Alan Dershowitz, for another example, the editor-author explorations for his next subject took a somewhat different path: after reviewing Alan's suggestion for an account of his recent cases, I suggested to him that the audience for *Chutzpah* had not yet been sated by the issue and answers in that book, but in fact had been merely aroused. I asked Alan to think about where that topic led, and the answer was *Is There a Future for Us?* Its examination of the issue of assimilation for Jews then suggested certain subthemes, such as Jewish humor in a postghetto era and the differences between the way white-collar Jewish defendants and Wasp defendants are treated, that will give the book added dimensionality.

Because no editor publishes in a vacuum, once I have a proposal and sample material, once I have determined that the project interests me and is one for which I see sales potential, I will consult with one or more of my colleagues at Little, Brown. An editor always wants to galvanize the key people at her firm to share her enthusiasm. I may show the material to our marketing or sales directors, who must sell the book into the independent bookstores and book chains, and to our subsidiary rights director, who has expertise in the paperback, book club, and audio rights markets. The president of the division is also part of the decision process since he is ultimately responsible for every book the house publishes. At the proposal stage, we then determine what we will offer for the book, and either directly make that offer to the author's agent, or if the proposal has been submitted to more than one house (called "multiple submissions"), we express our interest to the agent, who may then set up an auction. Yes, it is just as it sounds—or as it occurs in the art, jewelry, stamp, antiques, and other markets. You bid (on the phone); the bidding goes in rounds (from lowest advance to highest), and usually the bidder who offers the highest figure will end up publishing the book. Experienced literary agents, however, will state in writing that the "author reserves the right to choose other than the highest bidder." Perhaps one house has offered a more ambitious or innovative plan to market the book; perhaps the author has a preference for one editor he has met or the reputation of a particular house.

If we succeed in buying the book, we then draw up a contract. At that point I talk to the author about exactly how we will proceed editorially. If it is an author I have not worked with before, I find it prudent to specify that I would like to see a part of the manuscript rather than wait until there is a draft of the entire book. Or if the author would prefer to show me individual chapters, I am happy to review them: my objective is to serve the author in whatever way makes him most productive and comfortable. By seeing partial material I have an opportunity to determine the author's direction, style, and substance—and to suggest corrections before the mix solidifies in a completed manuscript and changes or shifts are more difficult to achieve: if you only have to alter a voice or refine the idea in the first fifty pages, the task is less forbidding than facing a rewrite after four hundred pages. And because I know the author is eager for my reaction once he has let the material leave his hands for mine, I call him to tell him I have received it and that I will read it that day, that week, the next weekend. The editor is the author's umbilical cord to the outside world—will she like it or not? will they?—and I try to help him deal with that stress of separation at once.

At the first stage, and in subsequent drafts, I ask myself as I read the material, is the author accomplishing what he set out to do, and if not, what does he need to do? It may be that his analysis needs articulation, that the drama of an incident needs to open a chapter, not conclude it; it may be her sentences are complex when more direct communication will liven the style; it may be that assertions need additional documentation. I take notes as I read, and once I have identified the problems I see—and the successes as well—I write an editorial letter. In that letter, which may range from three to fifteen pages depending upon the length of the material submitted and its complexity, I praise what is good and right, identify what I see as stumbling blocks, and suggest solutions. I try to be as specific as possible. I further buttress those comments with yellow Post-it slips on every relevant page of the manuscript, my dialogue with the author about the work paragraph by paragraph—line by line, if need be. When I look back at *Chutzpah,* for example, as provocative as the book was in its first draft, I also knew that it needed to galvanize its potential audience at once. Some books may find their focus as they move along; I look for an irresistible imperative in the opening lines. And so I suggested that the author move one of his conclusions to his opening statement, turning those lines into a rallying cry and an organizing principle for the book. With his statement that Jews are second-class citizens in America and that anti-Semitism is on the rise, he acknowledged the "Holocaust mentality" I referred to earlier and showed his understanding from the outset. The point is that what the author had to say was now clearly aligned to a perception of the natural audience for the book. Clarifying thought and intent serves both the editorial process and sales (remember this book's resultant success).

From first draft to final, there are usually three distinct editorial stages, or revisions of the manuscript. With the first draft (the editor is reading it for the first time although the author may have written and rewritten his pages many times), the editorial letter and the yellow slips address the larger problems of the manuscript and suggest exact solutions: the book needs to be more analytical and/or more anecdotal; its theme is not clear; the organization of the material is confused. The second draft (once the author has handled those matters) refines the material further: perhaps the argument is articulated now but needs additional tracing through the chapters to reinforce that larger theme. This is usually the time to give greater detail to characterizations—not just who and what they are in the book but how they distinguish themselves (physical gesture, verbal dialogue). Again, I will yellow-slip the pages and write an editorial letter that both congratulates the writer on his progress and notes the work that remains to be done. At this point the yellow slips are usually fewer and the letter shorter than on my first effort. By the third draft, the larger questions have been answered, the initial problems solved, the style and passages smoothed. Only the final touches remain: shifting passages for ultimate drama, playing out one character's role for balance or impact, delineating atmosphere (what blue was the sky that fateful day?), polishing the ending to leave an emotional or intellectual reverberation that stays with the reader beyond the final page.

At the finish, the work has been transformed from a typed outline to a fully fleshed portrait, rich in color and detail. The letters and yellow slips together are my way of being "there" for the writer, with a lengthy discourse of advice and support. In this enterprise, I am the writer's best professional friend: next to her, I want her success most. But an effective editor is not only an admiring friend; she must also be an articulate critic. I like the benediction that James Thurber once provided: "I have never written a piece that I thought could not be improved."

When the writer and I realize we have each done all that we could with the material, we have fulfilled separately and together the editor-author relationship. If the book reaches its potential, then the author's work will be acclaimed. For no matter the extent of an editor's backstage contributions, the book is first, foremost, and always the author's success. And that's the way it should be. The editor's satisfaction comes from knowing he did the first of several editorial jobs well, that of helping the author articulate his ideas to the very best of his abilities. Even with marketing expertise, the rest is in the hands of the often capricious gods, for only a small fraction of the almost 50,000 books published every year—perhaps only several hundred—will be both acclaimed and sold in significant numbers. As one colleague said, "You have to pray that you will be lucky!"

For an editor to survive and thrive in this highly competitive business he needs to believe in his books—this book is terrific; the next one will be even better! He must have the stamina and willingness to work an extended day and week: there are simply not enough hours in the conventional working day to read and edit, since between nine-thirty and five-thirty what an editor actually does do in the office is *meet* (with publicity, advertising, and marketing people; with editorial colleagues over their/your problems and projects; with agents over future books; with the legal department over questions that arise in a manuscript; with the contracts department over negotiation points; with the subsidiary rights director to determine when to sell a book into paperback). Reading manuscripts and even proposals—the starting point of it all—comes at the end of the day: the phones begin to quiet down at five-thirty, and I usually work in the office for another two hours; two or three nights a week, I'll read and sometimes edit for another few hours after dinner. To give the pages at hand uninterrupted attention, however, sustained reading and editorial work is best done—by this editor, at least—one full day each weekend.

Is it worth it? Editing certainly does not make most editors rich or famous. However, when you deal with nonfiction subjects, the material is literally as broad as the world around you, and your reward as an editor is to have the opportunity to continue to learn: every day you are bombarded with stimulating ideas—the luxury of multiple majors in a university of subjects. You also meet, and get to know for the duration of the book or books, fascinating, quirky, well-informed authors who are usually more crazed, charming, and accomplished than most people. Above all, you are among the lucky few whose life's work does make a difference: the books you publish will affect their readers.

And there are some delightful perks in an editor's life. Sometimes you must travel to where the writer is—and perhaps once a year, if you are fortunate, she's in Los Angeles and not Boston. And sometimes you do, indeed, take authors to glamorous restaurants for lunch. One of my favorite acknowledgments, from the anthropologist Lionel Tiger, appeared in his recent book, *The Pursuit of Pleasure*. Referring to the article in the *New Republic* that caused a furor in our business by dividing editors into those who literally edit the manuscript versus those who only "acquire" the work at lunch at the Four Seasons (and then turn the line editing over to an anonymous assistant editor), Lionel said ". . . for the sake of histories of modern publishing, I am happy to record the wholly eccentric fact that my entire benign cooperation with F.S.F. was not once catalyzed by a publisher's lunch." Not to be outdone, I called him and said immediately, "Lunch, Lionel—your choice." He said, "Lutèce." Lutèce it was, wonderful it was. And best of all, by dessert we had planned the next book.

Is that a true story? Buy Lionel Tiger's next book, read the dedication—and judge for yourself!

Editing the Science-Fiction and Fantasy Novel

The Importance of Calling Everyone Fred

John W. Silbersack

JOHN W. SILBERSACK *has been an editor of one sort or another since the age of thirteen, when he prompted Everett F. Bleiler at Dover Publications to reprint Montague Rhodes James's* Collected Stories *and was paid in copies. In 1992, after the deadline for this article, he became editor-in-chief of Questar, a division of Warner Books. He was the founder and former editorial director of ROC Books, the science-fiction division of Penguin Books, and also coordinated the science-fiction program of the Berkley Publishing Corporation from 1978 to 1981. He is the author of several books, including the best-selling science-fiction pastiche* No Frills Science Fiction.

"During 1991, science fiction and fantasy became a two-billion-dollar-plus commodity in the United States alone," writes John W. Silbersack in this all-inclusive, often controversial essay that examines the varied roles, problems, pleasures and pains, fulfillments and frustrations of the science-fiction editor and the importance of SF and fantasy in our culture. "Take science fiction and fantasy out of the equation of the last fifty years (itself a science-fictional concept) and the world we would find would be not only very different but very limited as well."

Among the many aspects of contemporary science fiction Mr. Silbersack discusses are editing SF writers ("What I try to offer authors is attention to the shape of their books and careers"), the opportunity given to SF writers "to experiment with plot, theme, character, and idea in a publishing climate that has otherwise all but abolished experiment, at least of the trial-and-

*error sort," the freedom granted an SF editor to build an imprint within a
larger corporate framework, the special way SF is marketed to its author-
driven readers, and the impact of SF on the American culture, and vice
versa.*

*"New writers seem to spend a lot of time worrying the editor-author
relationship to death—in most cases before such a relationship exists. I
have only two criteria for that relationship, and they are the same criteria
I use to buy books for publication: 'Is it worth the effort?' and 'Will it
work?'... I must have some sense going in not only that the book is good
and marketable but that the author and I have something we can offer each
other, other than, of course, a sizable advance and a stack of manuscript.
... So my advice to young SF and fantasy editors," Mr. Silbersack offers,
"is to stop labeling themselves. My advice to young writers is the same."*

Editing the Science-Fiction and Fantasy Novel

The Importance of Calling Everyone Fred

During 1991, science fiction and fantasy became a two-billion-dollar-plus
commodity in the United States alone, according to statistics compiled by
Locus: The Newspaper of the Science Fiction Field. As science fiction
marches on toward that icon of the future, the year 2001, the numbers are
bound to grow past understanding, just as they have since the days, over
fifty years ago, when, with revolutionary effect, mass-market paperbacks
were first launched on the world.

Until the motion picture release of *Star Wars* in 1977, this science-fiction
juggernaut was, in effect, propelled and controlled by a handful of dedicated
SF specialist editors at no more than six publishing houses worldwide, most
here in the United States. Fifteen years later, the juggernaut is on a roll,
uncontrolled by those creative and editorial pioneers that led SF out of a
desert of neglect, and the future booming along is in the hands of no one
man or group. Financial and popular success has shaped a transition from
science fiction as an insular culture dedicated to the future into, paradoxi-
cally, a multicultural (and multimedia) celebration of science fiction's own
success. In the process, what science fiction *is*—or, for that matter, what an
editor like myself comes to call science fiction—has become so elastic as to
have little meaning except as a marketing convenience or a way to define a
disappearing average. For anyone interested in writing, publishing, or read-

ing science fiction, particularly for aspiring writers, understanding the process by which this came about is crucial.

Once confined to the ghettoized world of pulp magazines, ratty paperbacks, and the literary equivalent (if literature needs one) of secret handshakes, SF has become truly global since World War II. Equally to the point, the language peculiar to science fiction and fantasy, the apparatus of thought and concept required to understand it, has become part of the cultural vocabulary of nearly every literate person on earth. In fifty short years SF has developed from a minor, limited cult to full-blown cultural acceptance. Ironically, this acceptance is in every sphere except where it all started—among the core of the true believers who today are more concerned with defining science fiction in terms of what it isn't rather than what it is. As a publishing genre, SF is still unassimilated, still relegated to a ghetto. Except when it isn't.

To discuss SF and fantasy without reference to the media explosion that has attended its fortunes since the mid-1960s is to miss the whole point of one of the most marked (and least remarked upon) evolutions of mass culture since fiction attained a truly global reach. The growth, the truly astonishing emergence of SF as a multi-billion-dollar industry, has been almost entirely in what are called the electronic media, encompassing everything from television to video games. Today, the forces that propel science fiction as a literary genre are often quite alien to the written word, or at best they are distant cousins. Yet like most editors, perhaps more than most, all SF editors I know got into this line of work for pure love of books. As book publishing gives way to other media, and as purity gives way to pragmatism and commerce, I try to keep my balance as I send myself warily into the path of the juggernaut.

It didn't start that way, or at least agility wasn't uppermost in my mind as I embarked on my editorial career. I knew science fiction as a reader does, not by virtue of any special study or even interest. SF was just one area that my precollege reading had covered. Still, like most readers of science fiction I had read what I *had* read attentively, even though all of this was in my early teens. I had read all the acknowledged classics of the literature called SF; had a pretty thorough knowledge of the major authors and their careers; even had an inkling as to who had published them. (And here let me pause to say that throughout this essay, unless I distinguish between them, I think of science fiction, or SF, as embracing fantasy as well. Though it might actually be more accurate to claim that fantasy embraces SF.) I had done all this not with an early eye toward an editorial career but merely because I fit the model for the core SF reader: my reading patterns are author driven.

That simple phrase—"author driven"—it turned out, was enormously important in publishing terms, and important too, I found, for my career.

It means simply that certain readers are given to paying attention to who wrote the book they last read and (if they liked the book) make at least modest efforts to find something else by the same author. The very notion is a publisher's dream at any time, but particularly so in this age of conglomerated and corporately modeled publishing. Why? Because it overcomes the one obstacle that publishing has traditionally presented to big business—the virtual impossibility of mass-merchandising its wares.

The marketing of anything in a country of 250 million is an expensive proposition. The things that get sold effectively are dishwashing soaps and candy bars, major appliances and soda. Even though it costs millions a year, you can afford to advertise Coca-Cola; you know that next year and ten years later the same old Coke will be there to reap the benefit (that is, if they don't decide to change the formula again).

By comparison, Joe Writer's first novel, complete with over-the-top reviews and the praise of literary lions, may be a work of art, but money invested in it for advertising or promotion *may* pay dividends during a two-month on-sale period in a few major markets. The formula, quoted *ad nauseam* in all introductions to publishing—and more often noted with approval than disfavor—observes that publishing is one of the very few industries where *every single product*—i.e., each title—is unique, to be sold from scratch. The ascendance of "best-selling authors" proves a powerful exception, but in the world of midlist fiction everyone still seems to be anonymous. And today, "midlist" means everyone who hasn't come to own the *New York Times* best-seller list—perhaps twenty authors own it all.

A year from now, or two or three, depending on the rate of Joe's creativity, you, as Joe's editor, must start from scratch, if you are lucky. An unfortunate trend among booksellers that have computerized—a relatively recent phenomenon—is to order from net, i.e., to base their order of an author's newest book on what they actually sold of the author's last. Strictly followed, this pattern sends the gross distribution bar graph plummeting into the depths of print-order hell.

But SF is different.

Science fiction attracts author-driven readers. The sale of one book and the money spent on it by the publisher *can* be built upon by the author's next, and so on down a long prolific line, culminating in an appearance on the best-seller list of your choice. There are plenty of other publishing categories that share this trait. But SF seems to stand out for the flexibility the readers allow the writers—and, I must add, their editors.

What SF offers is the freedom of a genre that seems peculiarly unable to define itself. Some of the terms bandied about—speculative fiction, fantasist, technothriller, scientifiction, horror, dark fantasy—only begin to suggest the confusion even SF's most determined codifiers have shared. As I write this, the Science Fiction Writers of America (SFWA) has just renamed itself the Science Fiction and Fantasy Writers of America (SFFWA), but not without a fight. For good or ill, confusion over what SF *is* means that SF is what the ambitious SF writer or editor says it is. I trust that all my colleagues push the limit, as I try to do. Gatekeepers we are (to invoke a thesis applied compellingly to my own former company);* no censors we.

It's a running joke that every ambitious new SF novel is labeled by its publisher (and before that by the agent) as on the "cutting edge." Fantasy, similarly, breaks ground—or tries to—by introducing unfamiliar backgrounds or elements or by striving for an untraditional degree of characterization. Yet, SF in every daily respect—and that goes fivefold for the editing of it—is a deeply conservative enterprise. Actually, the science-fiction editor lives his or her life (by 1990 the sexes finally achieved parity in science-fiction editing) in the midst of oppositions, familiar in their absurdity but rather startling in their *fin de siècle* portentousness. On the one hand, SF offers the writer greater freedom than any other publishing niche I can think of; on the other, that freedom is often more than anyone is comfortable with. It is a freedom squandered on the often irrational hope (it could hardly be considered a likelihood) that the next book can earn its writer and publisher a fortune—or even a decent living. Too many writers, in part fearful of editorial censorship but also in part greedy for the golden ring of commercial success, seem to turn from the experimentalism (both conceptual and stylistic), the political and social critique, and the inspired deviltry that the field still offers (and that editors still publish) in favor of much safer and potentially more lucrative novels crafted for the popular taste. As all wage earners know, nothing is more calculated to make a fellow careful than a predictable check.

It's ironic that while every category of publishing has its stars—best-selling authors who transcend not the subject matter but the average sales of their genre—only SF seems to support not only best-sellers but also a wide cadre of midlist authors who can make a living off their writing. The prominent success of SF's most original and idiosyncratic thinkers (both authors *and* editors) seems to promote a copycat mentality geared to the lowest common denominator. The best that can be said for the copycat mentality is that it does ultimately celebrate creativity, and support it, too. The worst: that it distracts us from the originality of the real thing, the groundbreaking work itself.

At its best, science fiction, and fantasy too, is a literature of revolution.

---

*Thomas L. Bonn, *Heavy Traffic and High Culture: New American Library as Literary Gatekeeper in the Paperback Revolution* (New York: Meridian, 1990).

The core purpose, of course, of any work of fabulism, whether science fiction or fantasy, is the questioning of established things. SF takes this principle to extremes, and it is not only with its talk of outer space, alien monsters, and furry-toed hobbits that it seems to avoid the present, the real, the status quo. Most such improbabilities are mere window dressing. The best science fiction and fantasy of the last century, from Wells to Tolkien, from Heinlein to Herbert and LeGuin, from Haldeman to Russ and Delany, has been profoundly about social change, much more so than about the ostensible adventures of any of their characters. In its unreal way, SF is the most political of literatures. By the same token, in the most real of countries, such as China, and the former Soviet Union, the dictatorships of South America, science fiction and fantasy have been modes of expression that have consistently escaped censorship. Whether called magic realism or fairy tale, these genres provide a freedom to say what must be said. Even here in the West, few popular novels have so often shaped the mood of their time as Vonnegut's *Slaughterhouse Five,* Heinlein's *Stranger in a Strange Land,* Frank Herbert's *Dune,* or LeGuin's *Left Hand of Darkness.* Since the advent of paperbacks, mass culture has embraced an outpouring of societally aware imaginings from every source, but as a category SF and fantasy stood out.

Yet, as I have said, the ideal is revolutionary in a way that adheres neither to the left *nor* the right of the political spectrum, but the practice is often boringly predictable. Strangely enough, I think authors are more often conservative, in the sense of pulling their punches, than the editors sometimes are. Granted the writers are probably furnishing what they think or know we editors will publish: they have to; they need to make a living. For their part, in the process of earning their own living, most editors I know find time and courage to at least occasionally back a dark and unpopular horse. But then, an editor's living isn't measured out by the book.

And of course, making a living—a good living, we hope—built of our labor and passion is the goal of writers and editors both. I can't speak for all SF editors, of course (though almost all without exception are my friends), but I think that in addition to *making* a living we all have a sense of living on the edge.

In one sense that edge is a function of the otherness that seems to earmark SF as something different. I don't have to describe the difference. Everyone in and out of publishing seems to understand just how SF and fantasy stand apart without quite being able to put it into words, except perhaps to make a joke of it. And that last, sadly, might be at the core of SF's difference. It *is* a big joke, all the jollier for protestations of seriousness. Just synopsizing the plots of even famous SF and fantasy novels is an exercise in absurdity; funnier still to do it before a group of cynical sales reps. But in a classic

Catch-22, true levity is reserved for anything that holds itself apart, and SF holds itself apart from a mainstream world that laughs at it. In my experience SF is different because of an assumption that you have to be a little weird to *get* it. In publishing terms that means that the SF editor is very much on his own, pursuing his career among colleagues who would never think to admit ignorance of politics or literature or popular culture but who freely admit of SF that they "just don't get it. After all, it's pretty silly stuff on the whole. Right?"

Apart as they are, SF editors do not work in the vacuum of Space. They work in big offices because only the very biggest companies have the luxury of specialization that a science-fiction department entails. But no large organization commands in every department — sales, promotion, publicity, fulfillment, copywriting, advertising, etc. — the specialized skills needed to reach the SF reader. It makes sense that all this should be coordinated by the SF editor, and often out of dire expediency it is. The SF editor, no matter his or her job title, has learned to function not only as an editor but also as a publisher when need arises. That means that the SF editor at most major publishing houses, usually at an early age, takes on responsibilities that otherwise might be years in coming. At twenty-two, the age I was when I negotiated my first six-figure deal, my authors were two, three, or even four times my age; my colleagues were toughened veterans of the publishing wars. And I was in seventh heaven, because of all the freedoms that SF allows its editors, the greatest is the opportunity to immerse oneself in publishing, to get involved and to learn. This may be the reason there are a disproportionate number of former SF editors who run publishing houses today: Lou Aronica at Bantam, Malcolm Edwards at Grafton/HarperCollins UK, Elaine Koster at NAL, Nanscy Neiman at Warner — the list is impressive.

For the science-fiction editor, responsibility has its attractions and its repulsions. The appeal of that responsibility has much to do with the management of small, discrete publishing entities within larger organizations. What is less attractive has to do with coping with a heightened sense of the conflicting demands of commerce and art. My guess is that the SF editor is called upon more than most of his colleagues to juggle the two; the object is to keep them both in the air at once.

For all these reasons, science fiction is in many ways a place between oppositions. It is a place where publishing seems warily to bridge commerce and literature, entertainment and education, science and fantasy, and the marketing strategies of direct and wholesale sales, independent and chain sales, specialty and mass-market books. These are the issues that will form the curricula of twenty-first-century publishing. The landscape I share with my colleagues by no means follows a straight and narrow trail, and we all approach our jobs from many viewpoints. To begin with, the label "science fiction" itself . . .

There is little that is particular to *science* in what the SF editor does. Actually, the science-fiction editor of most major publishing houses is also responsible for what many might think the opposite of "scientific" fiction, that is, fantasy. Indeed, except for the distinction on the spine and the (slightly) differentiated covers, science fiction and fantasy are indistinguishable publishing genres.

The distinction between what *can* be, as SF is often described, and what *can't* be, as fantasy often is, diminishes materially when viewed against the undifferentiating reality of what merely *is*—i.e., the rest of everything *else* written. By that I mean fiction pure and simple according to the criteria that distinguish between "mainstream" (best-seller and also literary fiction) and genre. But science fiction is not "pure and simple," according to its critics and not a few of its fans. The former complain that SF offers something less; the latter claim something more. Who is right? The truth, as every editor knows, is that it is the individual book and author that delivers; not the genre, not the jacket promises, not the whole rigamarole of concept (high or not), message, or hype. Above all else, not the publisher's label. What is pure and simple, in the last analysis, is that the truth is in the writing.

The best books I edit *should* be read by what is generally called a mainstream audience. It would shake them up and wouldn't hurt my bottom line either. But the fact of the matter is that those readers are generally inattentive in a way that bookish readers are not. That is, they aren't adventurous in their reading, they don't compulsively look to broaden their reading experience, they don't *work* at it.

Science fiction's readers are bookish in the sense that they *do* work at it. Sadly, few of them do so to the point of puncturing the comforting bubble of their favorite genre, SF or fantasy, but within their chosen world they are all a publisher could ever ask for. They read compulsively, and experiment with new authors, and trade books among themselves, and follow their favorite authors to the ends of the galaxies and back. These are the reasons publishers have learned to love them.

The P and L (profit and loss statement) is very simple: SF attracts publishers because, as an author-driven genre, it commands a high percentage of initial sale (sell-through) and substantial backlist sales. The SF editor relies in fact on comparatively modest initial sales with a high degree of marketing efficiency. For example, a typical mass-market midlist work of fiction may sell perhaps only 50 percent of copies advanced—a truly shocking figure, but average nonetheless. But the astute SF editor might manage a 70 percent sell-through. All else being equal, the margin of profitability to the corporate bottom line should be accordingly high.

While the best books are good enough to be read by anybody, not all books should be. Books that don't deliver, or don't deliver completely, are routinely published. What, anyone might ask, does the SF editor see in the trash that we all acknowledge is sometimes published? The answer is, as any editor might answer, a combination of optimism, stupidity, honest mistake, and in the SF arena something further—a devotion to something sometimes called "the novel of ideas." No other genre seems to think such an unlikely conjunction could yield a book, much less a commercial one. SF does—to its credit, and to its loss.

That is because fiction is not necessarily what SF is about, at least not wholly and not in the sense that academics or any well-schooled reader recognizes fiction. The SF writer, to a degree unknown in other popular literature, is judged against a criterion that categorizes SF as a literature of ideas. In most instances, of course, it is anything but, yet there are still plenty of writers, novels, and what pass as genre classics that offer little *but* an Idea with a capital *I*, while relegating character, plot, and style to far more subordinate roles. To go further, the border between fiction and polemic can be hairline thin and is notoriously treacherous, but no one disputes the fact that SF, under the guise of entertainment, often offers a message as well. SF is the only genre I know where authors are remembered, blurbed, and praised for their predictions, even the invention of spacecraft and satellites, nuclear piles and solar sails.

Yes, science fiction likes to think it has pioneered an edge for itself between popular literature and the real thing, with a lot of prediction to boot. And in some authentic ways it has. (Here at last, incidentally, is a point where fantasy strays from parallel pursuits, since fantasy, unlike SF, seems to turn inward as a genre, unheeding of uncomfortable realities.) And yet, the literature of the future is very much the literature of the past, unforgiving of invention and stylistic effrontery. David Hartwell, in the previous edition of this volume, wrote very interestingly of the historical reasons for this. Suffice to say that for the working science-fiction editor, commercial imperatives scorn avant-garde invention on the page but reward tales of invention in the old-fashioned Thomas Edison sense. Within certain corporate strictures, editors in this genre are almost given something rare in publishing, freedom to publish what they like. What they like and what sells are sometimes hard to reconcile, but that is the essence of the job. Sometimes the balance is drawn in one direction, sometimes the other; but most editors I know strive to strike a balance, however unwieldly. For better or worse, I believe that this affords the writer his or her greatest chance to experiment with plot, theme, character, and idea in a publishing climate that has otherwise all but abolished experiment, at least of the trial-and-error sort.

. . .

In one sense it seems to me that every book I publish is an experiment and that the whole apparatus of the publishing process—and quite an apparatus it is—is dedicated to making sense (and cents) of what is really a completely intuitive process: the selection and effective marketing of a pile of manuscript. My day-to-day, workaday life argues against this, spent as it is in meetings ranging from editorial to cover conferences, promotion, paging and pricing, sales, and postmortems of past titles. All of this would be intolerable if it achieved nothing but hours spent in a chair, but in fact quite a lot seems to get accomplished; enough so that the collaborative process of publishing seems to me to be the most vigorous and exciting business on earth. The results of our deliberations (i.e., the books we publish) still smack of trial and error, of a guess hazarded at whim, but we publish books in great number and corporately live or die by the attention, importance, and sales they achieve; and corporately, publishing seems to flourish. Personally, it rewards.

When not at a meeting table, editors spend most of their time on the telephone with authors, agents, and "contacts" in high and low places. The popular image of editors comfortably ensconced in overheated offices and overstuffed armchairs reading the day away is completely foreign to my experience and may never have had any reality at all.

If it ever had, it referred to a pre–World War II world of low-volume hardcover houses like Charles Scribner's Sons, Alfred A. Knopf, E. P. Dutton, or G. P. Putnam's Sons. It did not refer to the mammoth mass-market paperback publishers that dominate publishing today and virtually define the SF publishing arena. I am constantly amazed by the new authors (and science fiction authors at that) who assume, aggressively in some instances, that time has not moved on, that the prewar era is still in force.

Today publishing is anything but high-tech, but it is changed. As I said above, science fiction has found its haven in the paperback houses, publishing entities that specialize in volume (expressed as both distribution and numbers of titles). According to *Locus* more than 3,000 SF and fantasy titles are scheduled to be published in 1993 in the United States alone. The top five SF publishing houses (numerically by number of titles) will publish more than 800 original science-fiction and fantasy novels, or an average of 160 books apiece. Not all those books will originate in SF departments, but many will. And most of those departments will be pressed to give each book the attention it deserves, or even more to the point, the attention its author *thinks* it deserves.

For my part, I work on a list of between five and six original SF or fantasy novels a month, most published in paperback, some published in trade paperback or hardcover. All these books need some share of editing, packaging, and marketing, and much of that burden must be borne by my office. I'm helped in this by an editorial colleague and an assistant we share. My department of three reads an average of forty-two new manuscripts submitted each month from agents or authors with some sort of introduction to our publishing house. Many more manuscripts get at least a cursory screening from the slush pile. We manage all this for the most part on our own time; office hours are devoted to merchandising the art our off-hours reading discovers.

The mathematically minded reader will swiftly conclude that my life is a misery of work and more work. It is anything but, in part because every book is a fresh experience to be savored, very often even if it is very bad, and because editing (any kind of editing) *is* a kind of treasure hunt that promises surprise and reward around every corner. Like most editors, I think my job should be fun and it often is.

When it isn't fun that is almost invariably because what we laughingly call the author-editor relationship goes awry. I say "laughingly" because this isn't a relationship, it's a marriage, with all the emotional and contractual baggage that the term implies. Too often, I get the sense, the aspiring writer is so determined to be businesslike in his dealings with prospective publishers that he or she forgets we have some aspirations too. New writers seem to spend a lot of time worrying the editor-author relationship to death—in most cases before such a relationship exists. I have only two criteria for that relationship, and they are the same criteria I use to buy books for publication: *"Is it worth the effort?"* and *"Will it work?"* As applied to the author-editor relationship I mean, roughly, that I must have some sense going in not only that the book is good and marketable but that the author and I have something we can offer each other, other than, of course, a sizable advance and a stack of manuscript.

What I try to offer authors is attention to the shape of their books and careers. My attention is not always, or even often, expressed in lavish red-penciling. For obvious reasons I avoid like the plague books that need that degree of work. Today I try to buy books that need little or no line work and instead focus my attention on issues of structure, plot, and characterizaton. But even this has become a kind of step child to the more important (in terms of my sales and an author's career) issue of author development. More than not, my editorial input is expressed in terms of a kind of loose career guidance. I try to steer my authors in the direction that I feel will best benefit their development as commercial authors, and in so doing benefit, of course, my list. This mirrors in many cases the direction or shape I seek for the list I publish as a whole. My guidance is not that of an avuncular Perkins, I rush to add. I urge my advice with the tools in my hand—unequal leverage of persuasion, demonstration, and the power of exchequer. It's all part of the give-and-take of what we might call the social contract between author and editor, as opposed to the legal document drawn up between Corporation and Proprietor. In any event, our shared agenda is growth.

It's in this, I think, that the difference between editing science fiction and fantasy and editing anything else finally lies (if, indeed, there *is* a difference, because in most ways there is very little to distinguish between the two). For instance, I tell all my new editorial assistants (who, by the way, are *not* chosen for their knowledge of SF) that I want them to read genre submissions as they would read any book; and if they stumble over the often silly nomenclature of alien names, I tell them to call everyone Fred. By and large the advice works because, as with every work of fiction, whether set in the Bowery in 1960 or in Middle-Earth, each book must succeed on its own terms. So my advice to young SF and fantasy editors is to stop labeling themselves. My advice to young writers is the same.

But I said that I thought there might be a difference. If there is, it is in the SF editor's relationship to his special little corner of the publishing list as a whole. I think, and I hope, that most SF editors are more than usually aware not just of each book *as* a book, but of the way it fits among a number of books published as each month unfolds. And, over the space of a year, and numbers of years, how each book contributes to the shape and direction that gives a publishing line its particular character.

I think that's a good thing (though there may well be many authors who would fail to see the applicability to their own good), but I can't say, and don't want to say, that it is a trait reserved to science fiction. All good editors are, I think, empire builders in some quiet but forceful sense. I mean only to suggest that SF editors as a group are taught to think this way from an early age for reasons bound up in the history of SF publishing.

• • •

Some authorities name Mary Wollstonecraft Shelley's *Frankenstein* as the founding document of science fiction. Others name H. G. Wells's scientific "romances," while others reach back to classic and medieval flights of fancy directed to ends quite different from what we intend now.

More provincially, maybe more accurately, many date the modern SF era from the day a journalistic hack named Hugo Gernsback turned his attention to the foundation of a new "scientifiction" magazine named *Amazing Stories.* Interestingly, an editor, not a writer, defined modern SF, at least literally, since he coined the phrase.

Today's SF editors are the heirs in perhaps equal parts of Maxwell Perkins (*every* editor's hero), Ian Ballantine (the editor as enthusiast and entrepreneur, out of fashion but the best of our kind), and Judy Lynne Del Rey (the superbly proficient specialist). From these three, all successful SF editors, like Frankenstein's monster bringing us back to first things, may be manufactured.

There were many others in the science-fiction universe that played equally important roles in fashioning a publishing genre from scratch. To name just a few among book publishers: Donald A. Wollheim (Ace and DAW Books), Lester Del Rey (Del Rey), Truman Talley (NAL), and Terry Carr (Ace). And of course from the pantheon of nearly legendary magazine editors, John W. Campbell (*Astounding, Analog*), to name just one, probably exerts as much influence today as he did fifty years ago. Today their collective heirs (vastly more weighted toward books) continue, founding dedicated SF publishing companies (Tom Doherty at TOR and Jim Baen at Baen Books) and revitalizing older imprints (Susan Allison at Ace, Owen Locke at Del Rey, and Betsy Wollheim at DAW). Others convince corporate newcomers to form divisions dedicated to their beloved genre (John Douglas at AvoNova, Brian Thomsen at Questar, Lou Aronica at Bantam Spectra, David Hartwell, first at Pocket Books, then at Arbor House, then at William Morrow, or myself at Penguin/ROC Books). The point, of course, is that science fiction as a vital publishing genre has been proselytizing and refashioning some part of the publishing universe into a separate world of congenial editorial freedoms for many years.

Interestingly, individuals rather than corporations have truly defined science fiction as a genre. Just note the number of imprints that bear their editors' names.

But whether fashioned by the entrepreneurial skills of practiced businessmen-editors or the marketing and managerial skills of equally alert corporate committees, the operative impulse has always been to set science fiction somehow apart. Unlike mysteries, romance, or westerns, science fiction seems to thrive best as a publishing category with a clearly drawn distinction between itself and the rest of all publishing.

Perhaps it is no accident that, as some have argued, the fissure between "high" and "low" culture that opened in the nineteenth century included the publication of seminal science-fiction novels and begins to close in the late twentieth with authors often published first in the SF field, such as Kurt Vonnegut, T. Coraghessan Boyle, J. G. Ballard, Ursula LeGuin, and others. Other quite clearly literary and also "mainstream" authors such as Doris Lessing, Margaret Atwood, and Mark Helprin unashamedly embrace SF techniques in their fiction. And of course South American fiction under the rubric of "magic realism" leads where once Poe and Lovecraft held sway.

Still other writers that seem to belong in both camps but remain somehow obscure are Samuel R. Delany, Joanna Russ, Gene Wolfe, perhaps a dozen others. The gap, if not closed, *can* close, and the science-fiction editor is ever conscious of the leap in acclaim, revenue, and career that closure can afford (in a way that perhaps editors for westerns and romance are not and could not be). Still, on reflection it might be a very dicey thing that science-fiction editors and writers have one foot sunk in the mire (as all will acknowledge) and the other in the stars. There are altogether too many awards in the SF field and most writers would do well to heed them as little as their readers do, judging by the number of Hugo and Nebula Award–winning novels now out of print or the disappointing sales most such rewards leave in their wake.

Even more troublesome is the insistence and attention that this whole division occasions. Science fiction as an institution is too anxious to be included in the real world, and too proud to make an overture that would admit the truth: that we're not there yet. The net result is a kind of editorial paralysis that fails to follow where our successes lead. After all, in the last five years science fiction, or what might be called so, has come to occupy a significant proportion of the major best-seller lists, has become a staple of "literary" fiction, and in sheer dollar figures has become respectable indeed. Though it will be hard and scary work, eventually this most exuberant of genres will take hold. In fact, I am convinced that the vigor of genre SF and fantasy publishing has already contributed mightily to current thought and debate. Certainly this is so in regard to our understanding of technology and its ramifications, or the pursuit of such metaphysics as human consciousness itself. Take science fiction and fantasy out of the equation of the last fifty years (itself a science-fictional concept) and the world we would find would be not only very different but very limited as well.

Editing Children's Books

Phyllis J. Fogelman

PHYLLIS J. FOGELMAN *is president, publisher, and editor-in-chief of Dial Books for Young Readers. She began her career in children's books in 1961 as production editor at what is now HarperCollins. In late 1966 she left her position as senior editor at Harper to join The Dial Press as editor-in-chief of the new children's book department. In 1976 she was named vice-president, and in 1982 when the company's name was changed to Dial Books for Young Readers, she became publisher as well. She was named president of Dial in 1986.*

Some of the authors and artists Ms. Fogelman has worked with are Leo and Diane Dillon, Susan Jeffers, Steven Kellogg, Julius Lester, Mercer Mayer, Jerry Pinkney, Mildred D. Taylor, and Rosemary Wells.

Ms. Fogelman's knowledgeable voyage into the special world of the children's book editor expresses her ardent dedication to the enrichment and expansion of the child's imagination and understanding of the reality and diversity of the world. She describes the uniquely creative pleasure children's book editors experience in working with artists and authors to fashion an interesting, well-written, entertaining book that will endure. ("In most cases, however, the author is not involved in the choice of who will illustrate the story and will never even speak with the artist as the book is being developed.")

Aware that in choosing which books to publish for children the editor must also appeal to adults, who buy the books before they actually reach children, she notes that "it is most important that editors of juvenile books have a sense of what children will like. It's helpful if the editor can remember what it felt like to be a child."

Ms. Fogelman's essay offers an expert review of the business, sales, and marketing components that determine whether to take on a book, but ultimately it's her personal passion for a project that is the most influential factor. "If I'm excited by a project, interested in what it has to say, personally moved, and believe it will appeal to children, I will first make a decision that it should be published, and then figure out just how it should be done."

Ms. Fogelman sees publishing as one of the few fields remaining in which the individual has real impact in selecting and shaping the end result. "One reason I'm in this field is that I'm aware of how important books are to and for children. A good book can change their lives; it can affect how they think and feel about any number of subjects. It's not only very interesting to be involved in that process, it's also a great responsibility, one that is an integral part of publishing for children."

Editing Children's Books

One of the most satisfying aspects of editing and publishing books for children is discovering the potential in an author's or an artist's work. When a manuscript comes to me, it is my job to evaluate its chances of becoming a fine children's book, one that will stand the test of time. Part of this decision depends on personal taste, part on a knowledge of the market. But first and foremost I have to be emotionally moved.

Like children's book authors, children's book publishers become known for particular kinds of books. Publishing is one of the few fields remaining today in which the individual has real impact in selecting and shaping the end result. Nowhere is this truer than in the editorial process. And children's books have the great advantage of allowing—almost requiring—that an editor also work with artists, a part of the job that I've loved from the beginning.

Another of the great pleasures of editing children's books is the wide variety in the types of books being published. Books for children range from board books and picture books for babies and young children through middle-grade and young adult fiction and nonfiction. Although the subjects and formats are extremely varied, the criteria for selection are similar for all of them. Whether it's a picture book for the toddler or a novel for young adults, it's important for the text to be interesting and well written and the subject appealing to the age group for whom the book is intended. In children's fiction the plot and characterization must also be compelling. Nonfiction children's books have to be factually accurate, of course, and the quality of the writing should be as fine and lively as in a good work of fiction. All of this is also true of acquiring and editing books for adults. In choosing which children's books to publish, however, we must also appeal to adults in order to reach our ultimate audience: the children for whom the book is meant in the first place. It is generally adults who buy the books before they actually reach children, although teenagers do choose books— mainly paperbacks—for themselves. But even these books must first be filtered through booksellers and librarians—more adults.

Beyond the special ability of knowing what older people will buy for the young, it is most important that editors of juvenile books have a sense of what *children* will like. It's helpful if the editor can remember what it *felt* like to be a child. I've never known whether I have considerable recall of my childhood feelings because I'm a children's book editor and I often call upon those memories, or if it's because of those feelings that I decided to edit children's rather than adult books.

But one reason I'm in this field is that I'm aware of how important books are to and for children. A good book can change their lives; it can affect how they think and feel about any number of subjects. It's not only very interesting to be involved in that process, it's also a great responsibility, one that is an integral part of publishing for children. Unlike textbooks, children's trade books—those found in bookstores and libraries—are read for pleasure. Good literature—not basal textbooks—will not only provide that pleasure, but also can and should expand the imagination as well as foster knowledge and children's understanding of the world and the people in it.

The young are far more impressionable and vulnerable than are adults, and not surprisingly there is wide disagreement on what is appropriate for children to read. Some editors, like some parents, would like to protect children from knowledge of the dangers and ills in our society. Not every good subject for a book is appropriate for *young* children, but I believe that it's generally knowledge, not a lack of it, that arms children and helps to prepare them for the world as it is, rather than what we would like it to be. Even those who live in a very protected environment have easy access to TV and movies, and these often carry a stronger, harsher sense of reality than do most children's books, which are likely to deal with tough issues in a more sensitive way.

One such issue is AIDS. Recently we published *Ryan White: My Own Story,* a book for ages ten through adult. Ryan's five-year fight against AIDS until his death at age eighteen, and especially his fight against the sometimes violent prejudice he encountered, was, I believed, an extremely important story. But from the moment I contracted for the manuscript, I knew a special effort would be needed to gain a wide audience for a book on a subject many people don't want to read about. It was necessary, we felt, to have a publicity campaign to bring attention to Ryan's autobiography. Although the book was on the *New York Times* best-seller list, some book buyers still were deterred by the subject matter from buying or stocking it.

Children's books should represent the diversity in our nation. The United States has never been an all-white country, but especially prior to the 1970s one would not have known that from reading children's books. I've felt since I was a teenager that it's very important that all children read books by and about as many of the minorities in the United States as possible. As a child in a New England city of thirty thousand people, I had read every children's book in the public library by the age of nine. None of them was by or about black people, and I never even thought about it until four years later when I found, at home, *Black Boy* by Richard Wright and then a year or two later his first published novel, *Native Son.* I suddenly remembered clearly, as I do now, that the only time African Americans were mentioned in any book I'd read previously was in the study of the Civil War in my fourth- or fifth-grade social studies class. The passage in our textbook stated that although slavery was wrong, most slaves were well taken care of and were happy. Though I wasn't ordinarily the kind of child who questioned what I was told in school, I instantly knew that could not be true. Slaves were not happy being owned as a piece of furniture was owned; how could they be? The two Richard Wright books and the passage on slavery had a profound effect on me, as I think happens only when you're young. I'm sure that this was a major factor in my publishing books by and about blacks beginning in the late 1960s, when I arrived at Dial, and continuing into the 1990s.

Soon after I joined Dial as editor-in-chief of Books for Young Readers, I read a copy of a manuscript entitled *Look out, Whitey!* that the adult department was planning to publish. It was clear that the author, Julius Lester, was a wonderful writer, and I suggested to him that he consider writing for children. A few weeks later he came into my office with four or five ideas, and when he said he'd done research in the Library of Congress, where he had collected quotations from ex-slaves, I said immediately, "That's it, start with that one." Finally there would be a book for children that would tell what it was *really* like to be a slave. And so I published *To Be a Slave* in 1968, and it was chosen as a Newbery Honor Book—unusual for nonfiction and a first for a black writer at that time. And since then many fourth- and fifth-grade classes have used the book for the study of slavery. Even now I still think of *To Be a Slave* as one of the most important and most gratifying books I've ever published, and I've continued my commitment to developing talented writers and artists from different racial and ethnic backgrounds.

Just this week, I received *The Last Tales of Uncle Remus,* the fourth and final book of Julius Lester's extraordinary retellings of the largest single body of African American folktales we have. I originally suggested this major project to him in 1985, and the first book, *The Tales of Uncle Remus,* was published in 1987. *Last Tales,* which is the tenth book we've worked on together, will be published in 1993.

Some of the social and political progress brought about by the civil rights movement inspired the blossoming of writers and illustrators from various racial groups in the sixties and seventies, especially African Americans. One of the results of the new ferment was that a number of black people whose works I subsequently published went to Africa, particularly Ghana, and returned to write or illustrate books. Motifs from African art and design, as well as the Swahili language, brought a new dimension to children's books. To my mind this was the true birth of the multicultural movement, which has become such a strong force in children's books today.

When Muriel Feelings submitted her idea for *Moja Means One: A Swahili Counting Book,* she planned to use her simple linoleum block art for illustrations. I convinced her to allow Tom Feelings, whom I had asked to illustrate *To Be a Slave* and to whom she was then married, to illustrate the book, and his beautiful paintings gave the work the stature it deserved. As a result, in 1972 Tom became the first black artist to win a Caldecott Honor— runner-up for the Caldecott Medal. In 1975 he again received a Caldecott Honor for *Jambo Means Hello: A Swahili Alphabet Book.*

I had asked Leo and Diane Dillon to illustrate their first picture book, *The Ring in the Prairie: A Shawnee Legend,* which I published in 1970. A few years later I told them I thought they could do wonderful artwork for an African folktale I'd found for them. They did, and in 1976 *Why Mosquitoes Buzz in People's Ears* won the Caldecott Medal, making Leo the first black artist to win the Caldecott. The Dillons also won the Caldecott Medal in 1977 for *Ashanti to Zulu: African Traditions,* the same year that another Dial book, *Roll of Thunder, Hear My Cry* by Mildred D. Taylor, won the Newbery Medal. Mildred is only the second black writer to receive this prestigious honor and she continues to win many awards for her books, which are based on her own family in Depression-era Mississippi. Jerry Pinkney, an African American artist who created the artwork for the Uncle Remus books, also illustrated Robert D. San Souci's *The Talking Eggs,* a 1989 Caldecott Honor Book as well as a Coretta Scott King Award winner.

Beginning in the sixties and seventies we published books of American Indian folktales, and in 1991 Susan Jeffers illustrated *Brother Eagle, Sister Sky: A Message from Chief Seattle.* This beautiful book was on the *New*

York Times best-seller list, among others, for several months in 1992 in large part because of the environmental message that we are the caretakers rather than the owners of the land—a philosophy that has always been a part of Native American beliefs.

Considering that there are many millions of Latino Americans in this country, it is distressing that so few Latino authors are writing for children. A major author is Nicholasa Mohr, and I edited the three books she published with Dial. *In Nueva York* is a group of interrelated stories and was an ALA Notable and Best Book for Young Adults. *Felita* and *Going Home,* for younger children, are based on some of the author's experiences growing up in New York City and going to Puerto Rico for the first time— books that have brought in many letters from children going through similar experiences.

I am sometimes asked what the best training is for the profession of children's book editor. Two essential ingredients are a lifelong love of books of all kinds and an interest in a wide range of subjects and issues. One should also have the ability to develop into someone who can in the space of a few moments move comfortably from negotiating a contract to encouraging an author to complete a book, which may involve a little lay psychology. Then one should be able to immediately decide on the format of a picture book with an artist and estimate how many copies are likely to sell (before the manuscript is revised or the art begun), so that production costs can be estimated. And that may all be in less than a half hour after arriving at the office. A children's book editor should not only know how to select and edit manuscripts for publication and be able to work with all different kinds of artists, but should also have a good understanding of design, production, marketing, publicity, and subsidiary rights.

Despite all this, at the very start of the publishing process there is simply an editor alone in an office reading a manuscript. Well, not usually alone. Since I am also president and publisher of Dial, I'm rarely alone long enough to read manuscripts in my office. In fact I'm happy if I can read my mail! So it's even more likely that I'm on a crowded subway reading the manuscript, or at home at eleven at night reading it on the couch. The job is so demanding that there's just not enough time to read in the office.

But wherever I am, at this stage I'm just a reader, reacting to a writer's work. If the project is a picture book by an author-illustrator, I am also a viewer, looking at and evaluating artwork, usually sketches in dummy form at this point. In any case, if I'm excited by a project, interested in what it has to say, personally moved, *and believe it will appeal to children,* I will first make a decision that it should be published, and then figure out just how it should be done.

A major part of the editorial process is working with the author or author-illustrator, and in my experience the most important ingredient in that relationship is trust. The author must trust that the editor knows what she or he is talking about when asking for revisions. This is one reason that I like to meet with a new author before contracting for a project. A considerable degree of rapport is necessary for a productive working relationship, and whenever possible I like to discuss in person what kind of revisions I think are needed and see as well as hear how the author responds.

Trust and honesty are as important in an editorial relationship as they are in any good relationship—always a two-way street. I've also realized in recent years that the longer I've worked with an author or illustrator, the more *I* bring to the editorial relationship because I know the person I'm working with much better with each book. This also works in reverse for the author, who understands what kind of guidance is possible from his or her particular editor and what is reasonable to expect. People differ widely on what they require from an editor. Some want to discuss ideas before pursuing them; others send complete manuscripts and/or dummies before involving their editor.

I've worked with Rosemary Wells since 1970 and in that time have edited and published more than forty of her books: picture books, board books, middle-grade and young adult novels, as well as a cookbook spoof for adults. In addition to editing, part of what Rosemary expects from me is help in deciding which of the several ideas she has (simultaneously) she should work on and in what order.

One day in 1977 I picked up the phone and heard a familiar voice saying a familiar phrase: "Phyllis, I've got three ideas and I want you to tell me which to do first." (In the 1990s this type of call from Rosemary comes more often, and it's now generally four or five good ideas she's juggling.) She described them as one of her "usual" picture books, the young adult novel we'd been discussing, and something new: a short picture book for the very young. After listening to her briefly describe the latter, I immediately said, "Do the young book first."

A month later Rosemary walked into my office with a dummy for *Max's First Word.* It was marvelous. I sent her home to do three more young books about Max and Ruby, the brother and sister rabbits, and in 1979 I published four Max and Ruby books, which were the first high-quality board books in the United States. They were different from any that preceded them because the texts were wonderful little stories with a beginning, middle, and end. They were immediately successful and quickly spawned a huge number of board books here and abroad. My first contribution in this case was to tell Rosemary to concentrate on these books, but after getting production estimates, and even before editing them, I needed to figure out a way to successfully sell a huge quantity of Max board books in the first year. Board books must be priced very low, which means a large number must be printed in order to keep costs down. In the 1970s the idea of a high-quality, non-mass-market publisher like Dial selling that many books, almost exclusively to bookstores, was certainly a gamble, but they were so successful that we had to reprint them very quickly. We published Rosemary's second set of board books in 1985, and they continue to be popular, as are her Max picture books, which are larger and for a somewhat older, but still a mainly preschool, audience.

After publication Rosemary and I forgot just how much work had gone into them until years later, when we were asked to do an author/editor talk on the board books. I went through our files and had slides made from the early dummies to show how the books had evolved, so we could point up the editor-author working relationship, which was the theme of the conference. When we got to *Max's Breakfast* but before I showed the slide, which Rosemary had not yet seen, she said, "That one was easy to do." What she had forgotten was just how much work she had done before she made it, as I've always thought, a perfect book.

Max's Breakfast now starts: " 'Eat your egg, Max,' said Max's sister, Ruby. 'BAD EGG,' said Max."

When the *original* dummy was flashed on the screen, it showed Ruby's same opening sentence, but that dummied version continued: " 'POISON,' said Max." Ruby then proceeded to drag Max throughout the house pointing out all the *real* poisons to avoid. My major contribution to that book was to point out that although an instructional story about household poisons was important, this was not the book to do it in. The metamorphosis of *Max's Breakfast* from its original form couldn't have happened without Rosemary's willingness to rethink and reshape her initial concept.

I've always felt that the major aspect of the editor-author relationship is the revision process itself. With hard work on both sides, a talented writer or artist can grow and turn a good story into an even better book. However, without the author's willingness to do revisions, some manuscripts just miss being published, and others are accepted for publication that could be much improved. An editor's suggestions must make sense to the author, and it's important for an editor to make it clear why the change is important.

At best, most professional writers listen carefully, take suggestions, and revise, while writers who are unsure of themselves are less likely to revise well. Rosemary Wells has told me of a "Phyllis who sits on my typewriter." At this point in our long association she often can anticipate how I'm likely to react to something before I've even seen it.

Even the word *revision* is anathema to a number of writers and would-be writers, but the night Mildred Taylor received the Newbery Medal for her second book and first novel, *Roll of Thunder, Hear My Cry,* she told me that

she'd come to Dial with her first book, *Song of the Trees,* turning down two
higher offers from other publishers, specifically *because* I'd asked her to
revise it. (*Song of the Trees* had won the Council on Interracial Books
Award in 1973, after which the council sent a number of publishers the
winning manuscript.) Mildred continues to be a meticulous reviser, as well
as an excellent writer.

Manuscripts come to children's book publishers in many different ways.
But when an author or author-artist whom we have published previously
brings in a new manuscript, the chances of its being right for our list are far
better than average. Often the new work will have been "talked out" long
before it was ever written down.

But finding new talent is important too. It is the lifeblood of a publishing
house, and there have been new writers and artists every season at Dial.
Many new people come to us through recommendations; others through
literary agents. For unpublished authors, however, getting an agent can be
as difficult as getting published, and every publisher receives thousands of
unsolicited manuscripts every year from aspiring authors all around the
country. In an average year we log in approximately six thousand such
manuscripts, and we read each one. Although this is an enormous job, it is
one I am committed to, and from time to time we do find books in this way.

One such book is John Bellairs's *The House with a Clock in Its Walls,*
which we published in 1973. A few years before, John had sent in an
unsolicited three-hundred-page manuscript. A young editorial assistant,
Karen Andersen—now an author-artist—wrote to him to say that if he
would cut it in half and make the main character the boy instead of the
middle-aged uncle, we'd like to see the manuscript again. The revision
appeared unheralded a year later and became the first of thirteen successful
novels we've published by John Bellairs, all of which are still in print in
hardcover as well as in paperback. Over the past few years, we've contracted
for several picture books and two novels that have arrived over the transom—not a high percentage, but I do feel that the chance of discovering a
gem makes reading the unsolicited manuscripts worthwhile.

Some of the greatest publishing successes have been repeatedly turned
down by other publishers. A first novel, *Summer of My German Soldier,* is
one such book. Soon after publication Bette Greene told me that her
manuscript had been rejected by eleven houses before her agent sent it to
me. It proved to be an enormous success when we published it in 1973.
Considering how many rewrites and changes had to be made before publication, it is perhaps understandable why other publishers had chosen not to
take on such a major job. But from the first time I read the manuscript, I
was hooked by both the story and the emotional content. *Summer of My
German Soldier* is still in print in Dial hardcover, it has sold well over a

million copies in paperback, and it was a two-hour prime-time television show. But there were many times before the manuscript was ready for publication when I wondered if I had made the right decision.

Then too, there are the times when I see something and say to myself: It's brilliant, but is it a children's book? If it's really special, I'll often take a gamble with someone who just might be able to expand the horizons of children's books. This is true of illustrators as well as writers. From the moment a manuscript first comes in, we at Dial ask ourselves: What kind of child would like this? Will it have meaning and importance for children? And if it's a picture book, what artwork will bring it to life?

The selection of an illustrator is perhaps the single most important and also difficult choice to be made in publishing a picture book, the success of which depends on a harmonious interplay of text and artwork. I do not look for a literal "picturing" of the story, which is likely to be dull and repetitive. Instead I want to find an artist who can emphasize or balance certain elements in a story—its humor, its warmth, its beauty, etc. But the right artwork can also extend a book's meaning and even add a totally new dimension.

In cases when an artist both writes and illustrates a book, the dummy is usually the form in which an editor will first see it. This makes sense of course when you consider that an artist must work out ideas visually. From the dummy the editor can see what the artist is trying to say—the story he or she is telling—and thereby help to work out both the text and the artwork. Often there won't even be a manuscript separate from the dummy until the concept is quite far along and it's time to have the printer set the type that will be in the finished book. Both aspects of a picture book, text and art, are thus thought about and worked on by the editor *together* rather than as separate entities.

Steven Kellogg and I have worked on twenty-seven books together, and fifteen of them are picture books he has both written and illustrated. Steven is a wonderful writer and illustrator, and many of his books have gone easily and quickly, with the final books following the general outlines of his original dummies. *The Christmas Witch,* his most recent book, is one of these. With others, the process has been more complicated. An example of this is *Best Friends.* Several years ago when we were both asked to speak at the Vassar Summer Publishing Institute, we decided to discuss *Best Friends,* a picture book that captures the sometimes exhilarating, sometimes troubling emotions of childhood in a warm and humorous manner. Steven sent me his original dummies so I could have slides made to illustrate our talk. His accompanying note said: "Dear Phyllis, How's this for nostalgia: old dummies from *Best Friends.* You saw the first one twelve years ago!" The six dummies—each with some notes of mine—showed a fascinating progression from an interesting, very promising idea to a wonderful, fully realized book.

When a manuscript we plan to publish comes in, Atha Tehon, Dial's art director, becomes involved in both the choice of illustrator for, and the concept of, a picture book. Every house operates differently, but at Dial we all work together as a team and can easily switch roles, each going between a consideration of the text to a close, hard look at the artwork and back again. A good picture book should be a collaboration between two talents if the author is not also the artist. In most cases, however, the author is not involved in the choice of who will illustrate the story and will never even speak with the artist as the book is being developed. The author's vision tends to be quite specific and personal, and it *can* limit the artist's freedom and work against the book. It really is a situation—and as far as I know the only one—in which the "separate but equal" principle applies and should be put to use.

As a publisher and editor-in-chief I need to know what the market is for a particular book in order to decide whether it is worth our while to publish. Sometimes I discuss new projects in their early stages with our sales and marketing people to get their input about the potential market for a book and other considerations, such as how many copies they think could be sold. More often than not these are "novelty" books, such as pop-ups. It's often hard to discuss authors' ideas with sales and marketing people—even those as talented and supportive as ours—when most of the book is still in the discussion stage between author and editor.

There is always an element of risk and adventure in working on children's books: No one can be sure at the beginning of a project whether it will ultimately be successful with children, or reviewers for that matter! But taking such risks is one of the reasons I have found it such a pleasure to be involved in this field. The discovery of a promising new writer, the challenge of helping an artist attain his or her particular vision, and the satisfaction involved in creative, collaborative work are some of the things that make editing and publishing children's books continuously worthwhile.

Editing Reference Books

Linda Halvorson Morse

LINDA HALVORSON MORSE *is executive editor at Oxford University Press in New York, responsible for the Press's Trade Reference Department, whose core projects include "Companions" (one-volume encyclopedias), richly illustrated narrative histories, and edited anthologies. Ms. Morse began her publishing career at Macmillan Publishing Company, with responsibility for a major academic encyclopedia, then spent several years at D. C. Heath & Company in Lexington, Massachusetts, acquiring textbooks in history and political science.*

Today more publishers are producing more reference works on more topics than ever before. "We live in a world," Ms. Morse writes, "in which people need and want easy access to systematized knowledge."

Ms. Morse defines academic reference books as often multivolume "works planned for academic or professional readerships [and that] find a substantial portion of their market through libraries and other institutions," and trade reference books as usually one-volume works "written to satisfy the avocational interests of a broad general readership . . . and [that] are available through retail bookstores, in addition to direct mail and other channels."

Single-author reference works are edited in much the same way general nonfiction is handled. "Multiauthor reference projects, however, bring with them unique issues of intellectual coherence, teamwork, and long-term project administration." Ms. Morse uses as her model for discussion "a multiauthor trade reference encyclopedia; though directed to a more spe-

*cialized audience, a multiauthor academic reference work would present the
same kinds of editorial challenges, writ large."*

*Ms. Morse's encyclopedic essay touches on every important aspect of
editing reference works: from planning subject areas in which to publish, to
selecting and working with editorial boards and contributors, to developing
the content of a volume, to overseeing long-range project administration.*

*Looking to the future, Ms. Morse sees increasingly sophisticated use of
computers affording reference book editors greater speed and flexibility in
handling detailed editorial development and administrative work and more
choices in how "the material we generate reaches its audiences, with brave
new technologies (CD-ROM, on-line services, and the like) coexisting
with—but, we know in our hearts, never replacing!—the wonderful, reassuring bulk of a reference book."*

Editing Reference Books

Reference publishing is *not,* by most definitions, high drama. It is made
possible by slow accretions of scholarly knowledge, and in its most serious
forms is itself a deliberate, thorough, and painstaking process. Since the first
encyclopedists and dictionary makers turned their attention to collecting
and structuring human knowledge, their efforts have been replicated count-
less times up to the present in works great and small. The essence of the
intellectual process remains the same yet, clearly, the environment in which
this process takes place is vastly different. Today there is a marked increase
in the number of publishers that produce reference works, in the array of
topics treated, and in the sheer number of such works published. Behind it
all are the realities of demand and supply. We live in a world in which
people need and want easy access to systematized knowledge, and publishers, like any other businesses, will provide the "products" that their markets
demand.

What Is a Reference Book?

Reference works exist in many formats. Although the impressive array of
types defies a single, narrow description, we know reference works when we
see them: general encyclopedias, specialized encyclopedias, "Companions,"
guides, handbooks, dictionaries, glossaries, bibliographies, indexes, al-
manacs, atlases, anthologies. Narrative histories or overviews might be

included as well, when they are sufficiently comprehensive and authoritative to be considered "encyclopedic" in their teaching about a field.

Reference books can, of course, be shaped for various audiences. Works planned for academic or professional readerships find a substantial portion of their market through libraries and other institutions, and are packaged and priced accordingly. At this writing, such works typically approach one hundred dollars per volume, and can run to thousands of pages, in several volumes. Whether frequently updated handbooks or once-per-generation summations of scholarly learning in a field, these works are of strong professional interest to their intended readerships. Trade reference works are written to satisfy the avocational interests of a broad general readership; in addition, they may serve as a "resource of first resort" for scholars or professionals in related fields. They are most often planned to extend to one volume, are priced to be accessible to individual book buyers (currently, books priced at fifty dollars approach the upper limits), and are available through retail bookstores, in addition to direct mail and other channels.

What do these books have in common? We might first approach the question by considering the use to which most readers will put them. Generally speaking, a reference work is not meant to be read sequentially from beginning to end; rather, it is meant to be consulted for specific information. The transparent and readily accessible structure of the work, perhaps alphabetical, thematic, or chronological, and the editorial apparatus built into it (for example, the extensive patterns of cross-references found in encyclopedias) make it possible for the reader to find a particular piece of information without having to sort through daunting amounts of extraneous material. Reference works systematize knowledge and allow for easy access to it on the part of the reader.

A second view of reference works is from the standpoint of their financial profile. In common publishing parlance, reference books are known to "backlist" well, meaning that they are not only major titles in the years when they are published, but go on to reach their markets for some time, perhaps even for generations in successive editions. They are viewed as long-term, steady, and relatively predictable income producers when compared to, say, a best-selling romance novel. The other side of the equation is that they are generally quite expensive to produce. They involve substantial editorial costs, including in-house development efforts that may require several years, and substantial marketing expenses that are ongoing for the life of the book. Reference books endure.

The Need for Reference Books

Publishers are (or ought to be) sensitive to audience demand. If new parents need a guide to the latest wisdom on childrearing, if attorneys need a systematic handbook of new tax law, if general readers want a reference source for ideas in fields as diverse as music and archaeology, chances are that observant publishers will eventually respond. They will do so either by initiating projects themselves or by looking carefully at projects that are proposed to them from outside by prospective authors. Large audiences exist for specialized reference sources in business, law, medicine, engineering, and other areas of professional practice; scholarly audiences seek systematized knowledge across the full spectrum of academic disciplines from the sciences to the humanities to the arts. And there are avid general readerships for authoritative information in subjects ranging from gardening to politics to literature.

What makes a field particularly fertile ground for reference publishing? An *emerging* area of scholarship, where the challenge of structuring or systematizing knowledge still remains, yields wonderful opportunities for such projects. Women's writing, a focus of concentrated scholarly effort only in the relatively recent past, is one area in which exciting original research is now being synthesized in reference works of various types. *Advancing* areas, altered sometimes radically by significant new directions in scholarship, also provide rich possibilities for reference works. Military history, now expanded much beyond the traditional "drums and trumpets" to include important societal dimensions, is a good example. And some areas—advances in scholarship or not—are just perennial favorites for general audiences who never tire of information in whatever form it is served up: the American West, the Civil War, and Sherlock Holmes, to name a few.

Editing a Multiauthor Reference Work

Packaging, pricing, and marketing variations aside, there exists very little difference in the kind of editorial challenge posed by academic and trade reference works. A more significant gulf, in my experience, lies between single-author and multiauthor volumes. Single-author reference works—though charged with the special burdens of comprehensiveness, balance, authority, and lasting appeal attendant to any reference work—mirror the editorial process described in other chapters of this volume, and thus need not be a special concern here. Multiauthor reference projects, however, bring with them unique issues of intellectual coherence, teamwork, and long-term project administration; for this reason, they are an appropriate focus for this chapter.

I will use as my model here a multiauthor trade reference encyclopedia; though directed to a more specialized audience, a multiauthor academic reference work would present the same kinds of editorial challenges, writ large.

The commitment to publish a major reference work is substantial by any measure—not just in dollars spent, but in time spent, as well. The editorial process from idea to finished manuscript may take the better part of two or three years, or even considerably longer. In view of this commitment, the editorial process will likely be an exacting one, with a great deal of advance discussion of substantive issues and administrative procedures, and as little as possible left to chance throughout the course of the project. In the following pages I will touch on the principal phases encountered in editing reference works (of course, there are as many variations in this process as there are reference book publishers), together with aspects of the author-editor relationship that emerge along the way. In this kind of long-term association, shared work styles and intellectual ambitions contribute not only to the success, but also to the enjoyment, of the process.

Acquisitions

An obvious priority to the publisher at this stage is exploring the soundness of an idea, whether generated in-house or by outside sources. The acquiring editor conducts informal research, following a network of advice from scholars in the field, librarians, bookstore managers, and sales and marketing colleagues to answer a set of crucial questions.

Some questions concern the market for the work. How have other major works in the field fared in initial and long-term sales, and do competitive works exist that have an unyielding grip on the market? A busy market signals opportunity; a choked one, just the opposite. What audiences (or a blend of them) would be interested enough in the work to buy a copy? An ideal trade reference work, from the publisher's standpoint, attracts a wide range of readerships. Consider, for example, the appeal of a comprehensive and authoritative trade reference volume on world politics to scholars in comparative politics, international relations, history, economics, and related fields; to professionals in journalism, international business, and international diplomacy; and to lay readers ambitious in their learning about the world in which they live. The encyclopedia format allows for discussions ranging from straightforward description, to synthesis (bringing together, and providing context for understanding, a range of views on a particular topic), to interpretation (providing original thinking on a subject), allowing each readership to benefit from the work in distinct ways.

Other questions concern the substance of the volume. Is the field a new one, or is it advancing in such a way that there is a real general-interest, scholarly, or professional need for a reference work? A subject area in its extreme infancy may not yet be well enough articulated to lend itself to this kind of treatment; a field in which there is active, mature scholarship and enlivening debate is ideal. Other important questions: What "take" on the subject would allow the proposed book to make a unique contribution to the available literature and, therefore, stand a good chance of becoming a standard reference source? What should the substantive scope of the project be?

Finally, the publisher is likely to consider the selection of an outside general editor the single most crucial step in the process of commissioning a new reference work. I use the designation *general editor* instead of *author* purposely; while this person may contribute much of her own writing to such a volume, she must also function in a higher capacity, orchestrating the writing efforts of perhaps several hundred contributors. The general editor's credentials—academic, professional, or experiential—are vitally important. They signal mastery of the material, and also the likelihood of acceptance by audiences and critics rightly concerned with the authority of the volume.

The publisher will look for a general editor who has contributed substantially and visibly to the field in question, and who has wide-ranging knowledge of the field's outer boundaries, controversial areas, noteworthy new directions, and outstanding scholarly or professional voices. The publisher will favor a general editor who is widely networked in a field, and who can encourage participation in the project (as fellow editors, as advisers, or as contributors) by a wide array of distinguished colleagues. An important consideration as well is the prospective general editor's instinctive sense of the volume's potential audiences, and the myriad kinds of editorial "fine-tuning" that can be done to shape the volume to their particular needs and interests. A general editor who possesses a strong sense of audience will also be equipped to lend creative ideas to the eventual, all-important marketing effort.

During this period, the general editor and acquiring editor work closely together to establish preliminary plans for the volume—often in the form of a project proposal. I encourage prospective general editors to wrestle with all dimensions of the project, even if easy answers do not present themselves; at least in this way we know what issues need fuller resolution as the project moves forward. The proposal outline that I ask prospective general editors to work from focuses on such issues as the state of scholarly research and public interest in the field (i.e., what is interesting about this field, and *why* is there a market for the proposed work?), the work's intended audiences, and the work's likely substantive range and organizational principles, as well as administrative issues including scheduling and the division of labor between general editor and publisher. Outside reviewers are asked to comment on the proposal, which may then go through several rounds of revision before final in-house approval.

"Personnel" issues need to be resolved during this time. Typically the general editor will select, and work closely with, an editorial board of some four to five fellow scholars or practitioners who bring complementary expertise to the project, and who assume responsibility for a portion of the editorial work. Expansive reference works are rarely within the ken of a single individual; the collective vision of an editorial board helps to ensure that coverage in the volume is both comprehensive and balanced. In this kind of arrangement, the general editor serves as the main liaison with the publisher, and is charged with final decision-making authority on behalf of the editorial board.

Finally, an additional layer of specialist knowledge is often brought to bear on the project through the creation of an advisory board. While the editorial board actively *creates,* the advisory board serves in a more reactive capacity, for example by reviewing successive generations of the table of contents and offering suggestions for possible contributors in their areas of expertise.

Development

With the signing of a publishing agreement, the long-term partnership between publisher and general editor (or editorial board) officially begins. At this point the publisher may assign an in-house development editor to the project to guide the editorial board in the many decisions, great and small, that it must make about the organization and content of the book. The major accomplishment during development will be the completion of a detailed table of contents, a creative process that may require a year or much more of intensive editorial work. ("List of entry terms" is a more accurate expression to use than "table of contents" in the context of an alphabetical reference work. In such a work the reader looks up a topic of interest alphabetically in the body of the text, under a label known as the "entry term." The entry term literally gives the reader "entry" into the content of the volume; thus, no table of contents is needed.) Although a considerable amount of thought will have been given to matters of scope and content during acquisitions, the detailed mapping of the internal struc-

ture of a major project can only begin in earnest once all editorial participants, as described above, have signed on.

Primary goals in any serious reference work are comprehensiveness and
balance: making sure that all dimensions of the field or topic are covered
thoroughly, with an apportionment of space to various subtopics that
accurately reflects their relative importance. In a typical arrangement, each
editorial board member develops a list of entries within his area of editorial
responsibility; the individual lists are then amalgamated into one master
list; and the overall coherence of the list is then assessed by the editorial
board through successive revisions. The advisory board is also periodically
called on to point out afresh any gaps of coverage, imbalances, or other
deficiencies. During this time, the editorial board will also research and
nominate prospective contributors, who will themselves be recognized
specialists.

A central challenge in any multiauthor reference work obviously comes
from the fact that, instead of one mind at work on the project, there are
many. The kind of coherence that grows organically out of the work of a
single author—one perspective, one narrative, one voice—here must be
imposed from outside, beginning with the development process. In order to
approach their individual tasks with any uniformity of purpose, future
contributors will need to be informed about the project's overall organization and content, and about the unique substantive roles their own articles
will play in the larger scheme of the volume—that is, what will be covered
in their particular pieces that the reader will find nowhere else. It is of
special importance that contributors also understand the work's intended
readerships, so that they can tailor their presentations accordingly.

During development, the editorial board and in-house editors create
materials that will be sent to contributors to clarify these issues. In addition
to a general project description, a device that colleagues and I have come
to employ is the "scope description"—a paragraph prepared for each
article describing its intended coverage and focus, indicating specific examples or topics that need to be introduced in the article in order to ensure
proper overall coverage in the volume, and listing articles on related topics
that are also planned for inclusion in the volume. This paragraph is
amended as necessary in discussion with the contributor so that publisher
and contributor have a firm agreement about the objectives of the piece
right from the start. This step, replicated with each contributor, provides
insurance against gaps of coverage or undue repetition across the network
of articles. Contributors also need technical instruction on issues of editorial and bibliographical style, and guidelines for preparing copy in manuscript or electronic format. Explicit guidance to contributors in these areas
eliminates needless complication in later editorial stages.

Having witnessed and participated in the development of many reference works, I can state two things with relative certainty. One is that development of a list of entries is always more complicated than one ever anticipates. Layers of conceptual complexity will gradually emerge in any substantial project, and all involved may come to wonder why they ever agreed to take part in such a hopeless and interminable endeavor. Persistence pays off, though, and with much the same feeling as donning a pair of glasses and having the world come into focus, the structure and content of a complex encyclopedic work will eventually fall into place. Another truism is that it is worth every penny of cost to bring an editorial board together, in one room, to sort through initial questions of substance and organization. The group spirit that emerges in these sessions—in addition to an intense and productive focus on important editorial issues—provides glue that holds a team together through the inevitable trying times.

Administrative

Once the list of entries is in final form and prospective contributors have been identified, administrative work on the project begins. Here, the division of labor set out in early planning of the project begins to come into play. One common arrangement is for the publisher to assume responsibility for the administrative aspects of the project—inviting contributors, preparing and sending out contributor contracts, receiving manuscripts from contributors and routing them to the editorial board for review, and recordkeeping—thereby allowing the editorial board to restrict its focus largely to important issues of content. This arrangement is possible only if the publisher has on staff and assigns to the project an in-house project editor to follow through with the stunningly large number of administrative details that must be tended to assiduously every day. There is, of course, added expense to the publisher in assigning a project editor (who may handle several projects at a given time) to the work; the clear benefit is insurance that the project will keep moving at a brisk pace toward publication. Whatever the specifics of the administrative arrangement, all involved must be committed to keeping each piece of writing moving as quickly as possible through the editorial process.

Recordkeeping is a central challenge in any project involving hundreds of contributors and at least as many individual pieces of writing. The publisher may be ideally situated, with the benefit of its substantial computer capabilities, to create and then to maintain a project database—a constantly updated electronic record of article titles and descriptions, article lengths, due dates, payment terms, and editorial status. Using such a database, an in-house project editor can with relative ease produce stacks of individual-

ized, routine correspondence or generate a list of overdue articles for follow-up. (When I was first involved more than a decade ago in a major
multiauthor reference project, computers had not yet taken over. We used
a large wall chart to keep track of each piece of writing as it moved through
the sequence of editorial steps.) Of course, if the general editor is equipped
with proper computer capabilities or other suitable means for tracking this
kind of complex effort, there is no particular need for the publisher to
handle this work. The decision is really a practical one: who is best set up
to exert rigorous, day-to-day control over the inevitable details of recordkeeping, scheduling, and trafficking of materials? Interestingly, the computer has also become an important ally in the development process
described earlier; databases that orchestrate mass mailings can also sort
through lengthy lists of entry terms to identify problems of coverage and
balance.

Editing

Since the administrative work described above is ongoing for the life of the
project, editing in fact runs concurrently with it. Even as editing of individual articles proceeds, records need to be kept, reminder letters sent to tardy
contributors, and manuscripts routed to the editorial board for review.
During the period of editing, articles commissioned for the volume move
through a rigorous process of substantive and stylistic review, revision, and
final copy editing, a process typically orchestrated by the in-house project
editor. Article due dates are staggered by projected length—anywhere from
three to four months from the date of the invitation for the shortest article
(fewer than one thousand words), to the better part of a year for the longest
(perhaps six to seven thousand words).

In most projects an effective arrangement is one in which each article is
reviewed by at least two editorial board members—the editor (often called
the "section editor") in whose specific area of editorial responsibility the
article falls, as well as the general editor (who, having overall responsibility,
reads every piece in the volume). Typically, the section editor communicates
with the contributor about needed revisions and approves the article in its
final form. If the prescriptive efforts of the earlier development process have
been successful, most articles will need little more than modest fine-tuning
at this point.

Because readers will be disappointed (rightly) to find coverage that is
incomplete or that reflects a narrow interpretive stance or point of view, the
section editor must review each piece for balance, accuracy, and fullness of
coverage and provide the contributor with specific directions for remedying
any deficiencies. At the same time, the general editor must critique the

article from the perspective of its fit within the volume's network of articles on related topics. Another important focus throughout the process of review and revision is attention to the components of good writing—among them a clear line of argument, engaging examples to back up points being made, and high interest level—which apply every bit as much to reference works as to other kinds of writing projects. The contributor may be asked to work through stylistic problems with the help of detailed suggestions supplied by the section editor, or the section editor may attempt a line edit in the course of reviewing the article. Minor infelicities that persist can be dealt with in final copy editing. Of course, whenever changes are made in a manuscript it is important that the contributor be given an opportunity to review and approve them.

In the final stage of editing, individual contributions, each in final form, are brought together in a cohesive alphabetical manuscript. The editorial apparatus (cross-referencing systems and the like) that guides readers to specific information that they seek is devised at this point and inserted into the manuscript; the index, a very important access point in most reference works, is completed at proof stage. Since these final efforts require knowledge of the entire contents of the volume, and of the patterns of interrelated articles, they are most efficiently handled by the general editor working in concert with in-house editors. One need only experience the frustration of being unable to locate a needed piece of information in a reference work to appreciate the importance of this particular stage of editorial work. The manuscript is now ready for production and manufacturing, and, with any luck, will appear within several months as a finished book.

A Look toward the Future

A slight variation on an old adage sums up rather well the nature of reference publishing: the more things stay the same, the more they change. I imagine that in coming years much that is familiar to me about the world of reference publishing will not change all that much. My colleagues and I will continue to look for promising areas in which to publish, taking fresh looks at "old" topics and invigorating looks at new topics, trying to keep pace with reader interests. We will labor intensively over complicated projects that bring with them both substantial costs and substantial rewards. And we will go along our way feeling that, just maybe, we are involved in something that really matters, that makes the world a better place in which to live. *What* we do, then, is likely to remain pretty much the same, although we may have to do it faster, and better, to keep pace in an increasingly competitive marketplace. Change will come more in the realm of *how* we do

The Editor of Lives

Peter Davison

PETER DAVISON *entered publishing in 1950 with the firm of Harcourt, Brace and Company. Since then he has edited books for, successively, Harvard University Press, the Atlantic Monthly Press (of which he was director from 1964 to 1979), and Houghton Mifflin Company, where he now publishes under the Peter Davison imprint. He is also poetry editor for the* Atlantic Monthly. *He is the author of nine books of poetry (most recently* The Great Ledge, *Knopf, 1989), an autobiography (*Half Remembered, *1973 [revised edition, Story Line Press, 1991]), and a book on poetry (*One of the Dangerous Trades: Essays on the Work and Workings of Poetry, *Michigan, 1991).*

"The life of biography is in the details," writes Mr. Davison in this elegant essay that biographers, autobiographers, and editors of both will enjoy for its sage advice and wry wit.

An editor of biographies for over forty years, among them Diane Middlebrook's Anne Sexton: A Biography *(he offers a fascinating editorial evaluation of the controversy surrounding the publication of excerpts of tapes of Ms. Sexton's sessions with her psychiatrist), Mr. Davison is generous in sharing his expertise with editor and writer. He writes intimately and knowingly about editorial details, problems, and considerations relevant to editing biography and autobiography: finding and gaining legal access to vital papers; dealing with the laws of copyright and public domain in terms of personal letters; obtaining vital permissions to quote text and use photographs, and securing releases from persons depicted and quoted; handling the egos of those who want to tell too little or too much; coping with the spouse of a biographical subject still living or only lately dead; staving off*

327

the threats and punishments of libel; choosing a biographer who will not come to either admire or hate the subject too much; suggesting to the writer a compelling opening and a satisfying conclusion to the biography or autobiography; recommending to the biographer a reevaluation of the subject of the biography; and more.

Recalling the witticism of French critic Roland Barthes that biography is fiction that dare not tell its name, Mr. Davison dares to tell some trenchant truths about the art of editing people's lives, among them:

"Should the autobiographer plan to begin his tale at the beginning? Usually not: the exit from the womb takes pretty much the same course for all of us and is of principal interest to obstetricians."

"The editor's approach to the autobiographer has to be one of parental tenderness, even though parental strictness may also be called for to keep the memoir believable."

"The biographer's genius lies in having the sympathy and imagination to create the story of a life of which the subject would say, if he or she could, 'That's as close to me as anybody else could be expected to know.' The biographer's worst temptation is to transform the subject into someone preferable to the original."

"Editorial lesson: It is important for the sake of truth and history to have written the best biography of your subject; but it can be more lucrative to be first on the scene."

The Editor of Lives

For forty years I have been editing biographies and autobiographies, large and small, light and heavy, but usually reputable, ranging in biographical subject matter from Enrico Caruso (my first) and Katharine Cornell to Anne Sexton, from Justice Holmes and Ezra Pound to Adam Clayton Powell, Jr. (my current project); and in autobiographical subject matter from Alfred Kazin to Farley Mowat, from the elegant memoirs of Louis Kronenberger's *No Whippings, No Gold Watches* to the adoring rhapsody, *Discretions,* of Ezra Pound's daughter, Mary de Rachewiltz. I have even written an autobiography myself, entitled *Half Remembered,* and then, nearly twenty years after its first publication, revised and enlarged the book for paperback, even though I still could not remember the other half.

I have no experience in editing "celebrity" biographies like the fourteen extant "lives" of Marilyn Monroe nor in editing that particular breed of book that boasts of its "unauthorized" status in order to produce the maximum in sensationalism and thus provide free advertising—a sort of relay race with the libel lawyers. Such books, these days, are baldly announced as unauthorized in order to suggest to the public that they contain everything the celebrity would have given his or her eyeteeth for you not to find out. You will search in vain through this essay for suggestions on how to write such a book: in fact, I'd suggest you don't even try. It's a dangerous game, requiring *chutzpah* in the highest and ill will toward its subject.

. . .

The French critic Roland Barthes once wrote that biography is fiction that dare not tell its name. The same applies even more keenly to autobiography, since memoirs (like first novels) are written, invariably, by the living and usually for the living to read, and they have a tendency to paint a self-portrait in the most flattering colors, unless they fall into the rare self-revelatory category shared by the *Confessions* of Saint Augustine or of Jean-Jacques Rousseau. Most autobiographies treat the self as an example, or as a victim, or as a source of wisdom, or, sometimes, as the butt of humor. The living autobiographer, after all, still has to look the living reader in the eye. An editor, first and foremost, must determine which of these attitudes his author intends to take toward the subject of his personal story. He is responsible for understanding the writer and the story well enough to help the author choose. This is not easy when the editor doesn't yet know the story and has to drag the mere truth out of some notable who is swollen with self-importance. It's even harder when the editor does not know the author—though the author's reputation will probably have preceded him, or the subject would not likely have exerted sufficient public appeal for the publisher to have commissioned the book in the first place. (We need not dwell on the unusual instance, these days, of a notable person who actually writes his memoirs and then seeks a publisher: in the Era of the Literary Agent it happens the other way around.)

I have worked with autobiographers who want to tell too much about themselves; but with more (one of them this week) who do not want to tell enough, who cannot imagine describing themselves in a bad light, or in what the author's adoring—or divorced—spouse (the spouse is the hole card in every autobiography) regards as a bad light. The editor's approach to the autobiographer has to be one of parental tenderness, even though parental strictness may also be called for to keep the memoir believable. Nobody wants to drop his pants in public except for the randiest exhibitionist, some of whom do in fact write great autobiographies, like Henry Miller, whose books are for some reason called novels. Worse: dropping somebody else's pants in public, which is the bane of the editor's—and the author's—lawyers.

Should the autobiographer plan to begin his tale at the beginning? Usu-

ally not: the exit from the womb takes pretty much the same course for all
of us and is of principal interest to obstetricians. If the autobiographer can
settle on a later, essentially formative scene or an episode, in childhood or
adulthood, that somehow opens the door to the style and tilt for the whole
book, the story stands a better chance of telling itself from start to finish in
such a way as to cast the most revealing angle of light over its events. Agnes
De Mille, who has written half a dozen volumes of memoirs and, in her
eighties, a biography of Martha Graham, never began at the very beginning
in any of her books: even in her very first, *Dance to the Piper,* she began with
her discovery, at ten, of Hollywood, where she moved when her father gave
up directing plays and went into the direction of movies, before it was
revealed to her that she was a dancer, a gift that she exploited relatively late
in life but that colored everything that came before and after. Justin Kaplan
began his masterly biography of Mark Twain when his subject was thirty-
one because "the central drama of his mature literary life was his discovery
of the usable past."

Bertrand Russell, Victorian to the core, did begin at the beginning ("My
first vivid recollection is my arrival at Pembroke Lodge in February 1876"),
identifying his lordly grandparents (his grandfather was a prime minister)
before arriving at his unfortunate and sickly parents, who died in sequence,
leaving the grandparents to bring up Bertie and his older brother Frank,
wards in chancery, in high palatial splendor. Being set apart from other
children would make Russell for over ninety years yearn to sympathize with
others—with all mankind! Few, his childhood told him, had sympathized
with the lonely orphan in the lordly estate, but the boy early and often
found ways of consoling himself with philosophy, protecting his tender
feelings with his brilliant mind, and having opinions on *everything.*

Autobiography depends not only on the nature of the subject, but on the
audience imagined for it, to which the editor must be sensitive indeed. Those
who read the magnificent memoirs of George F. Kennan knew him beforehand as a behind-the-scenes adviser on foreign relations whose influential
articulation of the "containment" policy was written anonymously; but
Kennan also had a personal story to tell. Accordingly, he began, very
tentatively, with his happy childhood in the Middle West, in a dream
country that, as a lifelong diplomat, he would never return to: "There are,
of course, great variations in people's capacity to remember consciously
their early growth. My own falls, I fear, at the weaker end of the spectrum."
On his return to his native land after years of foreign service, the rural
simplicities of Wisconsin had long since disappeared. Kennan's memoirs
beneath their surface croon a lament for an imagined innocent America
while advocating an informed realism in foreign affairs. It's not strange that
his sympathy with contemporary America is limited and often so expressed.

I think that autobiography requires, more than anything else, a most particular attention to tone: what tone does the author take toward himself? Kennan is nostalgic, Russell is witty; Mary de Rachewiltz, the daughter of Ezra Pound and Olga Rudge, begins by exulting in the simplicities of the peasant upbringing that her foster parents gave her in the Tyrolean uplands for years before she even knew who her true parents were—a theme that would never leave her alone. Throughout her adored father's stormy career she would keep hoping that she could create once more that Alpine simplicity, and somehow include him in it—the last thing he wanted for himself, which was the last thing she discovered about him. In my work with her I encouraged her to play up her adoration and play down his anti-Semitism: not everyone who knew Ezra Pound found him so adorable.

Autobiographies have a lot of trouble ending themselves, because the hero or heroine by definition is still alive as the final words are written. The choices are all unsatisfactory: leave 'em laughing is probably the best—and most infrequent—choice. Marry (usually for the second or third time) and live happily ever after is a very frequent and unconvincing terminus. To conclude with the death of a loved one—wife, parent, or child—can be deeply touching, but it cannot help raising the question of the author's motive in telling us all this. The editor may well be able to suggest something remarkable. Frank Conroy's *Stop-Time* ends with one of the great unforgettable flourishes in contemporary autobiography, as his car skids, at ninety, across an English road: "But the front wheel caught a low curb and the car spun around the fountain like a baton around a cheerleader's wrist. . . . Then, with a slight lurch, everything stopped. . . ."

. . .

Turning to biography, I would like to distinguish between two entirely different problems: the life of the safely dead, and the life of the recently dead. The first depends for its existence on the discovery of papers and sources; the second usually depends on the good will of living people: widows or widowers or literary executors, or—God save the mark—attorneys. The two varieties require different approaches, and different kinds of help from their editor. But in either category the first thing an editor should do is to make absolutely certain that the writer has the deepest possible admiration for and identification with the subject under discussion. Why? Because the chances are that the biographer will have to live with this subject for at least five and sometimes longer than ten years—longer than most American marriages—and will discover things he or she never imagined possible. The biographer of Thomas Hardy discovers that Hardy was sexually excited by the sight and sound of the hangings of criminals and mourned his dead wife (very publicly and beautifully) in a long sequence of poems that did his second marriage no good, even though the first couple did not in fact get on well at all. Orwell's biographer learns that, despite his deep sympathies for the lower classes of mankind, Orwell was in person a surly and unpleasant friend. The biographer of Josephine Herbst revealed to the biographer of Katherine Anne Porter that Porter turned in Josie, her closest friend, to the FBI. Of the biographical subjects I have encountered, only Anton Chekhov seems to have been without serious fault or flaw, the easiest of all subjects for a biographer to live with, though one of the most elusive to understand.

If the biographer chooses a subject for exposure, knowing the subject's shortcomings, there is a chance that it may take twice as long as expected to write the book, for it is difficult for an author to force himself to write with sympathy about someone whose actions he or she detests. No woman except his widow has yet, to my knowledge, written objectively about randy, lewd, drunken, self-destructive Dylan Thomas, though in his life protective women flocked to his bed. But Thomas died young, at thirty-nine: a man who lives to ninety will unavoidably have left a long, long paper trail a-winding, a trail it may take years and years to follow. Will author, will editor, survive till the end comes? Scott Donaldson, the experienced and professional biographer of Hemingway, Cheever, Winfield Townley Scott, and others, found his scrupulously calculated deadlines went glimmering when he tackled the very long and highly eventful life of Archibald Mac-Leish; and, despite his original intentions, the book outgrew his expectations for it. The editor's task is to know, and to persuade the author, that enough is enough. Sometimes the text may be shortened; sometimes it will do to shorten the apparatus, the bibliography or notes. From a commercial point of view, buyers will pay a certain price to read the life of an admired person, but every story has a ceiling.

The second cautionary question for the safely dead is: Where are the papers? Who controls them? May they be quoted from? This can supersede any question of the passage of time: the Boswell papers, after all, did not turn up for 150 years after his death, on the precincts of Malahide Castle, where no one would have expected them to surface—and then ownership had to be established.

The third thing the editor can do to help the author of such a biography is to encourage the reevaluation of the figure of the protagonist in contemporary terms. Carolyn Heilbrun, in her cogent and discerning little book, *Writing a Woman's Life,* raises a number of challenging questions about the way biographers, male or female, write the lives of women; and since so many biographers these days are discovering the unwritten lives of women, her values are worth testing for any biography that contains women, in whatever role.

. . .

The second variety of biography is perhaps the most difficult: the life of the recently dead, whose papers and whose memories reside in the cupboards and the diaries and heads of the still living, most of whom have a particular interest in seeing that the life of the beloved (or nonbeloved) is written "accurately." No biographer needs more tact than one whose subject died young, mourned by some and unmourned by others, and whose papers reside, copyrighted, in the charge of a suspicious executor. The most striking recent example of this is poor Sylvia Plath, who committed suicide at thirty, leaving her literary effects to the care of the husband whom she had not yet divorced. As a result, every would-be biographer since her death in 1963 (I can count up to at least nine, only five of whom actually completed their books) has had either to clear permission for every line of poetry quoted from the Plath estate, in which case the estate required the biographer to submit the text of the book for inspection; or to omit quotations from the very poetry that had made Plath famous in order to avoid the necessity for the estate's approval of the text. (The approval of the text included the estate's defending itself against invasions of privacy or defamation, of which more below.) Biographers of T. S. Eliot have had similar problems, though in that instance the cost of the permissions was fiscal rather than censorial.

I happened to know Sylvia Plath and her husband and had been interviewed by nearly everyone who wanted to write about her life, but it was not until twenty-four years after her death that I was approached by Olwyn Hughes, agent for the estate, to edit a biography of Plath by Anne Stevenson, a poet and critic whose work I much admired, then and now. The biographer created version after version in order to fulfill the estate's requirements for correctness (and self-defense), and finally reached an impasse. At this stage all parties decided to surrender the manuscript to me to create a text, coherent with the author's views and style, that would pass the strict construction of the estate. This meant rewriting the book, page by page, reconciling Stevenson's version of Plath's life and poetry with that of the people who had been left by chance in charge of her poetry, and who were not only fiduciaries of the estate but characters in the book. My version, while hewing to biographical integrity, had to satisfy both the creative dignity of the biographer and the self-interest—and, to be fair, the deep involvement—of Plath's husband and sister-in-law. It was the most harrowing editorial task I have ever undertaken, because the estate had the legal right to do what it wished, and the author had the moral right to speak her mind. The editorial process lasted two years after the book's first draft was concluded. Essential to the endless negotiations were the careful ministrations of a gifted attorney at Houghton Mifflin Company. Despite all these hurdles, *Bitter Fame: A Life of Sylvia Plath* is still, to those of us who knew her, the most penetrating and eloquent life of the woman who was, at her reckless heart, a superb poet while attempting in her life to be everything else as well—novelist, mother, journalist, housewife, cook, intellectual, amoureuse, beekeeper, everything but the feminist that her misguided admirers imagined her to be.

As an example of the opposite solution to a similar problem, take *Anne Sexton: A Biography* by Diane Middlebrook. This biography, of another suicidal poet, took ten years from its commission to its publication and ran through four editors before it saw print. Jonathan Galassi, with Anne Sexton's elder daughter, who was also her literary executor, found Stanford University's Professor Middlebrook and offered her a Houghton Mifflin contract to write the book; and, with the assistance of foundation grants and private funds, Middlebrook was able to weave her fabric of interviews, research, and documentation for over five years. Only then did Sexton's primary psychiatrist, Dr. Martin Orne, come forward and agree to cooperate with the biographer, even offering her the audiotapes of some three hundred hours of psychiatric interviews. Middlebrook, who had by this time already drafted much of her text, first asked the literary executor whether she might hear and use the material in this most private of documents. With the estate's concurrence, she set aside her keyboard and spent most of a year listening to and annotating the interviews, and then rewrote her book with the sound of the analysand's voice in her ears, discovering as she advanced how closely Anne Sexton's poetry was related to the psychiatric interaction. By this time I had become the fourth and final editor of the book. The first editor helped find the right author for the book; the second contributed patience and moral support; the third guided the author through the complex of libel, invasion of privacy, and defamation that threatened to hedge in the tale of a woman who had loved many men, who had persisted in a most unorthodox marriage, who had given much love to many friends, and who had sacrificed a lacerated life for a career that preserved her tottering sanity.

My job, as the editor who finally saw the book into print, was—with the advice of the same attorney who had so admirably helped *Bitter Fame* into print, and with the scrupulous cooperation and support of Anne Sexton's daughter and her lawyer husband—to advise Diane Middlebrook on the creation of the final text. Every word was Diane Middlebrook's own, but it had to avoid giving offense to family and friends while telling the searing truth about Sexton's life. The direct quotations from her letters and poetry—and from letters to her from friends and lovers—had to be cleared with husband, children, every friend, every lover, every colleague. The scrupulousness and professionalism with which Middlebrook carried out her biographical duties were staggering. My principal contribution, aside from line-by-line examination of her splendid text, and advice as to how to keep the length of the book within tolerable limits, was, from my personal knowledge of Sexton's surroundings, to steer Middlebrook to certain acquaintances of Sexton's who might have more to tell or who might grant permission if approached this way rather than that.

After three years on the editorial job, I was proud to see Middlebrook's work at an end—only to find, to my astonishment, that the very first advance review, in *Publishers Weekly,* had solicited the opinion of an expert on the ethics of psychiatry, who, without reading a word of the book, condemned the morality of the biographer's use of the psychiatric tapes. The next thing we knew, to our complete surprise, was that we had a controversy on our hands, with articles in the London papers, on the front page of the daily *New York Times,* and throughout the press—all this three months before our biography actually saw publication. We had expected controversy over Anne Sexton's life, and even over her psychiatric history (a second psychiatrist had in fact conducted a two-year affair with his patient, writing her love poems as he collected his professional fees; but the psychiatric profession preferred to avoid mention of this peccadillo). The result, thanks to wonderful reviews and a brilliant publicity campaign orchestrated by the publisher and doughtily carried out by the author, was a best-seller as well as a literary triumph.

In short, the biography of the lately dead, especially literary figures, presents challenges that do not apply to subjects who have been off the scene long enough for their printed works to be out of copyright, though the law still requires the approval of the estate of a dead person to quote unpublished letters and other documents written by the protagonist, unless those are the public papers of a public person. Even now the courts, in the wake of the famous *Salinger* case, in which J. D. Salinger prevented Ian Hamilton from quoting his letters, or even paraphrasing them, are still wrangling over this subject. The editor of biographies has work to do in keeping up with the case law on the subject—or in keeping up with an attorney who knows.

It is for this reason that the editor of biographies needs to pay especial attention to the dreary particulars of permissions to quote, to releases from persons depicted and quoted, to finding and arranging permission to reproduce the best photographs. In such wastelands as these the vulture of libel is always hovering overhead. Yes, the publisher's contract sets such duties in the hands of the author, but today, when the publisher is asked to insure the author against damages, the publisher has to bear much of the load. An experienced editor, who has been involved with more biographies than most biographers, will not do his or her duty unless she lends a hand to make sure that the particulars are taken care of. The life of biography is in the details.

If there were a perfect biographer, he or she would have the following abilities: to be a real writer, one who understands how to construct and recount a flexible and sensuous narrative; to be a master of research, both of documents and interviews; to be tactful in dealings with relatives, librarians, lovers, executors, children, parents, and editors; to be so cannily devoted to the personality of the subject of the biography as to pursue every true lead and abandon every false one; to care so deeply about the precision of the text as to check every fact again and again, every document, every photograph, every rumor. But, beyond the conscientious practice of these mere skills, the biographer's genius lies in having the sympathy and imagination to create the story of a life of which the subject would say, if he or she could, "That's as close to me as anybody else could be expected to know." The biographer's worst temptation is to transform the subject into someone preferable to the original.

Anne Stevenson, as she wrote her life of Sylvia Plath, deepened in understanding of her subject and came to sympathize with Plath more deeply at the end than at the outset, perhaps more deeply than Plath's own family. Diane Middlebrook learned more about her subject than she had ever dreamed possible, and came to admire the way in which Sexton shored her poetry against the ruins of her life. Ronald Steel, in writing his biography of Walter Lippmann ("Walter Lippmann," he began, "was brought up to be a gentleman"), began to find himself losing accord with Lippmann's temperament, with Lippmann's attitude toward his own and other people's Judaism, and with other aspects of Lippmann's life. Steel's editor was the late, great Edward Weeks, who had himself been a close friend of Lippmann's and had edited many of Lippmann's books. Steel cast about, seeking perhaps to find a newer, younger editor under the publisher's roof who would show more sympathy to him and less to Lippmann, and as he did so the years passed until the book had exceeded its delivery date by a dozen years. Weeks exercised the most potent weapon an editor can wield: patience. Little, Brown, especially the sales department, grew restive: Lippmann was by this time long dead (though he had been alive and even vigorous when the task was begun), and the sales department could not imagine who would any longer be interested in reading his life. The editorial moral here is not always to listen too carefully to the lamentations of sales departments, for as it turned out every first-class reviewer in America chose to give close and admiring attention to *Walter Lippmann and the American Century* when it was published in 1980; it sold fifty thousand copies, won the Bancroft Prize, the National Book Critics Circle Award, and the Los Angeles Times Book Prize.

. . .

The agony of identification between biographer and subject had been worth the years of struggle, as it had been for Diane Middlebrook. The story of Anne Stevenson and Sylvia Plath does not have quite so happy an ending. Her life of Plath did not make its entrance until after two prior books, one deeply inaccurate and the other simply obtuse, and after Plath had, for very peculiar reasons, been elevated posthumously into an illusory icon of the feminist movement. Stevenson's laboriously truthful book was attacked, misinterpreted, and harangued by ideologue critics and relatively ignored by the American public, though in England, where the critics had attacked with even sharper vitriol, the public bought more copies. Of the three books I have just described, only *Bitter Fame* did not become a best-seller.

Editorial lesson: It is important for the sake of truth and history to have written the best biography of your subject; but it can be more lucrative to be first on the scene. John Malcolm Brinnin's agonized and agonizing personal memoir, *Dylan Thomas in America,* the first portrait, has outsold the half-dozen full-scale biographies of Dylan Thomas published since, for example Constantine FitzGibbon's solid *Life,* authorized by the Trustees for the Copyrights of Dylan Thomas a decade later. Brinnin's book was also made into a play that has showered both the author and the Trustees with royalties. If a legend is to be created, try to do it quickly.

Most lamentable of all is the case of Robert Frost, who had the misfortune to choose his own biographer, a Princeton librarian named Lawrance Thompson, and to outlive the appointment by twenty-five years, by which time Thompson had not only gathered up all the materials for a three-volume biography (which even he did not live to finish unaided), but had developed an antipathy for his subject that may prove as poisonous to the reputation of Robert Frost as Rufus Griswold's disapproving life of Edgar Allan Poe was to Poe's. No major American figure more desperately needs a rehabilitative biography than Robert Frost, and none is less likely to get his deserts until the executors are all dead and the interested parties disinterested. The "friends of Marse Robert," as Allen Tate once called them, gathered around the poet's posthumous reputation like Myrmidons surrounding the body of Patroclus, in their attempt to preserve the vulgar yet conventional image of the hayseed sage. The only American poet ever to read at a presidential inauguration, whose image appears on postage stamps, and who produced a body of the most beautiful, witty, and heartbreaking poetry in our literary history, is least likely to receive an adequate biography because he lived too long, authorized his own biographer, the wrong one, too early, and for whatever reason earned the biographer's secret enmity. For this fate no editor has a remedy.

Editing Popular Psychology and Self-Help Books

Toni Burbank

TONI BURBANK *joined Bantam Books as an assistant editor in the school and college department more than twenty years ago and is currently vice-president and executive editor. She has edited early works of the women's movement, maternity and child-care titles, and books on New Age psychology, health and healing, recovery, and mental health. Among authors with whom she has worked are Susan Forward, John Bradshaw, and Deepak Chopra. Other, non-self-help authors include Robert Pirsig, Alvin Toffler, and Natalie Goldberg.*

"At their best . . . popular psychology and self-help books are part of the huge democratization of knowledge. (At their worst, they imply that no one has the common sense to come in out of the rain.) . . . They also seem to me distinctively American—a reminder of our old faith in self-improvement, self-reliance, and human perfectability, married to the can-do temperament of management: just find the right technique, and you can make life work for you!"

So writes Toni Burbank in her crisp, instructive essay on the essential components of writing and editing these books. She points out that *"self-help books are topic driven. Unlike best-selling novelists, previously best-selling self-help writers can fail dramatically if their next topic does not speak directly to their readers' needs."*

Because self-help books are so dependent on publicity, Ms. Burbank notes that *"the author/spokesperson still comes first in editorial decision making."* That means the author must have impressive credentials, be *articulate, do well on talk shows, give workshops, and be well connected to other leading authors in the field.*

What the editor looks for, Ms. Burbank stresses, is not a book written to formula but one "with some tooth-marks on it, some signs of turmoil. . . . For me the best self-help writer is the person who has personally wrestled with and overcome a problem."

Incorporating examples from her own career, Ms. Burbank's essay covers such topics as selecting the subject matter of the book; acquisition; working with the author on the development, organization, and line editing of the work; marketing; and a look at what's next in the self-help field. Her essay is a portrait of a happy marriage between an editor and her work. "Every self-help book I edit changes my own life in some way, and I trust it does the same for its readers."

Editing Popular Psychology and Self-Help Books

Before I knew what an editor was, I wanted to be a teacher: a professor of Renaissance literature, to be exact. From the slum apartment of a graduate student, I looked down on "popular" anything. The only psychological theories I knew were those needed to explain lines of Shakespeare or Milton. It took me a long, painful time to realize that I was more a quick study than a scholar, and that teaching was only one way to spend my days talking about what shapes people's lives.

I have given up trying to justify the books I edit to my former academic colleagues. Popular psychology is the bread and butter of publishing, the "instant backlist," the surprise best-seller. It is also a genre of ill repute. I once heard Rebecca Sinkler, editor of the *New York Times Book Review,* state categorically that the *NYTBR* would never review self-help books, and most publications follow suit. Self-help books are also segregated onto the *Times*'s "Advice, How-to and Miscellaneous" best-seller list, where they have recently had to fight it out each week with a little fellow in glasses named Waldo.

At their best, however, popular psychology and self-help books are part of the huge democratization of knowledge. (At their worst, they imply that no one has the common sense to come in out of the rain.) Sometimes only a few weeks go by between a presentation at the annual meeting of the American Psychiatric Association and the book proposal that lands on my desk. They also seem to me distinctively American—a reminder of our old faith in self-improvement, self-reliance, and human perfectability, married to the can-do temperament of management: just find the right technique, and you can make life work for you!

The last decade has seen a tremendous deepening of the literature of self-help. One of my memorable mistakes as an editor was failing to go after reprint rights to Robin Norwood's *Women Who Love Too Much* because I thought "most women" could not relate to the pathological behavior that book described—which included kleptomania, bulimia, and suicide attempts. Since then, of course, the recovery movement has made serious dysfunction the stuff of talk shows. The suggestions and programs self-help books offer today are also dramatically more sophisticated, drawing on material as diverse as new discoveries in biopsychiatry to the spiritual traditions popularized by the New Age movement.

Acquiring the Book

Self-help books are topic driven. Unlike best-selling novelists, previously best-selling self-help writers can fail dramatically if their next topic does not speak directly to their readers' needs. And when a topic is hot, it often pays to publish a second-best book on the subject even if another publisher clearly has the dominant title. In the early days of recovery, the long-term bestsellerdom of Janet Woititz's *Adult Children of Alcoholics* spurred very respectable sales for similar but less celebrated titles. The trick is getting out before the glut. (Failing that, one can always edit a trendy word like "codependency" out of the text, as I have found myself doing lately. The problems are perennial; the labels change.)

That said, the author/spokesperson still comes first in editorial decision making. Because they are so little reviewed, self-help books are dependent on publicity. What are the author's professional credentials? How long has he or she worked with the method the book espouses? Is she articulate and personable, a likely talk-show guest? Is he "on the circuit," with frequent workshop appearances that will support the book over the long term? Is she in the network of other leading authors in the field (Bantam's New Age list, in particular, is like a big extended family), or does she have access to top-level endorsements?

In a few cases, we will match a particularly attractive senior author with a co-writer, but the majority of proposals today come in with the match already made if one is needed. The credentials of the co-writer are considered just as carefully. Many co-writers today bring to the project tremendous subject-matter expertise; they are by no means simply wordsmiths.

It helps, of course, to have a wonderful title—like *You Don't Have to Go Home from Work Exhausted!*, a book that my colleagues were sold on—with accompanying groans and guffaws—before they knew any more about it. I bristle, however, when I hear agents or editors use words like "gimmick" or "hook" or "handle," as if all we had to do was be clever and manipulative. (The Hollywood term "high concept" is only slightly better—somewhat closer to ideas than to kitchen gadgets.)

In fact, I believe that readers know when they are being manipulated, and when a book, no matter how accomplished, is written to formula. I'd rather have a book with some tooth-marks on it, some signs of turmoil. As I read a proposal, my own level of attention—my sheer alertness, as opposed to my judgment—is often the most useful clue. In books, as in people, we respond to that elusive quality called "presence" or "authenticity," and no amount of editing can supply it if it is missing.

For me, the best self-help writer is the person who has personally wrestled with and overcome a problem. How much of this struggle will be revealed in the book is a matter of personal taste; it may emerge only as a sense of passionate advocacy. I have urged some writers to be more self-revealing, and I have told others that I thought their self-exposure could hurt them. (In several very successful matches, the co-writer has had a personal stake as well, and I look for this level of commitment.)

I also pay attention to my own stake in the project. Of course I look for books that will balance the list and that fit well with Bantam's strengths. But there are too many days in publishing when professionalism alone will not sustain you; I am looking for a deeper energy to draw on. Sometimes the title of a proposal makes me laugh out loud and throw my arms wide—"this one's for me!"—it has struck my need so absolutely. Or perhaps I find myself introducing the concepts of the proposal into every conversation in the next week. Or I may privately dedicate a project to a friend or family member. And because I have thin genes, I have never done a diet book.

Working with the Author

Most self-help books are bought at the proposal stage, so my editorial role begins early, with basic focus and development. John Bradshaw, educated in a Catholic seminary, brings a Thomistic architecture to his projects, but other authors struggle with organization until the very end. I dislike the current practice of going directly into page proofs because in the old days of galleys, I sometimes moved portions of chapters even after the book was set.

Most first-time authors ask, "What is your standard editorial procedure?" and I always answer, "There is none." Each book, each author, requires a different approach. Most authors prefer to send in early chapters as they are completed, so that we can discuss tone and spot potential problems early. The point-by-point editorial memo and the Post-it marginal flags tend to come at a later stage, when we are filling in gaps. I much prefer working over substantive issues in person or by phone. Then the author or coauthor and I (or sometimes all three of us) can really cook.

The great gift of such meetings is the opportunity to expand and deepen the book, to listen for what the author thinks and feels but has not yet said. Professional circumspection reinforces the chill that descends on many writers before the blank page. (As I once heard Joel Gurin, then editor of *American Health,* tell a group of physicians, "The same surgeon who strides like a god into the operating room and decisively makes the first cut often turns into a cautious bureaucrat on paper, unable to say anything without qualification.") I go after my authors—their humor, their personal passions and compassion, their fascination with human behavior—and try to persuade them that these qualities are exactly what the reader wants and needs from them.

Experience has made me much bolder and freer at these fishing expeditions than I was when I was younger. I tease and challenge and cheerlead and get a sense of how hard I can push. I tell authors what particularly excites me about what we are doing together—and where I lose interest. I'm beginning, after a lifetime of reticence, to be more self-revealing. And I'm more comfortable with going off track, with not "working" every minute. Sometimes the best things emerge during breaks or over lunch. John Bradshaw's delight in taking me on a tour of his new garden prompted me to ask him to write about it; the resulting passage became the very moving introduction to part two of his new book, *Creating Love.*

These are wonderful high, heady hours—the best part of the job. But much of the editing I do falls under the old-fashioned discipline of rhetoric. Popular psychology and self-help aim to change consciousness and to change behavior. (In 1989, Daniel Goleman reported in the *New York Times* that one study had found selected self-help books nearly as useful as therapy in treating mild to moderate problems.) Such change requires an alliance with the reader that must begin on the opening page and be reinforced throughout. How does the author present him or herself, and whom does he or she identify as the audience? I often quote to authors the words of my first boss, Marc Jaffe: "There is no such thing as a mass market. There are only individual readers." I suggest that therapists write for their most interesting and attractive clients; or for their college reunion group. The writer is an authority (otherwise, why trust the book?), but the reader is also intelligent, conscientious, and responsive (after all, he or she bought the book!). Once this is established, any tendency to talk down usually disappears.

In John Bradshaw's *Homecoming,* there is a passage on the "triune brain," describing a major modern theory of brain evolution and structure. Several early readers suggested that it be cut—a needless complication. I worked very hard with John to make it clear and relevant, but kept it in. The clash of levels—moving from down-home examples to brain research complete with scholarly citations—seemed to me pure Bradshaw, part of his fascination and depth. And if the reader was nonplussed, the passage came deep enough into the book for him to tolerate it before returning to more comfortable ground.

The movement of a self-help book often falls into three parts: identification of the problem, interpretation and exploration of its roots, and the solution. But there are no neat formulas for how these parts are related and meted out. Obviously, a reader has identified with a problem before picking up a book, just as a therapy client does in entering therapy. But the book must create a safe space in which to explore the problem; it takes time to be able to act even on the best advice. Authors with clinical experience grasp this analogy easily. If the first chapter gives away too much, I might ask, "Would you introduce this material in a first therapy session?"

I warn my authors that I have a hobbyhorse about the table of contents and subheads. These can take hours of tinkering, getting the chapter titles as evocative as the main title, showing parallelism where it exists. Subheads should create a dramatic sense of progression within each chapter, and part of my editorial process is nearly always to create an abstract of the subheads to see if they "read," and to check that the sequence of subordination is correct. Later, the contents and heads often become key marketing tools, providing exactly the focus and phrases that will sell the book.

This marketing consciousness extends to the look of the book as well, beginning with my design memo requesting an "open, accessible self-help style as in *X*" (some previous title) and specifying the special features I want highlighted: exercises or meditations, boxed lists, diagrams. *The Personality Self-Portrait,* by John Oldham, M.D., and Lois Morris, contained a very sophisticated self-test with an equally complex scoring procedure. We went through at least four trial designs of the scoring sheet until we had achieved a design that the authors and I agreed was as clear and user-friendly as it could be.

In a book's specifically how-to sections, practicality and the detailed anticipation of problems are key. Exercises developed for workshops have to be adapted for individual work. A relationship book must have significant work for those out of a relationship, or for those with recalcitrant partners. My role here is to play a reader who takes everything very literally.

The margins start to bristle with yellow slips: "When should I open my eyes again?" "What if he gets furious when I say this and stomps out?" "What does it mean if I answer yes to this question?"

I believe that the author should also acknowledge when the book is not enough. One day during the writing of *Men Who Hate Women and the Women Who Love Them,* Susan Forward called me sounding very agitated. "When they get to this stage of the work," she said, "a tremendous amount of anger is going to be released. I don't think readers can handle it on their own. They need to get help, and they need to be careful not to act on their anger impulsively. I feel dishonest implying this is a do-it-yourself process." "That's great, Susan," I said. "Please write exactly what you just told me."

In *Homecoming,* John Bradshaw included very stringent warnings about stopping the experiential work if certain feelings came up, and about people who should not do the work at all. It is now common, as well, to warn those with addictions to drugs or alcohol that they should address those before undertaking other self-help work. This is a matter of basic integrity, not something done to satisfy our lawyers.

The writer's art is particularly apparent in the handling of two perennial elements of popular psychology, the case history and the typology. In this, of course, every writer stands on Freud's shoulders; who wouldn't be proud to come up with "Little Hans," "the Wolf-Man," and "the Oedipus complex." Case histories can be hackneyed and formulaic, implying that the client "gets well" in two therapy sessions after imbibing several miraculous interpretations (or, these days, swallowing a couple of Prozac). But there is no reason case histories can't rather give us a sense of the many manifestations of a given problem, of the complexity of change, and of the value of the struggle for insight. How fully characters should be developed, how case histories are carried through the book (if at all), their placement and pacing relative to interpretation, and whether they all have to be resolved are key topics for discussion.

Robin Casarjian's *Forgiveness: A Bold Choice for a Peaceful Heart* was her first book, and we struggled together over the issue of case histories. "Too abstract," I said of the first draft; "Not authentic, not me," she said of the model cases I suggested. The logjam broke when Robin sent out a call to her friends and workshop clients for personal stories of forgiveness. The letters that came back were too long to fit smoothly into the chapters, but they were also some of the most moving, dramatic testimony I had ever read. We created special "interchapters" to accommodate them, and when it came time for the sales department to see samples of the book, I chose these sections to send them.

And in the end, I think stories are what it's all about. People learn best when their emotions are engaged, and the self-help book is also a dramatic form and an entertainment, like a detective novel or a romance. We each see our own life as a narrative, and the large promise of self-help is that we can change the way the story comes out. A "self-help junkie" may not be someone who can't get it together, but rather someone who enjoys this particular form of a very old story: of downfall and redemption, of order out of chaos, of triumph against the odds.

What's Next in Self-Help?

Those of us who have been deeply involved in recovery books now have our noses in the air for the next major "trend." I am personally fascinated by the emerging field of biopsychiatry and how our new knowledge of genetics, inborn temperament, neurology, and brain chemistry will interact with psychodynamic and behavioral approaches. I have just finished work on *A Brilliant Madness,* a new book by actress Patty Duke and medical journalist Gloria Hochman, that combines the personal example of Patty Duke's manic-depression with information about the latest research on this complex disease. I see this as part of a larger movement to destigmatize mental illness and to broaden our definition of "normal" behavior.

I believe that the boundaries of self-help will also continue to expand into the areas opened by New Age, recovery, and transpersonal psychology, so that increasing attention will be paid to spiritual concerns. The new interest in religion, service, and life purpose takes us well beyond the psychological limits of the "culture of narcissism."

I am also curious to see how the new emphasis on multiculturalism will affect self-help writing. We are perhaps ready to confront the fact that our models of psychological health are, at least in part, culturally determined. Is separation from the family the only route to full maturity? Is self-sacrifice noble—or "codependent"? Is aggression essential to male identity? Self-help books are notoriously hard to sell in translation because of differences in national attitudes. Nathaniel Branden, in his new work, *The Six Pillars of Self-Esteem,* is the first popular writer I know who is addressing the issue of cultural norms.

Finally, driven by demographics and the presence of AIDS, we are turning again to the human verities of aging and death, and new publishing categories are being born to fill the need. I presume a largely middle-aged audience for books on growing old; those of us who are suddenly "next in line" after the death of a parent feel a special urgency about getting it right. And our new consciousness is making dying itself a final stage of growth— one that we must wrest back from hospitals and machines for ourselves and our families.

Back in my Eng. lit. days, I remember hooting with laughter when I first heard the titles of Jeremy Taylor's classics: *Holy Living* and *Holy Dying*. It was an age of irony, and I suspect I was embarrassed by the directness of Taylor's concerns. Now I am very happy to be working with writers who are his spiritual descendants. Every self-help book I edit changes my own life in some way, and I trust it does the same for its readers.

Editing the Romance Novel

Linda Marrow

LINDA MARROW *is a senior editor at Pocket Books, where she has worked since 1982, acquiring and editing romance novels as well as mysteries, thrillers, true-crime, and mainstream women's fiction. The romance authors she has worked with include Jude Deveraux, Julie Garwood, and Judith McNaught.*

Covering contemporary and historical romances ("A historical romance is usually set somewhere between the Norman Invasion in 1066 and about 1900"), Ms. Marrow's essay charts a clear course for both editor and writer to realize the best that each genre has to offer.

Both the writer and editor of romance fiction should be aware that "the reader of romance fiction can and will expect that both the hero and heroine will be alive and well and thoroughly in love with each other at the close of the story; that the hero and heroine will not be separated for lengthy sections of the book; and that the story will end at the point at which there is the most hope for their relationship."

Ms. Marrow shows the writer of historical romances how to research effectively to re-create a bygone age with authenticity and populate it with believable people. But she warns not to flaunt the research so that it slows down the narrative.

She offers valuable advice about handling dialogue (strike a balance between historical accuracy and contemporary readability) and creating characters (let the characters grow and develop during the course of the novel). And, whether writing historical or contemporary romances, Ms.

Marrow advises against "assigning only positive character traits . . . to their heroes and heroines. Readers will immediately feel distanced from a character with only virtues and no flaws, problems, or mild neuroses."

In the course of her cogent and clearheaded essay, Ms. Marrow makes many valuable suggestions about matters vital to the successful editing and writing of romance fiction, among them: how graphic sex scenes should be; handling sensuality, sexuality, and sexual tension; creating a fairy-tale, romantic atmosphere; and the importance of following publishers' guidelines for writing different kinds of romance novels.

Ms. Marrow sums up why so many women read romance novels when she quotes Kate Duffy, editor of Kismet Books: "If romance were as common as rudeness, I'd be unemployed."

Editing the Romance Novel

Novels published in the romance genre constitute a large and profitable area of the paperback world and are also becoming increasingly important in hardcover publishing. Like other genres (mystery, horror, science fiction, etc.), romance is an umbrella that covers several kinds of novels, all of which tell the story of two people falling in love.

Most romance novels published now fall into one of two fairly broad groups: historical romances or contemporary romances. A contemporary romance of course has a modern setting. A historical romance is usually set somewhere between the Norman Invasion in 1066 and about 1900.

Every genre has rules and/or reader expectations that must be satisfied; the romance category is no different. Just as a reader of crime fiction expects a dead body to appear early in the pages of a murder mystery, the reader of romance fiction can and will expect that both the hero and heroine will be alive and well and thoroughly in love with each other at the close of the story; that the hero and heroine will not be separated for lengthy sections of the book; and that the story will end at the point at which there is the most hope for their relationship. Some publishing companies, especially publishers of contemporary romance, have very specific rules or guidelines for the contents of the romances they publish. These rules can usually be found in the form of tipsheets, about which more later.

·   ·   ·

When beginning a historical romance, the writer confronts a host of challenges, some of which are quite different from those facing her contemporary romance colleagues. The most obvious of these is research. The historical romance writer must be able to re-create, authentically and con-vincingly, a fully realized world far different from the one her readers live in—a world full of the sights, sounds, smells, and social customs of the place and time of the story.

At no time should the writer lose sight of the fact that she needs to tell a story that is so compelling that readers cannot bear to put down her novel for even a moment. Editors and writers must remember that there is no place in the novel for a lecture (even a short one) flaunting the writer's newfound knowledge. The research should provide details that will enhance the story rather than slow it down, detract or digress from it. It is awkward and amateurish for the writer to choke the story with large clumps of information learned while researching the setting, if these clumps do noth-ing to propel the story forward or to develop its characters or to keep the reader reading. Every sentence should add something necessary to charac-terization or plot. Take as a rule what Chekhov once said about playwrit-ing: if a gun is hanging on the wall in the first act, it must fire in the last.

Researching the historical period a writer has chosen for her romance can be very daunting. Where does one start? I usually suggest to my writers that they determine to what extent actual historical events figure in the plot. Will any of the characters be directly involved? If so, the writer should learn the facts about that moment in history from every angle. Otherwise she'll have a hard time persuading readers that they have entered the world of her story and characters.

I've learned that merely knowing about (and being able to write about) a particular event isn't enough. A writer needs to be able to create a world full of characters that spring to life for the reader. What are these characters going to talk about? What do they see upon waking up from a nap or when walking down the stairs of their houses?

Even during the most important historical occurrences—war or eco-nomic uncertainty or national prosperity—real people don't speak only of the events or politics of the day. Fictional characters who do so seem stiff and stilted. Romance writers and editors should remember that real people talk to each other about the trivial as well as the significant: clothes, food, entertainment, gossip, illness. Interesting, well-drawn characters do the same. So after the writer knows the basic facts of the time she's chosen, it's time for her to find out what made up the fabric of the lives she'll be writing about.

As an editor, I'm often called upon to suggest ways that romance writers can learn more about the historical periods they are writing about. I recom-mend they look at books describing the clothing worn during the time. Read magazines published during the period that your characters might have read. Diaries or journals from the period provide invaluable material for writers, frequently giving not only the details of daily life but also information on what people were thinking about. Were people worried about where their next meal would come from? Did they have so much time and money that they could devote themselves to leisure? One can get clues from popular recipes of the period too: were they concerned with conserving fresh ingredients like eggs, milk, and beef? From the fashions of the time one can learn whether an adolescent girl might have been insecure because she thought her figure was developing too slowly—or too quickly. Read biographies of people like the main characters. It's easy to find material about kings and queens or great leaders of political and religious movements; it's harder to find information about the wife of a small-town mayor, or the least important young lady who waited upon the least important young duchess at a royal court.

Learn about the etiquette of the time: What was considered good manners and good taste and what was considered vulgar? Why did these rules exist? Would the hero and heroine of this novel heed them? Just like today, certain behavior was probably considered appropriate for one socioeconomic group and not for another. Think very carefully about who your characters are. A world of difference would probably exist between what was considered correct for the daughter of a farmer and what was proper for the daughter of a duke.

This kind of difference can be put to good use in plotting or in sparking conflict between the hero and heroine. An example of this might be a story in which the heroine is the daughter of a dairy farmer and the hero is a wealthy young man who left the village as an impoverished boy eager to seek his fortune. Now he has returned to claim the farmer's daughter as his own true love. What could possibly go wrong? Well, what if our plain-spoken, down-to-earth heroine finds our hero (eager to please and impress the girl of his dreams) to be condescending and affected? What if she loudly proclaims in front of the entire assembled village that he has put on airs since he left and now acts as though he were better than his old friends? You'll have a furious, embarrassed hero, a bold, no-nonsense heroine—a thoroughly and understandably estranged couple in an amusing conflict that came from your research into social custom and etiquette.

*   *   *

The characters in a romance—particularly the hero and heroine—are the most important element of the novel. None of the writer's efforts at researching the time period, plotting the story, or evoking a sense of place and time will amount to much if the fictional world she creates isn't inhabited by believable characters.

The two most common characterization problems I see new writers struggle with are assigning only positive character traits and attaching too many positive personality qualities to their heroes and heroines. Readers will immediately feel distanced from a character with only virtues and no flaws, problems, or mild neuroses; the writer will have created only a cardboard cutout instead of a fully fleshed-out person capable of bringing the reader to laughter or tears. Editors and writers alike should consider the characters they've found most memorable in their own reading. Frequently the personalities of the most successful ones are built around only one or two important qualities. In addition, the same quality can be both a strength and a weakness in a character. For example, the writer might have created a heroine who always acts impulsively. On several occasions her quick actions could create amusing and/or troublesome results for her. But ultimately her behavior could cause her to save the day for someone by dashing headlong into a situation that a more careful person would have flinched at or avoided altogether.

Another problem new writers should watch out for is not continuing the development of the characters throughout the entire novel. It's an easy mistake to create a hero and heroine in the first chapter and then let the story move those two people around for the rest of the book while their personalities remain static. This is a common and always fatal flaw in many romance novels I see: books with great beginnings that become less and less compelling when the characters' motivations, choices, and evolving personalities stop driving the story. The main characters and some of the important secondary characters must evolve and change because of what they experience during the course of the novel.

·   ·   ·

One of the first actions a novel's characters will take is to say something. Dialogue is immensely important in any novel because it is used simultaneously both to develop characters and to tell the story. It can be particularly troublesome for the writer of a historical romance to establish the right tone. The dialogue must sound true to the time period of the novel and yet not be stiff or full of archaic constructions that sound awkward and contrived to the modern ear. On the other hand, both editors and writers should watch for phrasing that is so modern as to be anachronistic. As far as letting the characters speak in dialect—be warned: I have seldom seen this accomplished in any way that is natural and readable. In one particular case, a marvelous novel I had acquired was somewhat difficult to read because of the heavy Scottish dialect used in most of the dialogue. After a lot of discussion, the author and I agreed that it was best to remove all but a touch of dialect from the speech of the novel's main characters and to allow the book's secondary characters to speak in a slightly heavier dialect.

. . .

The same challenge that applies to dialogue—striking the right balance between historical accuracy and the needs of the contemporary mass-market reader—applies to the overall tone and content of the novel. The writer must decide how much she will adhere to historical realism. If she's unsure, then I suggest she closely read the historical romances that are currently being published. She must find out how much or how little realism is accepted by the readers and then decide what balance between truth and fantasy works for her.

Writers who want to write within the genre of historical romance must not write a story so filled with archaic constructions that it no longer qualifies as accessible, escapist entertainment. Some years ago I fell so in love with one historical novel I acquired that I ignored completely the fact that the writer had done such a thorough job of re-creating the past that the book in no way worked as light entertainment. It wasn't until after the book's publication, when many fewer copies were sold than expected, that I admitted the truth: this was a beautifully written novel by a talented writer, but it was not a fast-paced mass-market read.

Although it may strike some editors and writers as heresy, for many writers a fairy-tale-like approach works best and has won the hearts of many readers. The novels written by these writers frequently have a dreamy "Once upon a time" quality to them. Sometimes these stories seem to belong to no specific year but will embrace instead a modern fantasy idea of the Middle Ages or Regency England or the American West. Generally fast-paced and lighthearted, the action in these romances is often driven by emotion rather than historical events.

If this lighter, less realistic approach appeals to the writer, both she and her editor must still be very careful to be accurate in describing the attitudes and values held by the people of the period being written about.

There is a very thin line between an acceptably relaxed treatment of historical accuracy and characters' thoughts and actions that are so ana-chronistic that they render the story totally unbelievable and uninteresting to the reader. In general, the writer should take great care with the charac-ters' opinions and their thought processes. For example, a heroine in Re-gency England simply would not have the same casual attitude toward birth control as an American in the early 1990s might, nor to the subject of divorce. The writer must strike the right balance: one that will allow the readers to suspend their disbelief and lose themselves in the world of the characters and the story.

. . .

The world of contemporary romance publishing is a very different one from that of historical romance publishing. Publishers like Harlequin, Silhouette, Loveswept, and Kismet publish various romance series or lines and each line has its own very specific guidelines and reader expectations to meet. To learn how to write for these different lines, writers should read several books in each series and also study and follow the tipsheets, in which publishers tell how they would like books shaped for their lines. To get the tipsheets, writers should look in *Literary Market Place (LMP)*, usually available at the reference desk in libraries, for the names and addresses of the publishers and editors of the series they're interested in.

The writer of a contemporary romance must excel at many of the same things as a writer of historical romance: plotting, characterization, dialogue, creating the right chemistry and sexual tension between the hero and the heroine, and frequently research. Although the contemporary romance writer does not need to research a historical time period, she will have to find out about the novel's setting and the careers of her main characters and evoke them believably and authentically.

In order for a contemporary romance plot to be successful it must do three things: satisfy the reader expectations of the romance genre; meet the requirements of the specific line you are writing for; and tell a wonderful, compulsively readable story. Contemporary romance editors should know not only what their own line requires but also how the line they acquire for and edit is different from the other romance lines of their competitors. Various lines differ in length of manuscript, complexity of plot, and approach to characterization. The editors of some lines encourage writers to develop subplots in their stories; in other lines the plots must concentrate more fully on the developing relationship between the hero and heroine.

A romance editor must be able to recognize when a writer's ability to tell a story and convey emotional depth outweighs writing flaws that can be corrected either in revisions or when the novel is edited. "If I feel that the writer is delivering the emotional depth I'm looking for then I might acquire a novel that needs a bit of plot help," says Leslie Wainger, senior editor and editorial coordinator for Silhouette Books. "Sometimes I'll get very involved in brainstorming about the story with an author who I know can make the love story work. On the other hand I might turn down a novel that tells a story that's more appropriate for my line, but that didn't convey the emotional intensity I'm looking for in a romance novel."

Kate Duffy, editor-in-chief of the Meteor Publishing Corporation, the company that produces Kismet Books, a line of contemporary romance, says that she needs to be confident that what needs to be fixed in a manuscript can be fixed before she'll acquire a writer's work. "If the writer has a good idea but no ability to execute it, then nothing would compel me to buy it," said Duffy, who was the first editor-in-chief of Silhouette Books.

Because these books have a modern setting, real cultural and current events affect the contemporary romance world. "Because of Clarence Thomas and Anita Hill we're having trouble acquiring and editing books where the hero is the boss and the heroine is his employee," says Duffy.

However, the fact that it generally takes from ten to twenty months to publish a book after it's acquired has an important effect on how up-to-date a plot can be. According to Wainger, "We can't be too current because the publication schedule can't keep up with the timelines. It's most important that the novel work as a romance. If an author seems to be giving a speech on a subject or issue, then it's up to the editor to take it out. We can't cross too far over the line between reality and romantic fantasy when romantic fantasy is what the readers are coming for."

Sensuality is an important element of the romance novel and is what many people think of first in connection with romances. However, it's a mistake to think that the writer can substitute a few fractious conversations and several sex scenes for authentic sexual tension and sexuality between the hero and the heroine. If a novel doesn't communicate the necessary emotional intensity without the sex scenes, then adding them will not achieve the necessary depth of feeling.

Leslie Wainger says that one of the main differences among the contemporary romance lines is the sexual intensity and explicitness of their books. An example of this can be found in Silhouette's tipsheets. The guidelines for the Silhouette Romance line read, "Although the hero and heroine don't actually make love unless married, sexual tension is a vitally important element." Compare this with their suggestion for the Silhouette Desire line: "The characters don't have to be married to make love, but lovemaking is never taken lightly."

Writers are frequently unsure about how graphic the sex scenes in a romance should be. While a certain minimal level of sensuality is expected by most romance readers, it's up to the writer how far she goes. To become familiar with the various levels of sensuality currently popular, once again I suggest that writers read a number of romances. Always make sure that the sex scenes are emotionally well motivated, that they never feel as though they were gratuitously and arbitrarily inserted into the novel. It's essential that editors and writers remember that sex is merely one element of what gives the romance novel its tremendous appeal.

. . .

At the heart of every romance novel is a subject that is of enormous interest to a lot of women: how a relationship between a man and a woman develops into love. Most successful romances explore in various amusing, exciting, and dramatic ways the problems men and women have communicating with each other and negotiating their roles within a relationship. At their best, these novels can make the reader believe for a few hours that the couple they're reading about is falling in love and experiencing all of love's excitement, frustration, sadness, and joys. Everyday life, of course, often fails to equal such an exhilarating slate—and from that gap between dream and reality springs the power and appeal of romance novels. Or, as Kate Duffy puts it, "If romance were as common as rudeness, I'd be unemployed."

Editing Male-Oriented Escapist Fiction

Greg Tobin

Just previous to becoming the editorial director of the Book-of-the-Month Club's Quality Paperback Book Club in August of 1992, GREG TOBIN was an associate publisher at Bantam Books, where he directed Bantam's frontier and historical publishing program under the Domain imprint, and was also publishing director for the Doubleday western program. He acquired fiction and nonfiction for both hardcover and paperback.

An editor and publisher, Mr. Tobin has been a member of Western Writers of America since 1981 and is the author of several westerns under pen names and his own. His latest novel written under his own byline is Big Horn *(Ballantine, 1989).*

Mr. Tobin sees category fiction (mysteries, westerns, SF and fantasy, war, romance, adventure, etc.) as addressing "the tastes of voracious readers who are looking for an exciting reading experience within a specific type of story but outside the norm: escape from boredom to exotic and dangerous places, identification with heroic but very human characters, clear choices and challenges in the realm of adventure and romance that make a difference, often a life-or-death difference."

Mr. Tobin believes that the disciplines imposed by category writing "expose the writer's shortcomings and bring out the best that is within him," and as a result "category fiction is the cause of good writing as much as it is the beneficiary of good writing."

Category fiction, Mr. Tobin writes, "is a means by which many new authors break into the business, get their first one or two or three books published—get the kinks out of their writing, learn the fundamentals of the storyteller's art. If an author brings some talent and ambition to the party,

356

if he focuses on the story rather than on the money he is not making, if he reads and learns from other books and authors in the same category and is aware of what the marketplace can support—then I am very interested in those words on the manuscript page."

Mr. Tobin describes the editorial, sales, and marketing factors that made him take on a new action series, shows how he worked with the author to develop its editorial content (the writer had never written book-length fiction before) and how he created a publishing program to support it, and examines the causes of the series' decline and eventual cancellation. In another instance, he reveals how he used his editorial and marketing expertise to discover "fresh means to address established markets"—specifically frontier fiction.

Mr. Tobin sees his responsibility as always to be "loyal to the ultimate decision maker on any book: the reader. He's the guy who counts the most. Without his loyalty, I'd be out of a job."

Editing Male-Oriented Escapist Fiction

My first job in book publishing provided the foundation for a career that has been an adventure—in more ways than one.

I came to New York City in the late seventies with the ambition to "break into the business" as an editor, and I landed a temporary job at a small, feisty mass-market house that published primarily category fiction in paperback.

What do I mean by *category fiction*? I mean westerns, mysteries, romances, horror stories, science fiction, war tales, and series of all kinds. Category fiction addresses the very particular needs of distributors and wholesale-supplied retailers such as drugstores, supermarkets, and newsstands. Category fiction also addresses the tastes of voracious readers who are looking for an exciting reading experience within a specific type of story but outside the norm: escape from boredom to exotic and dangerous places, identification with heroic but very human characters, clear choices and challenges in the realm of adventure and romance that make a difference, often a life-or-death difference.

Do you remember the experience of reading your first Hardy Boys or Nancy Drew book? Perhaps it was Jules Verne, Edgar Rice Burroughs, or Zane Grey who first transported you from the ordinary to an imagined world beyond the known and expected. For me it was all of the above-mentioned books and authors—and more—but I gave little thought to who actually published the popular fiction that so many young people and adults devoured so passionately.

A college education and a reverence for western literature were wedged into my brain between my Conan Doyle days and my paperback publishing career. Today, I am still recovering from my formal education, even as I learn and relearn fundamentals of reading, writing, and publishing.

I began learning these fundamentals in my first job in the book business, a post that illustrates rather starkly just what publishing (and my particular niche therein) is all about. For me the experience was analogous to being a young ballplayer shipped to a Double A farm team for a few seasons before joining the perennial pennant-winning club. It was terrific training from day one because I had to do a bit of everything: from copywriting to proofreading to negotiating contracts to scheduling to policing advance and royalty payments to reading the slush pile. Occasionally—very occasionally—I even did some editing!

Of course, all of these functions are still very much a part of my job today. I work for a very large publishing corporation, but the basic process of making a salable book from a raw manuscript or the glimmer of an idea is exactly the same.

The crucial factor for me was this business of seeking and publishing books in very well defined categories. As I read submissions (agented and unagented) and worked on books already under contract, I discovered something that excites me and motivates me to this day: I found that some excellent writing was evident in war and horror novels, mysteries, westerns, and action-adventure series. My natural interest was in categories that seem to attract male readers and so I eventually carved out a position at the house that allowed me to "specialize" in these categories that—not incidentally—contributed significantly to the house's income.

In other words, I was turned on. Intrigued. Hooked. The adventure of editing had commenced. I had made an irreversible decision: I was going to have fun at this. I had always enjoyed escapist stories—now I would be able to make them into books.

Let's examine for just a moment one of the underlying principles that inform my approach to men's-interest category publishing—and it is *my* approach. Others may or may not agree. But it works for me. Early on I asked myself this question: Is the solid writing and storytelling I find in these books *because* they are category books or *in spite of* that fact? In my opinion (then and now, with years of experience to back it up), category fiction is the *cause* of good writing as much as it is the beneficiary of good writing.

Why is this so? Any category imposes a discipline upon the author, whether it be particular conventions of plot that must be observed (or at least played against), whether it be demands of character and relationships (especially in the romance genre), or whether it be requirements of length (often imposed by the publisher, who seeks to keep the book at a certain cover price). These disciplines require a writer to develop his storytelling skills by working within a certain framework that is almost always more difficult than the budding writer realizes. These disciplines expose the writer's shortcomings and bring out the best that is within him.

When I speak at writers' conferences I recommend that every fiction writer try his hand at a mystery novel. I put it this way: In a "mainstream" novel you can get away with murder; in a mystery you cannot.

An example: One of our greatest best-selling authors of the past three decades, John le Carré, chose to channel his formidable skills through the mystery and espionage forms. You can't do any better than that.

Further, category writing develops an author's skills. It is a means by which many new authors break into the business, get their first one or two or three books published—get the kinks out of their writing, learn the fundamentals of the storyteller's art. If an author brings some talent and ambition to the party, if he focuses on the story rather than on the money he is not making, if he reads and learns from other books and authors in the same category and is aware of what the marketplace can support—then I am very interested in those words on the manuscript page.

The category—be it mystery or western or novel of adventure—gives the writer, both the novice and the veteran, a framework in which to create a story for a given readership, and that is no easy task. There are no *formulas* per se, but, as I alluded to above, there are *conventions,* which the talented writer can turn to his advantage. Example: The action-adventure hero must, at some point in the story, summon a near-superhuman physical capacity to elude danger and kill an improbable number of the enemy, or he must turn to an improbable gadget or weapon to escape with his skin. Example: In a traditional western, similarly, the protagonist is morally upright (not necessarily uptight), with a black-and-white view of the world; the bad guys are *bad.* Example: In the mystery novel there must always be a crime or a puzzle to be solved—period—end of discussion.

In addition to advising the author on the shaping and content of the manuscript, a very important function of the contemporary editor is that of de facto marketing manager. In recent years, a poor overall economy has affected the book business as it has nearly every other business. Publishers have been forced to reduce the total number of employees and other expenses.

This new financial reality, coupled with a trend over the past decade or

more away from acquiring editors actually line editing books, has caused us
to wear an extra hat or two in the office. In my case, it is fair to say that one
of those hats is that of marketing "idea man." The philosophy behind this
is simple: The editor who acquires books in a given category surely knows
the market for that category better than anyone in house—or else what is
he doing there in the first place?

At first, the hat was an awkward fit. I have never been formally trained
as a marketing expert and, because I have worked with a number of terrific
marketing colleagues over the years, I appreciate the need for training and
experience in that field. Besides, with all the other responsibilities an editor
is expected to fulfill (just look at the other essays in this book), who has the
time? Still, I kept an open mind.

At some point I realized that I also had never had any formal training to
be an editor. I just picked it up as I went along from mentors and colleagues,
borrowing and adapting editorial and negotiating techniques, breathing in
the experience of others. I have since approached the marketing and editorial functions from the same starting point: determined to learn as much as
I could and to learn by doing. This has more or less worked for me, and
here's how.

First, every book I acquire has to answer at least this one basic question:
What overall market or segment of the market will buy this book? From
that answer flow the editorial, publishing, marketing, and sales strategies.

A perfect example to illustrate this question-and-answer scenario is an
action-adventure series that I acquired and published very recently. I remember vividly the first telephone call from the agent, which occurred a few
days before our December sales conference. He described the series concept,
which was to place two contemporary Special Forces veterans in a specially
equipped eighteen-wheeler to conduct a war on crime (mobsters, kidnap-
pers, drug lords, smugglers, bad bike gangs, and the like) on the open
highways—fully sanctioned by federal authority that, in the books themselves, included a president very much like the current incumbent.

The idea appealed strongly to me on an editorial level for two reasons:
First, the story line had action aplenty, good characters, and gadgets and
techno-gimmickry enough to satisfy the tinkerer and fantasist in any red-
blooded American male; and second, I was seeking a strong entry into the
action-adventure series market, an area my company traditionally had not
concentrated on as strongly as did many other mass-market houses. We saw
this series proposal as one of three we were willing to take on and build an
action-adventure publishing program around.

The idea appealed strongly to me on a sales and marketing level because
my company had been the very first to exploit the truck-stop market as a
nontraditional outlet for paperback book sales. Our sales reps, in years

past, had opened up truck-stop accounts for book sales and installed racks and filled those racks and maintained those racks with religious fervor. Of course, we published (and still do) Louis L'Amour, the best-selling western storyteller of all time, and a huge proportion of these truck-stop accounts sold that author even though they were not all that interested—initially—in increasing their book sales in general.

Clearly, the agent had called the right editor at the right publishing house (no dummy, he), and we practically concluded the deal over the phone right then and there. My gut was on overdrive, but I requested the proposal and told him I'd talk to "my people" and see what we could do. Well, instead of a proposal came a full and complete manuscript for the first book in the series.

Again, I remember that *feeling* upon reading the manuscript: I knew I held something very unique, written by an author who knew his stuff and could convey the authenticity of his experience (of vital importance in any of the categories I deal with). But *he had never written book-length fiction before.* This was painfully apparent—but, ah, therein lay the challenge! I attacked the manuscript with gusto and arranged to meet the author and the agent for an editorial discussion.

I flew to a major city in the mid-South, and the author and agent drove a sizable distance to meet me at a truck stop located near a major interstate highway, where we breakfasted (one terrific meal, I must say) and, over a dozen cups of coffee each, reviewed the manuscript page by page, line by line, in some cases word by word. It was one of my favorite publishing experiences because I remember how the light went on in his eyes when he made the leap—literally right before my eyes—from amateur to professional writer. He *saw,* he understood, he made the connections.

First, there were straightforward issues of spelling, grammar, and punctuation—which not every author has mastered, some even at much later stages in their careers. Then, most interestingly to me, there was the issue of "efficiency" in relating the story: Is every "he said" or "she said" absolutely necessary? Are three adjectives really needed? How can you delete clichés and create new ways to express very familiar actions and ideas? Does each sentence really say what you intend it to say?

The author did his job. From that point, the publisher had plenty of work to do, especially in the realm of cover "packaging," since this book and the ones to follow would be paperback original novels. Here, the editorial content of the series lent itself beautifully to strong, high-tech, action-oriented images, and our art department "discovered" a new artist who had great rapport with the project and came up with a striking format and illustrations that perfectly targeted the books' readers.

I was proud to see the first book, and eventually the entire series, develop from concept to finished product. We broke new ground in the cover packaging, as well as editorially. The books attracted a cadre of devoted fans and delivered the escape entertainment they wanted.

P.S. The story does *not* have a happily-ever-after ending, however. The series sold strongly at first, but then began to decline until, after more than two years and a dozen books, we decided not to continue publishing it. This experience caused me to evaluate how and why it happened.

Ultimately I identified two direct causes. First, the action-adventure market had withered drastically. Mega-selling male-oriented fiction by authors such as Tom Clancy had brought men into the hardcover-buying cycle and was delivering bigger, more fulfilling story lines, thus creating needs and expectations that the category books could not fill. Hence, with the exception of very deeply established series such as Mack Bolan, sales of category-level books had tailed off into oblivion. A second cause was the fact that the sales structure of the publishing house had changed radically within that two-year span. No longer were individual sales reps opening new truck-stop accounts or servicing the truck stops as closely as they had in previous years; our company had merged with another and had become a huge publishing corporation.

A second example of an editor combining marketing and editorial approaches involves looking for fresh means to address established markets. Let's consider frontier fiction. For a number of years, I have edited category westerns, which can to a degree be fixed comfortably within the present context of men's-interest mass-market fiction.

In examining the frontier fiction marketplace—what was working for my house, what others were publishing, what categories and subcategories were not working—I determined that there was room for a quality category-level series of "mountain man" tales. One of the greatest novels in frontier fiction is Vardis Fisher's *Mountain Man* (from which the movie *Jeremiah Johnson* was made). And in the last decade a number of authors have written modern classics on the life of the hunters, trappers, and fur traders of the very early nineteenth century, the rugged individuals we know as the mountain men.

I also became aware of a very sizable community of readers who were (and still are) very passionate about these books and about re-creating the "black powder" lifestyle of the old-time mountain men. It's a world of muzzle-loading shooting competitions and primitive rendezvous where entire families camp the way they did in the mountain man and "buckskinner" era. Though there already were a couple of mountain man series being published as original paperbacks by smaller houses, I suggested my company produce a new original series—publishing possibly as many as three titles per year—in this category.

I discreetly queried an agent or two, then one day decided to spill the entire idea to one agent friend, who responded warmly but did not have an available client whom we both thought qualified to take on this project. He very much wanted to participate in this project, however, and we both agreed to keep it foremost in our minds.

Shortly thereafter, at a luncheon meeting with another agent (whom I did not know as well as the first fellow), I learned that *he* represented a versatile and prolific writer whom I had long respected. I blurted out the thought that perhaps this writer would be appropriate for the mountain man project.

Now there were two interested agents and one potential author involved. More than I had bargained for, but we negotiated an arrangement that satisfied all parties. Agent No. 1, with whom I had agreed to work in the first place, became the packager (also called book producer), whose job it was to guarantee delivery of an acceptable manuscript. Agent No. 2, representing the writer, participated with a standard commission. The author has written three books to date.

Both true-life stories show how I prefer to mine the fields of men's-interest mass-market fiction: by generating ideas and seeking authors myself, and by keeping an ear to the rails for the rumbling of that approaching Main Chance Express. I am not untypical, I think, among the editorial community in this.

I tend to listen to myself, to follow my own tastes, and to seek out books and authors who are in the slipstream rather than the mainstream, so to speak. When mega-authors such as Louis L'Amour, Tom Clancy, and Stephen King began to pull *men* into bookstores (where traditionally, and still today, women are the primary customers and actual purchasers of books), we in the book-publishing business became much more open to new forms of men's entertainment and new genres of fiction. My heavy involvement in military fiction (as well as nonfiction) stems directly from my responsibility to cover this market for my house. I have begun to develop much more of an affinity with and personal interest in military history because of this professional involvement. Much the same happened for me with westerns and frontier fiction, in which I continue to specialize.

· · ·

With the male reader primarily (but not exclusively) in mind, what do I look for in a given manuscript or proposal? There are two *a*'s for me: *a*ction and *a*uthenticity. These apply in all the men's-interest categories. Let's take military fiction as an example.

Today's reader of a novel about the air war in Vietnam wants and needs to escape from his present situation and to *be there*, to experience as intimately as possible the thoughts and feelings of the characters flying the planes and dodging enemy SAMs. In a manuscript that came to me from a first-rate young agent a couple of years ago, I was drawn from page 1 into such a story. It was a first novel, written by a decorated veteran of the war, and the manuscript possessed an immediacy of storytelling and depth of technical detail that I had not seen (especially in such a felicitous combination) in a very long time. The story moved, the characters *did things* (a simple achievement, perhaps, but too often I see static, uninteresting characters who think a lot but don't *do* very much at all), and the level of technical detail was just right: it didn't interfere with the storytelling and gave the reader the correct amount of information at the correct time. Wow! A natural!

We made a two-book deal with the agent and have since signed up another novel by this author.

In frontier fiction, from category westerns to epic novels of North American history, always I seek to learn something from my reading: perhaps about the culture of a particular Native American people who have not been written about much in popular fiction; perhaps about a particular weapon that was, in its time, revolutionary; perhaps about how the land itself was and still is today (in conflicts about water rights and logging, for example) a primary cause of events and not just a pretty backdrop. The day of the old shoot-'em-up is, I believe, past. The day of action-driven novels with real characters in authentic situations—yes, published as upscale, distinguished-looking paperback originals—is upon us. Action and authenticity are the rules to live (and publish) by.

Series publishing is another essential of mass-market publishing, one that is very important in men's-interest escapist fiction. It is also a vital factor in the decision making of marketing-oriented editors.

Look at any drugstore or supermarket paperback rack and count the number of series in any and all categories. Depending on the total amount of rack space, I wager you'll find a minimum of four and often up to a dozen different series. Why is this? Because a mass-market publisher looks for the largest possible audience for a book or category of books, and if that market has been identified, it profits (and pleases) both publisher and author to keep "feeding" it. No greater satisfaction exists for any editor than having an author who is happy and prosperous and a publisher whose bottom line is drawn in black ink.

Series publishing also gives the as-yet-unestablished author (such as the author of my trucker action-adventure books) a shot in a crowded world of best-selling "brand names." Brand X offers good quality at a low price. But there are tremendous roadblocks to getting Brand X onto the shelves in the first place. (One formidable roadblock in publishing original paperbacks is the lack of any book reviews.) Series support from a publisher and series identity in the racks help immeasurably.

The big if, of course, is: *if* it works. At what point does the publisher take the more fiscally prudent approach and discontinue the series? Usually this occurs when the initial distribution decreases to a point of unprofitability for a given title; most often, category series do not have any backlist life (though there are rare exceptions).

Currently I am editing three series in the frontier category that are well beyond the twenty-title mark and each with between four million and twenty-six million copies in print. We're not going to abandon any of those very soon. But for the less successful author? You can always sign him to write a *new* series. . . .

The adventure for me has been in discovering these "principles," if you will, and in modifying, adapting, and molding them to help my authors succeed in an increasingly hostile economic environment. The challenge has been in learning to discipline (and to be disciplined by) the marketplace, and always to be loyal to the ultimate decision maker on any book: the *reader*. He's the guy who counts the most. Without *his* loyalty, I'd be out of a job.

An Annotated Bibliography of Books on Editing and Publishing

Jean-Louis Brindamour and Joseph M. Lubow

JEAN-LOUIS BRINDAMOUR *joined Columbia University Press in 1960; since then he has worked in virtually every facet of the business, and in every type of publishing. He founded Strawberry Hill Press in San Francisco in 1973 and moved it to Portland, Oregon, at the end of 1990.*

JOSEPH M. LUBOW, a noted researcher, is senior editor of Strawberry Hill Press. He is the author of Reaching for Answers: Bill Belton's Story, *published by Strawberry Hill Press in 1993.*

Divided into two sections—"The World of Publishing" and "The Editing Process"—and comprising over ninety titles, the following annotated bibliography is derived from a much larger document created by Messrs. Brindamour and Lubow and used in the Certificate of Publishing Program, University of California Extension, Berkeley, California, where Dr. Brindamour taught for fourteen years.

An indispensible guide for editors and writers to further essential readings in the art and craft of editing and the world of publishing, the bibliography cites, describes, and critically comments on the most important general trade books and reference works on these subjects. It has been revised and updated especially for this edition of Editors on Editing.

An Annotated Bibliography of Books on Editing and Publishing

Publishing is a vast topic, covering all aspects from the original idea to the sale of the printed work. It would be nearly impossible, and probably very unwise, to compile a complete list of writings in the field. Instead, a *sampling* of works is listed and annotated. Some of the works are currently out-of-print (indicated by "o.p." after the entry), but lack of availability does not make them unimportant in the world of editors. For works that are reissued frequently, and for "annuals," no year of publication is given. And because editors, as is so with authors, are always "growing," several examples of books dealing with "genre writing" are included.

The World of Publishing

APPELBAUM, JUDITH. *How to Get Happily Published: A Complete and Candid Guide.* 4th ed. New York: HarperCollins, 1992. A down-to-earth, practical approach, especially for authors, concerning what one really *must* know to get the most out of the publishing process.

BAILEY, HERBERT S., JR. *The Art and Science of Book Publishing.* Athens, OH: Ohio University Press, 1990. An analysis of the problems of management in publishing, written by the former director of Princeton University Press. It discusses the economics, organization, planning process, and environments affecting publishing.

BALKIN, RICHARD. *A Writer's Guide to Book Publishing.* 2d ed. New York: Hawthorn/Dutton, 1981. A textbook-like discussion of the machinations of the general trade book industry, it gives the writer a picture of what to expect once a publisher has been approached. (o.p.)

BERNSTEIN, LEONARD S. *Getting Published: The Writer in the Combat Zone.* New York: William Morrow, 1986. A highly personal, quite entertaining view of "getting published."

BROOKS, PAUL. *Two Park Street: A Publishing Memoir.* Boston: Houghton Mifflin, 1986. History of a major publishing house, and of a publishing career.

BROWNSTONE, DAVID M., and IRENE M. FRANCK. *The Dictionary of Publishing.* New York: Van Nostrand Reinhold, 1982. A dictionary of terms covering all aspects of the publishing process including printing, journalism, art, photography, computer science, sales, marketing, and bookselling. (o.p.)

BUSCH, FREDERICK. *When People Publish: Essays on Writers and Writing.* Iowa City, IA: University of Iowa Press, 1986. His reflections on becoming an author give a sense of the thinking, motives, working conditions, and frustrations of authors.

A Checklist of American Imprints, 1801–1819. Metuchen, NJ: Scarecrow Press, 1982. One of a series of important historical reference works constituting the most complete list of American publications from the first third of the nineteenth century.

DELLIVEAU, FRED, ed. *One Hundred and Fifty Years of Publishing: 1837–1987.* Boston: Little, Brown, 1987. Another history of a major contributor to the American publishing scene.

DESSAUER, JOHN B. *Book Publishing: A Basic Introduction.* Rev. ed. New York: Continuum (Harper), 1989. An overall view of the publishing industry and profession, this text looks at the history and environments of publishing and takes us through its processes, products, and markets. An excellent survey of publishing.

DU BOFF, LEONARD D. *Book Publishers' Legal Guide.* Redmond, WA: Butterworth Legal Publishers, 1984, with 1987 paper supplement. Publishing history; business organizational structures; accounting; financing the business; contracts; author-publisher contracts; publisher-supplier contracts; secured transactions; how publishers find authors; copyright law; censorship; defamation; right of privacy; antitrust; unfair trade practices; and more.

DUKE, JUDITH S. *Children's Books and Magazines: A Market Study.* White Plains, NY: Knowledge Industry Publications, 1979. A thorough look at the children's book industry at the time, analyzing the economic and social trends, the markets, and the future of children's book publishing. (o.p.)

————, *Religious Publishing and Communications.* White Plains, NY: Knowledge Industry Publications, 1981. Analyzes the religious book industry and the religious communications fields, looking at the economic and social trends, markets, and finances. Includes profiles of some of the major organizations in the industry. (o.p.)

GEISER, ELIZABETH, et al., eds. *The Business of Book Publishing: Papers by Practitioners.* Boulder, CO: Westview Press, 1986. Aimed at the beginner, it covers every phase and function of the book publishing process as well as specialized types of publishing.

GRANNIS, CHANDLER B., ed. *What Happens in Book Publishing.* 2d ed. New York: Columbia University Press, 1967. A collection of essays by members of the industry on the book trade, from philosophy to production to sales.

GREENFIELD, HOWARD. *Books: From Writer to Reader.* Rev. ed. New York: Crown Publishers, 1988. Another helpful view.

GROSS, GERALD, ed. *Publishers on Publishing.* New York: R. R. Bowker, 1961. Self-portraits of publishers of the time give insight into the decision-making process. A classic! (Sadly, presently o.p.)

HOROWITZ, IRVING LOUIS. *Communicating Ideas: The Crisis of Publishing in a Post-Industrial Society.* New York: Oxford University Press, 1986. A scholarly overview of where publishing is going today.

Information Market Place. New Providence, NJ: R. R. Bowker. One of many in the "Market Place" series. Published annually.

International Literary Market Place. New Providence, NJ: R. R. Bowker. A reasonably comprehensive directory of publishers, distributors, agents, libraries, and other book-related organizations in 160 countries other than the U.S. Published annually each April.

Literary Market Place: The Directory of the American Book Publishing Industry. New Providence, NJ: R. R. Bowker. In this one vital volume, often referred to as the "bible of the industry," are names, addresses, telephone numbers, and other business data of the people and companies in all aspects of the book business—from publisher to bookstore, from word processing to marketing. Until recently *the* indispensable book for anyone interested in publishing, because the publisher has recently begun slyly removing materials into others of their "Market Place" series, this book is somewhat less complete than was previously so, while costing more.

MELCHER, DANIEL, and MARY LARRICK. *Printing and Promotion Handbook.* 3d ed. New York: McGraw-Hill, 1966. How to produce and market any printed item, arranged alphabetically by terminology. (o.p.)

One Book/Five Ways: The Publishing Procedures of Five University Presses. Los Altos, CA: William Kaufmann, 1978. A fascinating case study of the publishing history of a single manuscript at five academic presses: University of Chicago Press, MIT Press, University of North Carolina Press, University of Texas Press, and University of Toronto Press. Looks at acquisition and administration, editorial process, production and design, and sales and promotion. One wishes there were a similar book from the position of trade publishers. (o.p.)

PETERS, JEAN, ed. *The Bookman's Glossary.* 6th ed. New Providence, NJ: R. R. Bowker, 1983. A practical guide to terminology used throughout the publishing industry, from editor to bookseller.

SMITH, DATUS C., JR. *A Guide to Book Publishing.* Rev. ed. Seattle, WA: University of Washington Press, 1989. A handbook explaining the general principles of book publishing, this book looks for universals for would-be publishers to adapt to their particular environments.

TEBBEL, JOHN. *Between Covers: The Rise and Transformation of Book Publishing in America.* New York: Oxford University Press, 1987. A one-volume condensation of his monumental work (below).

————. *A History of Book Publishing in the United States.* 4 vols. New Providence, NJ: R. R. Bowker. A comprehensive history of the development and progress of the American publishing industry. *Must* reading for anybody interested in the history of publishing in this country.

TEBBEL, JOHN, and MARY E. WALLER-ZUCKERMAN. *The Magazine in America, 1740–1990.* New York: Oxford University Press, 1991. Additional *must* reading for an awareness of how our industry came to be.

UNWIN, SIR STANLEY. *The Truth about Publishing.* 8th ed. Revised and partly rewritten by Philip Unwin. London: George Allen & Unwin, 1976. Originally written more than eighty years ago, this classic on the book trade has been updated factually but holds to its original intent—to provide a publisher's perspective on the industry.

The Editing Process

American Heritage Dictionary of the English Language, The, 3rd ed. Boston: Houghton Mifflin Co., 1992. More permissive than many, its approximately 200,000 main entries make it an excellant example of its genre.

AMERICAN SOCIETY OF INDEXERS, INC. *Register of Indexers.* Washington, DC: American Society of Indexers. A self-selected list of free-lance indexers who are willing to accept free-lance index assignments.

ANDERSON, MARGARET J. *The Christian Writer's Handbook.* San Francisco: Harper San Francisco. Religious-oriented writing is quite specialized. This manual is designed to lead writers of Christian works through the publishing process and bring them to the Christian publisher's perspective.

Art Index. Bronx, NY: H. W. Wilson. Articles in domestic and foreign art periodicals, as well as some yearbooks and museum bulletins, indexed by subject and author.

ARTH, MARVIN, and HELEN ASHMORE. *The Newsletter Editor's Desk Book.* 3d ed. Shawnee Mission, KS: Parkway Press, 1984. A concise review of journalism principles applied to special-audience periodicals.

BEACH, MARK. *Editing Your Newsletter: A Guide to Writing, Design and Production.* 3d ed. Portland, OR: Coast to Coast Books, 1988. Offers guidance to the newsletter editor and publisher, including techniques in interviewing and working with volunteers, developments in word processing, and alternatives to help new and poorer organizations develop their newsletters as cost-effectively as possible.

Book Review Digest. Bronx, NY: H. W. Wilson. Published monthly except February and July. Excerpts of reviews of current fiction and nonfiction in the English language. Listed alphabetically by author, indexed by title and subject. Of extreme value when checking for the competition.

Books in Print. New Providence, NJ: R. R. Bowker. Multiple volumes—title and author indexes—listing available books, new and old. The final volume of the title listings includes publisher information. Annual, published in October.

Books in Print Supplement. New Providence, NJ: R. R. Bowker. Annual, published in April as a supplement to *BIP.*

Books Out-of-Print. New Providence, NJ: R. R. Bowker. Listings of titles declared out-of-print during the year. Annual, issued in November.

British Books in Print: The Reference Catalogue of Current Literature. London: J. Whitaker & Sons. Distributed in the U.S. by R. R. Bowker. The British version of *BIP.* Vol. 1 includes list of publishers and their addresses. Annual.

Business and Economics Books and Serials in Print. New Providence, NJ: R. R. Bowker. Published irregularly.

Chicago Guide to Preparing Electronic Manuscripts for Authors and Publishers. Chicago: University of Chicago Press, 1987. A handy reference dealing with types of computers, preparing the manuscript for submission to the publisher, publishing the electronic manuscript, coding, copy editing, etc. It also details some of the particular responsibilities of the acquisitions editor, copy editor, designer, and production coordinator.

The Chicago Manual of Style. 13th ed. Prepared by the editorial staff of the University of Chicago Press. Chicago: University of Chicago Press, 1982. A primary authority for much of the American publishing industry. Subtitled *For Authors, Editors, and Copywriters,* this manual is a settler of disputes and a teacher of usage and grammar for much of the book trade.

Children's Books in Print. New Providence, NJ: R. R. Bowker. Lists hardcover and paperbound editions of titles published for children to grade 12. Indexed by author, title, and illustrator. Annual, in November.

COMMINS, DOROTHY. *What Is an Editor? Saxe Commins at Work.* Chicago: University of Chicago Press, 1978. A classic study of one editor's ways. (o.p.)

Computer Books and Serials in Print. New Providence, NJ: R. R. Bowker. Annual, published in May.

Contemporary Authors: A Bio-bibliographical Guide to Current Writers in Fiction, Non-Fiction, Poetry, Journalism, Drama, Motion Pictures, Television, and Other Fields. Detroit: Gale Research. One place for an acquisitions editor to find information on the competition.

Current Biography. Bronx, NY: H. W. Wilson. Monthly magazine presents biographical articles on prominent figures throughout the world. Cumulated and bound yearly.

DOLAN, EDWARD F., JR. *How to Sell Your Book before You Write It: Writing Book Proposals, Chapter Outlines, Synopses.* San Rafael, CA: A Writer's Press, 1985. With special chapters on fiction by Irma Ruth Walker. A handy book that can be of considerable assistance to editors and/or writers, particularly beginners.

DOWNEY, BILL. *Right Brain . . . Write On! Overcoming Writer's Block and Achieving Your Creative Potential.* Englewood Cliffs, NJ: Prentice-Hall, 1984. Every editor, and writer, and agent, needs this book; a gem!

EHRENS, CHERYL R. *Cumulative Book Index.* Bronx, NY: H. W. Wilson. International bibliography of English-language books, indexed by author, title, and subject. Published monthly except August, cumulated and bound annually.

FLESCH, RUDOLF. *The A B C of Style: A Guide to Plain English.* New York: HarperCollins, 1964. A dictionary/thesaurus of basic English usage. (o.p.)

Forthcoming Books. New Providence, NJ: R. R. Bowker. Bimonthly cumulation listing forthcoming titles and titles published after July of each year.

FOWLER, HENRY W. *A Dictionary of Modern English Usage.* 2d ed. Revised and edited by Sir Ernest Gowers. New York: Oxford University Press, 1987. A good reference for answers to style and grammar questions.

GAGE, DIANE, and MARCIA HIBSCH COPPESS. *Get Published: Editors from the Nation's Top Magazines Tell You What They Want.* New York: Henry Holt, 1986. The title tells you all!

GOLDBERG, NATALIE. *Writing Down the Bones: Freeing the Writer Within.* Boston: Shambhala Publications, 1986. A wonderful book for editor and author alike.

GRAFTON, SUE, ed. *Writing Mysteries: A Handbook by the Mystery Writers of America.* Cincinnati, OH: Writer's Digest Books, 1992. Its value, for editors, is the background exposition by writers on how mysteries are conceived and executed.

GROSS, GERALD, ed. *Editors on Editing.* 3d ed. New York: Grove Press, 1993. Comments by many of the most prestigious editors in the business. Addresses all aspects of editing—structural, theoretical, practical—with wit and insight.

HODGES, JOHN C., and MARY E. WHITTEN. *Harbrace College Handbook.* 11th ed. New York: Harcourt Brace Jovanovich, 1990. A good basic reference for grammar and usage.

HOWELL, JOHN BRUCE. *Style Manuals of the English-Speaking World: A Guide.* Phoenix, AZ.: Oryx Press, 1983. Lists annotations for 231 English-language style manuals from all over the world.

JORDAN, LEWIS, ed. *New York Times Manual of Style and Usage: A Desk Book of Guidelines for Writers and Editors.* New York: Times Books. The style book used by the editors of the *New York Times,* it is one of the important guides in the non–book publishing field.

JUDD, KAREN. *Copyediting: A Practical Guide.* 2d ed. Los Altos, CA: Crisp Publications, 1989. Solid background and guidance for the beginning copy editor, giving an overview of the industry and the copy editor's role and position in it; takes the reader through the basics of the process, from learning awareness to bibliographies, typemarking, and tables.

KUNITZ, STANLEY, and HOWARD HAYCRAFT. *Twentieth Century Authors: A Biographical Dictionary of Modern Literature.* Bronx, NY: H. W. Wilson. See WAKEMAN for companion volume. A standard for editors.

LA BEAU, DENNIS. *Author Biographies Master Index.* Detroit: Gale Research. Index to biographical data on living and dead authors as they appear in selected biographical dictionaries.

Large Type Books in Print. New Providence, NJ: R. R. Bowker. Published biennially.

LARSEN, MICHAEL. *How to Write a Book Proposal.* Cincinnati, OH: Writer's Digest Books, 1990. Takes one through every step of writing a nonfiction book proposal, including a complete sample proposal to use as a guide. The author is a successful literary agent.

LONGYEAR, MARIE, ed. *The McGraw-Hill Style Manual: A Concise Guide for Writers and Editors.* New York: McGraw-Hill, 1989. A comprehensive guide to how to write for this book company. The book is a combination of in-house manuals written to the specifications of the needs of the house, especially in typemarking and typesetting.

MCCABE, JAMES PATRICK. *Critical Guide to Catholic Reference Books.* Littleton, CO: Libraries Unlimited, 1980. An annotated bibliography of books by and/or about Catholics or Catholicism. Arranged by subject matter and cross-indexed by author and title. (o.p.)

MCNEIL, BARBARA, and MIRANDA HERBERT. *Author Biographies Master Index Supplement.* Detroit: Gale Research. See LA BEAU.

MAREK, RICHARD. *Works of Genius.* New York: Atheneum, 1987. A major American editor writes about the business.

Medical Books and Serials in Print: An Index to Literature in the Health Sciences. New Providence, NJ: R. R. Bowker. Two-volume set published annually in May.

Microcomputer Market Place. New Providence, NJ: R. R. Bowker. Similar to all of their other "Market Place" titles.

MILLER, MARA. *Where to Go for What: How to Research, Organize, and Present Your Ideas.* Englewood Cliffs, NJ: Prentice-Hall, 1981. A unique sourcebook; it includes how to use libraries, reference books, and government information systems, and how to interview—by telephone and in person. (o.p.)

MURPHEY, ROBERT W. *How and Where to Look It Up: A Guide to Standard Sources of Information.* New York: McGraw-Hill, 1958. Designed to guide the layperson through the use of reference materials, it lists basic books available in a variety of subject areas. (o.p.)

Paperbound Books in Print. New Providence, NJ: R. R. Bowker. Multivolume set indexed by author, title, and subject. Final volume has publisher information and keys to abbreviations. Published semiannually in spring and fall editions.

PITZER, SARA. *How to Write a Cookbook and Get It Published.* Cincinnati, OH: Writer's Digest Books, 1984. A step-by-step guide to finding and testing recipes, designing, writing, and publishing a cookbook, and distributing the final product. (o.p.)

PLATT, SUZY, ed. *Respectfully Quoted: A Dictionary of Quotations Requested from the Congressional Research Service.* Washington, DC: Library of Congress, 1989. 2,100 quotations—humor, majesty, gravity, bitterness, insults, smears "from the real world of cut and thrust politics." A significant contribution to the lexicon of American politics.

The Reader's Adviser. New Providence, NJ: R. R. Bowker. An annotated bibliography on books in print. Especially helpful for an acquisitions editor and for the beginner. See especially the section "Books on Books," a good bibliography on publishing.

Religious Books and Serials in Print: An Index to Religious Literature Including Philosophy. New Providence, NJ: R. R. Bowker. Published biennially in the fall.

Roget's International Thesaurus. 5th ed. Ed. by Robert L. Chapman. New York: HarperCollins, 1992. The *classic*, this is a good place to look for a better word.

Scientific and Technical Books and Serials in Print. New Providence, NJ: R. R. Bowker. Two-volume set published annually in December.

SHEEHY, EUGENE P. *Guide to Reference Books.* 10th ed. Chicago: American Library Association, 1986. This guide is *the first place to look* for annotations on reference tools available throughout the world.

SKILLIN, MARJORIE E., and ROBERT M. GAY. *Words into Type.* 3d ed. Englewood Cliffs, NJ: Prentice-Hall, 1986. One of the standard manuals of style recognized by the publishing industry, it is often used in specialized fields in place of *Chicago Manual of Style.*

SOLOTAROFF, TED. *A Few Good Voices in My Head: Occasional Pieces on Writing, Editing, and Reading My Contemporaries.* New York: Harper-Collins, 1987. His criticisms of the industry—especially its "corporate mentality"—are strong and clear.

The Source: A Guidebook of American Genealogy. Edited by Arlene Eakle and Johni Cerny. Salt Lake City, UT: Ancestry Publishing, 1984. Comprehensive manual on U.S. record sources, stringently analyzed in terms of location, usability for specific time periods, and the nature of the information provided.

STRUNK, WILLIAM, JR., and E. B. WHITE. *The Elements of Style.* 3d ed. New York: Macmillan, 1979. A concise view of style and usage. Almost everyone uses it.

Subject Guide to Books in Print. New Providence, NJ: R. R. Bowker. A companion volume to *BIP,* it indexes in-print titles by Library of Congress subject headings. Published annually in October. There is also a *Subject Guide to Children's Books in Print* (published annually in November) and a *Subject Guide to Forthcoming Books* (published bimonthly).

TOMPKINS, JANE. *West of Everything: The Inner Life of Westerns.* New York: Oxford University Press, 1992. An excellent examination of the genre's elements. A *must* for all editors of westerns.

United States Government Printing Office Style Manual. Washington, DC: U.S. Government Printing Office. This stylebook establishes the standards for submission of materials to the Government Printing Office, giving guidance on form, style, grammar, binding, type size, etc., for all government publications. Revised and reissued every few years.

WAKEMAN, JOHN, ed. *World Authors, 1950–1970.* Bronx, NY: H. W. Wilson, 1975. A companion volume to *Twentieth Century Authors.* Another standard for editors.

Webster's Ninth New Collegiate Dictionary. Springfield, MA: Merriam-Webster, 1983. This abridgement is based on the *Third New International Dictionary.*

Webster's Third New International Dictionary of the English Language, Unabridged. Edited by Philip Babcock Gove. Springfield, MA: Merriam-Webster. A major resource when dealing with American English.

Writer's Market: Where to Sell, What to Write. Cincinnati, OH: Writer's Digest Books. The writer's practical guide to the (primarily magazine) publishing market. Compiled from responses to questionnaires sent to editors, publishers, and program directors, listings include basic information plus whom to contact, who buys free-lance material, editorial slant or focus, special needs, payment rates, etc. It is used broadly by authors.